Journal of Contemporary History: 3

1914:
THE COMING OF
THE FIRST WORLD WAR

hARpER ⚜ ͲΟRChBOOKS

*A reference-list of Harper Torchbooks, classified
by subjects, is printed at the end of this volume.*

Journal of Contemporary History

Edited by Walter Laqueur & George L. Mosse

Published

Edited by Walter Laqueur & George L. Mosse

1914:
THE COMING OF
THE FIRST WORLD WAR

Charles A. Fisher
Jonathan Steinberg
Wolfgang J. Mommsen
Immanuel Geiss
I. V. Bestuzhev
Leo Valiani
Christopher Andrew
Norman Stone
Glenn E. Torrey
Klaus Epstein
S. W. Roskill
Hans Rogger
Robert C. Williams
Ulrich Trumpener

HARPER TORCHBOOKS ❦ The Academy Library
Harper & Row, Publishers, New York

1914: THE COMING OF THE FIRST WORLD WAR

First HARPER TORCHBOOK edition published 1966 by
Harper & Row, Publishers, Incorporated
49 East 33rd Street
New York, N.Y. 10016.

Contents

Journal of Contemporary History: 3

1914:
THE COMING OF
THE FIRST WORLD WAR

The Changing Dimensions of Europe

Charles A. Fisher

The war which broke out in the summer of 1914 and swiftly engulfed the greater part of Europe is rightly regarded as one of the series of major disturbances which, at intervals of roughly a century following the peace of Westphalia, completely destroyed the carefully constructed equipoise of Europe and made necessary its reconstruction in substantially modified form. Compared with the situation which existed during the intervening periods between previous such disturbances, however, Europe appeared during the century following the settlement of Vienna to be relatively free from the running scourge of lesser wars, and this is the more remarkable in view of both the exceptionally explosive ideas released and widely disseminated by the French Revolution and the wars which it unleashed, and the no less significant changes which the Industrial Revolution produced in what may be called the technological foundations of political power.

It was, indeed, one manifestation of the new technology, namely the shrinkage of effective distance, which, by bringing Europe into far closer contact than ever before with the extra-European world, drew off much of the pressure which these new forces were producing, and in thus allowing it to disperse, usually against almost negligible resistance, in the outer world, gave rise to an illusion of stability within Europe itself. In general, however, both historians and statesmen have given far greater attention to the creative forces of ideas and ideologies, which by tradition are their stock in trade, than to the constraints imposed by geography and technology, with which such forces must needs come to terms. But while for this reason I propose to concentrate primarily upon the latter, to do so in isolation from the former would contribute little to our understanding of events, for the two sets of factors continually inter-acted upon one another.

3

Both the French Revolution and the Industrial Revolution were creatures of the Western extremities of Europe and, in the spread eastwards across the continent of these approximately contemporaneous manifestations of Western culture, both encountered increasingly divergent geographical and social conditions from those in which they had originated.

Notwithstanding the determination of the key participants in the Congress of Vienna to do all in their power to restrain any further revolutionary outbursts which might disturb the peace they had so painstakingly reconstructed, the ideals of liberty, equality, and fraternity continued to spread like a fire which, damped out in one place, reappeared with equal ferocity in another. However, whereas in the discrete peninsular and island compartments of Western Europe, where the concept of the nation-state was already established, these rising aspirations expressed themselves primarily in demands for greater social justice and the extension of the democratic franchise, in those regions where territorial unification had not yet been extended over peoples of basically similar speech and culture, as in the Italian peninsula and more especially in the great sprawl of German territories north and south of the main waterparting of Central Europe, the new ideals achieved their main fulfilment in the growth of nationalist sentiment leading to the eventual creation of new nation-states.

Still further to the east and south, both in the non-German territories which Austria had earlier acquired through the gradual repulse of the Turks from the ethnically heterogeneous lands of the middle Danube basin, and in the similarly diverse Balkan territories which in 1815 still remained within the Ottoman Empire, nationalist sentiments were openly revolutionary in their opposition to alien rule. And while similar nationalist aspirations were also present among the minority peoples along the western borders of Russia, in Russia itself the problems posed by an extremely retarded social evolution relative to the rest of Europe were only partially solved by the ending of serfdom in 1861, and continued to provide fertile soil for a later-flowering variety of revolutionary activity.

While the treaty-makers assembled at Vienna were understandably preoccupied with the threat of political revolution, though their lack of sympathy with its aims doubtless affected their judgment of its potential, they seem to have been totally unaware that the series of textile inventions and Watt's perfection of the steam engine, which had taken place in Britain shortly before the revolution broke out in France, had already set in motion forces which within a century would produce profound changes in the relative economic, territorial, and military ranking of the component states of Europe.

Yet within only a few decades the revolutionary reduction in travelling time, both on land and on sea, which had already been foreshadowed by Puffing Billy and the Charlotte Dundas, was beginning to make possible effective administrative control over far larger political entities than most of the then existing European states. Moreover, in combination with the new mass production of factory goods and the related demand alike for markets and primary produce, the improvements in transport were bound to transform the relationships of the more rapidly industrializing powers, both with their continental neighbours and with the world overseas. And finally, this new ability to draw upon basic foodstuffs and other vital materials from farther and farther afield, coupled with new advances in hygiene and sanitation, made possible an unprecedentedly rapid growth of population, which in its turn was to give rise to new international tensions, and at the same time provide more cannon fodder to feed the vastly greater military machines which industrialized powers could command in furtherance of their national purposes.

Theoretically, like the ideals of the French Revolution, the new industrial technology was assumed to be generally applicable, at least in the so-called civilized lands of Europe. But in practice its scope varied greatly both with the educational and social preparedness of individual countries to master it – a readiness which, as nineteenth-century Germany and twentieth-century Russia subsequently demonstrated, bore less relationship to democratic institutions than many in the West liked to think – and with the geographical distribution of relevant industrial resources. Among these last, accessible deposits of coal were by far the most important single localizing factor throughout the nineteenth century. The fact that all the most important of these were found in a relatively narrow band stretching from west to east along the median latitude of the continent, spreading itself generously in Britain, reappearing in France in only niggardly fashion in the north-east but underlying much of Belgium and the vast Ruhr, and continuing through Saxony, the Czech lands, and Silesia to the great Donbas of Russia, proved to be the operative feature in shaping the industrial geography of Europe before the first world war.

In these circumstances, therefore, Scandinavia to the north and also most of Mediterranean Europe to the south were largely by-passed by the major industrial developments of the nineteenth century. And even France, whose hitherto pre-eminent strength, based upon the agricultural richness of its soil and the energies of the large population which the latter supported, had twice enabled it to challenge the European order, was destined to suffer a partial eclipse. For although France was among the first and most assiduous of the continental powers to apply the new industrial techniques, the war of 1914–18 arose basically out of the problem of containing the new Germany, which both nationalist sentiment and changing economic geography had combined during the nineteenth century to make into the greatest concentration of power on the mainland of Europe, and it was Britain rather than France which by 1914 had become its principal adversary. How this came to be so may best be shown by examining briefly the responses of the leading European states to the new forces with which they were confronted.

Notwithstanding the unconcern of the diplomats with the new technology, the more perspicacious of the home ministers of continental Europe were anxious after 1815 to lose no further time in making up some of the industrial leeway they had lost to Britain. In particular, Chaptal in France was the first to appreciate the truth that the quickest way to industrialize is by copying the achievements of those who have already done so, and his encouragement of British manufacturers to set up factories in France, so that Frenchmen could then copy their methods, set the fashion for the rapid dissemination of British industrial know-how right across Europe, though it took until 1869 before John Hughes blew in the first blast furnace at Yuzovka, appropriately named after him, in the Donbas.

However, despite the considerable benefits which Britain obtained from its important share in the supplying of industrial centres in many parts of Europe, such developments were bound in the long run to reduce the continental demand for the commonest types of British manufactures. Thus they served to strengthen the ingrained propensity of a nation which, since the eighteenth century, had become the richest colonial power in the world, to look farther afield for its markets. And since the potential extra-European demand for the main textiles and metal goods, in the mass production of which it had an immensely advantageous head start, was balanced by the rapidly growing demand of an increasingly wealthy and populous Britain for food and industrial raw materials, the volume of such ocean-borne trade began to grow in an unprecedented fashion.

Nor was the change only a matter of volume. Hitherto colonies had been valued primarily for the commodities which they could produce for the mother country's benefit; now the emphasis was rather on their capacity to buy a growing quantity of its manufactures. Thus the arguments pointed ever more strongly in favour of the *laissez faire* doctrine of allowing the colonies to produce whatever paid best, for sale to whoever would buy. For in so doing they would increase their own capacity to purchase manufactures and, since those produced in Britain were unquestionably best, the choice in this respect also could safely be left to them.

Already, therefore, the old *raison d'être* of a colonial empire was itself becoming obsolescent, and though this was not fully appreciated at the time, the British government was not anxious for many decades after 1815 to expand its empire overseas. If a country like the United States, which had broken away from colonial rule, was nevertheless capable of buying more and more British goods without costing Britain a penny to administer, there seemed little point in wishing to assume further responsibilities in similar circumstances. Only where particular countries deliberately obstructed the free flow of trade did the British now attempt to intervene. For fifty years after 1824 the minute Straits Settlements were enough to give Britain the entry to most of South-east Asia, and Hong Kong, plus privileged footholds in a few treaty ports, sufficed to prise open the vast oyster of China. From now on, thanks to the fortunate way in which three-quarters of the world's population lived within a few hundred miles of the sea, all that appeared necessary to ensure Britain's continued commercial pre-eminence was to guarantee freedom and safety of movement upon the high seas and, where appropriate, upon the rivers draining into them. All trade would then gravitate to the world's seaways, and all of these would continue to lead to Britain.

Nevertheless, while the extent of Britain's tropical dependencies was not greatly increased during the half century after 1815, the Empire did begin to expand spectacularly in temperate latitudes, primarily as the result of the pioneering efforts of British settler colonists pushing onwards from footholds already obtained in Canada, Australasia, and the southern tip of Africa.

These developments, which reached their peak at varying dates after the middle of the century, also owed much to the demonstration which the United States had meanwhile begun to provide of what the new technology could do to open up the world's emptier lands. By 1869 it had become possible to travel from Washington to the Pacific coast within a week, roughly the same time that had been required to get from London and Paris respectively to the outer limits of Britain and France a century earlier. Henceforth it would be possible to hold together an area of sub-continental proportions at least as efficiently as the European nation-states had been integrated in the pre-industrial era. Equally important, it was in these sparsely populated lands of the New World that labour-saving machinery of all kinds really came into its own, and began to offer spectacular *per capita* returns to an immigrant population settling in far lower density than was typical of the increasingly congested lands of Europe.

In the process of thus expanding in temperate latitudes the British empire began to undergo a significant change in its political character. From its experience with the original American colonies Britain had learned that it was foolish to try to cramp local initiatives related to circumstances quite different from those of the mother country, and had come to realize that, notwithstanding the shrinkage of distance at sea, an empire whose farthest outposts were many weeks steaming from home could be effectively held together only on a loose rein. However, given the presence of the British navy operating from bases which put it within range of all the main ocean highways, a loose rein was all that was required, not only for the task of holding the empire together, but also for safeguarding the rights of British commerce throughout the world.

Indeed this latter task had clearly become the over-riding consideration, and the empire was no longer seen as an end in itself, but rather as the essential framework required to maintain the *pax*

Britannica, under whose benevolent auspices the entire world would gradually but ineluctably be drawn into a single great trading system, with its primary focus not in Westminster but in the adjacent City of London.

Yet in fact contrary forces were already at work. Notwithstanding the essentially unplanned manner in which this extraordinary growth of British influence had taken place, nationals of other countries had for many years been speculating on the nature of the relationship which they suspected must exist between the territorial growth of the British empire and the expansion of Britain's overseas trade.

In France the absence of large resources of coal proved to be an increasingly serious handicap in achieving British-style industrialization, and the earlier struggles against the British had already deprived France of any major overseas possession which could be exploited – as it was assumed the British had exploited India – for the benefit of the mother country. Moreover, the extreme caution which characterized the peasant and bourgeois elements in postrevolutionary France was reflected in a marked decline in the French birthrate and a deep-rooted tendency to national introversion, both of which in turn served to discourage fresh ventures overseas.

Against these, however, there were other elements, particularly in ruling circles, which, despite the setbacks of the previous half century, were obsessed with the desire to preserve the tradition of French pre-eminence in Europe. And although this objective seemed at first to be best served by a concentration of effort within that continent, the growing international stature which their British rival was deriving from its extra-European activities, combined with a deepening conviction that its industrial successes depended largely upon control of overseas markets and materials, tended to push the French into a new round of imperial competition with the British.

After initial moves in Algeria and the south-western Pacific during 1830–55, they focussed their imperialist ambitions for the next twenty-five years on the China trade, just as a century earlier they had centred upon India. And in recalling Talleyrand's argument that the short-circuiting of the British sea route to India, via a route across the Suez isthmus, would prove as disastrous to Britain as the discovery of the Cape route had itself been for Venice, the French proceeded to formulate a whole series of inter-related projects for the harnessing of modern engineering to the task of undercutting the British position in Asia.

Of these, which included the Suez canal, another canal across the Kra isthmus of Siam to short-circuit Singapore, and the opening of backdoor routes to China, by-passing Hong Kong, via the Mekong and later via the Song-koi, only the first came to fruition (in 1869), though the last two led indirectly to the establishment of France's richest overseas possession, the Union of Indochina. But as the humiliation of the Franco-Prussian war followed swift upon the triumph of Suez, many in France became convinced that, in its obsessive rivalry with Britain outside Europe, French leadership had been pursuing a mirage instead of facing realities nearer home, where the rising challenge to France's position had long been apparent in the more rapid growth of population beyond the eastern frontier. For while between 1800 and 1870 the population of France had increased only from 27 to 36 million, that of the German territories united in Bismarck's Reich had grown from 23 to 41 million. Nevertheless the colonialists contended that the best means of redressing France's man-power deficiency lay in the acquisition of still more overseas territories, from which colonial troops could be recruited to fight in the mother country's service. And while this view won widespread acceptance in France, it did not deter Bismarck from encouraging French colonialist expansion, primarily as a means of deflecting French thoughts from a revanchist policy in Europe.

Meanwhile, their concern for colonial man-power strengthened the French addiction to the assimilationist doctrine which, in both its political and its economic aspects, was completely at variance with the more liberal concepts of the British. But in a geopolitical sense the French empire remained essentially a second-best imitation of the British oceanic model, with the important qualification that it consisted overwhelmingly of *colonies d'exploitation*, with *colonies de peuplement* limited almost entirely to a narrow strip of north Africa. In these circumstances, therefore, the much expanded but still not particularly productive French empire of the early twentieth century, though certainly opposed in spirit and practice to the British dream of a single world-wide trading system, posed no fundamental threat to either Britain or the British empire, a fact which ultimately made possible the entente of 1904,

10

in the face of the growing menace which German aspirations were coming to present to both countries.

The problem of resolving the conflicting pulls of overseas and European ambitions did not arise until much later in Germany, with its relatively short coastline and no direct frontage on to the open ocean. Furthermore, for over half a century after 1815 the essentially land-minded Germans were grappling with the much more immediate problem of rearranging their fragmented political geography under the combined pressures of rising nationalism and the growing realization that the minuscule units of the *Klein-staaterei* presented a decisive obstacle to the effective utilization of industrial technology.

To a continental people like that inhabiting the vast plains of northern Germany, the methods which the United States was beginning to adopt in harnessing the new technology to such very different geographical circumstances from those of Britain, were of particular interest, and it was in the light of what he had seen of the revolutionary potential of the long distance railway in the United States that, as early as 1833, the economist Friedrich List recommended the creation of an all-German railway network centred in Berlin.

Indeed, although nationalist sentiments provided the more obvious driving force behind the move towards German unification, List's whole politico-economic philosophy, with its emphasis on the protection of infant industries and the necessity for state planning, gradually came to exert as decisive an effect on the economic and geopolitical evolution of the new Germany as the radically different doctrines of Adam Smith and the Manchester school had done upon that of nineteenth-century Britain.

It was, however, under the more traditionally-minded leadership of Bismarck that the political unification of Germany was accomplished in 1871, and though Austria had been deliberately excluded by the war of 1866, and many other areas of German speech and culture were also left outside, the new Reich henceforward represented the largest concentration of population in any single European state to the west of Russia. Only at this stage did extensive industrialization, on a scale commensurate with the great reserves of coal and iron which Germany possessed, really get under way, but in the course of the next three decades tremendous advances occurred, most strikingly in the heavy industries which had already been helped by the recent military activities of a power that laid great stress on the importance of the artillery.

Like other nations in the throes of rapid economic growth, the new Germany at first showed little interest in colonial matters, and it seems clear that Bismarck to the end of his days had no desire to see Germany expand overseas or extend its home territories beyond the manageable limits which he believed it to have reached in 1871. Nevertheless by the 1880s and 90s many Germans were beginning to think much more seriously about colonialism and, like others before them, to speculate about the connection between economic growth, population increase, and territorial expansion. Being Germans, moreover, they did so with much greater thoroughness than any of their neighbours had done, and, generalizing from the diverse experience particularly of British, Dutch, and French expansion overseas, and the contemporary but no less spectacular American advance overland, German geographers subsequently propounded the doctrine that a growing population must ultimately require more territory from which to draw its livelihood, and hence that increasingly congested industrialized lands like those of western Europe and the eastern United States needed *Ergänzungsräume*, or complementary regions of lower density, to provide them with primary produce, markets, and perhaps also outlets for settler colonists.

While it is easy to ridicule the excesses with which others later distorted Ratzel's concept of *Lebensraum*,[1] the fact remains that all the major industrial powers except Germany had obtained *Ergänzungsräume* on a very extensive scale during the preceding century. Indeed the tempo of colonial expansion had undergone a notable acceleration following the American Civil War which, by depriving European manufacturers of cotton, their principal imported raw material, had given a new twist to the old argument that tropical colonies were needed to provide reliable sources of vital commodities which the mother countries could not produce themselves.

Such considerations, reinforced by the growing industrial de-

[1] Friedrich Ratzel was the pioneer exponent of German political geography. Among his numerous writings particular reference should be made to 'Die Gesetze des räumlichen Wachstums der Staaten', *Petermanns Mitteilungen*, 42, 1896, pp. 62–88, and 'Der Lebensraum: eine biogeographische Studie', in *Festschrift für Albert Schäffle* (Tübingen, 1901), pp. 103–89.

mand for vegetable oils and coarse fibres, played a major part in provoking the final great scramble for colonial territory, above all in the hitherto largely neglected African tropics, after the mid-1870s. And while the French made the greatest territorial gains, the British now also joined in and obtained most of the richest areas, and in addition both Belgium and the newly-united Italy participated for the first time in the colonial steeplechase.

In such circumstances it was scarcely surprising that in Germany also the clamour for colonies grew louder. German policy, it was argued, had for too long concerned itself exclusively with Europe, and unless it was quickly projected upon the wider world stage while the going was good, the country would be left disastrously behind. Moreover, while rapid industrialization was at last providing sufficient economic opportunities at home to check the tide of emigration, which hitherto had been second only to that from the United Kingdom, this merely underlined the need for Germany to be assured of reliable markets and controlled sources of raw material overseas. In any case, emigration had by no means ceased, and since to a military-minded people like the Germans the continued loss of potential man-power to the United States was becoming increasingly unpalatable, the possibility of finding new outlets under their own jurisdiction, as the British were doing in their settler colonies, provided a further incentive to colonial expansion.

Thus it was that in 1884 Bismarck, apparently acting against his own inclinations though with no visible diminution of virtuosity on that account, succeeded in staking out claims to most of the best pieces of real estate that remained, respectively in north-east New Guinea, and west, east, and south-west Africa.

After this round, and the riposte of further claims by rival imperial powers which it provoked, their remained scarcely any worthwhile territory in the world which was not already within the recognized orbit of some established western or Asian state, but it was soon clear that Wilhelm II, who came to the throne in 1888 and dispensed with Bismarck's services two years later, was not disposed to curb Germany's territorial aspirations because of that. To an even greater extent than Napoleon and his spiritual heirs, Wilhelm was consumed with an overpowering sense of rivalry towards Britain, and a determination to contest the unique position which it had won, both as a naval and as an imperial power. To this end he quickly added a vast naval building programme to Germany's already massive expenditure on its army, and the rush for naval *points d'appui* led to the occupation of Kiaochow in China in 1897 and to the two Moroccan crises of 1905 and 1911, both of which implied an intention to provide the German navy with the means to operate against the British sea route, via Gibraltar, to the East.

In addition, Wilhelm clearly hoped to extend Germany's colonial territories at the expense of such older empires as were threatened with disintegration. And although in the event it was the United States which obtained the Philippines, the only remaining prize of the Spanish empire, the Turkish possessions in the Middle East continued to hold out tantalizing prospects for German footholds there, from which Britain's colonial and commercial interests in both India and eastern Africa could in turn be threatened.

Undoubtedly the Kaiser's expansionist aims enjoyed great popular support in Germany, although there were many who wondered whether in fact Germany might not be better advised to continue its historical tradition of giving prior concern to Europe. Since by no means all the Germans had been included in the Reich of 1871, the Pan-German League of 1893 advocated the inclusion of Austria, German-speaking Switzerland, and, for good measure, the Netherlands, and in addition to these there were millions more, scattered in pockets and clusters throughout eastern and south-eastern Europe.

Bismarck had been content with a relatively small and compact Reich, which with the help of the railway and a Prussian-style administration he had made into the most tightly knit and efficiently run state in all Europe. But why should Germany stop there, any more than the United States had stopped short on the threshold of the Middle West? Did not Germany's natural *Ergänzungsraum* also lie on its own doorstep, in lands already linked with it by railways built largely with German capital? Why should not Germany find its future in a *Drang nach Süden* or a *Drang nach Osten*? Southern and eastern Europe were much less densely populated than Germany, and their predominantly Slavic inhabitants were unquestionably regarded by most Germans as cultural inferiors. Among these lesser breeds countless Germans had for centuries settled and, as landowning aristocrats, skilled artisans, and superior farmers, had functioned as the bearers of a higher culture. Their descendants, still living there, formed sizable elite minorities which, if actively supported from outside, could with characteristic efficiency organize these predominantly agrarian lands so as to double or treble their productivity as *Ergänzungsräume* for industrialized Germany.

Certainly no technical or geographical obstacles stood in the way of introducing such a policy in the relatively under-developed lands either to the east or the south, and although it would have run completely counter to the nationalist aspirations of the various non-German peoples involved, this would have been of little account to the Germans who had come to regard small states merely as obstacles to technical efficiency and the march of destiny. However, while an advance eastwards would inevitably have involved a head-on collision with Russia, which for all its backwardness was still the great power whose apparently unconquerable spaces had defeated Napoleon, a south-eastern policy, besides offering the possibility of avoiding such dangers, had positive advantages of its own. For in this direction it was possible for Germany, following its alliance of 1879 with Austria, to make use of the latter as a catspaw in probing ever deeper into the Balkans, and in so doing to combine a policy of overland expansion along the Berlin–Baghdad axis with the schemes of the naval expansionists for undermining British maritime supremacy in the Indian Ocean, after acquiring a new German sphere of influence in the Middle East. The granting by Turkey of a concession for the building of the so-called Berlin–Baghdad railway through its territory in 1899 seemed to mark a decisive step in this direction.

In effect the furthering of such aims involved Germany in the curiously ambivalent policy of trying to shore up Austria and Turkey until the time was ripe to take over these ramshackle empires. Until early in the nineteenth century these two had occupied between them the entire territory from the Tirol to the Persian Gulf, but whereas previously each successive Turkish retreat had been matched by a corresponding increase in Austrian territory, after 1815 the various Balkan peoples, whose nationalism erupted into a series of rebellions against the Turks, were not absorbed into Austria but instead succeeded one by one in establishing their independence. Since the first of these peoples to break away, namely the Serbians, were Slavs like the Czechs, Slovaks, Poles, and others represented among Austria's own minority peoples, the Serbian example became an increasing irritant to the unhealthy body politic of the Austrian empire. And in 1867, which saw the Vienna government, weakened by the defeat of Königgratz, agree to grant its Hungarian subjects the equality of status implied in the concept of the Dual Monarchy, the prospect of further nationalist-inspired disintegration was intensified by the birth in Russia of the unofficial but widely approved Pan-Slav movement, which professed Russian support for the Balkan Slavs languishing under alien rule.

Preoccupied with the problems of such internal and external nationalist pressures, the Austro-Hungarian Empire lagged further and further behind Germany in its economic development, a situation aggravated by the fact that its principal deposits of coal lay in the peripheral Czech lands of Bohemia and Moravia and the Polish areas of Silesia. Accordingly the German programme of expansion envisaged as its first stage the incorporation of the existing Austria–Hungary within a new German *Mitteleuropa*, to be followed by an extension of economic and political influence along the Berlin–Baghdad axis to the Persian Gulf, and an eventual bid for oceanic domination beyond. In the meantime, however, it was desirable to support Austria–Hungary and Turkey in order to block any Russian designs upon the Balkans, which had appeared particularly sinister at the time of the break-away of Bulgaria from Turkey in 1878.

It was at this stage that Austria–Hungary, with German support, obtained the right to occupy the outlying Turkish provinces of Bosnia–Herzegovina, and Germany likewise found no conflict of interests in giving moral support to Vienna's desire to continue its newly resumed advance at Turkey's expense by gaining an outlet to the Mediterranean via Salonika, which *inter alia* might provide yet another threat to the British sea route to the East.

The interest which the German expansionists showed in the British route to the East should have given no cause for surprise. Ever since Britain had been master of India, virtually all its rivals, beginning with the French and the Dutch, seem to have assumed that Indian-derived wealth was vital to Britain's economic prosperity. Moreover the British themselves consistently regarded the route to India as the life-line of empire and, perhaps mindful of Peter the Great's dictum that 'the commerce of India is the commerce of the world', had considered every advance of nineteenth-century Russia into Inner Asia as a potential threat to their position in the East. Indeed, it was Russia's policy of consolidating its hold over continental Asia, by building the Trans-Siberian Railway between 1892 and 1902, which brought about Britain's final abandonment of splendid isolation through the conclusion in 1902 of the Anglo-Japanese alliance, the first attempt to contain Russian expansionism by concerted action from outside.

Potentially at least, the completion of the Trans-Siberian Railway represented a major geopolitical revolution, which had been foreshadowed by the first trans-continental lines in the United States a generation earlier, but whose world-wide significance was appreciated only when the new railway reduced the travelling time from St Petersburg to Vladivostok from a couple of months to less than a fortnight. To the British geographer, Halford Mackinder,[2] this latest manifestation of the shrinkage of distance marked the beginning of the end of the Western dominance of Asia by means of the tenuous maritime route around the continental periphery.

Since the steamship, unlike its contemporary invention the steam locomotive, did not need to have a track built for it, the oceanic routes had experienced the steam-induced shrinkage of distance half a century before the first railways were built across the major continents. But, once the latter had been accomplished, the advantages of greater speed and shorter and more easily defensible inner lines of communication on land were to prove decisive, and in his paper of 1904, Mackinder put forward the startling suggestion that the 'heartland' of central Asia, which was impregnable against the attacks of sea power and could now be developed by similar techniques to those used in the American West and linked by rail to the surrounding territories of China, India, the Middle East, and Europe, might become the strategic pivot of the world, from which a well-organized aggressor power could, in effect, revive the strategy of the earlier steppe nomads, who had more than once attacked these several marginal areas with devastating results.

In making this blood-curdling prophecy only a fortnight before the outbreak of the Russo-Japanese war, Mackinder implicitly admitted what was soon to be demonstrated, namely that Russia on its own was in no state to play such a role. But in pointing to the

2 H.J. Mackinder, 'The geographical pivot of history', *Geographical Journal*, 23, 1904, pp. 421–44.

ultimate threat that, if the whole of Eurasia were to be thus united, 'the empire of the world would be in sight', he added: 'This might happen if Germany were to ally herself with Russia'.[3]

The possibility that Germany might have tried to take over the organization of Russia, either via an Austrian-style alliance or by means of direct conquest, was subsequently implied by Brest Litovsk in 1918, and demonstrated by Hitler's attack on the Soviet Union in 1941. But in the early years of the twentieth century the south-eastern option seemed to be the preferred choice, and the extent of German preparation to this end was such that when the Austrian Archduke was murdered by a Serbian assassin at Sarajevo in Bosnia, the explosion could not be contained. Open and secret alliances, designed either to preserve or to overturn the balance of power, came into operation, and the holocaust began.

Whether a European war at this particular juncture was inevitable may well be argued; what can scarcely be disputed is that the continuance of the British and Germans actively to advance rival and in many respects contradictory concepts of the way in which the world should be ordered must sooner or later have led to a major collision. To most Britons, and perhaps to many others in the West, this wording may seem unduly harsh. For them the British view of a single world-wide trading system, apparently contributing, via the material improvement of all mankind, to the emergence of a single world order, and meanwhile flexible in its treatment of its own dependencies and basically tolerant of the attitudes of foreign powers, was both forward-looking and even inspiring. But against this the British were hypocritical, or at the least unduly complacent, in overlooking the extent to which the virtues of their system were the product of the sense of satisfaction and security which their position of unique pre-eminence had conferred upon them, and even more naïve in regarding this pre-eminence as the product of an innate superiority rather than of a merely transitory stage in the ongoing process of technical change.

By contrast, the ruthlessness of the German denial of rights of small nations was bound to unite most of their neighbours in implacable opposition. Yet this should not blind us to the insight of the Germans in appreciating that the revolutionary increase in the scale of economic and political organization, which the new

[3] Mackinder, *loc. cit.*, p. 436.

technology was coming to demand, would call for drastic changes in the political geography of Europe if the latter were to hold its own against such emerging extra-European giants as the United States.

In effect, therefore, both the British and the Germans had seized upon complementary facets of the truth about the way in which the world was evolving, but each had assumed that its own approach could be indefinitely pursued, primarily for its own benefit and under its own leadership.

To say this is really to assert that the concept of a self-contained European concert, to which most European statesmen continued blindly to cling, had in fact become dangerously irrelevant to the conditions of the early twentieth century. Such a concept had been valid only for so long as effective national integration had been limited, as it was before the nineteenth century, to the compact and discrete compartments of the insular and peninsular fringe of the continent. But once the Industrial Revolution had provided the means for the great mass of the German peoples straddling the central trunk of the continent to become similarly organized, their combined advantages of numerical strength, natural resources, and central situation were bound to put them in a position to dominate Europe. That, indeed, was what *Mitteleuropa* meant.

By extension, however, once these same technological forces could be effectively harnessed to the geographical resources of Eurasian Russia, the latter in its turn would require at least the whole of the rest of Europe as a counterweight. And meanwhile the concept of a European states system was also being by-passed by the way in which the leading states of western Europe were themselves outgrowing their restricted homelands. In this sense the overseas activities, above all of Britain, though less self-conscious than the policies of Germany within Europe, represented an equally significant reaction against the constraints imposed by limited national territories. As early as 1826 Canning had called the New World into existence to redress the balance of the Old; the contingents of troops from the overseas empires of Britain and France which arrived in Europe after August 1914, and the even more momentous entry of the United States into the war on the Allied side in 1917, were to show how much greater the need for such redress had meanwhile become.

Yet to say that Europe no longer existed as a world sufficient unto itself is not to dismiss the concept of European unity as dangerous and reactionary nonsense. The supreme tragedy of 1914 was that the great powers of Europe, in viewing their developing relations with the extra-European world in terms of old-fashioned European rivalries, failed completely to appreciate that only by drawing closer together in spirit and in practice could they begin to play the decisive role, for which long experience had prepared them, in shaping a truly effective balance in the wider world which they themselves had done so much to make one.

The Copenhagen Complex

Jonathan Steinberg

> *Der Rabe Ralf ruft schaurig: 'Kra!*
> *Das End ist da! Das End ist da!'*
>
> – CHRISTIAN MORGENSTERN,
> *Alle Galgenlieder* (1908)

To Germans in the days of Kaiser Wilhelm II, the word 'Kopen-hagen' meant more than the name of the Danish capital. It repre-sented a past event and a present fear, the fear that some day, per-haps on a peaceful afternoon as in the autumn of 1807, a British fleet would suddenly appear off Wilhelmshaven or Kiel and with-out warning attack the beautiful new ships of the Imperial Navy. Unsuspecting as they rode quietly at their moorings and unable to defend themselves, the great German capital ships would be pounded into smoking ruins and the world position and pretensions of the German Empire would at one blow be crushed beyond repair. The seizure of the Danish fleet and the bombardment of Copenhagen in 1807 had for a fleeting moment uncovered the true features of British power, its utter ruthlessness behind a humani-tarian mask. Who could say when that mask might fall again? The development of the Imperial Navy and Germany's world position were dangling on a thread which at any moment might be cut by a swift, ruthless stroke. The *englische Gefahr* represented an ever-present menace to German aspirations. This fear of a 'Kopen-hagen', hovering like an unquiet spirit in the background of Anglo-German relations, waxed and waned with the course of events during the years before 1914. It seeped into men's perceptions and became part of the vocabulary of political life. By becoming a fixed point in the German picture of the outside world, the 'Copenhagen complex' in its turn helped to shape the events themselves and played a part often as crucial in the formulation of German policy as the more tangible 'facts' of traditional diplomacy and military strategy. In the end, military and diplomatic policy-makers operate against a vision of the world at least in part of their own making. The nightmare is always real to the dreamer.

The idea that Great Britain had no scruples about the use of force exerted a powerful influence on important civilian leaders of the Wilhelmine era. Kurt Riezler, personal assistant and closest colleague of the German Chancellor Bethmann Hollweg, had little doubt on this point. In a book written on the eve of the first world war under the pseudonym, 'J.J. Ruedorffer', he drew the following lesson from British history:

When the English bombarded Copenhagen in 1807 in peacetime and seized the Danish fleet, the action aroused a storm of moral outrage everywhere except England, but the proclamation which England addressed to the Danish people before the seizure, justified even this action in a thoroughly naïve way by calling on the interests of freedom and the peace of the world. As in this case, so the history of English conquests has produced countless other documents of the same sort.[1]

British principles were in the end either hypocrisy or self-deception, and the sooner the Germans learned this lesson, as a Pan-German pamphletist suggested in 1897, the better:

Let people in Europe once and for all time stop this ludicrous complaint about 'perfidious Albion' and learn to judge that people more justly. The art of statecraft is one thing and the laws of morality another. Statecraft is battle and in it one cannot shoot with rosewater, least of all at inferior opponents.[2]

That British power and British principles had historically always been in screaming contrast seemed clear to men of such broad sympathies as Friedrich Naumann, the social reformer, and Gustav Schmoller, the distinguished economist. For Naumann, 'the entire English system of thought, the combination of puritanism and

---

[1] 'J.J. Ruedorffer', *Grundzüge der Weltpolitik in der Gegenwart* (Stuttgart/Berlin, 1913), p. 91. Cf. also Karl-Dietrich Erdmann, 'Zur Beurteilung Bethmann-Hollwegs', *Geschichte in Wissenschaft und Unterricht*, vol. 15, no. 9, September 1964, and for further discussion of Riezler–Ruedorffer, Imanuel Geiss, 'Zur Beurteilung der deutschen Reichspolitik im ersten Weltkrieg – Kritische Bemerkungen zur Interpretation des Riezler-Tagebuchs', in H. Pogge-v. Strandmann & Imanuel Geiss, *Die Erforderlichkeit des Unmöglichen*, Hamburger Studien zur neueren Geschichte, Band 2 (Frankfurt/Main, 1965).

[2] Fritz Bley, 'Die Weltstellung des Deutschtums', *Der Kampf um das Deutschtum*, Heft 1 (Munich, 1897), p. 11.

capitalism, seems to me moral hypocrisy',[3] and Schmoller saw Great Britain dominated by *Seeräubernaturen* inevitably thrown up by the processes of democracy. He drew a sharp distinction between Germany and Britain:

We are no commercial, capitalist, aristocratic republic, in which bourse and big capital, mining speculators and colonial railroad kings dictate wars. We lack all the preconditions in the character of the people and institutions of state for great colonial expansion and brutal trade wars. We lack the personalities, the traditions and the hard commercial egoism.[4]

'The hard commercial egoism' of the British must lead to an attempt to crush Germany. This fact seemed self-evident to a generation saturated with social-Darwinian ideas and attitudes. 'England would certainly have worked against the expansion of our power on the continent more ruthlessly and militarily with less restraint, the less she herself feared us', Tirpitz explained in his memoirs.[5] To him, as to so many of his contemporaries, the political and economic worlds were Darwinian jungles. States and firms behaved predictably. 'The older and stronger firm inevitably seeks to strangle the new and rising one before it is too late. That was the key to the Anglo-German conflict.'[6]

Germany seemed to be heading for a struggle which could neither be avoided nor postponed. The struggle for survival and self-realization had its roots in the essential nature of the modern state and not in the wills of men. Darwinian laws, Hegelian idealism, and Rankean realism blended to form a vision of the state which had life and inner principles of its own. Writing in 1908, Friedrich Meinecke argued that cosmopolitan and universal ideas had retarded the development of the modern German national state:

Both condemned as blind greed for power, what lay at the fundament of the nature of the state, what was the very expression of its self-

---

[3] Friedrich Naumann to Lujo Brentano, 31 July 1907, quoted in W. Conze, 'Friedrich Naumann, Grundlagen und Ansatz seiner Politik in der national-sozialen Zeit', in *Schicksalswege deutscher Vergangenheit* (Düsseldorf, 1960), p. 364.

[4] Gustav Schmoller, 'Die wirtschaftliche Zukunft Deutschlands und die Flottenvorlage', lecture delivered in Berlin, 28 November 1899, reprinted in G. Schmoller, *Zwanzig Jahre deutscher Politik* (Munich/Leipzig, 1920), p. 15 ff.

[5] Admiral Alfred von Tirpitz, *Erinnerungen* (Leipzig, 1920), p. 198.

[6] Admiral Alfred von Tirpitz, *Politische Dokumente*, vol. 1, 'Der Aufbau der deutschen Weltmacht' (Stuttgart/Berlin, 1924), p. 5.

preservation and self-determination . . . for, in addition to the universal side, morality also has an individually determined side, and it is from this latter aspect that the apparently immoral egoism of the state can be justified; for that which emerges from the deepest individual nature of a being can never be immoral.[7]

On the eve of the first world war, Meinecke rejected the attempt to limit the self-expression of the power-state by international congresses or agreements, a 'wretched idea, the fruit of a quietistic, universalist romanticism'.[8] The inner forces of historical development of the state could never be, and should never be, controlled. The history of the failure of the first attempt to unify Germany under Prussia revealed to Meinecke an iron law of historical process: 'There are battles in human history which must be inevitably fought out, even when defeat stands clearly in view'.[9]

The battle ahead for Germany need not end in defeat. The evidence pointed in the other direction and only a fool could ignore it. By 1900 Germany had completed an era of unexampled growth. To contemporaries, as to later observers, it was evident that the Reich had achieved 'a degree of material primacy in Europe which no power had possessed in Europe since 1815'.[10] Germany was rapidly becoming a European super-power, a development which Friedrich Naumann greeted with lyrical enthusiasm: 'The German race brings it. It brings army, navy, money and power . . . Modern, gigantic instruments of power are possible only when an entire people feels the spring-time juices in its organs'.[11]

Could this German 'spring-time' be a mere fluke? Surely the tremendous explosion of German power could only mean that the forces of history had called the Reich to its 'mission', to defend the variety of European culture against the Anglo-Saxon commercialism, the barbarism of the slumbering Slavic world, and the insidious decadence of the Latin peoples.[12] All the evidence, the

[7] Friedrich Meinecke, *Weltbürgertum und Nationalstaat*, Studien zur Genesis des deutschen Nationalstaates (Munich/Berlin, 1908), p. 88.

[8] Friedrich Meinecke, *Radowitz und die deutsche Revolution* (Berlin, 1913), p. 417.

[9] Ibid., p. 522.

[10] F.H. Hinsley, *Power and the Pursuit of Peace* (Cambridge, 1963), p. 301.

[11] Quoted in W. Conze, *op. cit.*, p. 363.

[12] For a brilliant discussion of Germany's 'mission', cf. Ludwig Dehio, *Deutschland und die Weltpolitik im zwanzigsten Jahrhundert* (Frankfurt, 1961), p. 63 ff.

wisdom of her great historians, the impressive figures supplied by her demographers, the bustle and noise of her huge ports, and the smoke and thunder of her great Ruhr factories, pointed towards an era of German world power and thus towards the inevitable combat with the sprawling world empire of Great Britain. Another of Germany's distinguished historians and publicists, Hans Delbrück, summed up what many Germans felt at the beginning of the new century:

We want to be a world power and pursue colonial policy in the grand manner. That is certain. Here there can be no step backward. The entire future of our people among the great nations depends on it. We can pursue this policy with England or without England. With England means in peace; against England means – through war.[13]

The task which such aspirations posed for Germany's naval strategists was formidable, and by the mid-1890s they had begun to face it squarely for the first time. The angry British reaction to the Kaiser's telegram to President Krüger of the Boer Republic in January 1896 marked the beginning of a new phase in Anglo-German relations, and shrewd Germans realized it. In a letter written in February 1896, Admiral Albrecht von Stosch, Chief of the Admiralty under Bismarck and Tirpitz's master in naval strategy, made the point to his star pupil:

The fury of the English against us, which found expression in the events of the Transvaal-Telegramme, has its real explanation in Germany's competition on the world market ... Since the foreign policy of England is determined exclusively by commercial interests, we must henceforth reckon with the opposition of that island people ... As a result, I have been considering the question, how can we wage a naval war against England with any hope of success?[14]

These questions were being considered in other quarters as well. On 3 May 1897, the Kaiser ordered the Chief of the High Command of the Navy, Admiral Wilhelm von Knorr, to prepare an operational study for war against England. The sheer size of the British naval forces and the dangers of a 'Copenhagen' made the task a difficult one for Korvetten-Kapitän Ludwig Schröder, the Admiralty Staff officer entrusted with the work. The solution

---

13 Hans Delbrück, 26 November 1899, *Die Preussischen Jahrbücher* (Berlin).
14 Stosch to Tirpitz, Oestrich im Rheingau, 12 February 1896, reproduced in Tirpitz, *Erinnerungen*, p. 53 ff.

seemed to him to lie in an attempt to out-Copenhagen the British by seizing Antwerp and the mouth of the Scheldt in a sudden *coup de main* before war had been declared, and from the Belgian coast mounting an invasion of England:

We must consider, first of all, that in a war between Germany and England our national wealth, the welfare of the German people, yes, perhaps, our very existence as a state would be at stake. In the face of such considerations, clinging to artificially constructed clauses of international law would be far more reprehensible from an ethical point of view than merely bending the law because circumstances force us to do so. If the life of the nation is at stake, disregarding the neutrality of Belgium and the Netherlands need not dismay us ... The history of war in every age shows us such examples. They will be repeated as long as wars are waged. England itself can serve as the best example. The English government has never hesitated to disregard the rights of neutral nations when British interests were at stake. Is there a more flagrant example than the *coup de main* against Copenhagen in 1807 ?[15]

The Schröder plan had strong advocates within the navy and a series of joint staff studies were made of its feasibility, but the main reason for its abandonment lay in its failure to deal seriously with the *englische Gefahr*. In 1898, the Reich Chancellor, Prince Hohenlohe, summoned the State Secretary of the Imperial Naval Office, Admiral Tirpitz, to a discussion on the Schröder plan, and Tirpitz made his distaste for such audacious ideas only too apparent. According to Hohenlohe, Tirpitz declared:

The idea of an invasion of England is insane. Even if we succeeded in landing two army corps in England, it would not help us, for two corps would not be strong enough to hold their positions in England without support from home. Tirpitz concludes that all hostile activity towards England must wait until we have a fleet as strong as the English.[16]

The Chancellor may well have misunderstood Tirpitz, for Tirpitz never advocated a fleet 'as strong as the English', but something both shrewder and more effective.

Tirpitz's answer to both the Copenhagen problem and the

---

[15] Quoted in Jonathan Steinberg, 'A German Plan for the Invasion of Holland and Belgium, 1897', *The Historical Journal*, vol. 6, no. 1 (Cambridge, 1963), p. 116.

[16] Diary entry, 24 October 1898, Fürst Chlodwig zu Hohenlohe-Schillingsfürst, *Denkwürdigkeiten der Reichskanzlerzeit*, ed. by K.A. von Müller (Stuttgart/ Berlin, 1931), p. 464.

achievement of a world position lay in his famous 'risk theory'. If Germany could develop and concentrate a powerful battle fleet in home waters, he argued, a relatively limited investment in German battleships could exercise a leverage on the Royal Navy with its world-wide commitments out of all proportion to the actual strength of the German fleet. In his first great memorandum to the Kaiser upon taking office in June 1897, he pointed out:

For Germany the most dangerous naval enemy at the present time is England. It is also the enemy against which we most urgently require a certain measure of naval force as a political power factor . . . Our fleet must be so constructed that it can unfold its greatest military potential between Heligoland and the Thames.[17]

The Kaiser's Chief of the Naval Cabinet, Admiral Freiherr von Senden, developed the logic of this position in correspondence with Vice-Admiral Valois, an advocate of the 'cruiser school' of naval strategy:

If we opted for cruiser warfare, the whole English fleet would be available for use against us militarily. If we develop ourselves for battleship warfare, the line from the Elbe to the Thames is the appropriate theatre of war . . . in other words, with our massed power to strike the weaker part of the total British sea force . . .[18]

Whatever the strategic merits of Tirpitz's risk theory, it had one obvious weakness. Would the slow, steady build-up of German naval power not invite the Copenhagen which it aimed to prevent? Would not the likelihood of a British attack be increased as the size of the German fleet, and thus the threat to Britain, grew? Tirpitz recognized the danger. He argued both at the time and after the first world war that the German Empire would inevitably have to pass through a 'danger zone' but that the danger zone would narrow the greater the risk to the opponent which a sizeable German fleet represented: 'Such a situation is dangerous, but it becomes untenable unless a considerable fleet greatly increases the risk to the enemy in every attempt to strike down his aspiring competitor'.[19]

The risk would have to be run, Tirpitz believed, but it could be

17 Quoted in Jonathan Steinberg, *Yesterday's Deterrent – Tirpitz and the Birth of the German Battle Fleet* (London, 1965), p. 209.

18 'Aufzeichnungen betr. Ansicht Valois über die deutsche Flottenpolitik gegen England', 1898, 'Nachlass Senden', quoted in ibid., p. 127, note 10.

19 Tirpitz, *Erinnerungen*, p. 198.

greatly reduced if German foreign policy and domestic expressions of opinion could be kept under control. Only a pacific and self-restrained foreign policy could provide the right atmosphere to allow Germany's gradual attainment of world power and equality at sea. His hopes were not fulfilled. In his own words,

We threw ourselves into the arms of others, then suddenly fell on them, we never missed an opportunity to demonstrate to others how splendidly we were doing. We never put ourselves into the position of others. We blew fanfares which never corresponded to our real position.[20]

This accurate summary of the course of German foreign policy between 1890 and 1914 reflects well on Tirpitz's political sagacity, but it begs an important question. How could the forces needed to mobilize German society for the attempt to achieve sea power be aroused without stirring up the explosions and demonstrations which Tirpitz so heartily disliked? Could the German Navy be built without generating such hostility to England that England would be alarmed?

The conduct of Germany's foreign policy could not escape the frame of mind which made the Copenhagen complex a reality. Many diplomats and statesmen shared the navy's view of England and the Kaiser believed unreservedly in the *englische Gefahr*. The Copenhagen complex acted to limit the options open to German foreign policy at the very moment when that foreign policy needed to be flexible and imaginative. As early as 1898, Baron Friedrich von Holstein, the most important strategist of the Wilhelmstrasse, recognized this possibility and tried to find a way to counter it. If only some sort of reassurance could be given to the Kaiser that the English had no such ideas, the missing flexibility could be restored. In a letter to his close friend, Count Paul von Hatzfeldt-Wildenburg, he suggested that Hatzfeldt should use his formal reports as Ambassador to Britain to allay the Kaiser's anxieties:

It would have a favourable effect if you could state – *in good conscience naturally* – that the danger of a sudden English attack at sea need not be taken into consideration. Actually I am astounded that it is still necessary to describe this fear as unfounded. In the present world situation it seems to me out of the question that England should attack Germany

[20] Ibid., p. 164.

with Russia and France watching, but there are people who hold a different view. The removal of this fear would lead to the disappearance of the inclination toward a closer relationship with Russia, a result which would please me.[21]

Pro-Russian 'inclinations' of the late 1890s were a minor disturbance for German foreign policy compared to the havoc wrought by Copenhagen fears during the Russo-Japanese War. In the two years between the outbreak of war in February 1904, and the close of the Algeciras conference in early 1906, German diplomacy staggered from one crisis to another, teetered on the brink of war with no fewer than three great powers, and permanently antagonized a fourth. By January 1906, German diplomacy had converted an initial position of strength into one of manifestly humiliating isolation, and only Austria–Hungary supported Germany unreservedly. It was the beginning of the period of *Einkreisung*. During these crucial two years, the Copenhagen complex exercised its most decisive and baneful influence on the course of German foreign policy and naval strategy, and in particular helped to generate the first serious 'war scare' for nearly twenty years. Anglo-German relations never recovered from the events of the winter of 1904–5.

The Russo-Japanese War began ominously. On the night of 8 February 1904, Admiral Togo's battle squadron suddenly appeared in the outer harbour of Port Arthur and pounded the pride of Russia's Pacific Squadron into smoking hulks. The Russian battleships, riding at anchor with their lights blazing, scarcely fired a shot. Here was the very stuff of the German nightmare, for the attack had occurred before war had been declared. The benign, not to say cynical, attitude of the British press to this ruthless act of their ally made the Germans uneasy. The *Daily Graphic* put it this way:

The indignation said to have been caused in St. Petersburg because Japan has assumed the offensive without a formal declaration of war is a curious illustration of the hold which traditional ideas have upon the popular imagination . . . As a matter of fact, declarations of war are as obsolete as the practice of sending heralds to announce hostilities.[22]

21 Holstein to Hatzfeldt, Berlin, 31 May 1898, *The Holstein Papers*, Memoirs, Diaries and Correspondence of Baron Friedrich von Holstein, ed. by Norman Rich and M.H. Fisher, 4 vols. (Cambridge, 1955–63), vol iv, no. 655, p. 80 ff.
22 *The Daily Graphic* (London), 10 February 1904.

As the war dragged on the Germans found themselves shifting towards Russia and away from strict neutrality. The balance of naval power in the Far East might tilt permanently against them if Russia were eliminated as an Asian naval force. The German colonial toehold in Shantung would then be at the mercy of the Anglo-Japanese coalition. By August 1904, the Germans were in very dangerous waters. Their neutrality had been openly compromised by the actions of the Hamburg–Amerika Line's colliers which were busily supplying Russian warships,[23] and secretly compromised both by the growing German commitment to a Russian victory and by the Kaiser's promise to protect the passage of the Second Pacific Squadron through the Baltic and North Seas. The Kaiser ordered the navy and the Ministry of Interior to be on the watch for 'suspicious Japanese with luggage',[24] who might try to plant mines in the path of Admiral Rozhdestvensky's armada. As the time for the departure of the squadron approached, the Russians grew more nervous. The German naval attaché, Kapitän Hintze, drew the attention of the Russian Admiralty to the danger of an English attack:

> The Russian military departments must be blind, if they failed to see that *England could begin the war at any moment, just as Japan has done.* That this fact has not been more widely expressed publicly arises from the inferiority of the Russian press ...[25] (Kaiser's emphasis)

The attempt to export the Copenhagen complex was accompanied by secret German moves to get the Russian fleet in the Pacific to attack the Japanese more vigorously.[26]

By the time of the Dogger Bank incident, on 22 October 1904, German nerves were nearly as strained as those of the jittery Russian commanders who fired on the Hull fishermen. The furious

[23] Cf. L.J.R. Cecil, 'Coal for the Fleet that had to die', *American Historical Review*, July 1964, p. 993.

[24] Wilhelm II to Imperial Naval Office, Very Secret, New Palace, 28 August 1904, Akten des Admiralstabs, Abteilung 'A' (German Naval Archive, Seeley Historical Library, University of Cambridge), II. R. 11.b., vol. 2.

[25] Kapitän zur See Paul Hintze to Imperial Naval Office, St. Petersburg, 29 August 1904, ibid., II. R. 11.a., vol. 2.

[26] Count Bülow to Foreign Ministry, 9 September 1904; Count Pourtalès to Bülow, 15 September 1904, *Die Grosse Politik der europäischen Kabinette*, vol. xix, no. 1, nos. 6053–4, p. 220 ff. Admiral von Tirpitz to Kapitän Hintze, 26 September 1904, Akten des Reichs-Marine-Amt, XVII, Archives of the Militärgeschichtliches Forschungsamt – Dokumentenzentrale, Freiburg im Breisgau (abbreviated below as MGFA–DZ), F. 2044, PG 66077.

reaction of British public opinion to the Russian blunder frightened the Germans quite as much as the Russians, and with good reason. By now the British were convinced that Germany was behind Russia and responsible for Russian intransigence. On 28 October 1904, Sir John Fisher, the First Sea Lord, wrote to his wife: 'Things look very serious. It's really the Germans behind it all. Peace seems assured tonight but one never knows, as that German Emperor is scheming all he knows to produce a war between us and Russia'.[27]

Sir John would have been surprised had he realized how frightened the German leadership actually was at the moment he was writing. Dogger Bank had suddenly made Germany's diplomatic situation desperate. If Britain went to war with Russia, the German colliers which were supplying Rozhdestvensky's squadron would become hostages to fortune. Anything might happen, and Germany had not so much as a promise of an alliance from the Russians. Hurriedly the Kaiser, Reich Chancellor Count Bülow, and Baron Holstein prepared the text of a Russo-German treaty of mutual defence. The Kaiser broached the idea in a private letter to the Tsar on 27 October.[28] The Tsar, himself very shaken by the ferocity of the British reaction to Dogger Bank, jumped at the offer.[29] On 30 October, Count Bülow submitted the draft of the treaty to the Kaiser. Germany had, he observed, reached a moment of 'world historical significance'.[30]

The Russo-German treaty was to inaugurate a new era. German neutrality, compromised by the coaling agreement with Russia, could be jettisoned. A new alignment of the powers would be brought about, and Germany's precarious diplomatic position secured by one daring diplomatic stroke. On 31 October, Bülow called a meeting of his senior diplomatic advisers and invited both Count Schlieffen, Chief of the General Staff, and Admiral von Tirpitz. Tirpitz was accompanied by Kapitän von Trotha, Chief of the *Zentralabteilung* of the Imperial Naval Office, who took careful notes. The advantages and disadvantages of the Russian alliance

[27] Quoted in A.J. Marder, *From Dreadnought to Scapa Flow*, vol. i, 'The Road to War' (Oxford, 1961), p. 111.
[28] Kaiser Wilhelm II to Tsar Nicholas II, Telegramme (in English), 27 October 1904, *Die Grosse Politik*, XIX, no. 6118, p. 303.
[29] Nicholas II to Wilhelm II, Telegramme (in English), 29 October 1904, ibid., no. 6119, p. 305.
[30] Bülow to Wilhelm II, ibid., no. 6120, p. 306.

were discussed at length. Holstein, supported by Bülow, pleaded for the alliance, but State Secretary of the Foreign Ministry Richthofen opposed it.[31] Tirpitz left the meeting very worried about the future, and on the following day wrote to Richthofen, who had been spokesman of the opponents, advancing further arguments against the Russian treaty:

The military significance of a Russian alliance for us in a war at sea is practically zero ... while on the other hand the danger of a military clash with England would be greatly increased, because the wrath of English public opinion would direct itself entirely against us, if the alliance became known ... Suppose for a moment that the most immediately significant case arises. England declares war on us alone and Russia would like to join on our side. The Dual Alliance with its provisions would hamper our freedom to act against France, while Russian help would be insubstantial.[32]

When the treaty negotiations lapsed because of Russian insistence on first informing France,[33] Bülow had already lost his earlier enthusiasm for the idea: 'The decisive point is as always whether an agreement, alliance or treaty of any kind with Russia would increase or decrease the danger threatening us from England ...'[34] That the *englische Gefahr* represented a real menace to Germany was scarcely questioned. The angry outbursts of anti-German sentiment in Great Britain exceeded anything that the Germans had ever encountered, and fears of a Copenhagen began to take on a grisly reality.

The Admiralty Staff was not caught by surprise. It had already made the Copenhagen complex the premise of its annual manoeuvres in the autumn of 1904:

General situation: Tension between Germany (blue) and a Western power (yellow) is suddenly sharpened by the latter with the intention of bringing about a break. It is known that a West squadron with cruisers and torpedoboats is lying in a Channel port cleared for sea. The

---

[31] Kapitän von Trotha, 'Sitzung beim Reichskanzler', Berlin, 31 October 1904, Akten des Reichs-Marine-Amts, XVII, MGFA–DZ: F. 2044. PG 66077.

[32] Tirpitz to Richthofen, Berlin, 1 November 1904, ibid.

[33] Nicholas II to Wilhelm II, 7 December 1904; Wilhelm II to Nicholas II, Bülow to Count Alvensleben, 12 December 1904; Alvensleben to Foreign Ministry, 13 December 1904; all in *Die Grosse Politik*, XIX, nos. 6130, 6131, 6135–8, p. 322 ff.

[34] Bülow to Holstein, 13 December 1904, *The Holstein Papers*, vol. iv, no. 867, p. 316.

German 'A' squadron is lying at Kiel; the 'B' squadron is on manoeuvres in Skagerrak.

First Phase of Manoeuvres:
Blue Party's Assignment: In Berlin, news arrives on 7 September, 11 a.m. that a West squadron steering an easterly course passed Dover on 7 September, 7 a.m. The German command assumes that this squadron has orders to enter by surprise the German Bight and to disrupt the mobilization of Heligoland and the Elbe defences. Yellow forces are to be regarded as hostile even if no declaration of war has been announced . . .[35]

Alarming reports from the naval attaché in London began to arrive in Berlin with great frequency during November and December 1904. 'By chance', Korvetten-Kapitän Coerper reported on 17 November, 'I heard on the following day that in the Admiralty a war game, Germany versus England, was being played, which is supposed to be finished before Christmas'. The Kaiser wrote in the margin, 'Before spring we must be ready for anything'.[36] Changes in the organization of the British fleet confirmed the Kaiser's anxieties and he sent the Chief of the Admiralty Staff to the Foreign Ministry to discuss the diplomatic consequences of the concentration of Germany's overseas squadrons at home, 'in order to prepare unobtrusively for the possibility of an English attack in the spring'.[37]

Much more drastic measures would surely be required than the unobtrusive recall of the overseas squadrons. Admiral Felix Bendemann, Station Commander, Wilhelmshaven, wrote a very secret memorandum for Tirpitz in which he outlined his 'Thoughts about the present critical situation'. In a series of questions and answers, he asserted both that 'England's war aim is to destroy the German merchant and battle fleets' and that 'the moment is favourable for carrying these aims out'.[38] On the same day that

---

[35] 'Zum Immediatvortrag – Das strategische Kaisermanöver', 10 August 1904, Akten des Admiralstabs, Abteilung 'C', I. 3–8, vol. 11, MGFA–DZ: F. 2027, PG 65964.

[36] Korvetten-Kapitän Coerper to State Secretary, Imperial Naval Office, Attaché Report, no. 907, London, 17 November 1904, Akten des Admiralstabs, Abteilung 'A' (Seeley Archive), II.E. 1.a., vol. 1.

[37] 'Aufzeichnung Richthofens', Berlin, 30 November 1904, Die Grosse Politik, XIX, no. 1, no. 6150, pp. 356–7.

[38] Admiral Felix Bendemann, 'Gedanken über die augenblickliche kritische Lage', ganz geheim, Wilhelmshaven, 3 December 1904, Akten des Reichs-Marine-Amts, XVII, MGFA–DZ: F. 2044, PG 66077.

Bendemann was writing his alarming appraisal of the situation, the Kaiser was discussing a much more daring proposal with the Chief of the General Staff, Count Schlieffen, and the Chief of the Admiralty Staff, Admiral Büchsel, a plan to out-manoeuvre the British by seizing Danish territory:

It is generally agreed that even if the war begins at first with a surprise attack by England alone, the participation of France will soon follow ... One thing is absolutely certain. Germany cannot afford to surrender her defences against an enemy attempt to penetrate the Belt. As a result, Germany must carry out certain acts of war in the Belt, i.e. within Danish territory, and thus must violate Danish neutrality. That is unavoidable![39]

Work began on what came to be known as 'Operationsplan II' under the terms of an All-Highest Cabinet Order of 3 December 1904. 'O.P. II' rested on the assumption that two army corps (IX and X) could be made available to carry out the seizure of Jutland, assuming that the Danes resisted. The Kaiser approved the plan and argued for it vigorously:

The seizure of Danish territory must take place, if only to gain control of Esbjerg, quite apart from the question of the closing of the Belt. He was of the opinion that the Army could and must spare the troops.[40]

'O.P. II' had a strange fate. After agreeing initially to the idea of a seizure of Danish territory, the Chief of the General Staff suddenly informed the Admiralty Staff in February of 1905 that:

The Army cannot spare the troops which would be needed for the occupation of Seeland in a war against England and France without jeopardising the chances of success against France. The Army indicated that it would be necessary to employ

	for Seeland	3 Divisions
	Friesen	1 Division
	Jutland	2 Divisions

plus cavalry.[41]

---

[39] 'Immediatvortrag: Verhandlungen mit dem Generalstab wegen Besetzung dänischen Gebiets bei einem Ueberfall durch England', ganz geheim, von Hand zu Hand, Berlin, 3 December 1904, Akten bes Admiralstabs, Abteilung 'C', I. 3–8, vol. 11, MGFA–DZ: F. 2017, PG 65964.

[40] Ibid., p. 2.

[41] 'Zum Immediatvortrag', A. 300 III, ganz geheim, 14 February 1905, Akten des Admiralstabs, Abteilung 'C', I. 3–8, vol. 11, MGFA–DZ: F. 2017, PG 65965.

The navy found itself robbed of its most important advanced defence plan, and Admiral Büchsel reported gloomily to the Kaiser that the present deployment of the English

made a surprise attack by English naval units on the most important points of our North Sea defences probable as the opening stage of the war . . .

The decision against the Danish plan

must force us to recognize that we no longer have satisfactory guarantees that we can compel the enemy to do what is most advantageous for us . . . Indeed, Admiral von Bendemann, when he presented to Your Majesty the elements of our earlier operational plans, always assumed as the unconditional prerequisite for success that we should be masters of the Danish waterways, which even in Admiral von Bendemann's opinion necessarily implied the seizure of Danish land areas . . .[42]

Naval special pleading was useless. The Schlieffen plan had priority, and the sudden eruption of the Morocco Crisis at this very moment shifted attention from the prospect of a war opened by Great Britain to one against France. It may well be that the sudden change of heart in the General Staff had something to do with Holstein's aggressive foreign policy, and it is known that Schlieffen and Holstein saw each other almost daily during the early months of 1905.[43]

While the Admiralty fought for its Danish invasion plan, the war scare was moving the fears of a Copenhagen to the very centre of the diplomatic relations between Great Britain and Germany. On Christmas Eve, 1904, Sir Frank Lascelles, the British Ambassador, was summoned to the Reich Chancellor's Palace for an important interview. In a dispatch to Lord Lansdowne, he reported that the

---

[42] 'Denkschrift zum Immediatvortrag über [OP II] (lined out in original) den Aufmarsch und die Verwendung S.M. Flotte im Kriege gegen England im Mobilmachungsjahre 1905', ganz geheim, von Hand zu Hand. A 738 IV, Berlin, 21 March 1905; Akten des Admiralstabs, Abteilung 'C', I. 3–8, vol. 11, MGFA–DZ: F. 2017, PG 65965.

[43] On the relations between Schlieffen and Holstein and the question of 'preventive war' in 1905, cf. Norman Rich, *Friedrich von Holstein – Politics and Diplomacy in the Era of Bismarck and Wilhelm II*, 2 vols. (Cambridge, 1965), I, p. 305.

discussion had revolved around the 'belief' that Britain was about to attack Germany:

This belief was so strong, His Excellency added very confidentially, that it was thought advisable to consult Count Metternich on the subject, and he had been summoned from London for that purpose. The Emperor had been assured by Count Metternich that there was not the slightest intention on the part of either His Majesty's Government or the vast majority of the English people to attack Germany, and His Majesty's apprehensions had been calmed.[44]

Lascelles was too optimistic. The First Sea Lord, Sir John Fisher, had in fact suggested earlier in the year to King Edward VII that it would be a good thing to Copenhagen the German fleet before it got too strong. The King replied: 'My God, Fisher, you must be mad!'[45] Mad or not, Sir John was after all Britain's First Sea Lord and, as the Kaiser told the British naval attaché, Captain Philip Dumas, in June 1906, 'Our officers think that Sir John Fisher's great aim is to fight us'.[46] These fears were by no means confined to the ranks of the navy. As Professor Marder remarks: 'The belief that "Fisher was coming" actually caused a panic at Kiel at the beginning of 1907, and cautious parents kept their children home from school for two days'.[47]

In November of 1905, the Mayor of the village of Tönning an der Eider in Schleswig-Holstein reflected a general anxiety in the German public when he wrote:

One thing we do know, that, if at all, the war can only come from England and will have as its goal in the first place the destruction of our fleet. In this view we are surely not alone in our assumption that England's first blow will fall directly after the declaration of war, or perhaps, even precede it . . .[48]

The Mayor's belief that Tönning an der Eider was the very spot which Sir John Fisher had chosen for a raid was not shared by the navy, but the fears undoubtedly were.

[44] Sir Frank Lascelles to the Marquis of Landsdowne, no. 32, Secret (telegraphic), Berlin, 25 December 1904, Foreign Office Confidential Print (Copy in Seeley Historical Library, Cambridge), vol. 8533, no. 286, p. 266 ff.

[45] A.J. Marder, *op. cit.*, p. 113.

[46] Ibid., p. 113 ff.

[47] Ibid., p. 114.

[48] The Mayor of Tönning an der Eider, Schleswig-Holstein, to the Chief of the Imperial Naval Cabinet, 14 November 1905, Akten des Kaiserlichen Marinekabinetts (Seeley Historical Library, Cambridge), XI. c.

On 3 February 1905, Mr Arthur Lee, the Civil Lord of the Admiralty, declared in a speech in his constituency that 'the Royal Navy would get its blow in first before the other side had time even to read in the papers that war had been declared'.[49] The Kaiser told Tirpitz that he had informed the British Ambassador that 'this revenge-breathing corsair must by tomorrow be disavowed and officially disciplined by the government'.[50] Admiral Müller took the occasion to lecture Tirpitz on the need for a much more rapid naval expansion than the somewhat ponderous Navy Laws permitted:

The fire-eating speech of Mr Lee gave His Majesty, the Emperor and King, the occasion to express himself to me to the effect that those persons were right who saw in the continued English threats the need to accelerate our naval arms programme and those who want to avoid a more rapid course in our fleet development for fear of England are denying any future to the German people. I need not say that this is also my own view.[51]

Anglo-German relations never recovered from the shock of the war scare. The experiences of 1904 and 1905 greatly encouraged those already powerful forces who demanded more battleships than the Imperial Naval Office seemed ready to provide. The German Navy League moved into a new and more aggressive phase. Its leaders dared now 'to declare war' on Tirpitz[52] and the forces of moderation were shouted down. Meanwhile, beyond Germany's frontiers, large-scale shifts in the alignments of the great powers were taking place, to the disadvantage of Germany. The collapse of Russian military power in the Far East and the outbreak of revolution at home threatened to remove the Tsarist Empire from the ranks of the great powers. An abyss opened beneath the feet of Europe's diplomats, while around them the fury of the Franco-

49 Korvetten-Kapitän Coerper to Imperial Naval Office, Attaché Report no. 8, London, 4 February 1905, Akten des Admiralstabs der Marine, Abteilung 'A' (Seeley Historical Library, Cambridge), II, E.30.

50 Kaiser Wilhelm II to Admiral von Tirpitz, 4 February 1905, RMA XVII, MGFA–DZ: F. 2044, PG 66077, also reprinted in Tirpitz, *Politische Dokumente*, vol. i, p. 14.

51 Admiral von Müller to Admiral von Tirpitz, ganz vertraulich, Berlin, 8 February 1905, Akten des Reichs-Marine-Amts, XVII, MGFA–DZ: F. 2044, PG 66077, also reprinted in Tirpitz, *Politische Dokumente*, I, p. 15.

52 Tirpitz to Bülow, Berlin, 8 November 1905, Akten des Reichs-Marine-Amts, XIX, MGFA–DZ: F. 2045, 66079.

German clash over Morocco seemed the overture to the great war of revenge.

By the time the Algeciras Conference had settled the Moroccan crisis, a considerable diplomatic revolution had taken place. The two years, 1904 and 1905, saw the solidification of the Anglo-Japanese alliance and the Anglo-French entente. Britain would now clearly not stand alone against Germany, nor was it so likely that she would have to strike suddenly before war had been declared. Panics continued to erupt in Anglo-German relations, but the jitters became commoner on the British side. Erskine Childers' *Riddle of the Sands* (almost uncannily close to the Schröder plan of 1897), William Le Queux's *The Invasion of 1910*, Spenser Wilkinson's *Britain at Bay*, and other alarmist books and articles foretold blood-curdling German plans for the invasion of Great Britain.[53] Le Queux's book, serialized in the *Daily Mail* during 1906, caused such a fuss that the Kaiser ordered the General and Admiralty Staffs to make formal reports on each instalment.[54] The arms race itself went into a new phase with the appearance of the 'Dreadnought' in 1906, and there was a nasty incident in 1908–9 when the British accused the Germans of building in secret more rapidly than the public terms of the Navy Laws indicated. Relations were, in short, not good, but the Copenhagen complex alone never exercised the same force on the German imagination and policy in the years after 1906 as it had before. By the end of 1907, the Anglo-Russian agreement completed the 'encirclement of Germany' and much more general fears of being overwhelmed from all sides displaced the specific fears of a sudden British attack. Writing in 1909, Count Schlieffen, now retired as Chief of the General Staff, expressed these encirclement fears dramatically:

An endeavour is afoot to bring all these Powers together for a concentrated attack on the Central Powers. At the given moment, the drawbridges are to be let down, the doors are to be opened and the million strong armies let loose, ravaging and destroying. Across the Vosges, the Meuse, the Niemen, the Bug and even the Isonzo and the Tyrolean Alps. The danger seems gigantic.[55]

[53] A.J. Marder, *op. cit.*, pp. 159–70 and 179–81.

[54] 'Zum Immediatvortrag', gehalten, 3 April 1906, Admiral Büchsel's handwritten memorandum, Akten des Admiralstabs, Abteilung 'A' (Seeley Historical Library, Cambridge) II, E. 30.

[55] Count Alfred von Schlieffen, 'Der Krieg in der Gegenwart', *Deutsche Revue* (Stuttgart/Leipzig), 1909, pp. 13–24. Cf. Gerhard Ritter, *The Schlieffen*

Count Schlieffen's successor, the younger Moltke, referred to by the Kaiser as *'der traurige Julius'* because of his melancholic temper, felt the same profound pessimism about Germany's prospects.

Behind all the glitter the Gorgon head of war grins at us ... We all live under a dull pressure which kills the joy of achievement and almost never can we begin something without hearing the inner voice say: 'What for? It is all in vain!'[56]

There is something incongruous about Schlieffen's and Moltke's apprehensiveness. As odd as the idea of Ludendorff in his bath was to John Maynard Keynes, the image of the aged Count Schlieffen sitting in his study obsessed by spectral hordes pouring over the frontiers of the Reich is surely odder? Here was Germany, the greatest power the continent of Europe had ever known, a land full of the noise and smells of industrial expansion, guarded by the world's most terrible land army, augmented by the world's second most powerful high seas fleet, a society literally bursting with every conceivable expression of strength, and here were her leaders, nervously expecting Sir John Fisher at any moment, or the hordes of invading Slavs. The normal techniques of historical analysis grind to a halt before this German *weltpolitische Angst*. Among the plentiful evidence of fear and pessimism, the Copenhagen complex is unusual only in its concreteness and the frequency of its appearance in the official documents. Yet these documents turn the usual problems of historical analysis onto their heads. This is not a case of an assertion which cannot be 'proved' by documentary evidence, but of documentary evidence which cannot in the ordinary way be asserted. To understand the Copenhagen complex, the historian must plunge into speculations which go beyond the events of traditional diplomatic or military history. It will not do to dismiss 'Kopenhagen' as a mere pretext for naval expansion, as Holstein tried to do:

The Kaiser has been afraid for some time that the English might suddenly attack us one day; Tirpitz shares this fear, and in his case I under-

---

Plan – *Critique of a Myth*, English ed. (London, 1958), p. 100, and *The Holstein Papers*, vol. i, p. 159 ff., for Holstein's furious rebuttal of Schlieffen's ideas.

[56] Diary entry, 25 August 1905, Generaloberst Helmuth von Moltke, *Erinnerungen, Briefe, Dokumente* (Stuttgart, 1922), p. 337.

stand it, for this fear is the most effective argument in favour of either giving up our colonies or increasing our fleet.[57]

Nor is it enough to throw up one's hands in despair with Professor Stadelmann and to say: 'What a strange and incomprehensible self-deception lay in this word "*Gefahr*"!'[58] The mere recognition of the phenomenon as 'irrational', as Professor Hubatsch suggests,[59] is only a start.

The first step must be to plumb the Copenhagen complex for its hard core of reality and to avoid the temptation to dismiss it as entirely groundless. Admiral Sir John Fisher was certainly capable of trying to Copenhagen the German fleet, and the Germans knew it. The possibility that Britain might have to strike such a foul blow could never be entirely dismissed. After all, they *had* bombarded Copenhagen and destroyed the Danish fleet in 1807. The Germans had not invented the historical fact, nor, as Churchill was to demonstrate with the French fleet in 1940, were the British wholly incapable of a repeat performance, if circumstances demanded it. What makes the Copenhagen complex so puzzling and intriguing is that it began to influence German policy *before* the Germans had a fleet worth 'Copenhagening'. Why should Britain risk international opprobrium and the dangers of a major war to destroy six or seven old tubs? In 1896 and 1897, when Copenhagen jitters began to afflict the Kaiser and his admirals, Germany had no more than five first-class modern battleships of the 'Brandenburg' and 'Kaiser' classes on duty, all of which were smaller and less powerful than the eight battleships of the 'Royal Sovereign' class, and the even larger eight battleships of the 'Majestic' class, quite apart from the vast armada of other craft available. The Royal Navy at war would hardly notice the few German ships, let alone trouble to 'Copenhagen' them. If, as the German theory of trade implied, the British were bent on destroying the commerce of their continental competitor, they could easily sweep the German merchant navy from the seas without going near Kiel or Wilhelmshaven.

Part of the trouble was that the Germans had got their history

[57] Holstein to Hatzfeldt, 3 May 1898, *The Holstein Papers*, IV, no. 656, pp. 81–2.

[58] Rudolf Stadelmann, 'Die Epoche der deutsch–englischen Flottenrivalität' in *Deutschland und Westeuropa* (Schloss Laupheim, Württemberg, 1948), p. 135.

[59] Walther Hubatsch, *Die Ära Tirpitz* (Göttingen, 1955), p. 13 ff.

wrong. They spoke repeatedly of a raid by the British in peace-time. Yet the peace of the summer of 1807 was no more than the beginning of the most desperate phase of Napoleon's attempt to strangle Britain's trade. As Admiral Mahan explained in his history of the role of sea-power in the Napoleonic Wars, the situa-tion had become desperate for Great Britain, and the attack on Copenhagen was justified: 'The transaction has been visited with the most severe, yet un-called for, condemnation. The British ministry knew the intention of Napoleon to invade Denmark, to force her into war, and that the fleet would soon pass into his hands, if not snatched away.'[60] For Mahan, it was not Copenhagen but the British Orders in Council of 11 November 1807 which 'trampled upon all previously received law, upon men's inbred ideas of their rights; and that by sheer uncontrolled force, the law of the strongest . . .'[61] Whether Mahan was right to exonerate Britain or not, the Germans consistently ignored the reality of the threat to Britain in 1807. They also confused the issue by identi-fying their position with the victims. The true historical parallel to the German position in the mid-1890s was not that of the Danes, but *that of the French*. In real terms Germany had assumed the position of continental predominance which France had once held. Neither the facts of the past event nor the assessment of present dangers can explain the persistence of the idea of an *'englische Gefahr'*.

The roots of the Copenhagen fears reached deeper than a mis-reading of past events or an opponent's motives. They descend into the love-hate relationship between a half-English Emperor and an England which never entirely accepted him, and, more generally, into that special ambivalence about England and the English way of life felt throughout the educated middle classes in Germany, and thus by the predominantly middle class officer corps of the navy. For the Kaiser, the sea and the navy were symbols of the British Empire's greatness, a greatness which he both admired and envied. As Michael Balfour puts it:

The desire to be an English gentleman was alternating all the time with the desire to be the Prussian prince – and each conspiring to frustrate the other. The tension between the two, superimposed on his physical

[60] Captain Alfred Thayer Mahan, USN, *The Influence of Sea Power upon the French Revolution and Empire*, 2 vols. (London, 1893), II, p. 276 ff.
[61] Ibld., p. 287 ff.

disability and upon the tensions already endemic in Prussian society, is the ultimate key to his character . . .[62]

In this respect the Kaiser reflected the feelings of many of his contemporaries. Admiral von Tirpitz, who in English eyes came to be the embodiment of the German menace, was never in the ordinary sense an enemy of England. His wife and daughters had been to Cheltenham Ladies College; he and his sons spoke excellent English, and the family's beloved 'Lady Hay', Miss Edith Hayward, the children's governess, belonged to the inner circle of family life during the very years when the Tirpitz fleet challenged British naval supremacy.[63] This anglophilia, reminiscent of the French dominance of German life during the eighteenth century, marked a break with the older Prussian mentality. Theodor Fontane's last novel, *Der Stechlin*, written between 1895 and 1897, expresses beautifully the *gemischte Gefühle* of an old Junker at the marriage of his son into an international, cosmopolitan, anglophilic family. The old Prussia was rapidly giving way, and Fontane sets the *Sonnenuntergang* of the Prussian past against the uncertain prospects of the German future. For the new Germany was not to everyone's liking. The Kaiser's speeches, *Weltpolitik*, the official bombast and byzantinism, the huge statues and monuments, were felt to be outer aspects of an inner uncertainty. A pessimism about Germany's future unites men as diverse as Moltke, Max Weber, Fontane and Gustav Schmoller.

Pessimism could not be stilled by the grandiose fleet plans of the Kaiser, for that fleet challenged Britain. The challenge provoked anxiety, and the anxiety rapidly manifested itself in fears of an *Ueberfall*. 'Kopenhagen' really stood for a fear of what the British might do if they once found out what the Germans wanted to do. But what was it they wanted to do? They wanted *Geltung*, *Anerkennung*, *Gleichberechtigung*, a whole host of emotionally loaded and psychologically revealing objectives. The need of the younger brother or the *parvenu* to be recognized is not a negotiable item, and it is consequently hardly surprising that the British could never quite make out what the Germans wanted, nor arrive at a 'deal' in the ordinary course of diplomacy. A nation ready to

[62] Michael Balfour, *The Kaiser and his Times* (London, 1964), p. 85.

[63] Information by courtesy of Korvetten-Kapitän a.D. Dr Wolfgang von Tirpitz, the Admiral's son.

declare war for a few South Pacific islands or a slice of a North African territory in which it had minimal interests can simply not be dealt with by the established devices of international accommodation. The Germans wanted what they thought the British had, but they wanted to have it without destroying Britain in the process. Germany could not enjoy *Gleichberechtigung* if the British Empire was destroyed to achieve it. These anxieties led to both the pessimism and the fear of a sudden calamitous blow. In part, the Germans half expected to be punished for the audacity of their aspirations. Writing in 1893, Fontane poured out his fears:

Two or three days ago, the great naval manoeuvres began in the Irish Sea, and upon my life, I am convinced there won't be a hundred Englishmen who will not have the feeling when they see this fleet: 'Come what may, the *seas* are still ours, and we'll destroy anyone who'll deny us this domination. And if our fleet should be lost, we would build another. We have the money for it, and the good will, and the confidence *that it must be so, that it cannot be any different.*' We do not have a trace of this confidence. Old Mrs Wangenheim always told me (putting on her most Catholic face as she did so) 'Prussia–Germany is without promise'. That is right. We are not mentioned in the Old Testament. The British act as though they *had* the promise . . .[64]

Fontane's uncertainty and pessimism were understandable. Not only must German *Weltpolitik* lead to a conflict with England both desired and feared, but it must threaten the institutions of the ramshackle Reich itself. Would the Empire not be found wanting in the moment of decision ? The Reich was undergoing one of the most rapid periods of industrial and population growth in modern history. Huge factories and sprawling, smoking cities were springing up everywhere but the institutions of society changed slowly. The industrial explosion occurred under archaic political institutions within a semi feudal social order in a loose and dangerously centrifugal federalist union. They churned up a society already riven by bitter religious divisions and torn by violent aspirations to complete the 'unfinished' nationalist revolution of 1871. As Thorstein Veblen shrewdly observed more than fifty years ago:

Comprising, rather than combining, certain archaic elements, together with some of the latest ramifications of mechanistic science and an un-

---

[64] Theodor Fontane to August von Heyden, 5 August 1893, quoted in Joachim Remak, *The Gentle Critic, Theodor Fontane and German Politics, 1848–98* (Syracuse University Press, 1964), pp. 77–8.

tempered application of the machine industry, it necessarily lacks that degree of homogeneity in its logic and orientation that would characterize a maturer cultural complex. The resulting want of poise is not to be accounted an infirmity, perhaps; it makes for versatility and acceleration of change; but it is also a clear warrant that the existing congeries of cultural elements do not constitute a stable compound.[65]

That 'clear warrant' was felt in Germany and has been only too brutally confirmed by the subsequent sequence of rumblings and upheavals. Germany in the Wilhelmine era was an unstable society, and that instability found its expression not only in the exaggerated bombast of public life, but in the exaggerated anxieties of private reflection. The Copenhagen complex was only one of its manifestations, though an influential one. It was a certain warning that Germany's leaders feared the consequences of their own hopes.

[65] Thorstein Veblen, *Imperial Germany and the Industrial Revolution* (New York, 1915), fourth ed. (New York, 1954), p. 239.

The Debate on German War Aims

Wolfgang J. Mommsen

Fritz Fischer's large-scale study of the political war aims of imperial Germany from 1914–18[1] created a sensation on its appearance in 1961 (since then there has already been a third, slightly amended edition) which was not confined to professional historians, but spread to the general public and has not yet subsided. The reason is clear; Fischer's inquiry touched one of the sore points of the German people's historical consciousness, which was just beginning to reawaken after the catastrophic end of the national-socialist era. Could it really be true that the whole of the recent German past, from the beginning of the twentieth century, was nothing more than the introductory phase of the 'greater Germany' imperialism of the national-socialists? Fischer himself does not formulate the basic theses of his work very precisely; ideas like the one just mentioned appear, as it were, incidentally, but they force themselves on the reader's attention, not least by reason of his provocative and relentless style.

In point of fact, Fischer's propositions are put forward in the form of an inexorable deployment of evidence and thus constitute a formidable challenge to the traditional concept of the history of the first world war which, with only a few modifications, was accepted in their turn by German historians after 1945. In the Weimar period it was regarded as the duty of German historians to work for the revision of the war-guilt clause (para. 231 of the Versailles treaty), which formed the legal foundation of the whole structure of reparations and discriminations imposed on Germany. These efforts appeared on the whole to have been successful, and a kind of international consensus seemed to have been achieved to the effect that historical sources had not confirmed that Germany alone –

[1] F. Fischer, *Griff nach der Weltmacht, Die Kriegszielpolitik des Kaiserlichen Deutschland* (Düsseldorf, 1961).

her dubious policies of July 1914 notwithstanding – bore the burden of guilt for starting the war. Fischer does not agree with this view and, although using the conclusions reached in Luigi Albertini's great work on the policies of the European cabinets in July 1914, he exaggerates them to the point of declaring that German policy was, in fact, the decisive factor in provoking war, with the object of obtaining by force equality of status with the three great world powers – the British Empire, Tsarist Russia, and the United States. Germany's war aims, he contends, were not the outcome of the war situation, but rather a blatant expression of the German nation's will to world power and thus preceded the outbreak of war itself. Fischer rejects the explanation that these aims received their final shape only under pressure of threats to the country's continental position. He presents instead a Germany engaged in a continuous struggle for power – a struggle which, far from being the result of an existing situation, was in fact the means by which events were to be shaped. This interpretation is obviously based largely on ethical convictions (although social, economic, and political motivations are often brought into the argument), reflected in the repeated condemnation of the extremism and recklessness of German nationalist and imperialist ambitions.

Previous research into this period did not ignore the popularity of extreme annexationist and imperialist views among large sections of the German people, but this was mainly ascribed to the war atmosphere and to the public's lack of information about the true state of affairs. Insofar as annexationist aims were officially put forward, these were regarded as largely tactical moves dictated by the military situation, or they were ascribed to the military leaders. With the possible exception of the extreme left, practically all groups were agreed that the government itself supported a comparatively moderate policy. This was not without influence on the course of historical research, nor on the German public's mental image of the events of that time.

What underlay this traditional interpretation of German policies? Contemporaries were clear in their own minds that the German nation was at that time split into two warring camps, on the one hand the supporters of the ideal of national self-sufficiency, on the other the imperialists of the pan-German stamp. Perhaps the most convincing account of this contemporary opinion is to be found in Ernst Troeltsch's courageous essay, published in the *Neue*

Rundschau in the spring of 1915, that is to say at a time when the battle in print about German war aims had reached its first climax. Essentially, two irreconcilably hostile forces confronted each other, the supporters of the traditional ideal of the nation-state against the enthusiastic adherents of imperialism. To the former the true purpose of the war was the victorious defence of the German Reich against a world of enemies; hence their positive war aims were directed solely towards ensuring the security of the empire: 'such limitations in our aims are forced upon us by the European balance of power, by our geographical situation and its boundaries, by our past history, and above all by a deep ethical conviction which drives us to achieve and maintain our own right of existence, but at the same time commands us to respect the independence of other nations and their own opportunities for genuine development'. Naturally Troeltsch looked on himself as a member of this group. He summed up the attitude of its opponents: 'What a German victory should aim to achieve is the permanent enfeeblement of the great world powers on its borders, namely the British and Russian empires; this would also remove for ever the French threat to Germany. German world power must supplant these weakened empires.'

This description of the war aims current at the time gives a fairly accurate picture of how the German people saw the situation, at least during the first years of the war. The annexationists in their turn also divided Germany into the same two camps, although using a very different vocabulary. They distinguished between those who possessed the will to power, the courage and toughness which were essential if a peace was to be won which would secure for all time Germany's position as a world power, and those others who, ensnared by humanitarian and sentimental illusions, failed to realize how serious the situation was and therefore pleaded for a 'weak-kneed' peace.

Not surprisingly, Chancellor von Bethmann Hollweg in particular was regarded as a member of the anti-imperialist camp. From the start of the war it was generally agreed that Germany could sign a peace treaty only if it brought some recompense for the immense sacrifices that had been made. The consequence was an unending stream of expansionist war aims of a truly incredible extravagance, which came pouring out from almost every quarter.

The Chancellor was, however, the soul of prudence, at any rate for the time being, and refused to take a public stand on this question; indeed, in the first months of the war he tried to discourage exaggerated nationalist expectations, so that almost from the start he gained the unenviable reputation of a defeatist and an anti-imperialist. On the other hand, the parties of the left, convinced that Bethmann Hollweg was no 'blind annexationist', gave him their support.[2]

Although as the war went on Bethmann was gradually forced to abandon discretion and to advance more or less unambiguous war aims, in the eyes of his right-wing critics he remained an unreliable fellow who was ready to renounce all annexationist claims if this would end the war. This was a point of view which – in spite of all the war-aims programmes discovered by Fritz Fischer – probably came very close to the Chancellor's inmost convictions. On the other side, the representatives of the left – with the exception of the insignificant Liebknecht group – continued until July 1917 to regard the Chancellor as an advocate of a compromise peace whom it was necessary to support in his struggle with the conservatives, despite the ambiguity of his declarations, public and private. Scheidemann's attempt in his speech at Breslau on 20 June 1916 to claim the Chancellor as his ally on the question of a peace without annexations was no doubt a good tactical move, but its success depended on the assumption that Bethmann Hollweg's efforts at negotiation on the basis of a peace without substantial annexations were genuine. It is clear that Scheidemann sincerely believed this, a belief that remained unshaken even after the war. Although exhorted to announce great and glorious war aims, which would arouse mass enthusiasm, the Chancellor continued to keep the door ajar for any possible development in the direction of negotiations, even in the face of a public opinion which in the main wanted annexations, and of a parliamentary majority united until July 1917 in its annexationist outlook. These tactics suggested that the Chancellor believed in a negotiated peace, but had not always managed to get his views accepted, an impression which received confirmation as he increasingly became the target of the military leaders.

The dispute determined the course of political events inside

---

[2] August von Stein, editor of the *Frankfurter Zeitung*, end of November 1914 to Haussmann. Quoted in Haussmann, *Schlaglichter* (Frankfurt, 1924), p. 14.

Germany in the later war years. Hence the attempt made retrospectively to distinguish between the 'genuine' opponents of annexations and all those who to a greater or lesser extent departed from the aim of the *status quo ante* cannot be taken as a reliable guide for assessing the state of mind of the warring groups in Germany from 1914 to 1918. In fact, the formula which opposed the proponents of a 'Hindenburg' peace to those of a 'Scheidemann' peace continued to dominate public debate even after the war. In particular, it determined the course of the discussions of the Committee of Investigation set up by the Weimar National Assembly to examine the causes of Germany's defeat. Bethmann Hollweg and Jagow had little difficulty in heaping on the former military leadership the main responsibility for the extremist war-aims programmes of 1916 and 1917, which alone had been made public at the time. The Committee, almost every member of which detested Ludendorff, readily accepted this approach. Significantly, the members omitted to question Bethmann Hollweg more closely and agreed with him that 'the virulent hatred with which the so-called annexationists hounded me' dispelled any doubts as to his attitude on war aims. When questioned about a conversation with the American ambassador, Gerard, in January 1917, during which he had informed the latter in a somewhat disguised form of Germany's current war aims, especially of the intention to maintain permanent indirect control of Belgium, Bethmann's reply was characteristic: 'But Gerard knew that I . . . was no annexationist. The whole of Germany knew that.' The ex-Chancellor had made a similar remark in a letter to Prince Max of Baden, written before the end of the war, which had come into the hands of the Committee of Investigation; 'The world knows that I was never in favour of annexationism, and the proof is the hatred with which its apostles pursued me'.[3]

These testimonials to himself fitted well into the picture of the vehement disputes between the civil and military authorities about war aims and the conduct of internal affairs, which were still fresh in everyone's memory. The political climate of the post-war years, poisoned by the stab-in-the-back legend and the agitation con-

---

[3] *Stenographic reports of the 15th sub-committee of the German National Assembly* (Berlin, 1920), vol. 1, pp. 128–33, 146, 232. Cf. James W. Gerard, *My four years in Germany*, p. 265, and Schulthess' *Europäischer Geschichtskalender*, vol. 58, Appx. 1, p. 1003. Bethmann cannot be wholly acquitted of the charge of having up to a point wilfully misled the committee.

cerning the war-guilt question, prevented a really objective view being taken of Germany's wartime policies. Bethmann Hollweg's undeniable bias in favour of a negotiated peace was entered far too quickly on the credit side of the war-guilt account, and the annexationist ambitions of official quarters, no secret at the time, were played down as being no more than concessions to the military leaders without any binding force.

Thus an image was created of a Chancellor who was a 'lover of peace' and a 'seeker after understanding', a man who had swum against the stream and stood up against the military. Otto Erich Volkmann, the expert attached to the Committee of Investigation, came to the conclusion that Bethmann 'at any time during the course of the war would have consented to a peace which confirmed the *status quo ante*'[4]; to be sure, he remarked on another occasion that the ex-Chancellor's policies – in spite of the fact that he was 'inwardly' in favour of a negotiated peace – had nonetheless scattered far and wide 'the seeds of the German policy of annexationism of the last war years'. The attitude of the social-democrats contributed to the genesis of this relatively favourable verdict on the Chancellor's policies.[5]

This comparatively favourable image of Bethmann Hollweg strongly influenced historical judgment on the period. Hitherto neither contemporaries nor historians had doubted that up to the time of their loss of effective power in the spring of 1917, the political leaders had been in favour of a moderate negotiated peace, whereas the military leaders, steeped in traditional concepts of a strategy of annihilation, had always striven for a peace of absolute victory and had constantly been at odds with the civil power on this question. Thus interest was concentrated on the intense struggle which took place between the supporters of a moderate peace and those of an overwhelmingly victorious peace, one of the main purposes of which would be to destroy England's mastery of

[4] O.E. Volkmann, *Die Annexionsfragen des Weltkrieges, Werk des Untersuchungsausschusses*, vol. 12, 1, pp. 48, 167.

[5] Cf. P. Scheidemann, *Der Zusammenbruch* (Berlin, 1921), p. 83, and *Memoiren eines Sozialdemokraten*, vol. 1, p. 279 ff. Bethmann Hollweg's *Betrachtungen zum Weltkriege* gave a similar impression; in it he explained why he had been unable to carry out his comparatively moderate policy, giving more importance to defending himself against the reproach of having failed to provide strong moral leadership than to a detailed discussion of war aims. Yet he stressed far more than was justified by the facts his opposition to the war aims of the Third Army high command.

the sea. In the opening years of the war this struggle was waged in secret as a battle of dossiers, but from the autumn of 1916 it was fought out in the open and with increasing bitterness. Yet very little was known publicly about developments in foreign policy during the war, particularly the numerous semi-official peace feelers that had been put out. Bethmann himself was generally regarded as a somewhat weak and indecisive personality, well-intentioned but unable to assert himself against the combined opposition of the military establishment, conservative circles, industry, and the parties of the right; there was general agreement that at any rate during his chancellorship, there had been no intention of making annexationist demands that did not admit of compromise in the event of peace negotiations; but there was not quite the same readiness to believe, as Volkmann did, that Bethmann Hollweg was prepared to sign a negotiated peace that included no annexations of any importance. Historical research has hitherto been inclined to attribute Germany's defeat to the succeeding Chancellors' abandonment of this moderate course under pressure from the military leaders and the annexationist politicians of the right, rather than to German policy on the outbreak of war and during its first years. Thus the personality and the policies of the first wartime Chancellor were regarded up to 1918 as the keys to an understanding of the history of the first world war.

In his study of Germany's war aims in the West, Hans Gatzke had already made a breach in the wall of traditional interpretations, although he had had access only to printed source material. Nevertheless, he too maintained that the war aims of the government in general and of Bethmann Hollweg in particular were 'on the whole moderate' in comparison with the extremist plans propagated among the German public. But it was Fritz Fischer, later backed up by Werner Basler and Imanuel Geiss,[6] who was the first to abandon the conventional pattern of two sharply contrasted camps, one annexationist, the other moderate and basically non-annexationist, substituting for it the thesis of the 'fundamental unanimity

---

6 Hans W. Gatzke, *Germany's drive to the West. A study of Germany's western war aims during the First World War* (Baltimore, 1950), p. 19 and *passim*; Werner Basler, *Deutschlands Annexionspolitik in Polen und im Baltikum 1914–18* (Berlin [East], 1962); Imanuel Geiss, *Der Polnische Grenzstreifen 1914–18* (Lübeck & Hamburg, 1960).

of will with regard to war aims that characterized all politically influential circles in Germany from the Kaiser himself, by way of the civil government and the military leadership, right down to the Reichstag majority and the German press'.[7] His examination leads Fischer to the conclusion that the differences of attitude were of only limited significance even though contemporaries may have felt them very deeply. Variations of opinion, whether in official circles or outside, were, he maintains, of little importance in face of that monolithic will to world power shared by all the influential groups and classes of the nation. To be sure, Fischer also points out that it was principally the army, heavy industry, and wide sections of the upper middle class which championed the most outrageous of the imperialist war aims; but the Social-Democratic Party and those members of the German intelligentsia who during the later stages of the war were the guiding spirits behind the 'People's Union for Freedom and Fatherland', are also found guilty of having lent temporary support to Germany's claim to world rule or, at any rate, world power. Thus, e.g. Ernst Troeltsch, Friedrich Meinecke, and Alfred Weber are implicitly counted among the imperialists, although not among the open ones. Only the extreme left and certain out-and-out pacifists like Friedrich Wilhelm Foerster can measure up to Fischer's inflexible yardstick of probity – support for the absolute *status quo ante*.[8]

In point of fact Fischer goes even beyond this. He does not confine himself to asserting that the antagonism between imperialists and so-called anti-imperialists was superficial; he states that the leaders of the Reich – not only the Kaiser and the High Command, but specifically also Bethmann Hollweg and his closest collaborators – were united in their resolve to extend Germany's power at the expense of each one of her enemies, that this resolve was faithfully, fully, and above all unbrokenly pursued during the whole course of the war, and that in view of this basic agreement the numerous conflicts between them are of secondary importance. In spite of differences of outlook on certain points, Fischer argues, they were united in working for the aggrandisement of German power and regarded this as the true object of the war. This very

[7] Fischer, *op. cit.* 3rd ed., p. 841.
[8] Characteristically, Foerster is not mentioned in Fischer's book, which deals only with those intoxicated by the dream of a victorious fight for a Greater Germany.

rigid black and white thesis is derived from a mass of documentary records and is presented as the actual and factual core of all the confusing quarrels between parties and groups and government departments of every shape and kind. The most important part of the argument is the attempt to prove that the views of the political leaders did not differ significantly from those of the military leaders but that, on the contrary, their common aim of fighting for German world power was in complete harmony with the desires of the overwhelming majority of the German people.

This presentation of the facts, whose objective accuracy is not under discussion at the moment, not only contrasts sharply with the traditional portrait of Bethmann Hollweg as the statesman of moderation and compromise, but is also the complete antithesis of the earlier views discussed above about the whole complex of German war-aims policies. According to Fischer, the entire German nation, with the exception of some small and unimportant groups, had to a greater or lesser degree become the victims of an overwhelming obsession with power, the desire to obtain for the German empire equality of status with the three great world powers. Fischer describes the first wartime Chancellor as a clear-headed politician who deliberately led Germany into the war and thereafter, while remaining flexible in his methods, worked tenaciously and unyieldingly for the expansion of German power. He seems bent on a complete reversal of those views on Bethmann Hollweg which had developed in the atmosphere of the struggle against the charge of war guilt, as of a man who was always 'prepared to negotiate', but who had been frustrated by an unfortunate conjunction of political obstacles. This interpretation is as mistaken as the earlier ones, since it once again reduces the whole question of Bethmann's war-aims policies to a matter of 'political attitudes', to a purely personal, patient, and unremitting effort to enhance Germany's power both eastwards and westwards. All the Chancellor's actions are inspected in this light, and when they do not fit the pattern[9] they are said to have been modified for tactical reasons only – a method used in the traditional interpretations, but in reverse. To this is added the further thesis of the continuity of Germany's war-aims policies, from September 1914 right up to the 1918 treaties with the enemies in eastern Europe. This, too, is

---

[9] See Fischer, 230 ff.

contrary to general opinion, which sees the transition to unlimited submarine warfare and the complete military takeover of both home and foreign affairs by Hindenburg and Ludendorff as a fundamental change of direction in war policy.

In general, Fischer reaches his conclusions by assessing attitudes and virtually disregarding differences of circumstance. The political actions of the persons and groups governing Germany during the first world war are attributed to their ethical outlook, measured in relation to specific principles of power politics, imperialism, etc., while all the external factors which may have influenced them are more or less ignored. Fischer and his pupil Geiss seem to be concerned above all to expose as unmistakably as possible an attitude of mind which they rightly detest; hence their obvious tendency to exploit to the limit the documents relating to war aims and to ignore the fact that in politics no less than in daily life deeds seldom match up to words. Fischer shows no interest in the greater or lesser differences of attitude hidden behind the positions adopted in public for tactical reasons by the different government departments and personalities. He confines himself to the literal wording of the documents, whatever the situation in which they were composed and whatever the specific object they served. In certain cases, as for instance the treatment of the war-aims conference at Kreuznach on 23 April 1917, the use of this method is particularly irritating, since it must be taken for granted that in politics points of view which are fundamentally different in their nature are practically always presented as being merely different in degree.

Moreover, Fischer is bent on producing not so much a narrative of events or reconstructing the chain of cause and effect, as a continual stream of new evidence for the sole purpose of proving his main theme – Germany's will to unlimited world power. Although it would be absurd and unjust to accuse Fischer of conscious tampering with the sources,[10] there are in his work many exaggerated and biased statements (some of which were subsequently withdrawn). For instance, he regards the German peace offer of 12 December 1916 as nothing more than a trick, the purpose of which was to hinder Wilson's inconvenient attempts at

[10] Gerhard Ritter, in particular, made this accusation at the German Historians' Congress in Berlin in 1964, reported in the supplement to *Geschichte in Wissenschaft und Unterricht*, 1961.

mediation and to make diplomatic preparations for unrestricted submarine warfare, whereas it is perfectly obvious that Bethmann Hollweg meant this offer quite seriously and, although he was not very optimistic about its chance of success, regarded it as the final attempt to avert the *ultima ratio* of the submarine war.

Thus, in spite of the profusion of source material which he for the first time made available to historical research, an achievement which merits unreserved recognition, Fischer's interpretation is open to attack on many points. But this does not fully explain why the discussion about his theories aroused so much heat, at any rate in its early stages. The reason is that his conclusions, put forward perhaps hastily, are in sharp contrast to the contemporary image of the period, which still influences our own historical consciousness. His work heralded a change in the character of our politico-historical thought. Attitudes which seemed to contemporaries consistent with the maintenance of the status quo and thus purely defensive in principle, have today the appearance of out-and-out annexationism or at the least of some variety of indirect rule. This conclusion is reinforced when German war aims are considered in isolation and not in relation to the war aims of the Allies.[11] Fischer's tendency to ignore power-political concepts to the point of denying them altogether, and his measurement of German war-aims policy by the standard of a complete territorial *status quo ante*, make nonsense of the history of the late Wilhelmian era; nowhere, it seems, is intelligent insight to be found; on every hand there is nothing but boundless, utopian nationalism, often tinged with *völkisch* ideas. Nor does he even consider this as due in part to the war atmosphere, which has at all times and everywhere had the effect of stirring up nationalist sentiments. On the contrary, he makes the war itself appear to be the outcome of this delusionary nationalist struggle for world power. Is the history of the late Wilhelmian era really nothing more than the introductory phase

11 It would be wrong to reproach Fischer because he does not concern himself with Allied war aims, but his argument does give the impression that Germany could have obtained peace by making the offer of the *status quo ante*. See Erwin Hölzle, 'Das Experiment des Friedens im ersten Weltkrieg', *Geschichte in Wissenschaft und Unterricht*, 1962. Cf. also A.J.P. Taylor's short but as yet un-excelled study, 'The War Aims of the Allies in the First World War', in *Essays presented to Sir Lewis Namier* (London, 1956); and, most recently, Pierre Renouvin, 'Les buts de guerre du gouvernement français (1914–18)', in *Revue historique*, March 1966; also published in *Geschichte in Wissenschaft und Unter-richt*, Jg. 17, Heft 3.

of the national-socialist hankering after world conquest? And was the Social-Democratic Party's celebrated declaration of loyalty to their country on 4 August 1914 also nothing more than a mixture of crude self-deception and unacknowledged nationalist imperialism?

It is these implications in Fischer's writing which account for the sometimes very harsh reviews of his work.[12] Had all the efforts to reach an objective clarification of the war-guilt question been meaningless and misdirected? Had Germany deliberately brought about not only the second but also the first world war? These questions are not discussed in detail by Fischer himself, but to the general public they seemed to constitute the quintessence of his argument. This of course opened up old wounds at a time when Germans were trying to understand their own historical past, and it is not surprising that this reaction gave rise in its turn to a series of unedifying feuds in the press.

A scholarly discussion of Fischer's theories had already begun before the appearance of *Griff nach der Weltmacht*, for he had made known his main conclusions in pre-publication extracts in the *Historische Zeitschrift*. Hans Herzfeld immediately questioned

---

[12] See for instance the articles by Golo Mann in the *Neue Zürcher Zeitung*, 28 April 1962, and of Gerhard Ritter in the *Hannoversche Zeitung*, 19/20 May 1962, as well as the one by Michael Freund with the significant title: 'Bethmann Hollweg – the Chancellor of the year 1914?' in the *Frankfurter Allgemeine Zeitung*, 28 March 1964. See also Paul Sethe in *Die Zeit*, 17 November 1961; Josef Engel in *Geschichte in Wissenschaft und Unterricht*, 1963, p. 517 ff; Erwin Hölzle in *Historisch-Politisches Buch*, Jg. 10, 1962, p. 65 ff; finally Giselher Wirsing's '. . . auch am ersten Weltkrieg schuld?' in *Christ und Welt*, 8 May 1964. Opinions of a generally favourable kind are expressed by Bracher in his *Neue politische Literatur*, 1962, p. 471 ff. and by Rudolf Neck (from an Austrian point of view) in *Mitteilungen des österreichischen Staatsarchivs*, Jg. 15, 1962, p. 565 ff. Very important is the balanced but critical judgment of Ludwig Dehio in *Der Monat*, no. 161, 1962, p. 66 ff. There is, in addition, a detailed review by Fritz T. Epstein, 'Die deutsche Ostpolitik im ersten Weltkrieg', in *Jahrbücher für die Geschichte Osteuropas*, Jg. 10, 1962, p. 381 ff. Hans Herzfeld was the first to make a summary of the discussion in an article entitled; 'Die deutsche Kriegspolitik im ersten Weltkrieg', in *Vierteljahrshefte für Zeitgeschichte*, Jg. 11, 1963, p. 224 ff., followed by Otto Ernst Schüddekopf with 'Politische Kriegsführung. Die Kriegszielpolitik der Mittelmächte während des 1. Weltkrieges', in *Neue Politische Literatur*, Jg. 3, 1965, and by Fritz Fellner, who forcefully stresses Fischer's merits in 'Zur Kontroverse über Fritz Fischers Buch "Griff nach der Weltmacht"', in *Mitteilungen des Instituts für österreichische Geschichtsforschung*, vol. 72, 1964, p. 507 ff. Several of these reviews were collected and published in 1964 under the title *Deutsche Kriegsziele 1914–18*, ed. Ernst Graf Lynar.

Fischer's views on Bethmann Hollweg. Using the diaries of Admiral Müller and the memoirs of Friedrich Meinecke[13], he pointed out how very moderate the Chancellor's attitude actually was, considering the heavy pressures to which he was subjected; he also doubted whether it was legitimate to talk about an unbroken line of German war-aims policy since August 1914.[14] Shortly after, Gerhard Ritter attacked Fischer's interpretation of German policy in the July crisis in an unusually sharply-worded article.[15] Subsequently the controversy spread to ever wider circles, as new aspects of the problem were revealed by further research. The subject is now too vast to be covered in a single article.

So far discussion has been concentrated in the main on two groups of problems: first, the causes of the war and the closely connected question of how far German war aims were foreshadowed in the policies of the pre-war years; second, the assessment of the war-aims policies themselves.

Given the importance which German historians in the twenties and thirties attached to the war-guilt question, it is not surprising that Fischer's pronouncements on German policy in the July crisis immediately aroused general attention and sharp opposition. His view that the ideas put forward by Friedrich v. Bernhardi in *Deutschland und der nächste Krieg*, published in 1912, rendered 'with absolute precision the intentions of official Germany', although the German Foreign Office, for one, tried at the time to have them rejected, provoked vigorous criticism in many quarters as an overstatement of an undeniable fact. Another of his theses that could not stand up to examination, at any rate in the form in which it was presented, was his assertion that the German political leadership, relying on British neutrality, was bent at the very least on inflicting a severe humiliation on Russia on the Balkan question, but was prepared to start a four-power war for the hegemony of Europe, in which England was expected to stand aside. It was pointed out in several quarters that if Germany became involved in a general war, then in the given circumstances it would automatic-

---

[13] *Regierte der Kaiser? Kriegstagebücher, Aufzeichnungen und Briefe des Chefs der Marine-Kabinetts Admiral Georg Alexander v. Müller 1914–18*; Friedrich Meinecke, *Strassburg–Freiburg–Berlin. Erinnerungen 1901–19* (Stuttgart, 1949).
[14] 'Zur deutschen Politik im ersten Weltkriege.' *Historische Zeitschrift*, vol. 191, p. 67 ff.; also Fischer's reply, ibid., p. 83 ff.
[15] 'Eine neue Kriegsschuldthese?' Ibid., p. 64 ff.

ally be waged against France, and Bethmann Hollweg fully expected that England in this event would join the enemy side, though perhaps not necessarily from the very beginning.[16] In view of this, one of the key assumptions of Fischer's original interpretation of German diplomacy in the July crisis falls away. In his introduction to the third volume of his *Staatskunst und Kriegshandwerk*, Ritter once again, in opposition to Fischer, identified the subordination of the political establishment to the military leaders as the decisive cause of the failure to preserve peace. Over and above this, he holds fast to his belief in the basically defensive character of German policy.[17] This is a view accepted by Karl Dietrich Erdmann as well, since he became acquainted with the diaries kept by Bethmann Hollweg's private secretary Riezler. To be sure, Erdmann has now conceded, contrary to his earlier view, that by 5 July 1914, the Chancellor was already fully conscious of the possibility of a general war breaking out in which England too would be involved. On the other hand, Egmont Zechlin has lately attempted to explain Germany's conduct in the July crisis as arising from secret information about a naval treaty between Russia and England that was said to be in course of preparation and which aroused fears of a closer alliance of the two powers. He considers that this ever-threatening danger of England taking sides with Germany's continental rivals, a step which was bound to have a catastrophic effect on Bethmann's long-term foreign policies, was the reason why the Reich, literally at the last moment and at the risk of world war, started a political offensive. Its purpose was both to give effective support to her only remaining ally, Austria–Hungary, and to force a show-down about the Balkan crisis that had been looming over Europe for years, at a moment still relatively favourable to

[16] Unequivocal proof is to be found in Lerchenfeld's report to Hertling of 4 June 1914 about a lengthy conversation with Bethmann Hollweg. *Bayrische Dokumente zum Kriegsausbruch*, ed. Dirr (Munich, 1922), p. 112; also Bassermann's letter to Schiffer of 5 June 1914: '. . . Bethmann said to me with fatalistic resignation: "If there is war with France, England will march against us to the last man".' *Schiffer Nachlass*, no. 6, Hauptarchiv Berlin–Dahlem. See also Zechlin, 'Deutschland zwischen Kabinetts- und Wirtschaftskrieg', in *Historische Zeitschrift*, vol. 199, p. 345 ff., and Karl Dietrich Erdmann, 'Zur Beurteilung Bethmann Hollwegs', *Geschichte in Wissenschaft und Unterricht*, Jg. 15, 1964, p. 536.

[17] *Staatskunst und Kriegshandwerk. Das Problem des 'Militarismus' in Deutschland*, vol. iii, *Die Tragödie der Staatskunst. Bethmann Hollweg als Kriegskanzler (1914–17)* (Munich, 1964), p. 15 ff.

Germany.[18] These interpretations do approximate to Fischer's point of view, since they agree on the growth of an attitude of fatalism, the belief that 'war will come for all that' which undoubtedly affected the decisions of Germany's political leaders, and also admit that the thought of a preventive war entered as one element into their political calculations.[19] Meanwhile, Imanuel Geiss, a pupil of Fritz Fischer, has compiled a collection of documents in two volumes, consisting with few exceptions of material already to be found in official publications, but with a very full commentary frankly designed to give documentary confirmation to Fischer's case.[20] It is a pity that the sole aim of this documentation is to throw light on the decisions of the German government, the diplomatic documents of the other powers concerned being included as it were as a mere sideline.

Latterly, however, Fischer has been rather letting his defenders down by becoming more and more radical in his views concerning Germany's responsibility for the outbreak of the war. In a lengthy essay in the *Historische Zeitschrift*, completed in 1963 but not published until 1964, he not only defends his previous ideas, but tries to strengthen his case by attributing Germany's decision to make war to the effects of a crisis in the development of her economic expansion in south-east Europe. The demonstration is unconvincing because there is no direct connection between the failure of German attempts at economic expansion in Greece, Bulgaria, and Turkey, and the decision of 5 July 1914 to give unconditional support to Austria–Hungary in the Serbian question. This decision must be considered as a complete reversal of the German Foreign Office's previous attitude, which had however already been undermined to some extent by Wilhelm's declarations to Archduke Ferdinand during his visit to Vienna in March 1913, under the pressure of military quarters. Economic issues do not seem to have affected it in any way.

18 E. Zechlin, *Deutschland zwischen Kabinetts- und Wirtschaftskrieg*. Also by the same author, 'Probleme des Kriegskalküls und der Kriegsbedingung im ersten Weltkrieg', in *Geschichte in Wissenschaft und Unterricht*, Jg. 16, 1965, p. 69 ff. See also his most recent contributions, 'Bethmann Hollweg, Kriegsrisiko und SPD 1914', in *Der Monat*, January 1966, and 'Motive und Taktik der Reichsleitung 1914. Ein Nachtrag', ibid., February 1966.

19 See Fischer's reply, 'Weltmacht oder Untergang. Deutschland im ersten Weltkrieg', in *Hamburger Studien zur neueren Geschichte*, vol. i (Frankfurt, 1965).

20 *Julikrise und Kriegsausbruch 1914. Eine Dokumentensammlung*, 2 vols. (Hannover, 1963/64)

But this is not all. Fischer took up an even more intransigent stand in a long article published in *Die Zeit* of 3 September 1965, in which he asserted that since 1913 Germany had been systematically making preparations to launch a world war: 'By the summer of 1914 the war had been well prepared intellectually, politically, diplomatically, and economically! All that remained to be done was to actually bring it about', and for this purpose the assassination at Sarajevo came at the right moment. A little later, in a volume of the series entitled *Weltmacht oder Untergang. Deutschland im 1. Weltkrieg*, Fischer again spoke out (this was obviously written before the article in *Die Zeit*, but appeared later). Here his tone was somewhat more moderate; 'Germany deliberately made use of the Sarajevo incident as an opportunity for overcoming the obstacles to German world-power policies'.[21] Granted the close connection between the longing of the German people in the years before the war to win successes in world politics and German policy after Sarajevo, do the sources confirm his main thesis, namely that the government of the Reich had since 1913 deliberately steered a course towards war because it considered that all prospects for a peaceful enhancement of Germany's world status had been blocked? Fischer is now preparing a new book in which he intends to supply the proof for this assertion; it is to be called *Der Krieg der Illusionen*, and is awaited with some eagerness. Nevertheless, the feeling remains that this radicalization of his opinions lessens the persuasive power of his arguments. Even granted that the German government since 1906 (the rights and wrongs of its actions are here not under discussion) felt itself compelled to embark on policies which steadily increased the risk of war, the theory that long before Sarajevo German statesmen were already determined to embark on a general war as an escape from their difficulties does not seem convincing, especially as there is general agreement that Bethmann himself was opposed to a preventive war. His original plan, certainly after 1912, was to edge cautiously towards an agreement with Russia and also and especially with England. He did not, as Fischer seems to assume, expect to achieve by this means an immediate increase of political elbow-room, but only a gradual improvement of the general political climate, in order to open up long-term prospects of success in the field of world politics. Argument will also go on as to the justification for

[21] *Hamburger Studien zur neueren Geschichte*, vol. 1 (Frankfurt, 1965), p. 52.

attributing one and all of the 1914 German war aims to political and economic aspirations of the pre-war period. Certainly the war aims of 1914 did not just fall from the sky; but the mere fact that they were given concrete shape only during the 1914 'state of siege' should surely be a warning against over-hasty back-dating.

Hitherto, when historians have asserted that in the years before the war Germany was mainly interested in economic expansion, they have based their opinion largely on the Ruedorffer–Riezler book *Grundzüge der Weltpolitik* (1914). Now that Erdmann has gone to the pages of the Riezler diary (unfortunately still not available for general use), to illustrate the comparative moderation of Bethmann Hollweg's policies, Riezler has also been drawn into the controversy. Imanuel Geiss has lately tried to prove that Riezler was most probably in favour of a war as a means of cutting the Gordian knot of world politics. It was the same Riezler who, during the first world war, as confirmed by the same sources, was attacked by Dietrich Schaefer as the protagonist of a feeble pacifism. More convincing is the approach of Hillgruber, who recently tried to distil from Riezler's writings a theory of the risks of war in the age of modern power politics which may have guided Bethmann Hollweg and his counsellors in the critical days of July 1914.[22] Yet, however Riezler's diary is interpreted, one thing is incontrovertible, namely the alarming spirit of fatalism in which wide circles of the German (and indeed not only the German) public, as well as their political leaders, awaited the approaching war. This was a frame of mind that, when the hour of crisis came, decisively weakened the will to preserve peace.

We now reach the second big group of problems – the evaluation of the policies followed by Germany during the war itself. Here the difficulties of trying to present a complete picture of the many different views which have been put forward during the discussion of Fischer's theses are even greater. An attempt will nevertheless be made to give at least a short summary of the different points of view which have emerged.

[22] See H. Pogge-von Strandmann and Imanuel Geiss, 'Die Erforderlichkeit des Unmöglichen. Deutschland am Vorabend des ersten Weltkrieges', *Hamburger Studien zur neueren Geschichte*, vol. 2 (Frankfurt, 1965); and Andreas Hillgruber, 'Riezlers Theorie des kalkulierten Risikos und Bethmann Hollwegs politische Konzeption in der Julikrise 1914', *Historische Zeitschrift*, vol. 202, Heft 1, 1966.

Criticism of Fischer's work was at first mainly concerned with his conception of the personality and policies of Chancellor Bethmann Hollweg. It is to Fischer's lasting credit that he was the first to survey the whole range of war-aims programmes drawn up by the various government departments on the Chancellor's instructions. But in his eagerness to give them an exact and pithy description, he went too far, at least in certain respects, in his opposition to the views that had prevailed hitherto. Even otherwise favourable reviews, such as Klaus Epstein's,[23] questioned Fischer's ready acceptance, as proof of his own opinion, of remarks made to third parties by Bethmann, although it was quite obvious that these only showed that he was deliberately being 'all things to all men'. Fischer's portrait of Bethmann Hollweg as a statesman steadily pursuing far-reaching power-political and imperialist aims, misses the essence of the Chancellor's personality. Even on the question of war aims he was always seeking points of agreement, and at the beginning of the war at least he tried to damp down the exaggerated expectations of the over-excited masses. In a penetrating study based on the Riezler diaries, Erdmann has recently described the great gulf between Bethmann and the Pan-Germans and their middle-class and conservative supporters with their naive aspirations.[24]

Janssen, too, in his brilliant book about the war-aims policies of the German federal states, draws special attention to the Chancellor's comparatively moderate political line.[25] And even Willibald Gutsche, an East German historian, attests in Bethmann's favour that his war aims were in conformity with the tendencies of the more moderate group within 'German monopoly capitalism', and that he was sharply opposed to the aims of heavy industry, which enjoyed the support of Bissing, governor-general of Belgium.[26] It can hardly be denied that Fischer limits his inquiry strictly to an

[23] Klaus Epstein, 'German war aims in World War I', *World Politics*, vol. xv (October 1962), p. 171 ff. This also appeared in the *Vierteljahrshefte für Zeitgeschichte*.

[24] Ibid., p. 539 ff.

[25] *Macht und Verblendung: Die kriegszielpolitik des deutschen Bundesstaates 1914–1918* (Göttingen, 1962), especially p. 125 ff.

[26] See Gutsche's interesting and – apart from its Marxist–Leninist trappings – serious study, 'Zu einigen Fragen der staatsmonopolistischen Verflechtung in den ersten Kriegsjahren', in *Politik im Krieg 1914–18* (Berlin [East], 1964). Cf., also his essay, 'Erst Europa dann die Welt', in *Zeitschrift für Geschichtswissenschaft*, 12. Jg., 1964.

exposure of Germany's struggle for power and does not give adequate consideration to the political difficulties which the Chancellor and his colleagues faced at home vis-à-vis both the general public and the military establishment. This situation forced them continually to temporize and to change their tactics. To those who have studied the sources it is disturbing that Bethmann Hollweg's bitter opposition to the Pan-Germans and the industrialists and ultra-conservatives behind them, which greatly increased his difficulties, is dealt with by Fischer as if it were of merely secondary importance. There was after all a world of difference between Bethmann's September Programme and Class's first big memorandum on war aims; it is misleading to suggest that the two are identical in attitude. In reply, Fischer argues with much justice that the question is not so much one of Bethmann Hollweg's personal views but rather of his political activities, and that he could not have acted otherwise than he did.[27] To prove this it would be necessary to supplement the analysis of Bethmann's personality and political strategy by a study in depth of the whole contemporary political system. Fischer makes a valuable start in this direction, but only a start, due to his predilection for explanations based on political attitudes and socio-economic laws.

Efforts of the same nature are to be found in Egmont Zechlin's numerous, discerning, but unfortunately widely-dispersed papers.[28] He is mainly concerned to show that Bethmann's policy was a 'cabinet' policy in the style of the nineteenth century, tuned from the first to a limited war followed by a peace negotiated between cabinets, public opinion being as far as possible excluded. He tries to make out, not always convincingly, that Bethmann Hollweg at first took the line that England would show restraint in the military field and might even be prepared to act as mediator, until he was forced to recognize that England intended to fight to a finish. He shows that the question of how the struggle against

---

[27] *Historische Zeitschrift*, vol. 199, p. 279 ff.

[28] *Friedensbestrebungen und Revolutionierungsversuche.* Beilagen zu *Das Parlament*, B. 20/61, B 24/61 and B 20/63 and B 22/63; 'Das "schlesische Angebot" und die italienische Kriegsgefahr', in *Geschichte in Wissenschaft und Unterricht*, Jg. 14, 1963, p. 533 ff; 'Deutschland zwischen Kabinettskrieg und Wirtschaftskrieg. Politik und Kriegführung in den ersten Monaten des Weltkrieges 1914', in *Historische Zeitschrift*, vol. 199, 1964, p. 347 ff; *Probleme des Kriegskalküls und der Kriegsbeendigung im ersten Weltkrieg*', in *Geschichte in Wissenschaft und Unterricht*, Jg. 16, 1965, p. 69 ff.

England was to be carried on in the event of a French defeat was of great importance in the genesis of the so-called September Programme. Indeed, there can hardly be a doubt that the *Vorläufige Richtlinien über unsere Politik beim Friedensschluss* implicitly rest on the assumption that England would go on with the war (as emerges also from the Chancellor's accompanying letter to Delbrück of 9 September 1914), otherwise it would be astonishing that England, in the eyes of the German public the main enemy, is not even mentioned in a Programme in which, according to Fischer, the basic aims of German policy for the whole course of the war are spelled out. In view of Rechenberg's catalogue of demands to France concerning rights in Channel ports and so forth for the duration of the war, which was obviously drawn up in the light of the September Programme,[29] and of the stock-phrase 'continental blockade' in Riezler's diary, it must have been drawn up, at least in part, as a programme for the war against England. For even after a French defeat, which at the time the Germans regarded as imminent, England and its Dominions were expected to carry on the war, or at least to deny Germany access to the open sea for the foreseeable future. Neither the September programme, nor the other private or public statements by the Chancellor, too numerous to be dealt with here in detail, can be said to have quite the conclusive force as regards his personal views on war aims that Fischer attributes to them; but it must be admitted, in Fischer's favour, that Bethmann Hollweg, moderate as he was, was not in a position to get his line of policy accepted in other government quarters. Whatever risks the Chancellor was prepared to take in flouting both official and public opinion, as in his readiness to cede a small part of Silesia to facilitate agreement between Vienna and Rome, he could never have prevailed against the more or less annexationist majority of the nation, and particularly the military. Perhaps he shrank from open battle on behalf of his moderate views, as was stated after his fall by Eugen Schiffer, a personal friend[30]; or again, the power of the

---

[29] See Rechenberg's notes of 18 September 1914, which list the concessions to be demanded in connection with the projected customs union in the event of a separate peace with France. For instance: 'Right of occupation, particularly of Channel ports and western (districts), if necessary until the war with England is over, the French army demobilized and moved correspondingly further south'. *Akten der Reichskanzlei*, no. 403, Deutsches Zentralarchiv Potsdam.

[30] Diary entry of 19 July 1917. *Schiffer Nachlass*, no. 3. Hauptarchiv Dahlem.

military establishment to extend its influence far beyond the limits of its own sphere of activities made such an outcome impossible. It is mainly to the elucidation of this last question that Gerhard Ritter devotes the third volume of his *Staatskunst und Kriegshandwerk*. This is a detailed study of the war years during which Bethmann Hollweg was Chancellor, and an admirably comprehensive summing-up of the results of recent research. Compared with Fischer's methods, it has the great advantage of being a lucid narrative, dealing also with the policies of the Allies and of the United States. Ritter as well as Fischer was able to make use of a great deal of unpublished official material, and also of a new edition of the files of German Foreign Office documents concerning Germany's efforts for a separate peace.[31] In contrast to Fischer, Ritter maintains that German policies were originally basically defensive in nature. He does not deny that in the course of the war they took on a more offensive character as efforts were made to strengthen and extend Germany's power on the Continent, either indirectly by economic hegemony or directly by open annexation; but he is far milder than Fischer in his interpretation of German war policy as a whole.

Fundamentally, the conclusions reached by the two writers are nonetheless not all that dissimilar. Ritter also believes that the 'unsolved "Belgian question" ' . . . became the curse of Germany's whole war policy'. But, unlike Fischer, he tries to show that there was some justification in Germany's attempt to acquire some form of permanent control over Belgium. Using King Albert's diary, he throws new light on the 1916 negotiations on Belgium (which Fischer was the first to present in detail), showing that there actually was a real chance of indirectly fitting the Belgian glacis into the German sphere of influence (although the question arises whether negotiations with a monarch that were taking place against the declared wish of the Belgian government could really have led to a permanent solution acceptable to both sides). Bethmann Hollweg took these hopes so seriously that in his catalogue of German war aims prepared for Wilson at the end of January 1917 he asked, on the

---

[31] *L'Allemagne et les problèmes de la paix pendant la première guerre mondiale. Documents extraits des archives de L'Office allemand des Affaires étrangères*, publiés et annotés par A. Scherer et J. Grunewald. So far only the first volume (Paris, 1962) has been published, but Ritter was able to use the documents being prepared for the second. Unfortunately the editing is slovenly; the work contains numerous errors of fact.

Belgian question, only for a free hand to settle it by bilateral agreement with King Albert. With regard to a peace settlement on the eastern front, Ritter's conclusions are once again more moderate than Fischer's. Bethmann, he says, believed 'national hopes of territorial acquisition should never stand in the way of a separate peace with Russia'. But this leaves certain questions unanswered, for example the extent of the annexations desired by Germany, and the degree to which even limited territorial claims, such as the Polish border strip, were an obstacle to a separate peace with Russia. There is in our view no doubt whatever that the High Command and the Kaiser were determined in 1917 to block any peace negotiations with Russia that assumed German renunciation of any large-scale annexations. This was a situation which Bethmann regretted, and which fatally compromised his position; but he did not openly resist.

Ritter's actual theme is, of course, the influence of the military establishment on political decisions, and here he is in full accord with earlier opinion, and perhaps goes further than is appropriate in emphasizing the point. Yet his approach is anything but conventional; in his appraisal of Falkenhayn and Ludendorff he carries out a noteworthy 'revaluation of values'. In complete contrast to the earlier literature, he draws a surprisingly favourable portrait of Falkenhayn, whereas Hindenburg and Ludendorff are painted in the blackest colours. Ritter praises not only Falkenhayn's comparatively moderate attitude in the war-aims question, but also his military strategy. This has traditionally been regarded as mistaken because of the failure of the great offensives at Ypres and Verdun, with their frightful casualties. Ritter maintains that there were only slight differences of opinion about war aims between Falkenhayn and Bethmann Hollweg; together they formed 'a united front against the tumultuous nationalism, "militarism", and annexationism of public opinion', and he is surprised that no closer relationship ever developed between the two. It is true that military anxieties and difficulties weighed heavily on Falkenhayn and explain his moderate attitude; but he was an extremely ambitious man with great influence on the Kaiser, and Bethmann had to be continually on the watch to frustrate the Chief of Staff's political proposals. The rumour circulating at that time that Falkenhayn was about to become Chancellor was not altogether without foundation. His efforts to force a separate peace with Russia and his attitude on the submarine question repeatedly endangered the Chancellor's position. In the end it was Bethmann Hollweg himself who caused Falkenhayn's fall and who did not hesitate to use the weapon of prolonged and patient intrigue to bring this about, when he realized that a peace settlement could not be reached in partnership with the general. Since the hard core of Ritter's account is an analysis of the antagonism between the political and military leaders, he criticizes Fischer for treating this question as secondary to the combined will of both sides to extend the power of the Reich to the utmost limits of what was possible.

This is certainly justified to some extent. On some points, however, he definitely overstates his case. For instance, the great crisis of confidence in the year 1917, of which Bethmann finally became the victim, was in point of fact less the result of soldiers dabbling in politics than the outcome of the deep disappointment at the failure of unrestricted submarine warfare, which German propaganda had presented as the 'infallible weapon' to bring the war to an end by summer at the very latest.

One other aspect of Ritter's book is also unsatisfactory – its marked anti-Austrian tone. It would seem that Ritter succumbed to the temptation to present German policies in a more favourable light by giving them, as a dark background, the partly defeatist, partly annexationist, and wholly dishonest conduct of the Emperor Charles and his foreign secretary Count Czernin. Ritter's assumption that there was a strong tendency in Vienna to conclude a separate peace with the Entente at the expense of her German ally is not confirmed by Wolfgang Steglich in his recent detailed study, *Politics of Peace of the Central Powers 1917–18*. Steglich does not gloss over the far-reaching annexationist aims of the Central Powers even in those years; nonetheless he arrives at the challenging conclusion that they might have agreed to a *Behauptungsfrieden* that was tantamount to a peace on the basis of the *status quo ante*, but that the Western Powers would not have agreed, since a negotiated peace by which Germany's status as a Great Power would have been acknowledged almost unimpaired, would have broken up the Entente.[32]

No doubt this is not the last word in the debate on German policies

[32] W. Steglich, *Die Friedenspolitik der Mittelmächte 1917-18*, vol. 1. (Wiesbaden, 1964).

during the first world war. The process of re-examining traditional concepts has been intensified and is being extended far beyond the problems of those years. The younger generation of German historians is striving, in a much more unbiased and critical state of mind than hitherto, to identify the sources of infection in German society which provided the seed-bed for the rise of nationalsocialism. Seen in this light, Fischer's studies have certain great and lasting merits. They have shattered some traditional beliefs and taboos, and directed historical research into new paths, and it is therefore a matter for regret that official government quarters have frowned on Fischer's theses and have attempted, if only indirectly, to hinder their dissemination.[33] It may also be doubted whether it was proper to reprint in the official Government bulletin the article entitled 'Die Last des Vorwurfs: Zweimal deutsche Kriegsschuld ?', in which Eugen Gerstenmaier gives his wholly negative views on Fischer's theses.[34] The manner in which official quarters took sides, until the daily press exposed their attitude, met with general disapproval by the German historians, even those highly critical of Fischer.

None of the protagonists in this heated debate denies that a thorough revision of the opinions held hitherto has now become necessary[35]. To be sure opinions are divided as to how far such a revision should go. The theoretical basis of the discussion seems to be changing ground and moving gradually towards what in the long run could become a closer approximation of the different points of view. The argumentation of Fischer and his school is increasingly based on economic and social history, aspects of the question hitherto virtually ignored except by Kehr, Hallgarten, and Vagts.[36] Yet much of the preparatory work in this field still remains to be done. The recent contributions from East Germany

[33] See Bernd Nellessen, 'Maulkorb für einen historiker ? Warum Bonn Fritz Fischer die Reise nach Amerika verwehrte', in Die Welt, 3 June 1964.

[34] Christ und Welt, 2 September 1964, reprinted with only slight alterations in the Bulletin der Bundesregierung, 4 September 1964.

[35] With the possible exception of Walter Hubatsch. See his essay 'Ursachen und Anlass des Weltkrieges 1914', in 1914–1939–1945. Schicksalsjahre deutscher Geschichte (1964).

[36] Eckart Kehr, Schlachtflottenbau und Parteipolitik 1894–1901 (Berlin, 1930); Der Primat der Innenpolitik, ed. Hans-Ulrich Wehler (Berlin, 1965); Alfred Vagts, 'M.M. Warburg und Co. Ein Bankhaus in der deutschen Weltpolitik', in Vierteljahrshefte für Sozial- und Wirtschaftsgeschichte, Jg. 45, 1958.

are not altogether satisfying owing to the pre-arranged explanatory pattern usually employed over there.[37]

It is noteworthy that it is the communist historians, too, who do not approve of some of Fischer's conclusions, though they welcome his exposure of the nationalistic antecedents of non-communist Germany. For Fischer does not place the whole burden of responsibility for Germany's far-reaching war aims on the shoulders of the so-called ruling and upper middle classes, especially the big industrialists, and this does not fit into the Marxist–Leninist pattern. Furthermore, he does not in their view lay enough stress on the opposition of the extreme left to the imperialist policy of the 'ruling classes'. On the contrary, he presents the socialist workers either as the 'fellow travellers' of government policy, or, in so far as they openly declared war on the latter, he simply dismisses them as having had little influence on the course of events. Moreover, Fischer implies that Germany bears, if not the sole, at all events the greatest share of the guilt for the outbreak of the war and for its pursuit to the point of utter exhaustion, in contrast to the Marxist–Leninist view, in which *all* capitalist states are inexorably driven to war.

In West German research there is a growing tendency to examine the domestic German situation to discover why, in 1914–18, German war aims were so unrealistic. The constitutional, political, and social structure of the German Empire, which was at that time passing through a period of crisis, must obviously provide a large part of the explanation, and Fischer recently asserted that German expansionist aims during the war were designed to preserve the 'traditional class and social structure of the Prusso–German Reich' in face of the mounting pressures of democracy. This is a tenable thesis, but in the loose and general formulations in which Fischer clothes it, it is neither very new nor very informative. Even at the time it was clearly realized, among others by Max Weber, that there was a direct connection between the extreme annexationist aims of the Right and the social and economic

---

[37] Cf. Lothar Rathmann, *Stossrichtung Nahost 1914–18* (Berlin [East], 1963); Werner Richter, *Gewerkschaften, Monopolkapital und Staat im ersten Weltkrieg* (Berlin, 1959); Joachim Petzold, 'Zu den Kriegszielen der deutschen Monopolkapitalisten im ersten Weltkrieg', in *Zeitschrift für Geschichtswissenschaft*, Jg. 8, 1960. The contributions to the symposium *Politik im Krieg 1914–18* (Berlin [East], 1964), are not concentrated so exclusively on economic and social aspects and are often interesting.

interests of their own group. One of the main future tasks of historical research will be to define and classify these interests more precisely and to analyse them within the framework of the political and social conditions of the last years of the Wilhelmian Reich. A beginning has already been made in the work of Reinhard Patemann, Willibald Gutsche, Pogge-Strandmann, and Egmont Zechlin.[38] One may hope that as research on these questions expands, the general discussion will gain in objectivity. Opinions on Germany's policies in the first world war have clashed with such unaccustomed bitterness because, during the years of national-socialist rule, students of German contemporary history were prevented from treating these burning questions of the immediate German past in an impartial and unprejudiced manner. And so the prejudices, opinions, and attitudes of contemporaries were kept alive in their original form, instead of undergoing the customary continuous process of revision. The debate on German war aims is itself a symptom of the fact that the Germans, because of the crises and upheavals in their history since 1918, have not yet found their way back to an undivided historical consciousness.

[38] R. Patemann, *Der Kampf um die preussische Wahlreform im Ersten Weltkrieg* (Dusseldorf, 1964); W. Gutsche, 'Bethmann Hollweg und die Politik der Neuorientierung', in *Zeitschrift fur Geschichtswissenschaft*, Jg. 13, 1965; Pogge-Strandmann, 'Staatsstreichpläne, Alldeutsche und Bethmann Hollweg', in *Die Erforderlichkeit des Unmöglichen*; E. Zechlin, 'Bethmann Hollweg, Kriegsrisiko und SPD 1914', in *Der Monat*, 18 Jg., Heft 208, 1966. See also E. Pickart, 'Der deutsche Reichstag und der Ausbruch des ersten Weltkrieges', *Der Staat*, vol. 5, 1966.

The Outbreak of the First World War and German War Aims

Imanuel Geiss

The Crisis of July 1914

German innocence – or at least relative innocence – for the outbreak of the 1914 war had for decades been something that could not be questioned in Germany. The function of this taboo varied according to the circumstances: in early August 1914 it was designed to impress both the SPD and Britain, in order to get the former into the war, and if possible to keep the latter out of it. During the war it was to convince neutrals and Germans alike of the righteousness of the Reich's cause. Immediately after the war, even the left-wing governments of 1918–19 clung in dealing with the Allies to the concept of German relative innocence, in the hope of getting a more lenient peace settlement. When they failed, later governments and public opinion in the Weimar Republic retreated from the relatively critical line of these earlier governments which, after all, had published the German documents and set up a Commission of Enquiry into the causes of Germany's defeat.

The Weimar Republic opened a sustained campaign against article 231 of the Versailles treaty; it hoped, by disputing Germany's responsibility for the war, to dismantle the treaty as a whole. The campaign had started at Versailles itself, where Bülow (later Secretary of State in the Auswärtiges Amt) mapped out and initiated the strategy.[1] In the Auswärtiges Amt a small sub-section, the Kriegsschuldreferat, inspired, directed, and financed the German innocence propaganda. Its chief instruments were two organizations, the Arbeitsausschuss Deutscher Verbände (ADV),

---

[1] What follows is only a preliminary sketch of a very complicated story, based so far on the study of about half of the rich archival material of the Kriegsschuldreferat in the Political Archive of the Auswärtiges Amt at Bonn.

71

and the Zentralstelle zur Erforschung der Kriegsschuldfrage. ADV, a federation of practically all reputable semi-political organizations, including the trade unions, looked after the general propaganda, while the Zentralstelle had to cover the scholarly aspects of the campaign.

The two organizations worked together, notwithstanding occasional rivalries and bickerings behind the scenes, and the Kriegsschuldreferat saw to the necessary finances and co-ordination. Each had a periodical, the more important one for the general historian being the Zentralstelle's *Kriegsschuldfrage*; for its launching it was possible to find money even in summer 1923, at the height of the inflation. The editor of *Kriegsschuldfrage* – later renamed *Berliner Monatshefte* – was Alfred von Wegerer, an ex-army officer. For tactical reasons he posed as an independent, but he was in fact employed by the Auswärtiges Amt, in a position ranking in salary and annual leave as a *Ministerialrat*. Both the budget and the literary activities of the Zentralstelle were controlled by the Kriegsschuldreferat, which in its turn gave Wegerer valuable information for pursuing the scholarly struggle against the 'Kriegsschuldlüge'.

A third, more subtle instrument consisted of a host of writers, none of them historians, engaged as part-time propagandists. For a moderate but regular monthly payment of a few hundred marks they wrote three or four articles a month in German dailies and/or periodicals on the war guilt question. The most prominent among them were Bernhard Schwertfeger, an ex-Colonel, and Hermann Lutz, a free-lance writer. The appearance of Lutz on the pay-roll of the Auswärtiges Amt is the more startling since, judging from his *Gutachten* for the work of the Commission of Enquiry,[2] he must have passed as an independent critic of the official line. A fourth means used was to subsidise publications which took the German line, although occasionally books with critical passages were allowed to pass in order not to arouse suspicions abroad. These publications ranged from *Die Grosse Politik* to insignificant pamphlets. The usual method was to buy a number of copies, often several hundred, in advance; these were afterwards sent to German missions abroad which distributed them free to key personalities in the respective countries. Many of the subsidised books were transla-

---

[2] Hermann Lutz, *Die europäische Politik in der Julikrise 1914. Das Werk des Untersuchungsausschusses*, 1. Reihe, Bd. 11 (Berlin, 1930).

tions into German. (The Auswärtiges Amt subsidy was much sought after by German publishers, and it is quite possible that without the financial assistance of the Kriegsschuldreferat many a book might not have appeared.) Probably only a few foreign authors received more than this kind of subsidy: one, Boghitchevitch, living in Switzerland, was paid by the Auswärtiges Amt in gold francs, a difficult thing to manage in 1919. Most of the foreign authors supporting the German cause were probably unaware of the subsidy, though it is difficult to say how many would have minded if they had known.

The Kriegsschuldreferat decided which publications criticizing the German line were to be attacked, how, by whom, and when and where, or whether they should be simply ignored. This is what happened to a booklet by Walter Fabian, now editor of *Gewerk-schaftliche Monatshefte*.[3] Similarly, it acted as internal censor for official or semi-official publications, in particular of the Unter-suchungsausschuss, an effort in which it was partly supported by the latter's secretary-general, Eugen Fischer-Baling. Together, they prevented the publication of Hermann Kantorowicz's *Gutachten* for the Untersuchungsausschuss, although it was completed and set up in type as early as 1927.[4] When, in 1932, the Untersuchungsausschuss wanted to publish five volumes of documents on German war aims, the Kriegsschuldreferat vetoed the proposal on the ground that the documents would prove to the whole world that German plans of conquest made nonsense of the German innocence campaign. Finally, the Kriegsschuldreferat prepared the many official statements of German chancellors and of President Hindenburg on the war guilt question during the Weimar period, statements which, perhaps more than anything else, helped to strengthen the taboo.

The campaign was the more effective since German historians lent it their great prestige. Most of them did not need official prompting but had only to follow their natural inclinations. Surprisingly enough, the contribution of professional German historians to a rational analysis of the causes of the war had been fairly slight. Most of the German campaigners were amateurs, and none of the few professionals who were prominently engaged (Hans

3 Walter Fabian, *Die Kriegsschuldfrage* (Leipzig, n.d. [1925]). The chapter on July 1914 was republished, unchanged, in August 1964; see W. Fabian, 'So brach 1914 der Krieg aus', in *Gewerkschaftliche Monatshefte*, vol. 15, no. 8.
4 I hope to be able to publish this *Gutachten* in the near future.

Delbrück, Friedrich Thimme, Paul Herre, Erich Brandenburg, Richard Fester, Hans Rothfels, Hans Herzfeld) ever wrote anything comparable to the great works of Pierre Renouvin, Bernadotte E. Schmitt, or Luigi Albertini. The defence of the German cause was mostly left either to foreigners, such as Barnes or Fay, or to amateurs such as Wegerer or Lutz.[5]

How effective the German innocence campaign had been became clear after the second world war. To the rest of the world this had only proved German responsibility for the first. Not so in Germany. After a few years of confusion and hesitation, which produced some criticism by Friedrich Meinecke, most German historians swung back to the old line. They contended that Germany (or rather Hitler) was responsible for the second but not for the first. There was no fresh research or re-interpretation of the causes of 1914. Although a few modifications were introduced by Gerhard Ritter,[6] Wegerer's authority was never questioned[7]; Albertini's massive work was almost completely ignored. The German public remained dependent on the meagre fare offered by professional historians in articles, textbooks, and short chapters or sub-chapters in a number of more general works.

It is only against this background that one can understand the terrific outburst of excitement over Fritz Fischer's book,[8] which quickly became known as the 'Fischer controversy'. For Fischer not only questioned the taboo built up over five decades by successive political regimes in Germany; he also broke the monopoly of knowledge held by conservative or mildly conservative-liberal historians, in a historical problem which may well rank as

[5] Pierre Renouvin, *Les origines immédiates de la guerre* (Paris, 1925); Bernadotte E. Schmitt, *The Coming of the War*. 2 vols. (New York, London, 1930); Luigi Albertini, *Le origini della guerra del 1914*. 3 vols. (Milan, 1942), English ed. *The Origins of the War of 1914*. 3 vols. (London, New York, Toronto, 1952/57); Harry E. Barnes, *The Genesis of the World War* (New York, 1927); Sydney B. Fay, *The Origins of the World War*. 2 vols. (New York, 1928); Alfred v. Wegerer, *Der Ausbruch des Weltkrieges 1914*. 2 vols. (Hamburg, 1939); for Lutz, see footnote 2.

[6] Gerhard Ritter, *Staatskunst und Kriegshandwerk*, 3 vols. (Munich, 1954–64), vol. 2, pp. 282–343.

[7] Ibid., p. 386, n. 9. Karl-Dietrich Erdmann, 'Die Zeit der Weltkriege', in: *Handbuch der deutschen Geschichte*, ed. Bruno Gebhardt, 8th ed. vol. iv (Stuttgart, 1961), p. 18.

[8] Fritz Fischer, *Griff nach der Weltmacht. Die Kriegszielpolitik des kaiserlichen Deutschland 1914/1918* (Düsseldorf, 1961), 3rd edition, 1964.

one of the most complicated and bewildering in modern history. He did it just by picking up Albertini and reading the documents published since 1919.

The leading German historians rushed angrily into print to denounce Fischer and closed ranks against the heretic. Vis-à-vis Fischer they all seemed to have forgotten their former squabbles and political disagreements. Erwin Hölzle from the right joined forces with Golo Mann, Ludwig Dehio, and Hans Herzfeld of the 'left',[9] while Gerhard Ritter from his centre position turned out to be Fischer's most persistent critic.[10] Taking real or imaginary defects as an excuse for condemning the effort as such, many concentrated their attacks on the chapter on July 1914. In the very year when their attacks reached an emotional climax in the shrill polemics of Michael Freund[11] and Giselher Wirsing,[12] the discussion took a turn for the better. After the initial formation of a united front against Fischer, three major groups emerged. One, led by Hans Rothfels, stuck to their traditional guns and said there was nothing to revise. A second, headed by Gerhard Ritter and Michael Freund, though criticizing the older German literature on July 1914 as 'too apologetic' (Ritter) or even denouncing the traditional line as the 'Unschuldslüge' (Freund), still maintained most of their old arguments.

A third group, represented by Egmont Zechlin and Karl-Dietrich Erdmann, have at least in part abandoned the old positions, although very discreetly and without giving any credit to Fischer. They now admit that Germany in July 1914 deliberately risked war, even with Britain, but they hedge this vital admission with a number of 'explanations' which only tend to obscure the central issue. Zechlin argues that Bethmann Hollweg, when taking the plunge in July 1914, only wanted a limited, 'rational' war in

9 Hölzle in *Das Historisch-Politische Buch*, March 1962, pp. 65–9; Golo Mann in *Neue Zürcher Zeitung*, 28 April 1962; Dehio in *Der Monat*, February 1962; Herzfeld in *Vierteljahrshefte für Zeitgeschichte*, July 1963, pp. 224–45.

10 Gerhard Ritter, 'Griff zur Weltmacht?' in *Lübecker Nachrichten*, 20 May 1962; 'Eine neue Kriegsschuldthese?' in *Historische Zeitschrift (HZ)* June 1962, pp. 646–68; *Staatskunst und Kriegshandwerk*, vol. 3 (Munich, 1964); *Der Erste Weltkrieg; Studien zum deutschen Geschichtsbild.* Schriftenreihe der Bundeszentrale für politische Bildung, no. 64 (Bonn, 1964); 'Zur Fischer-Kontroverse', in *HZ*, June 1965, pp. 783–7.

11 'Bethmann Hollweg, der Hitler des Jahres 1914?' in *Frankfurter Allgemeine Zeitung*, 28/29 March 1964.

12 '. . . auch am Ersten Weltkrieg schuld?' in *Christ und Welt*, 8 May 1964; 'Der Bauchredner', ibid., 10 July 1964.

eighteenth-century style, not a ferocious world war.[13] In two recent articles he has moved even closer to the position of those who criticize the traditional line, so that the differences between him and the Fischer group, on that point at least, have now been reduced to a few subtle shades of interpretation. On the other hand, these slight divergences give even less warrant for Zechlin's (and others') view that Fischer is all wrong, since Zechlin now maintains that Bethmann Hollweg consciously took the risk of British intervention.[14] Erdmann gives a psychological portrait of the Chancellor, based mainly on the diary of Kurt Riezler, Bethmann Hollweg's close adviser, and stresses the Chancellor's subjective honesty, his rejection of world domination for Germany (which, unfortunately, Erdmann confuses with the alleged rejection of achieving the status of a world power).[15] Both harp on the rediscovered story of the proposed Anglo-Russian naval convention. Still, Zechlin and Erdmann have introduced new tones into the debate and have made rational discussion possible. They set the final seal on the demolition of the traditional taboo.

Another myth has also to go for good – the myth of *Einkreisung*.[16] There was no 'encirclement' of Germany by enemies waiting to attack and crush her. The partition of Europe and the world into two power blocks, with the Triple Entente on the one hand, the Triple Alliance on the other, was largely a result of German policy, of the German desire to raise the Reich from the status of a continental power to that of a world power. The Triple Alliance itself came into being as a purely continental arrangement in the years 1879–82, in order to keep France isolated, and the Franco-Russian Alliance of 1894, the nucleus of the Triple Entente, was the French means of escaping that isolation. It was only after Germany started on her ambitious and ill-fated career of becoming a full-fledged

---

13 Egmont Zechlin, 'Deutschland zwischen Kabinettskrieg und Wirtschaftskrieg. Politik und Kriegführung in den ersten Monaten des Weltkrieges 1914', in *HZ*, 199/2, p. 361 ff.

14 E. Zechlin, ' Bethmann Hollweg, Kriegsrisiko und SPD 1914 ', in *Der Monat*, January 1966; 'Motive und Taktik der Reichsleitung 1914. Ein Nachtrag', ibid. February 1966.

15 'Zur Beurteilung Bethmann Hollwegs', in *Geschichte in Wissenschaft und Unterricht*, September 1964, pp. 525–40.

16 The best and most detailed study exploding the myth is the undeservedly forgotten book by Hermann Kantorowicz, *Der Geist der englischen Politik und das Gespenst der Einkreisung Deutschlands* (Berlin, 1929), in particular the last chapter.

world power in her own right that the world situation changed radically. Britain, challenged by Germany's naval programme more than by her territorial claims, notably in Africa, abandoned her 'splendid isolation' and sought alliances, first with Japan in 1902, then with France in 1904, and finally, in 1907, with Russia. What was – and to a certain extent still is – denounced in Germany as *Einkreisung*, amounted to the containment of German ambitions which ran counter to the interests of all other imperialist powers.

The concept of encirclement, however, played an important part immediately before the outbreak of war in 1914. In Germany the idea had become widespread that the only choice for the Reich was between rising to a full-fledged world power and stagnation. The German *Weltanschauung* saw only the unending struggle of all against all; this social-Darwinist concept was not limited to the lunatic fringe, but influenced even the most liberal spokesman of the Wilhelmian establishment, Riezler, Bethmann Hollweg's young protégé.[17] For him all nations had the desire for permanent expansion with world domination as the supreme goal. Since he looked upon any containment of German aspirations as a hostile act, Riezler's ideas, translated into official policy, were bound to make war unavoidable. Even Bethmann Hollweg thought in 1911 that war was necessary for the German people.[18]

The final logical conclusion was the idea of preventive war against those enemies who tried to block Germany's further rise. The traditional school in Germany always indignantly denied the existence of the preventive war concept even among the Prussian General Staff.[19] The prevailing spirit of militarism and social-Darwinism in Wilhelmian Germany made it, however, more than plausible. A new source, the private papers of Jagow, provides the missing link between Germany's pre-war *Weltpolitik* and the outbreak of war. At the end of May or early in June 1914 Moltke, Chief of the General Staff, asked Jagow, the German Secretary of State for Foreign Affairs, to start a preventive war as soon as possible, because militarily the situation for Germany was constantly deteriorating. Jagow refused, pointing to the improvement in the

---

[17] See Kurt Riezler, *Die Erforderlichkeit des Unmöglichen* (Munich, 1912), chap. vi; J.J. Ruedorffer (Riezler), *Grundzüge der Weltpolitik in der Gegenwart* (Stuttgart, 1914).

[18] K.D. Erdmann, *Zur Beurteilung Bethmann Hollwegs*, p. 534.

[19] A.v. Wegerer, *Ausbruch*, I, p. 355. G. Ritter, *Staatskunst und Kriegshandwerk*, vol. 2, p. 147.

German economic situation. But after the war he admitted that he was never *a limine* against the idea of preventive war – after all, Bismarck's wars had been preventive wars, according to Jagow – and that Moltke's words inspired him with confidence in military success when the crisis did come in July 1914.[20] Another recent find tallies with Jagow's point of view. In February 1918 ex-Chancellor Bethmann Hollweg, questioned privately by the liberal politician Conrad Haussmann, said: 'Yes, My God, in a certain sense it was a preventive war. But when war was hanging above us, when it had to come in two years even more dangerously and more inescapably, and when the generals said, now it is still possible, without defeat, but not in two years time. Yes, the generals!'[21]

Against that background the events after Sarajevo are easy to understand, for Sarajevo turned out to be hardly more than the cue for the Reich to rush into action, although Austria had to deal the first blow against Serbia. The Austrians, however, were originally divided in their counsels. Only the Chief of the General Staff, Conrad von Hötzendorf, pressed for immediate war against Serbia, supported by high officials in the Foreign Ministry and by most of the German press in Austria. Foreign Minister Berchtold, the Austrian and the Hungarian Prime Ministers, Stürgkh and Tisza, hesitated and were for less radical measures. But even Conrad realized that he could not wage war against Serbia without first making sure that Germany would cover Austria's rear against Russia.[22] Thus the real decision lay with Germany.

After Sarajevo Germany could not at once make up her mind which course to follow. The Auswärtiges Amt clearly saw the danger involved in Russia's trying to protect Serbia if Austria made war, namely, that a world war might result. This is why the Auswärtiges Amt from the first counselled moderation both to

---

[20] Nachlass Jagow, vol. viii; Politische Aufsätze. Politisches Archiv des Auswärtiges Amts, Bonn. The relevant document has meanwhile been published by E. Zechlin in *Der Monat*, February 1966.

[21] Wolfgang Steglich, *Die Friedenspolitik der Mittelmächte*, vol. I (Wiesbaden, 1964), p. 418, n. 3.

[22] To save space, references to well-known documents have been omitted. All the relevant material mentioned can be found, arranged in chronological order, in my *Julikrise und Kriegsausbruch 1914. Eine Dokumentensammlung* (2 vols. Hannover, 1963/64), and in a condensed pocket-book version: *Juli 1914. Die europäische Krise und der Ausbruch des Ersten Weltkriegs* (Munich, 1965).

Austria and to Serbia. The German General Staff, on the other hand, was ready to welcome Sarajevo as the golden opportunity for risking a preventive war. In this situation it was the Kaiser's word that proved decisive. Wilhelm II was incensed at the murder, perhaps most because it attacked his cherished monarchist principle. When he received the report of Tschirschky, the German ambassador to Vienna, of 30 June, telling of his moderating counsels to the Austrians, the Kaiser commented in his usual wild manner and provided the specious slogan 'Now or never'! which turned out to be the guiding star of German diplomacy in the crisis of July 1914.

On 5 July, Count Hoyos came to Berlin, bringing with him two documents on Austrian policy towards the Balkans. The Austrian ambassador, Szogyeny, handed them to the Kaiser at a special audience at the Potsdam Palace, in which he apparently used fairly warlike language, although the documents of his own government spoke of war, if at all, only by implication. After initial hesitation, Wilhelm II promised German support to the Dual Monarchy, whatever Austria did. His promise soon came to be called the German *carte blanche* to Austria. But the Kaiser was not satisfied with giving his ally a free hand against Serbia. He urged Vienna, which apparently had not made up its mind, to make war on Serbia, and that as soon as possible. Bethmann Hollweg and the Emperor's other civilian and military advisers duly endorsed these imperial decisions.

When Bethmann returned to Hohenfinow, he told Riezler what had happened at Potsdam. From what Riezler recorded in his by now famous diary, it appears that the Chancellor was not only fully aware of the possible consequences when taking his 'leap into the dark' – war with Britain, i.e. world war – but that already at that stage his first objective seems to have been war with Russia and France; a diplomatic victory – France dropping Russia, Russia dropping Serbia – would have been accepted only as a second best.[23]

Impressed by the German stand, Berchtold swung round in favour of Conrad's line. His colleagues in the Cabinet followed suit, last of all Tisza, and so did Emperor Francis Joseph. Preparations were made in Vienna and Berlin for the *coup* against Serbia: it was decided to confront Serbia with an ultimatum which

---

23 K.D. Erdmann, *Zur Beurteilung*, p. 536.

would be designed to be unacceptable as soon as the French president Poincaré and his prime minister Viviani had finished their state visit to Russia. That was to be on 23 July.

Meanwhile, the Austrian and German governments did everything to create a peaceful impression. The two emperors enjoyed their usual summer holidays, as did the leading generals of the Central Powers. But they returned to their respective capitals before or just after the ultimatum was handed over at Belgrade. Austria kept the German government informed of her intentions through the normal diplomatic channels, while the German government pressed Austria to start the action against Serbia as soon as possible. Privately the Germans aired serious misgivings at the lack of energy Austria displayed, and the Auswärtiges Amt suspected her of being unhappy about Germany's urgency. These suspicions were not unfounded: the Austrians had waited to make a decision until the German declaration of 5 July, but even then they moved slowly. According to Austrian plans, mobilization would begin after the rupture of diplomatic relations with Serbia, but it was originally intended to delay the actual declaration of war and the opening of hostilities until mobilization was completed, i.e., until approximately 12 August. The Wilhelmstrasse, however, deemed such delay absolutely intolerable. It was quick to see that the powers might intervene diplomatically during the interval to save Serbia from humiliation. As the German government was bent on preventing any mediation, it spurred Vienna on, as soon as it learned of the Austrian time-table, to declare war on Serbia immediately after the rupture with Belgrade and to open hostilities at once. On 25 July, Jagow told Szogyeny that the German government

takes it for granted that upon eventual negative reply from Serbia, our declaration of war will follow immediately, joined to military operations. Any delay in beginning warlike preparations is regarded here as a great danger in respect of intervention of other powers. We are urgently advised to go ahead at once and confront the world with a *fait accompli*.

On the other hand, Jagow justified his refusal to pass on British proposals of mediation to Vienna by the alleged fear that Vienna might react by rushing things and confronting the world with a *fait accompli*. Yet when Austria, giving way to German pressure, did declare war immediately, the German Secretary of State told the British Ambassador, Sir Edward Goschen, that now the very thing had happened he had always warned against: namely, Austria rushing things as an answer to proposals of mediation.

German pressure on Vienna to declare war on Serbia without delay had an immediate and telling effect: on 26 July, Berchtold, who had been wavering and who tended to be timid rather than aggressive, adopted the German idea, and in this he was vigorously supported by Tschirschky. Conrad, however, was far from happy. Although usually thought of as the most warlike on the side of the Central Powers,[24] he would have preferred to stick to the original timetable, but he gave in, and the Austrian government decided on an early declaration of war. On 27 July the final decision was taken to declare war the following day.

Now the German government had accomplished one of its short-term aims: Austria had confronted the world with a *fait accompli* in the form of an early declaration of war against Serbia, which was bound to undermine all attempts at mediation between Austria and Serbia. The following day, 29 July, the Austrians rushed things even more, again following German advice, when they started the bombardment of Belgrade.[25] The immediate effect was catastrophic: the Russians took the bombardment of Belgrade as the beginning of military operations against Serbia, as it was meant to be. They had, on 28 July, already ordered partial mobilization against Austria in order to deter her from actual warfare against Serbia. Now the Russian generals, thinking war with Austria and Germany imminent, successfully pressed for immediate general mobilization, since Russian mobilization was known to be far slower than Austrian or German. The Tsar ordered a halt to general mobilization and a return to partial mobilization after the receipt of a telegram from Wilhelm II late in the evening of 29 July, but the next afternoon the generals and the foreign minister Sazonov renewed their pressure on him. Nicholas gave

[24] As shown recently in G. Ritter, *Staatskunst*, vol. 2, p. 282.
[25] The German government was informed of Austrian preparations to shell Belgrade through a report by the German military attaché at Vienna, Count Kageneck, of 18 July: *Politisches Archiv des Auswärtiges Amts, Der Weltkrieg* (vol. 2). Kageneck's report is one of the documents not included in the German documents; it was published for the first time in *Julikrise* (137).

way and Russian general mobilization was ordered for a second time on 30 July, at 6 p.m.

The German government rushed things also in two more respects: on 27 July Jagow had assured Jules Cambon and Sir Horace Rumbold, the British chargé d'affaires in Berlin, that Germany would not mobilize so long as Russia mobilized only in the south, against Austria. Two days later, however, the Auswärtiges Amt received a lengthy memorandum from General Moltke, whose arguments boiled down to an insistence on German general mobilization. Again the Auswärtiges Amt followed the lead of the generals. After 30 July, Berlin demanded the cancellation of Russian mobilization not only against Germany, but also against Austria, and that demand was expressly included both in the German ultimatum to Russia on 31 July and in the declaration of war of 1 August. When the French ambassador reminded Jagow of his words only a few days earlier, Jagow apparently shrugged his shoulders and replied that the generals wanted to have it that way, and that his words had, after all, not been a binding statement.

The second point was at least as serious: while the Entente powers tried desperately to prevent a local war, in order to avert a continental and world war, by making a whole series of proposals of mediation, [26] the German government not only flatly rejected them or passed them on to Vienna without giving them support, but also stifled the only initiative from the German side which might have saved the general peace. This time, the initiative had come from the Kaiser. Wilhelm had returned from his sailing holiday in Norway after learning of the Austrian suspension of diplomatic relations with Serbia on 25 July. He arrived at Potsdam on the 27th. Early the following morning he read the Serbian answer to Austria's ultimatum. Like nearly everybody else in Europe outside Germany and Austria, the Kaiser was impressed by Serbia's answer, which had conceded practically everything except one point, and made only a few reservations. Suddenly all his warlike sentiments vanished and he minuted:

a brilliant achievement in a time-limit of only 48 hours! It is more than one could have expected! A great moral success for Vienna; but with it all reason for war is gone and Giesl ought to have quietly stayed on in Belgrade! After that I should never have ordered mobilization.

[26] In particular the suggestion to extend the time limit for answering the ultimatum and the British proposal to hold a four-power conference in London.

He immediately ordered the Auswärtiges Amt to draft a note for Vienna, telling the Austrians that they should accept the Serbian answer. To satisfy the army, and at the same time as a guarantee for what the Serbians had conceded, the Kaiser suggested that Austria should content herself with occupying Belgrade only and negotiate with the Serbians about the remaining reservations.

Apparently the Auswärtiges Amt took fright at their sovereign's weakness. The moment that had come during both Moroccan crises threatened to come again: that the Kaiser would lose his nerve and beat the retreat. This time, however, Bethmann Hollweg and the Auswärtiges Amt did not listen to their sovereign as they had done on 5 July. The Chancellor despatched the instructions to Tschirschky on the evening of 28 July, i.e., after he had learned that Austria had declared war on Serbia. Furthermore, he distorted the Kaiser's argument by omitting the crucial sentence that war was now no longer necessary. The occupation of Belgrade was not meant to be, in Bethmann's words, a safeguard for the implementation of Serbian concessions, but a means to enforce Serbia's total acceptance of the Austrian ultimatum. Finally, the Chancellor added a comment which was sure to defeat any conciliatory effect of his démarche, if any chance of this had remained.[27]

In these circumstances, the démarche, when executed by Tschirschky, had no effect whatsoever, nor did a later British proposal along similar lines.

When developments had gone so far, Bethmann Hollweg undertook his most important move, the bid for British neutrality. On 29 July he had despatched the ultimatum to Belgium to the German minister in Brussels. The violation of Belgian neutrality made it vital for Germany that at least British acquiescence be secured. During the evening of 29 July, Bethmann, returning from talks with the Kaiser and his military advisers at Potsdam, summoned the British ambassador. The Chancellor asked for England's neutrality in return for the promise that Germany would not annex French or Belgian territory. The reaction of the Foreign Office was scathing, as is borne out by Crowe's comment.

A British answer to the German demand was no longer needed, for, just after Goschen left the Chancellor, a telegram from London arrived: Lichnowsky reported Grey's warning that Britain would not remain neutral if France were involved in a continental war.

[27] Albertini, op. cit., II, p. 456 ff.

Now Grey – at last – had spoken in such a way that even the German Chancellor had to abandon his cherished hope of British neutrality, which would have meant certain victory for Germany in the imminent continental war. Bethmann Hollweg was dumbfounded, for he saw clearly the consequences of Grey's warning – a world war which Germany could hardly win. In his panic, he tried to salvage what seemed possible. He now pressed the Austrians in all sincerity to modify their stand, but did not go so far as to advise the Austrians to drop the whole idea of war against Serbia. He only pleaded with them to accept the British version of the 'halt-in-Belgrade' proposal and to open conversations with the Russians. In such conversations the Austrians were to repeat their promise not to annex Serbian territory, a pledge which, as the Chancellor knew quite well, was regarded by Russia as insufficient. Bethmann made his proposals in the vague hope that by shifting the blame to Russia the British might stay out after all. At the same time he wanted to persuade the German public, especially the social-democrats, to follow his policy by demonstrating his peaceful intentions. The Chancellor did not want to put an end to the local war, which had just seen its second day; what he wanted was to improve Germany's position in a major conflict.

Bethmann Hollweg failed in his first objective; he succeeded in his second only too well. The social-democrats supported the German war effort, and the Russians are still blamed in Germany today for having started the war. For this same reason – to shift the blame to Russia – Bethmann also resisted the pressure of the General Staff who pleaded for immediate German mobilization. The Chancellor urged that Russia be allowed to mobilize first against Germany, since, as he put it, he could not pursue military and political actions at the same time. In other words, he could not simultaneously put the blame on Russia and order German mobilization before Russian general mobilization.

On 29 July, the German generals still appreciated Bethmann Hollweg's policy. But during the 30th they became impatient. In the evening, about two hours after Russian general mobilization had been definitely ordered, they told the Chancellor that he had to make up his mind about German mobilization immediately. The Chancellor won a delay until noon next day, but there was little doubt which way the decision was meant to go. Bethmann Hollweg agreed, in the hope that the Russians might order general mobilization beforehand. During the morning of 31 July the Germans waited for the news of Russian general mobilization as their cue to rush into military action themselves. Luckily enough for Bethmann Hollweg and generations of German historians, Sazonov lost his nerve and had, in fact, already ordered Russian general mobilization.

At 11 a.m. Bethmann, Moltke, and Falkenhayn met again, anxiously waiting for news from Russia with only one hour left before the deadline they had set themselves. At five minutes to twelve a telegram from Pourtalès, the German ambassador to St Petersburg, was handed to them. It confirmed the rumours that Russian general mobilization had been ordered. Now they could order German mobilization with what they thought a clear conscience. Immediately after the receipt of the telegram the state of threatening war, the phase of military operations which immediately preceded general mobilization, was declared in Germany. The same afternoon, two ultimata went off – one to Russia demanding that she stop all military preparations not only against Germany but also against Austria, the other to France, asking about the stand France would take in a war between Germany and Russia. At the same time the Auswärtiges Amt prepared the declarations of war on both countries. Thus war had become inevitable, even more so since German general mobilization, according to the famous Schlieffen plan, meant opening hostilities against neutral Belgium a few days after mobilization had actually started.

After noon on 31 July, therefore, the catastrophe could no longer be averted. On 1 August, Germany ordered general mobilization, at the same hour as France. In the evening of that day, Germany declared war on Russia. An hour before, a curious and revealing incident had occurred. A telegram from Lichnowsky arrived suggesting that Britain might remain neutral if Germany were not to attack France. The Kaiser and his military, naval, and political advisers were happy, since their tough line during the July crisis seemed to be paying off after all. Only Moltke demurred. He was shocked by the idea of having to change his plan, and even feared that Russia might drop out as well. Late in the evening another telegram from London arrived, making the true position clear.

The French answer was evasive in form but firm in content: France would not forsake her ally. At the same time, France tried desperately to secure British support. The Russians, the French, and Crowe in the Foreign Office, urged Grey to make Britain's stand quite clear, that she would not remain neutral in a continental war. Grey had warned Germany before, but his language had not been straightforward enough to destroy German illusions. When Grey made the British policy unmistakably clear, even to the German Chancellor, it was too late.

How much Germany up to the last hour still hoped for British neutrality can be seen by the invention of a whole series of alleged border incidents, some of which were so crudely presented that outside Germany nobody believed them. They were part of the German manoeuvre to put the blame this time on France and to impress Britain. The German invasion of Belgium, however, removed the last hesitations: Britain sent an ultimatum to Germany demanding the immediate withdrawal of German troops from Belgium. When Germany refused, Britain entered the war automatically after the time-limit of the ultimatum had expired, i.e., at 11 p.m. Greenwich time on 4 August.

In trying to assess the shares of responsibility for the war two basic distinctions have to be made: on the one hand between the three stages of war connected with its outbreak: local war (Austria v. Serbia), continental war (Austria and Germany v. Russia and France), and world war (Britain joining the continental war). On the other hand, one has to distinguish between the will to start any of those three stages of war and the fact of merely causing them.

Since the world war developed out of a local war, then of continental war, the major share for causing it lies with that power which willed the local and/or continental war. That power was clearly Germany. She did not will the world war, as is borne out by her hopes of keeping out Britain, but she did urge Austria to make war on Serbia. Even if Austria had started the local war completely on her own – which, of course, she had not – Germany's share would still be bigger than Austria's, since a German veto could have effectively prevented it. Germany, furthermore, was the only power which had no objection to the continental war. So long as Britain kept out, she was confident of winning a war against Russia and France. Germany did nothing to prevent continental war, even at the risk of a world war, a risk which her government had seen from the beginning.

Austria, of course, wanted the local war, after – with German prodding – she had made up her mind, but feared a continental war. In fact, she hoped that Germany, by supporting her diplomatically, might frighten Russia into inaction.

Russia, France, and Britain tried to avert continental war. Their main argument for mediation between Serbia and Austria was precisely that to prevent the local war would be the best means of averting continental war. On the other hand, they contributed to the outbreak, each in her own way: Russia by committing the technical blunder of providing the cue for German mobilization, instead of waiting until Germany had mobilized. The French attitude was almost entirely correct; her only fault was that she could not hold back her Russian ally from precipitate general mobilization. Britain might have made her stand clear beyond any doubt much earlier, since this might have been a way of restraining Germany, although it is doubtful whether this would have altered the course of events to any appreciable degree. The share of the Entente powers is much smaller than Germany's, for it consisted mainly in reacting – not always in the best manner – to German action.

Looking back on the events from the mid-sixties, the outbreak of the first world war looks like the original example of faulty brinkmanship, of rapid escalation in a period of history when the mechanisms of alliances and mobilization schedules could still work unchecked by fear of the absolute weapon and the absolute destruction its use would bring in what would now be the third world war.

Russian foreign policy February–June 1914

I. V. Bestuzhev

The recent research work of Soviet historians into Russian foreign policy on the eve of the first world war[1] is distinguished by two characteristic features. First, they make use of a wide range of sources, in particular of archive material, among which the most important are the collections of documents in the Russian foreign policy archives, published in the volumes of *Mezhdunarodnye Otnosheniya v epokhu imperializma* (unfortunately the series is incomplete), and the collections held by the Central State Archives of the October Revolution and the Central State Historical Archives. Second, the research has been closely linked with research into the socio-economic history of Russia at that time. A large group of historians have worked in this field and have done a great deal to advance our understanding of the social and economic problems of Russian history in the imperialist epoch (1900–17).[2] The results of this research enable us to give a more profound analysis of tsarist foreign policy.

As a result of the greater availability of source material and of the increased attention given to the socio-economic foundations of foreign policy, it has been possible to give a more precise account

---

[1] Cf. V.I. Bovykin, *Ocherki Istorii vneshnei politiki Rossii: Konets XIX veka – 1917 god* (Moscow, 1960); ibid., *Iz Istorii vozniknoveniya pervoi mirovoi voiny: otnosheniya Rossii i Frantsii v 1912–14* (Moscow, 1961); P.N. Efremov, *Vneshnyaya politika Rossii 1907–14* (Moscow, 1961); A.V. Ignatiev, *Russko Angliiskie otnosheniya nakanune pervoi mirovoi voiny (1908–14)* (Moscow, 1962). Cf. also *Istoriya diplomatii*, 2nd revised ed., vol. 2, by V.M. Khvostov (Moscow, 1963); N.P. Poletika, *Voznikovenie pervoi mirovoi voiny (Iyulskii krizis, 1914)*, 2nd revised ed. (Moscow, 1964); K.B. Vinogradov, *Bosniiskii krizis 1908–9 – prolog pervoi mirovoi voiny* (Leningrad, 1964); I.V. Bestuzhev, *Borba v Rossii po voprosam vneshnei politiki 1906–10* (Moscow, 1961).

[2] In particular the latest work of A.L. Sidorov, I.F. Gindin, P.V. Volobuev, V.I. Bovykin, K.N. Tarnovsky and others. Cf. K.N. Tarnovsky, *Sovetskaya Istoriografiya Rossiiskovo Imperializma* (Moscow, 1964).

of Russia's position within the system of great powers at the beginning of the twentieth century. Study of the materials leads to the conclusion that it would be erroneous to present tsarist Russia on the eve of the first world war as a peculiar kind of semi-colony, merely an instrument of English and French policy, as was asserted in the *Short Course of the History of the CPSU*. Tsarism conducted an independent imperialist policy, even though it was becoming increasingly dependent on France and England. On the other hand, it would also be incorrect to present Russia as though it were on an equal footing, as a great power with pretensions to world supremacy, with England and Germany, which had such pretensions at that time.

The documents show that tsarism, pursuing its own imperialist aims, was compelled – as were France and Japan – to adjust itself to the struggle between the claimants to world supremacy. The question whether to begin or not to begin the war, and if to begin, then when, was decided in the final analysis in Berlin and London, although the question itself might have been raised in Paris and Petersburg and Vienna. The conclusive proof of this statement is given by the history of the Moroccan, Bosnian, Albanian, and Scutari crises, and the crisis over the Liman von Sanders mission (1905–14).

Reference to the documentary material also enables us to give a deeper analysis of the actions of the various governments, including the Russian, in the field of foreign policy, and to single out from the picture of each event as a whole the two linked aspects – the subjective intentions of the historical actors on the scene in undertaking the given action, and the objective significance and historical consequences of the action.

For example, the objective significance of the 1907 Anglo-Russian agreement was that it marked a further step in the formation of the two imperialist groups on the world stage. 'They are dividing Persia, Afghanistan, Tibet (they are preparing for war with Germany)' – that was Lenin's appraisal of the substance of the Anglo-Russian agreement.[3] But on that evidence alone it would be incorrect to assert that in 1907 the tsarist government was consciously moving towards a coalition with England against Germany. The documents show that at that time the tsarist government was

[3] V.I. Lenin, *Polnoe Sobranie Sochinenii*, 5th ed. vol. 28, p. 669.

not even dreaming of an alliance with England. In making the agreement, Nicholas II and his Foreign Minister Izvolsky were hoping to strengthen their position and to play the part of *tertius gaudens* in the approaching Anglo-German conflict. Berlin had not lost hope of neutralizing the agreement by a more far-reaching agreement between Germany and Russia.[4] But the course of developments led to the transformation of Russia into a member of the anti-German coalition (though not the leading one by far), and Russian diplomacy found on its agenda precisely that item of an alliance with England against Germany.

Another example: the known outcome of Russia's Balkan policy in 1912 was the failure of the attempt of the Russian ambassador in Constantinople, Charykov, to get for Russian warships exclusive rights of passage through the Bosphorus and the Dardanelles, and the establishment, with active Russian diplomatic participation, of a Balkan Union comprising Bulgaria, Serbia, and Greece. But it is clear from the documents that Charykov's démarche was only the unsuccessful last stage of a far bigger operation in diplomatic history. Charykov's mission, as revealed in the instructions of the President of the Russian Council of Ministers Stolypin over more than two years (from July 1909), was to work for the realization of a grandiose plan – the creation, under Russian auspices, of an all-Balkan alliance consisting of Turkey, Bulgaria, Serbia, Rumania, Greece, and Montenegro. This coalition was intended to serve as a powerful counter-weight to Austria–Hungary and to bring about a radical change in the balance of forces in the approaching world war.[5] The pursuit of this – alas, constantly receding – mirage lasted right up to 1914.

It was precisely the same with the July 1914 crisis. The contradictions among the great powers had by then reached such an extremely acute stage that world war had become unavoidable. The governments of all the powers, including Russia, shaped their policies on the assumption that war was near, but as regards preparedness for war tsarist Russia lagged considerably behind Germany. And just as it was a temptation for Germany to exploit this advantage, so it was desirable for the ruling circles of Russia to postpone the clash if only to 1916–17, when it was expected that the programme worked out in 1913 for strengthening the army and

[4] I.V. Bestuzhev, *op. cit.*, pp. 127–48.
[5] Ibid., pp. 338–44.

navy would have been carried out. 'What Russia desires in the next few years is a postponement of the final settlement of the Eastern question and the strict maintenance of the political status quo.' This was the task given to Russian diplomacy in the secret report of the Russian naval general staff dated 9/22 December 1913.[6] On the other hand the Russian military agent in Berlin, Colonel Bazarov, reported as early as 1912 that the German arms programme would be completed at the very latest in spring 1914, after which 'the critical moment will arrive when public opinion, the army, and those standing at the head of the state will come to realize that Germany is then in the most favourable position for beginning a successful war'.[7]

And in fact, as the State Secretary at the German Foreign Ministry, von Jagow, wrote in July 1914: 'Basically, Russia is not at the moment ready for war. Nor do France and England want war now. In a few years, on all reasonable assumptions, Russia will be ready. By then it will overwhelm us with the number of its troops; its Baltic fleet and strategic railways will have been constructed. Our own group will in the meantime have become much weaker' (Jagow was referring to the progressive disintegration of Austria–Hungary).[8]

In Petersburg they were bound to recognize that in these circumstances a war with Germany held the threat of defeat, and – as the experience of 1905 had shown – this would inevitably hasten a revolutionary explosion. Why then did the tsarist government in July 1914 consider it essential to risk these dangers, instead of making concessions which would gain them the time they so badly wanted – as it had done at the time of the Bosnian crisis and the crises of 1912–13? The answer to this question is to be found in the peculiarities of Russia's domestic and international position at the beginning of 1914; it was these which shaped the psychology of its ruling circles, make their aims intelligible, and explain why they chose this and not another course.

Russia's international position in February 1914, when the outcome of the crisis arising from Liman von Sanders' mission became clear, was characterized by the following important factors:

[6] *Krasny Arkhiv*, vol. 7, p. 34.

[7] Central State Military-Historical Archives, coll. 2000, schedule 1, file 687, folio 127.

[8] V.M. Khvostov, *op. cit.*, p. 776.

Relations with Germany, already strained, had become much worse. This was reflected in the 'newspaper war' of the two powers over the von Sanders' mission, which coincided with demands in the Russian press for a revision of the Russo-German commercial treaty of 1904, whose operations had been unfavourable to Russia, and, in the German press, for a preventive war against Russia.

Strained relations with Austria–Hungary, behind whom, again, stood Germany. The anti-Austrian campaign in the Russian press in 1914 reached white heat. It was inflamed by the no less embittered campaign against Russia in Austria–Hungary, one manifestation of which were the demonstrative trials of Ukrainian nationalists. In Petersburg Austria–Hungary was regarded as enemy no. 1. It was thought that the internal crisis coming to a head in that country might at any moment compel Vienna to a more active policy in the Balkans, or to a direct move against Russia.

Relations with England had deteriorated because of its more active policy of expansion in Tibet and particularly in Persia. Despite the Anglo-Russian agreement of 1907 the English government, taking advantage of the increasingly tense relations between Russia and Germany and Austria, and the consequent greater need of Russia for a further rapprochement with England, was in effect seeking Russian recognition of a British protectorate in Tibet and its agreement to the extension of the Anglo-Persian Oil Company's concession to the whole of Persia, including the Russian 'sphere of influence'. At the same time, London was trying to reinforce English influence on the Shah's government, to the obvious prejudice of tsarist influence, and to avoid an agreement on the Russian plan for a Trans-Persian railway, to which Petersburg attached great importance. As a result, in the words of the Russian ambassador in London, Benckendorff, the string of Anglo-Russian relations 'was so over-stretched' that it threatened to snap.[9]

Relations with France had become complicated. Petersburg had at that time accumulated a heavy score of grievances and claims against its ally, connected primarily with contradictions between the two powers in the Near East. These included resentment against the French position at the peace negotiations in Bucharest which concluded the Second Balkan War (August 1913), when France, together with England and Germany, took the side of Greece

---

[9] *Mezhdunarodnye otnosheniya v epokhu imperializma*, series 3, vol. 3, pp. 3–10.

against Bulgaria, whereas Petersburg considered support of Bulgaria essential to the re-establishment of the Balkan Alliance; dissatisfaction with the French position at the time of the Liman von Sanders crisis, when France in effect declined to give Russia active support, although it had put not a little effort into aggravating Russia's relations with Germany; anxiety over French efforts to get railway concessions in north-east Anatolia, that is, in an area adjacent to the Russo-Turkish frontier, thus seriously threatening to weaken Russia's economic and, more particularly, its strategic position there. Finally, friction arose in the course of the Franco-Russian negotiations then in progress concerning the actual realization of French loans to Russia for military needs and the means to obtain England's adherence to the Franco-Russian alliance.

Russia had obviously lost the game in the series being played for influence at Constantinople. The transformation of Turkey, after the Liman von Sanders mission had consolidated its position there, in effect into a German protectorate (this was how Russia's ruling circles assessed the position at the time) faced Russian diplomacy with the problem of preventing the final transfer of control over the Black Sea Straits to German hands. The question of the Straits took on a new sharpness.

Strengthening of the rapprochement with Serbia, after a certain cooling off in relations at the time of the Balkan Wars, when Belgrade expressed dissatisfaction with the trend in Petersburg towards compromise with Austria–Hungary and support for Bulgaria. The lack of clarity in the Bulgarian attitude induced the Russian government to place more value on its relations with Serbia.

Strengthening of the rapprochement with Montenegro after a marked cooling-off of relations during the Balkan Wars, when Russian subsidies were withdrawn from Montenegro because its king Nicholas Negosh (Petrovich) had started war on Turkey, thus frustrating Russian diplomatic efforts to construct an all-Balkan alliance on the basis of Macedonian autonomy (within the Ottoman Empire) and the division of this region into Serbian, Bulgarian, and Greek spheres of influence. Moreover, the unconciliatory attitude of the King at the time of the Scutari crisis made it much more difficult to reach a compromise with Austria–Hungary, and nearly provoked a premature (from Petersburg's point of view) collision with that country. Now the King needed Russian support

93

because of the growth in Montenegro of the movement for re-union with Serbia, whose ruling dynasty, the Karageorgeviches, was hostile to the Montenegrin Negosh dynasty.

An improvement in relations with Rumania which, it is true, were still not very firm, as Rumanian bourgeois-landlord circles turned more and more decisively towards Russia and against Austria–Hungary, while King Carol's court continued to lean towards the Triple Alliance.

Extreme intensification of the struggle with Austria–Hungary for influence in Sofia, with the object of bringing down the pro-Austrian government there and getting Bulgaria back into the bosom of the Balkan alliance.

Finally, progress in the rapprochement with Japan, which would secure the rear in the event of war in Europe. This process was brought to a conclusion with the Russo-Japanese agreement of 1916, which amounted in essence to an alliance between the two powers.

As to Russia's internal position, two factors deserve our attention in the context of the present analysis: A new rise of the revolutionary wave, reflecting the failure of the tsarist government's attempts to ward off the resurgent revolution by means of limited reforms of a bourgeois character which left untouched the powers of the autocracy and the inviolability of landlord property. This circumstance, of vital significance for the internal political situation, confronted tsarism with the problem of pursuing a more active foreign policy, as one of the traditional methods of 'stabilizing' the domestic situation.

A growth in the economic power of the big bourgeoisie, whose voice the government had to listen to more and more attentively as, with the growing acuteness of the country's situation, internal and international, it needed their support. This factor, it goes without saying, was less significant than the first, but in 1914 it became vital and cannot be left out of consideration.

Both factors played a decisive part in the struggle of classes and parties in Russia on questions of foreign policy. The peculiar feature of this struggle was that – in contrast to the struggle over questions of domestic policy, where there were relatively sharp differences concerning the scope and timing of reforms between the liberal-bourgeois and the conservative-landlord (black-hundred) camps – almost complete unanimity reigned among the liberal-bourgeois and the moderate right wing of the conservative-landlord camp, who advocated a vigorous struggle against Germany and Austria, and did not shrink even from open hostilities with them. Opposed to this course, as running too great a risk of military defeat and a new revolutionary explosion, were the extreme right wing of the black-hundred camp. They were comparatively few in number, but since they accounted for the majority of the court camarilla – those who really controlled tsarist policy – their influence was vast. It was this which gave its extreme intensity to the struggle over foreign policy in the press, in the Duma, and among the ruling circles.

By February–March 1914 some changes had occurred in this struggle: the growing strain in relations with Germany and Austria – more severe than any other foreign policy conflict – led to an ever-widening extension of the anti-German and anti-Austrian campaign among bourgeois-landlord circles.[10] There was a steady growth of pressure on the government by the imperialist bourgeoisie, acting through the commercial and industrial groups in the Duma and the State Council, through the council of representatives of trade and industry, committees of the Bourse and other organizations of large-scale capital. This pressure was reinforced by the growing number of landlords who were reorganizing their estates on capitalist lines. These too worked through the Duma and the State Council and also through the Council of representatives of finance and agriculture, and perhaps the council of the United Nobility (the position in regard to the last-named is not clear and requires further research in the archives). More frequent conferences were held between members of the government and leaders of the bourgeois-landlord parties, and with individual magnates such as Riabushinsky, Konovalov, and others.

These circles demanded a reinforcement of the alliance with France by an alliance with England, and a shift from defence to an offensive against Germany and Austria in the Near East. 'The chief object of our foreign policy', wrote *Novoe Vremya*, which may be taken as a fairly accurate barometer of sentiments among the ruling circles, 'should from now on be to break that tightening Teutonic ring around us which threatens Russia and the whole of Slavdom

10 See I.V. Bestuzhev, '*Borba v Rossii po voprosam vneshnei politiki nakanune pervoi mirovoi voiny*', in *Istoricheskie Zapiski*, vol. 75 (1965), pp. 44–85.

with fatal consequences ... And to do that it is up to us to exert all our strength to restore the Balkan alliance and to enter into direct treaty relations with the Slav powers which are part of it. Only such an unwavering policy can strengthen both our alliance with France and convert into a firm alliance our existing indecisive agreement with England'.[11]

If this text is compared with the actions of the Russian Foreign Ministry in the first half of 1914, it is clear that the entire foreign political programme followed undeviatingly along these lines right up to the July crisis.

In the course of the struggle over questions of foreign policy up to 1914 one curious shift became apparent: while the anti-German campaign had at first been headed by the Kadets, whereas the Octobrists and in particular the moderate right, had joined in only gradually and with serious misgivings, it was now the Octobrists and the moderate right who took over the advanced positions, although at one time they had been Stolypin's main pillars in his celebrated policy of 'twenty years of peace, at home and abroad'. Their voices counted more heavily in bourgeois-landlord opinion, the more so when the progressives and other groups, and later a part of the Kadets, joined more resolutely in the chorus.

It should be noted that differences on this question among the Kadets grew stronger; some went over to the Octobrists, others, led by Miliukov, advocated a more 'restrained' foreign policy, bringing them closer in this respect to their violent opponents on the extreme right. The only conceivable explanation of this attitude, at first glance so surprising, is that some Kadet leaders feared that the liberal opposition would lose all prestige if it supported an openly imperialist policy at a time when the revolutionary tide was rising.

At this point it is necessary to deal with the role of the Bolsheviks in the struggle to unite the revolutionary-democratic camp against militarism and the threat of war, and against tsarist imperialist policies as a whole. Until now Bolshevik activity in this respect has been described in isolation from the struggle going on among the political camps in Russia. At the same time the Bolsheviks represented the most consistent and active force in the revolutionary-democratic camp, and therefore their actions have to be considered

[11] *Novoe Vremya*, 23 December 1913 (5 January 1914).

in the context of the camp as a whole. It is of course extremely difficult to determine precisely the positions on foreign policy held by the Mensheviks, Socialist-Revolutionaries, and the Trudoviki fraction. Their public declarations frequently contained protests against militarism, but the objective substance of their policy was support for the pro-Entente Kadet tendency. But it is necessary to examine the specific features of the positions taken by the different groups in the revolutionary-democratic camp as the only means of establishing the Bolshevik line in contrast to the various currents of a petty-bourgeois character.

The anti-militarist struggle of the Bolsheviks was of immense importance. The core of the Russian working-class masses, headed by the Bolsheviks, did not succumb to the wave of chauvinism which swept over the countries of Europe in August 1914. The events of 1917 showed this clearly. 'By and large', Lenin noted, 'the Russian working class showed itself immune to chauvinism . . . The illegal Russian Social-Democratic Party (Bolsheviks) fulfilled its duty to the International. The banner of internationalism was held firmly in its hands'.[12]

Turning now to the question of the influence exercised by the struggle of classes and parties over matters of foreign policy on the psychology of the ruling circles at the time of the July crisis, we find that, between February and June 1914, the growing international tension and the revolutionary surge within the country called forth a twofold process – on the one hand, the consolidation of the right wing of the liberal-bourgeois camp (the Octobrists and the groups associated with them) and of the 'moderate' wing of the conservative-landlord camp (the moderate rights and their associated groups), and, on the other, the conflict at both poles of these camps (among the Kadets and the extreme right). Events similar to those occurring among the Kadets also took place on the extreme right, where the strongly pro-German front was visibly breaking up in the second half of 1913 and the early part of 1914. Many of its adherents moved over to join the moderate rights on questions of foreign policy.

Typical among them was one of the leaders of the extreme right,

---

12 Lenin, vol. 26, p. 331. On the Bolsheviks' anti-militarism see also I.V. Bestuzhev, 'Borba Lenina protiv militarizm' in the symposium *Bolshevistskaya Pechat i Rabochii Klass Rossii v gody revoliutsionnovo podema 1910–14* (Moscow, 1965).

Purishkevich. On the eve of the Balkan Wars his speeches on foreign policy did not differ in tone from the utterances of Rasputin (who also gave a press interview on this subject). The leitmotif of both was the same – to avoid at whatever cost a collision with Germany and Austria, and to achieve unity among the three neighbouring empires as the best guarantee against revolution. This was precisely the attitude of the pro-German majority in the camarilla, while at the time of the Balkan Wars only Rasputin 'reassured' newspaper correspondents with the statement – which shocked bourgeois-landlord opinion: 'A lot of nonsense is being talked about war. Can you really fear that our patriots will go to war? They're chattering and fighting without thinking'.[13] Purishkevich, on the other hand, in the name of these 'patriots', proclaimed openly from the tribune of the Duma that 'the hour has struck to settle accounts with our historic enemy, with that patchwork monarchy' – Austria–Hungary.[14]

In the first six months of 1914 this latter tendency became more clearly marked, reflecting the increasing strength of the anti-German group in the camarilla. Its existence had long been known. Its centre was the Copenhagen circle around the Tsar's mother, the Empress Maria Fedorovna, to which, incidentally, Izvolsky himself belonged until he became a Minister. But the tendency they represented had for a long time been stifled by the pro-German entourage of the Tsar. Now, given the changed situation within the country and internationally, the relation of forces was shifting. The anti-Germans, such as the future Commander in Chief the Grand Duke Nikolai Nikolaevich and General Yanushkevich, who had been appointed chief of the General Staff and played a most active role in the days of the July crisis, took front place in the camarilla. They were joined by Goremykin, appointed for the second time chairman of the Council of Ministers, who had at one time been wholeheartedly pro-German. This explains why the war with Germany was begun under a head of government who enjoyed the reputation of a Germanophile. Of course, Goremykin's role in determining policy was negligible, but his metamorphosis is indicative of the change in mood among the ruling circles.

The same shift in the attitude of the Tsar personally can be followed in his letters and statements between 1912 and 1914. Up

[13] *Rech*, 15 March 1913.
[14] *Novoe Vremya*, 8/21 December 1912.

to the Balkan Wars they give an impression of enmity towards England and a desire to settle 'misunderstandings' with Germany and Austria at any price. Curiously enough, even the Bosnian crisis was included by the Tsar in the category of 'misunderstandings'.[15] But gradually the tone of his utterances about England softened – and by the same token ever greater animosity characterized his comments on Germany and Austria – 'astonishing impudence' (this in regard to Germany) and 'The Austrians should be forgiven nothing. They must be made to pay for everything' (*vsiakoe lyko v stroku*).[16]

There can be little doubt about the Tsar's reaction, given this state of mind, to such arguments of his ministers in the July days as, for example, 'Russia would never forgive the sovereign' if he made further concessions.[17] Obviously, for Nicholas II, this had already become a fairly weighty argument.

All the attempts of the most determined Germanophiles at court and in circles close to them (Durnovo, Rozen, Taube, etc.) to convince the Tsar of the necessity for a rapprochement with Germany were, as we know, fruitless. The effort was made more than once, but, as Taube said, it was like hitting water: 'So long as I reign, peace will not be broken from the Russian side' – that was the most the Germanophiles could get from their monarch.[18]

No less interesting was the attitude of those directly in charge of the conduct of Russian foreign policy, which showed a gradual adaptation to correspond with the changing situation and the changes among those holding high office.

From May 1906 to roughly April 1909 (up to and including the outbreak of the Bosnian crisis) Izvolsky was the leading personage involved. Then Stolypin took over the conduct of foreign policy; at first he acted through Charykov, who was in full agreement with him and who until May 1909 held the post of under-secretary for foreign affairs. After Charykov's appointment as ambassador to Constantinople, Stolypin acted through Sazonov, his own creature to succeed Charykov at the Ministry (although Izvolsky remained the nominal head of the ministry for nearly eighteen months more,

---

15 M. Martchenko, *La catastrophe austro-hongroise* (Paris, 1920), p. 118.

16 Arkhiv vneshnei politiki Rossii, Chancery coll. 1913, file 7, folio 18; *Mezhdunarodnye otnosheniya* . . . series 3, vol. 1, p. 190, vol. 2, p. 413.

17 S.D. Sazonov, *Vospominaniya* (Paris–Berlin, 1927), p. 247.

18 M. Taube, *Der grossen Katastrophe entgegen* (Berlin–Leipzig, 1929), p. 301.

and even conducted a number of important negotiations; but only with Stolypin's agreement or by his direct instruction, whereas formerly the Foreign Minister had acted independently of the Chairman of the Ministerial Council, and was answerable only to the Tsar). While Stolypin was alive, both Sazonov and the new under-secretary Neratov, who deputized for Sazonov (officially appointed Minister in October 1910) when he was on leave or sick (Sazonov spent a great part of 1911 in bed), were in effect only executants of the orders given by the chairman of the ministerial council.

After Stolypin's death in September 1911, his role as the actual chief in Russian foreign policy was partly taken over by the new chairman of the Ministerial Council Kokovtsov. According to his evidence, Sazonov, right up to Kokovtsov's resignation in February 1914, undertook not a single serious action without consulting him and receiving his approval.[19] But from September 1911 Sazonov became in large degree independent, a man of experience who enjoyed the confidence of the Tsar. Consequently, Russian foreign policy from the end of 1911 to the beginning of 1914 may in a certain sense be called the Kokovtsov–Sazonov policy. Right up to the crisis arising from the von Sanders mission, the two consistently followed the line marked out by Stolypin, trying to avoid conflict with Russia's western neighbours and at the same time to bring the Balkan States closer to Turkey and to each other.

The Balkan Wars and the von Sanders mission struck a heavy blow at this policy. However, even up to February 1914 Kokovtsov retained in essentials the same position. His resignation was undoubtedly connected largely with the struggle among Russian ruling circles over questions of internal policy, but the foreign policy side of the affair also played a certain part. To all demands for a more active policy against Germany and Austria Kokovtsov invariably replied in the same terms as those used by Stolypin: 'it would not be desirable to be drawn into a European conflict'.[20]

In Stolypin's time this policy found support among a large section of the bourgeois-landlord groups. But with 1914 the situation changed: indeed, at the end of 1912 *Novoe Vremya* (8/21 December), expressing as it were the common sentiments of

[19] V.N. Kokovtsov, *Iz moevo proshlovo*, vol. 2 (Paris, 1933,) p. 101.
[20] E.A. Adamov, *Konstantinopol i Prolivy*, vol. 1 (Moscow, 1925), p. 67.

bourgeois-landlord opinion, remarked that Stolypin's slogan 'peace at whatever price' had become, in view of the irreconcilable differences with Germany and Austria, 'not only ignominious but dangerous'. And in February 1914 the Russian government in a semi-official article considered it necessary to appeal to 'public opinion' with a statement that 'for Russia the times are past for threats from outside; no clamour will frighten Russia; Russia is prepared for war', etc.[21] Kokovtsov was calumniated for his 'feeble and anti-Slav policy'. One member of the court circle, explaining the reasons for his resignation, used a phrase which was said to have originated with Nicholas II: Kokovtsov, in the words of the Tsar, was not 'a man of action', and, since the situation had become so involved 'what was needed was active, or at least decisive people'.[22] Whether or not the Tsar actually held that opinion (which is unlikely, in view of the appointment of Goremykin, an obviously passive and indecisive character), the fact that such remarks circulated at court is in itself significant.

In contrast to Kokovtsov, Sazonov turned out to be more flexible as a statesman, with the ability to grasp quickly changes in bourgeois-landlord opinion and corresponding changes of sentiment among the ruling circles. Precisely for that reason he was able to remain in office, despite efforts to get him out. It is easy to follow the evolution of the Foreign Minister's views from his instructions throughout 1913 and in the early part of 1914, and from his speeches at the Council of Ministers. And if, at the special government conferences in November–December 1912, Sazonov gave vigorous support to Kokovtsov, who was maintaining a 'prudent' line (that is, compromise with Austria) against all the other members of the Ministerial Council, at the special conference of 31 December 1913 (13 January 1914) he was already beginning to slide towards the position of his former opponents, and at the conference on 8/21 February 1914, like all the others taking part, to take as the starting point of his remarks the conviction of the inevitability in the near future of a general European war. At the time of this conference the essentials of an entire foreign policy programme were worked out, and this was now put into operation under the personal guidance of Sazonov right up to the time when the outbreak of war changed the situation and demanded a new outlook on

21 *Birzhevye Vedomosti*, 27 February 1914.
22 *Mezhdunarodnye otnosheniya* . . . series 3, vol. 1, p. 315.

foreign policy. It was these considerations which determined Sazonov's attitude and role in the July crisis.

The conference of 8/21 February did not draw up any document formulating the programme of foreign policy. Rather what emerged was a system of views, a set of programmatic arrangements in accordance with which Russia's foreign policy was shaped. The essence of these views may be summed up as follows:

It was recognized that Russia was not yet ready for large-scale war. At the same time it was assumed that the collapse of the Ottoman empire in the not distant future was inevitable, and that following this a clash with Germany over the Straits was also inevitable. This clash could not be conceived otherwise than in terms of a general European war. There was the possibility of an Austro-Serb or a Bulgaro-Serb conflict, and either might provoke a conflict with Austria which in the end would again mean a general European war. It was agreed – in full accord with bourgeois-land-lord opinion – to support Serbia against Austria up to and including open intervention on its side. At the same time, as already observed, it was considered desirable to postpone the collision at least until 1916–17.

All these considerations are clearly formulated in Sazonov's detailed memoranda of 23 November/6 December 1913 and 7/20 January 1914.[23]

What logically followed was the need to accelerate the carrying out of the tasks that had long stood on the agenda, such as the settlement of outstanding differences with France, the conclusion of an alliance with England, the uniting of Serbia and Montenegro against Austria, the replacement of the pro-Austrian Bulgarian government by a pro-Russian one, consolidation of the rapprochement with Rumania, undermining German influence in Turkey.

Negotiations with France, conducted through diplomatic channels, were taken up in Petersburg (between Sazonov and the French ambassador Paléologue) and in Paris (between Izvolsky and the French Premier Doumergue). The result may be described as a further rapprochement between the two powers in regard to improving their readiness for a general European war; a compromise was reached on the question of railway concessions in

---

[23] E.A. Adamov, *op. cit.*, pp. 70–6; *Mezhdunarodnye otnosheniya* . . . series 3, vol. 1, pp. 61–4.

Asia Minor and on a number of other Russian demands. It was also agreed that President Poincaré should pay a visit to Petersburg, with whom, it was suggested, outstanding questions would be settled personally. By the time of Poincaré's visit, however, the international crisis was already dominating the situation.

With England it had already been agreed at the time of the Balkan Wars to hold preliminary conversations on all important European questions between the British Foreign Secretary and the Russian and French ambassadors in London. This agreement was the penultimate step before the actual establishment of the Anglo-French–Russian alliance, a coalition of powers opposed to the Triple Alliance in so far as it was designed to reach an agreed three-power policy on the cardinal questions of the day. Negotiations were now begun on an Anglo-Russian naval convention, intended to complement the existing Anglo-French convention and to serve, in Sazonov's words, as 'a mighty step towards the closer association of England with the Franco-Russian alliance'. The ultimate aim was to turn the three-power alliance, 'whose actual existence is as little proved as the existence of the sea serpent', Sazonov wrote, into 'a defensive alliance'.[24]

These negotiations had no result, up to the outbreak of war, as the English government took an evasive attitude, dragging them out and even at the end breaking them off on the ground that references to the secret negotiations had appeared in the European press.[25] England's disinclination to transform the Entente into a formal alliance (although it was clear that it was not in her interests to leave France and Russia without support in the event of hostilities with Germany) was apparently due to the following considerations:

First, the English government was convinced that Russo-German contradictions had reached such a pitch that, in the event of Anglo-German hostilities, England would in any case be assured of Russian support, even without an alliance. Moreover, in not tying itself down by obligations incurred under an alliance, England retained freedom of manoeuvre in the event of a Russo-German clash, which, given the circumstances of the time, meant

24 Ibid., p. 360, vol. 3, p. 126.
25 G.M. Derenkovsky, 'Franko–Russkaya morskaya Konventsiya 1912 i Anglo-Russkie morskie peregovory nakanune pervoi mirovoi voiny', Istoricheskie Zapiski, vol. 29 (Moscow, 1949).

in effect that England could choose the moment for war with Germany which best suited itself.

Second, in dragging out the negotiations for an alliance which would guarantee Russia the support it strongly desired from England in the first days of any conflict with Germany, the English government automatically obtained from Russia a greater readiness to make concessions on those differences between the two powers in the Middle East to which reference was made earlier.

Third, in evading an alliance, England could avoid undertaking concrete obligations in regard to redistributing 'spheres of influence' in the East after a war from which, it seemed reasonable to assume, it would emerge far less weakened than Russia.

Finally, a formal alliance with tsarism was bound to provoke a vigorous protest from the English proletariat and from a significant section of the pacifist-minded bourgeoisie. This would have complicated the English government's position at a time when the domestic situation was already strained and difficult enough.

Thus, England's reluctance to turn the Entente into a formal alliance is to be explained not by the Foreign Secretary Grey's alleged desire for peace, as is sometimes asserted in western historical writing, but by a sober political calculation, in virtue of which England not only lost nothing, but on the contrary strengthened its leading position in the Entente, forcing France and Russia to set a greater value on their relations with her.[26] In short, what emerged was the uncertainty among the ruling circles of Petersburg and Paris (as well as Berlin and Vienna) of English support for France and Russia in a conflict with Germany, particularly in the opening stage of the war, which might prove decisive. This had a marked effect on the course of the July crisis.

As regards Serbia and Montenegro, the problem for Russian diplomacy was to delay as far as possible the reunion of the two states, which was strongly urged by public opinion in the two countries, and at the same time to get the maximum co-operation between them in the event of war with Austria. Taken as a whole, their reunion was to Russia's interest, but in this case Russian diplomatic attitudes were determined not so much by political as by dynastic considerations. King Nicholas was intriguing actively

[26] Cf. Khvostov, *op. cit.*, pp. 767–85.

against the Karageorgeviches in Petersburg, where he had the stronger ties in court circles as two of his daughters were married to Russian Grand Dukes.

There was another important factor at work. Austria had un-equivocally declared that it would not allow such a strengthening of Serbia, or would at least demand substantial compensation. Moreover, Serbia was already in conflict with Vienna over the former Turkish railways it had acquired after the Balkan Wars, and as it was not to Russia's advantage to force a premature Austro-Serbian clash, Petersburg tried to maintain the status quo, re-straining the Negosh (Petrovich) and the Karageorgeviches from dynastic conflict and Serbia from an open collision with Austria, while improving the preparedness of both Balkan countries for war.

In regard to Bulgaria, Sazonov as before made the greatest efforts to get an urgently-needed French loan for that war-devastated country. He hoped thereby to draw Bulgaria towards the Entente, overthrow its pro-Austrian government, and restore the Balkan alliance. These efforts remained fruitless. Berlin and Vienna managed to foist a German loan on Sofia, thus consolidat-ing their position in Bulgaria and pushing it nearer to an alliance with Turkey against Serbia and Greece. But Russia continued to struggle for a reorientation of Bulgarian foreign policy.

In Constantinople the Russian position was even weaker. Not only that; the move towards a rapprochement with Turkey after the Balkan Wars turned out to be highly unpopular in Russian bourgeois-landlord circles, which were now coming out in favour of a final division of the Ottoman empire. Nevertheless, Sazonov did not abandon hopes of getting Turkey at least to remain neutral in the approaching war. His maximum programme envisaged a gradual strengthening of the Russian position in Turkey and ultimately a return, in Russo-Turkish relations, to the position at the time of the treaty of Unkiar-Skelassi in 1833, which guaranteed Russia control of the Straits as ally and protector of Turkey.

With this object in view an entire system of measures was worked out to strengthen Russian influence in Turkey and undermine the German. It contemplated the formation of an autonomous Armenia under Russian protection as the most powerful means of exerting pressure on Constantinople, the admission of Russia as a member of the Ottoman Debt Council, that is, to a share in the control of Turkish finances, renewal of the agreements forbidding railway construction in the areas of Asia Minor adjoining the Russian frontier, the acquisition of a controlling interest in one of the leading Turkish banks. It was also planned to develop trade, bribe newspapers, put on exhibitions, etc. These were the goals pursued by Russian diplomats at Constantinople in the first half of 1914. In addition, a not insignificant place in their activities was taken by the attempt to reconcile Turkey and Greece, between whom a war over the Aegean Islands was coming to a head, which from Petersburg's point of view was premature and undesirable. That, despite failure on practically every point enumerated above, Sazonov persisted in the attempt to attain these ends is shown by the talks on a Russo-Turkish rapprochement held at Livadia in the Crimea in May 1914.

The visit of Nicholas II to Constanza in June 1914 equally clearly bears testimony to Sazonov's energetic efforts to reinforce Russo-Rumanian relations, for there was still no certainty of Rumanian support in the event of a Russo-Austrian conflict.

In assessing the results of Russian diplomacy up to June 1914, what stands out is the incompleteness of Russia's diplomatic preparation for war. It did not succeed in getting a guarantee of England's attitude. In the Balkans, instead of the all-Balkan alliance against Austria–Hungary which Russia desired, what was taking shape was not so much an anti-Austrian as the consolidation of an anti-Bulgarian and anti-Turkish coalition of Serbia, Greece, Rumania, and Montenegro. The Bulgarian–Turkish alliance, which Petersburg too pressed for, was directed not to the support of Serbia against Austria, but against Serbia (and Greece), which was certainly not in Russia's interests. And since Petersburg had not given up hopes of bringing these two groups into a single coalition, and, more important, of turning the Entente into a formal alliance, it is obvious that any complication in the international field was bound to appear premature and undesirable.

The incompleteness of diplomatic preparations for war, and the incompleteness of military preparations, made it supremely necessary for Russia to postpone the decisive conflict with Germany and Austria–Hungary. Hence the attempt of some Western historians to contrast tsarist foreign policy on the eve of the July crisis, as one deliberately designed to provoke a general European war, with the allegedly pacific policy of all the other powers, or at least of some of them, will not stand up to investigation.

Examination of the facts shows that the policy of all the great powers, including Russia, objectively led to world war. Responsibility for the war is borne by the ruling circles of all the great powers without exception, notwithstanding that the German and Austrian governments, which actually unleashed the war, displayed greater activity because Germany was better prepared for war and because the internal crisis in Austria was becoming progressively more acute, and notwithstanding the fact that the decision on when to unleash war was, in the final analysis, taken in effect in Germany and England.

Analysis of the history of international relations in the early years of the twentieth century leads to the conclusion that the July 1914 crisis was not an accidental catastrophe, but the consequence that was bound to follow from the objective conditions reflected in the policies of the imperialist powers.

Italian-Austro-Hungarian Negotiations 1914–1915

Leo Valiani

The assassination of Franz Ferdinand put an end to the Habsburg empire's projects of reform. The Austro-Hungarian government became convinced that only by means of a victorious war could the monarchy be preserved. The foreign minister, Count Berchtold, observed to Francis Joseph on 2 July 1914, that if Austria–Hungary wished to retain her name as a great power she could not avoid proceeding resolutely against Serbia. Tisza, the Hungarian Prime Minister, who viewed the international situation more realistically than his Austrian colleagues and was convinced, unlike them, that Russia would intervene in spite of German solidarity with Austria–Hungary, was unfavourable to a war at that moment; but his opposition was fatally weakened by his adding that he would have preferred a situation in which at least it would be possible to count upon Bulgarian participation in the attack on Serbia. On the other hand, Tisza was notoriously more opposed than anyone to the only real alternative to war, which was the satisfaction, within the framework of a reorganized Habsburg monarchy, of the national claims of Austria–Hungary's own southern Slavs. Consequently, during the two weeks when events began precisely to justify his anxiety by proving that Germany and Austria–Hungary would have to fight alone against Russia, France, and Serbia, at the very least, Tisza changed his views and adopted the thesis of a preventive war.

The entry of Great Britain into the war not only greatly diminished the chance of victory for Germany herself but also made it obvious that Austria–Hungary could escape defeat only on one condition: namely, that Italy, who after the British intervention would never join her allies of the Triple Alliance but who could, on the other hand, thanks to supplies guaranteed by the British fleet, consider turning against Austria, should nevertheless maintain indefinitely the neutrality proclaimed by the Rome government on 2 August 1914. Already at the Austro–Hungarian joint council of ministers on 8 August, when Berchtold reported that Rome was demanding compensation for the prospective Austro-Hungarian advance into the Balkans and that Berlin was recommending negotiations to this effect, it was confirmed by the chief of staff, General Conrad, that there were insufficient troops for war on a third front, against Italy. Until Sarajevo, Conrad had been in favour of preventive war against Italy. Now he was too slow to deduce from his own warning the conclusion imposed by the military situation, which was the necessity of adequate concessions to Italy in order to avoid being attacked by her; but from then on he repeated that Italian intervention would place Austria–Hungary in a position of disastrous military inferiority.

Since Austria–Hungary had staked everything on war with Serbia, and if necessary with Russia as well, it is worth exploring further the question why she did not put victory in this war above every other consideration, and why, when she became aware that she could not win it if she had to face an attack from Italy at the same time, she did not do everything humanly possible to make sure of Italian neutrality before it was too late. Even the recent biography of Count Berchtold, by such an elder historian as Hugo Hantsch, is reticent about this, although actually Berchtold was obliged to resign in January 1915 because he had at last perceived the necessity of making those concessions to Italy which might perhaps, at that time, have been able to avert her intervention.

The question needs to be re-examined with the help of the Vienna, Bonn, Budapest, and Rome archives, which several historians, including the present writer, have explored in the last few years, and of the recently published Italian diplomatic documents covering the period 28 June–2 August and 2 August–16 October 1914.

In the Austro-Hungarian joint council of ministers on 7 July, having reported that William II and the Reich Chancellor had assured him of 'Germany's most decided support' in the event of war, Berchtold added that 'we have now to reckon once again with Italy and Rumania; and here, in accord with the Berlin cabinet, it seemed to him better to act, and to wait for requests for compensation later'.

There was not so long to wait as Berchtold expected. As early as

14 July the Italian foreign minister, Marchese di Sangiuliano, defined the directives of Italian policy as follows to Bollati, the ambassador in Berlin, and the Duke of Avarna, the ambassador in Vienna, having already informed Flotow, the German ambassador in Rome: 'Our whole policy must be directed towards preventing ... any territorial aggrandisement of Austria, unless balanced by adequate territorial compensation for Italy'. At that time, as the whole context of his letter shows, Sangiuliano had not yet considered that the prospective Austro-Serbian conflict might develop into a European war; he therefore took it for granted that Italy would do well to remain for the time being in the Triple Alliance, though without indeed excluding the probability that she might leave it 'in a few years time, to join some other group or to remain neutral'. It was therefore in the interest of 'the solidity and efficacy of the Triple Alliance', in his opinion, that Germany should espouse the Italian view concerning compensation due to Italy in the event of an Austro-Hungarian advance. On 18 July, being now convinced that Russia would take the field in defence of Serbia (the day before, he had urgently requested the Italian ambassador in Petersburg to suggest to the Tsarist government a very clear explanation of its intention to the government in Vienna, hoping in this way to induce milder counsels), Sangiuliano charged Bollati to explain urgently to Berlin that by article 7 of the terms of the Triple Alliance compensation was due to Italy for every territorial occupation, temporary or permanent, effected by Austria–Hungary *dans les régions des Balcans* in the course of invading Serbia.

It was still a discussion between allies, though two of them were alienated by sharp divergences of interest upon which the third ally (Germany) had to arbitrate. When, on 22 July, the Russian ambassador reminded him that 'it was in Italy's interest not to allow Serbia to be crushed', so as to prevent an Austrian hegemony in the Balkans, Sangiuliano replied: 'That is true, but we can assist Serbia, within certain limits, by diplomatic methods; but we shall certainly not go to war with Austria to save her'. In reality the Italian government, no less pledged to power politics than the Austro-Hungarian, was primarily concerned not with saving Serbia but with ensuring Italy's predominance in Albania and in thwarting Austria's predominance in the Balkans generally.

Italy's diplomatic support for Serbian independence took the form of the following telegram from Sangiuliano to his ambassadors in Berlin and Vienna on 24 July, the day after the ultimatum to Belgrade: 'I beg your Excellency to declare urgently to the foreign minister that if Austria–Hungary occupies territory, even temporarily, without our previous consent, she will be acting in violation of article 7 of the treaty of alliance. We announce accordingly our fullest reservations. I think it opportune further to observe that the step taken by Austria–Hungary, which is liable to create dangerous complications, ought not, in my opinion, to have been taken without previous consent of her allies. . . . It is our desire to pursue policies in accord with our allies, but as regards Balkan questions . . . this will not be possible unless we can count upon an agreed interpretation of article 7; failing which, our policy must be directed towards preventing territorial agrandisement by Austria and must therefore concur with that of other powers which have the same interest. . . .'

The Italian government was informed officially of the ultimatum only after its delivery. Since Austria–Hungary had declared war without being the victim of aggression, the war could not be called a defensive one, and by the terms of the Triple Alliance, which made it a defensive alliance, the Italian government was under no obligation to intervene on the side of its ally. On 15 July, the day on which Austria–Hungary decided to go to war, Berchtold telegraphed instructions to Mérey, his ambassador in Rome, to inform Sangiuliano of the ultimatum a day *before* it was delivered to the Serbian government. But on 20 July he changed his mind and requested Mérey to make the communication a day *after* the sending of the ultimatum. Evidently he did not want the Italian government to have even so much as one day available for expressing a contrary opinion. Mérey himself, although much more Italophobe than was suitable in an ambassador accredited to Rome, would have preferred that Italy should have been informed at least a day in advance. Unquestionably, the Austro-Hungarian government had failed in a treaty obligation of the Triple Alliance by not previously informing its ally of the ultimatum. But Mérey hoped, nevertheless, that the successful invasion of Serbia, which he himself had unhesitatingly advocated, would restore Austria–Hungary's prestige in Italy. While considering it still possible that in the event of a European conflict Italy might prefer to side with Germany, Mérey recognized that in the meantime, in the Austro-Serbian war, Italy would take advantage of not having been consulted or even informed and would simply hold a watching brief, in readiness to claim compensation for every occupation by Austria–Hungary of Serbian territory. And although he feared that Berlin would support Rome in this, he still advised that Vienna should refuse all concessions. 'In my view', he reported, 'there would be no serious danger. The unsatisfactory state of her army and her finances, the frequent internal disorders, the weakness of her present government, and her difficulties in Libya, the Dodecanese, and Asia Minor, make any large-scale action by Italy impossible ... she will not abandon the Triple Alliance, if only because three-quarters of the population would disapprove. The worst that could happen would be some action in southern Albania.'

When he wrote this, Mérey evidently did not know the exact terms of the directive issued by Sangiuliano on 24 July. If he could have seen it he would have realized that the Italian foreign minister had framed the request for compensation, as provided in article 7 of the treaty, in such a way that its rejection would at once put Italy virtually in the camp of Austria–Hungary's enemies. This cannot have been realized by Giolitti either, because he (being equally ignorant of Sangiuliano's directives) declared himself in full accord with the Italian government's attitude at that time and, consequently, with its interpretation of article 7, but without suspecting that this interpretation involved from the outset the possibility of war with Austria–Hungary.

In fact, Sangiuliano considered himself justified *a priori* in joining the powers hostile to Austria–Hungary, if she failed to make concessions acceptable to Italy, in compliance with article 7. It would certainly have been fairer if he had openly warned her that in the event of insuperable disagreement he would denounce the Triple Alliance; and, moreover, this warning (if made before 28 July) would have been an effective method of pressure to dissuade her from going to war. But Sangiuliano felt that such frankness would be too dangerous for Italy and he instructed the ambassador in Vienna to transmit his observations of 24 July in softened terms.

It was impossible, however, for Berchtold to ignore the gravity of the warning he received a few days later from the King of Rumania, who had failed, in the crown council, to induce his government to march with Austria–Hungary in conformity with the pact then in force between Vienna and Bucharest. On 6 August the Austro-Hungarian minister in Rumania, Czernin, telegraphed as follows to Berchtold from the royal residence of Sinaia:

King informs me he does *not* exclude the possibility of Italy's attacking us also. Italian public opinion would be heavily against us. Italian minister here contributed greatly to crown council's decision by informing all members just before meeting that Italy does not accept *casus foederis*. Role and influence of Italy were decisive for negative attitude of crown council. Italian minister has informed King, with maximum secrecy, that the whole Italian atmosphere would change in our favour and active cooperation become possible, if we would cede Trento.

In the joint council of ministers on 8 August Berchtold spoke about Italy's claim to the Trentino, but he correctly deduced that even if the claim were satisfied Italy would only remain neutral and would not make war on France and England. Tisza, who was concerned above all to avoid any precedent which might encourage similar aspirations on the part of Rumania for Transylvanian, that is, Hungarian territory, said that he personally felt sure that if Italy got something from Austria–Hungary today she would ask for something more tomorrow. On the other hand, it failed to occur to him that precisely these increasing Italian demands, which he feared, might have the effect, if they were satisfied, of bringing Italy, although unwillingly, to favour the victory of the Central Powers because it would safeguard her gains, and to fear that of the Entente. Yet it was obvious that the Entente, and particularly Russia, who claimed to be defending Serbia as a Slav nation, would resent Italy's endorsement of Austro-Hungarian conquests of Balkan territory in exchange for the cession of Austrian territory, because, if the Trentino did not suffice, this could only be Adriatic territory with a mixed population of Italians and Yugo-Slavs. An Italo-Austrian agreement which reinforced the Triple Alliance would necessarily make Italy appear to the Entente to be aligned with the Central Powers. It would be only a matter of time for the Italian government to become convinced that, just as an irreconcilable difference with Austria–Hungary over article 7 would place Italy alongside that country's enemies, so a satisfactory agreement upon the article should place her alongside the Central Powers.

But naturally, after the preliminary refusal to cede even the Trentino, all thought of keeping Italy, in the long run, opposed to the Entente was out of the question. What did however arise was the opposite possibility, as expressed at that meeting by the Austrian prime minister, Stürgkh. He wondered if it was prudent to wait passively for Italy to attack, and whether it would not be better 'to deceive her with a kind of secret agreement. . . . No diplomatic trick is too low in dealing with such brigands as the Italians now are'. Stürgkh proposed – thus justifying in advance Italy's insistence in the spring of 1915 upon the immediate fulfilment of the concessions then offered by Austria–Hungary – that Germany should promise Italy the Trentino, by a secret treaty, on condition that Italy assisted her allies of the Triple Alliance and endorsed, after the war, the measures taken by Austria–Hungary in the Balkans. Since one of these measures would be the suppression of Montenegro, which for family reasons it would be impossible for Victor Emmanuel III to accept, Italy would find herself obliged to renounce the Trentino. The Hungarian ministers – Tisza and Burian, the minister attached to the sovereign – rejected this idea, observing that Italy would certainly not be deceived. But the fact that the head of the Austrian government could entertain such an idea is further proof of the lack of realism among the leaders of the Central Powers. On 9 August the Austro-Hungarian ambassador in Berlin telegraphed to Berchtold that both William II and the German chief of staff had suggested to the Austro-Hungarian military attaché that the Trentino should be promised to Italy and then, after the war, some pretext be found for not keeping the promise. In the council of ministers on 19 August, faced with information from a German source that Italy had not only 'already spoken about the Trentino' but had set on foot 'vast military preparations', so that she could attack at any moment, Berchtold announced that since it was desirable to remove as far as possible the chance of a war with Italy, he was holding conversations with the Italian government to make them believe that certain concessions might perhaps be made. At a later meeting (9 September) he specified that he was thinking of concessions in Albania. With this, and also with the need to prepare in the meantime for defence against Italy, Tisza was in agreement; but he advised against doing anything that Italy could regard as provocation.

Meanwhile, Mérey in Rome had collapsed under the nervous

tension and complications of the war and had been replaced as ambassador by Baron Macchio. Prince Bülow and other more disinterested observers have justly criticized Macchio's rigidity and failure of initiative; and yet his despatches reveal that he did not lack a serious political foundation. On 15 August, the day after his arrival in Rome, where he had immediately visited the secretary-general of the Consulta, Macchio telegraphed that in the Italian capital 'the public still seems to be wavering, the desire to maintain neutrality is prevalent and the fear of complications with allies is at least as strong as the impulse to provoke them. . . .' He deplored the German military attaché's reports, which made the government in Berlin believe that an Italian attack might be imminent.

The truth is that the Germans were deliberately exaggerating, in the hope that the Austrian government would be frightened into making those sacrifices which might induce Italy to enter the war on the side of her Triple Alliance partners and thus make possible the defeat of France, where the German offensive was already proceeding. But the Italian diplomatic documents make it clear that Italy had no intention of taking up arms against the Entente, with which she was already conducting top-secret discussions about a possible intervention at some time against Austria–Hungary. The choice before the makers of Italian policy was always and only, as they saw it, between absolute neutrality and war against Austria–Hungary. It was, in fact, only in the first months of 1915 that they made a final and definite choice; and so Macchio was right when he deflated his German colleague's illusions and also when he said that the time for Italy's irrevocable choice had not yet come, but he was wrong in ignoring the fact that, in Rome, time was against Austria, and the directive given him from Vienna to work to delay Italy's decision was profoundly mistaken. With the passing of time, Italy's demands would have increased, not diminished. Oppressed as she was by the weight of the Russian offensive, Austria–Hungary was in no position to detail a large detachment of troops for the Italian frontier. The Italian army, on the other hand, took advantage of the interval to remedy its material and technical shortcomings. It was a pure chance that the Russian defeat at Gorlice, a day before Italy's repudiation of the Triple Alliance and three weeks before she entered the war, enabled the Austrian high command to despatch a few divisions post haste to the Italian arena. Though the time thus gained was certainly invaluable at that moment, it was due not to precise forecasting by Vienna, but to the desire of Sonnino, the new Italian foreign minister, to extort the maximum territorial advantage from the Entente in Albania, Dalmatia, etc., and so to be able to justify his rejection of Giolitti's plea for an agreement with Austria–Hungary on the basis of Prince Bülow's offers.

But what Macchio and the government in Vienna ought to have foreseen was that the propaganda of the Entente, and especially of France, would inevitably prevail sooner or later in Italy unless counteracted by Austria–Hungary with some bold diplomatic gesture. This was clearly perceived by the most strongly neutralist Giolittian deputies, such as Guido Fusinato and Camillo Peano, who sounded the alarm in vibrant tones in their letters to Giolitti of 19 and 25 August. But Giolitti himself, Italy's authoritative former prime minister, who was a long way from Rome, attached no importance to the warning and did not return. And Macchio, too, whose country was running mortal risks and who saw with his own eyes the anti-Austrian demonstrations by students outside his embassy, continued to believe that the situation was not urgent. Writing to Berchtold on 29 November, he said that he could not believe that Sonnino, who had such a reputation for honesty and who had always supported, since its inception in 1882, the Triple Alliance, could want to begin his work at the Consulta (he had replaced Sangiuliano, who died the previous month) with an act of treachery. Of Cadorna, the head of the Italian general staff, the ambassador knew that he was Austro-phobe but did not think that he would be able to make the government adopt his policy in place of their own. What escaped the Austrian diplomats was this: Article 7 was well known in Italy (it had been published as long ago as 1903 in the *Corriere della Sera*), and since public opinion has decisive weight in an authentic parliamentary regime (such as existed in Italy but not in Austria), the government would not be allowed to resign itself to being left empty-handed.

When the Italian parliament reassembled at the beginning of December 1914, Giolitti spoke in the debate on the government's announcements. With the apparent aim of supporting the government's view – that Italy was not obliged to take up arms on behalf of her Triple Alliance partners, who had not been attacked, whereas one of them had taken the initiative in attacking the Serbs – he made a sensational disclosure. He revealed that in August 1913, when he was head of the Italian government, Vienna had requested his support for an Austrian action against Serbia, and that he had refused. Salandra, the actual prime minister, to whom Macchio expressed his amazement at such an unheard-of disclosure among allies, replied that he, too, was 'painfully affected' by it. 'He added confidentially', the ambassador reported, 'that with Giolitti one must always allow for personal considerations'. In effect, Salandra interpreted Giolitti's gesture as intended to reinforce the decisive weight which he aimed always to exert upon Italian policy. On further information, Macchio reported that Giolitti had been jealous of the success of Salandra's declarations and had therefore made his disclosure in order to prevent the government from adjourning the Chamber *sine die* (Giolitti had far more influence over the majority in the Chamber than over the ministry), and to oblige it to name a date for reassembly, which was eventually fixed as 18 February 1915. In addition, Macchio reported that Giolitti 'sent me word, confidentially through a friend, that he fully recognized the unusual character of his so-called revelation. But he had simply wanted to show, in a comprehensible manner, that already in his day the question of the *casus foederis* had been discussed in connection with a possible European conflict, and to deduce therefrom that Italy's neutrality would not be incompatible, in certain circumstances, with loyalty to the Triple Alliance. At the same time he had wished to insist that Italy ought to continue to stand firmly by the Alliance, and to make the Chamber more clearly aware of this.'

As regards Salandra and Sonnino, Macchio liked to think that '*somme toute*, the solid position of the government is a guarantee against the violent impulsiveness of irresponsible elements. But the cabinet itself, in view of the increased economic depression, ought to demonstrate to the country, as against the milliard voted for war preparations, some compensating value sufficient to make an out-and-out policy of neutrality seem satisfactory to the Italians' calculating instinct'. Macchio was here replying to Berchtold's information that the Italian ambassador in Vienna had insisted, in Sonnino's name, that the Austro-Hungarian advance into Serbia, which had just begun, called for the application of article 7. Although Macchio agreed that the Italian government was committed to obtaining tangible results, he did not think that Italy had any serious intention of going to war; she hoped, simply by threats, to obtain something at Austria–Hungary's expense if things went badly for the Central Powers, or from the other side if the Entente were the loser. Prince Bülow, who had meanwhile arrived in Rome as German envoy extraordinary, took a graver view of the situation and had no doubt that the cession of the Trentino was indispensable to ensure Italy's continued neutrality. Nevertheless, in a letter to a friend of his and Giolitti's, a man highly placed in Italian financial circles and in whose judgment both of them had great and justified confidence, Bülow wrote on 3 January 1915, that 'Salandra makes a very good impression, shrewd and cultured'.

The objective situation was such as to encourage Italy to reach a decision. To general surprise, the Austro-Hungarian expeditionary force had been beaten by the Serbs and obliged to evacuate Belgrade. As Macchio was to observe, so far from deducing from this event that an agreement on article 7 concerning a modification of the *status quo* in the Balkans had become less urgent, Italy deduced that the Habsburg monarchy was sufficiently weakened for a war against it not to be excessively risky. Bülow and his colleagues had sensed it precisely. At the end of 1914, Count Berchen, counsellor at the German embassy in Rome, had addressed himself directly to Hoyos, the head of Berchtold's cabinet, to explain that Italy would certainly go to war unless the Trentino was ceded and that Rumania would follow suit. And the Austro-Hungarian military attaché telegraphed to his high command that he knew from a reliable source that General Cadorna had said that in view of the expense and scale of Italy's rearmament, her entry into the war was inevitable. According to the German military attaché this would take place in the spring; but he, unlike his Austrian colleague, still believed that at the price of the Trentino and Albania Italy could be turned against France.

Macchio and his colleague at the Vatican, Prince Schönburg, did not share the illusions of the German military diplomats – who were only playing into the hands of those in Vienna who ruled out all concessions *a priori* and who, being easily able to disprove the possibility of Italy's risking war against the Entente, deduced that she was equally unlikely to attack Austria–Hungary; but they nevertheless reached the conclusion that Italian policy was evolving towards intervention. On 6 January Sonnino reminded the Austro-Hungarian ambassador that the compensation provided for in article 7 must be defined without delay and gave him to understand that Italy demanded the Trentino. On the same day Macchio wrote a long private letter to Berchtold, advising him for the safety of the monarchy to resign himself to a sacrifice of territory in return for an undertaking by Italy to render her ally some service later on. Failing this, he was convinced that Italy would attack sooner or later, if only from fear of a republican uprising by the interventionists.

Being urgently advised in the same sense by the German ambassador in Vienna, who gave him Bülow's alarming secret reports to read, Berchtold resigned himself. On 9 January he proposed to Francis Joseph that the Trentino be ceded; but the Emperor, who regarded this territory as particularly dear to his house, refused to hear of it. The next day, in spite of a message from Conrad with the warning, typical of the incoherence of soldiers playing politics, that the precariousness of the situation would make any concession appear as a sign of weakness, Berchtold repeated to Stürgkh, Tisza, and Burian the arguments he had used with the Emperor. Tisza objected that it was premature to speak of concessions, the situation on the Russian front not being so grave as to justify them. After a lunch with the German ambassador, who warned him that Vienna's obstinacy would be its ruin, the Hungarian prime minister informed Berchtold that he would call for his resignation. The minister for foreign affairs immediately expressed his willingness to resign. Francis Joseph suggested to Tisza that he himself should take over the foreign ministry, but Tisza declined on the ground that he could influence Vienna from Budapest but could not govern Hungary from Vienna; he arranged instead for Burian to be nominated. On 11 January, before his resignation was made public, Berchtold had still to receive the Italian ambassador and reply negatively to his request that Austria Hungary should consent to cede a part of her own territory in compliance with her obligations under article 7. According to Vienna, Italy's recent occupation of Valona in Albania ought to satisfy her.

Berchtold himself said of his successor that it was not true, as was hinted in certain quarters, that Burian was a mere docile instrument of Tisza; on the contrary, he was a man of courage who thought for himself. And indeed he is revealed as such in his unpublished diary, which we have consulted in Budapest, and which confirms that, especially in 1917–18, he was frequently in disagreement with Tisza. Forgach, departmental head at the Vienna foreign ministry, wrote to Macchio on 3 February that it would be difficult to imagine a greater contrast than that between the personalities of Berchtold and Burian, the former always hesitant and the latter too self-confident, but he concluded, 'in any case, we now have firm direction'. It was not, however, in the right direction. According to the Duke of Avarna, Italian ambassador, Burian had 'the mind of a lawyer rather than a diplomat'. On 24 February Forgach himself confessed to anxiety about Burian's action: 'If he continues like this we shall be at war with Italy and Rumania in two months. The minister says he would rather have that than voluntarily give up a single square yard of territory!!!' This was only the outburst of an official who, having played a decisive part in promoting the war against Serbia, was all the more anxious now to miss no chance of winning it. What Burian would never accept was the cession of Hungarian territory; he would not have refused to cede the Trentino to Italy, and perhaps even Austrian Bukovina to Rumania, if he became convinced there was no other way to avoid being attacked. And this is what he and Tisza made clear in the joint council of ministers on 2 February, the latter emphasizing the greater urgency of the Rumanian menace. At that session Burian informed the ministers that the Italian army was not yet ready and the Italian government not so mad as to decide upon war until it was. And in the meantime, so Tisza and Burian hoped, things might begin to go much better for Austria–Hungary on the Russian front.

It was obviously a gamble, this hope of something turning up to cancel a burdensome debt before the final day when it must be paid. The German leaders, beginning with the Chancellor, Bethmann Hollweg, saw more clearly that the war could be won only in France, to whom the security offered by a benevolently neutral Italy would be very helpful; they wanted to avoid the need for sending further German troops to assist Austria–Hungary, and, on the other hand, to oblige France herself to employ troops to protect her Italian frontier. On 6 and 10 February Bethmann Hollweg had long interviews with the Austro-Hungarian ambassador, begging him to persuade Vienna to come to an agreement with Italy, so as to keep her from intervening, which, he repeated, would be a catastrophe for the Central Powers.

From this time onwards Macchio's despatches report an increasingly warlike tendency in the Italian government. The difference between Salandra and Giolitti, he wrote on 27 January – a few days before the publication of Giolitti's letter on the concessions he thought Vienna could make and which, he advised, should eventually be accepted – was widening. Giolitti's followers wanted to get back into power; but, according to Macchio, Giolitti himself, who was accustomed to act as a kind of autocrat, seemed 'with advancing age to have lost some of his energy'; he had little desire to assume the burden of government in a situation in which Salandra, if forced to retire, would be in a strong position to criticise him for having neglected the upkeep of the Italian army after the Libyan war, and without even benefiting the Italian treasury thereby. It was probable that Giolitti preferred to await an opportunity to substitute for Salandra someone more amenable to his own control, without having to assume the burden of government himself. On 10 February Macchio reported further that the demonstrations by Giolittian deputies in favour of neutrality and the success of the socialist meetings proved that the Italian people did not want war; but there was a danger that the very weakness of his internal position would cause Salandra 'to seek help from an external policy which would keep him in the saddle under the banner of national aspirations'. Writing on 2 March, he described Salandra's difficult position, having deluded his supporters with the belief that he would extract something from Austria–Hungary and then having got nothing. 'But Giolitti, with his sensitive feeling for internal political affairs, which are more and more the cornerstone of external affairs in this country', had no desire to risk his own prestige and save Salandra from his predicament by replacing him in the negotiations with Austria–Hungary. Far from wanting to be in power at the moment, Giolitti 'is enjoying the role of benevolent uncle to the Salandra cabinet, to which he is again promising support, while thankful to have escaped the evil fate of being at the helm at such an awkward moment'. The government newspapers in Vienna had unanimously rejected Giolitti's plea for concessions to Italy, though for the opposite reason to that of the Italian interventionist press; in other words, because it called for sacrifices from Austria, and this – as Macchio did not fail to point out – had convinced the former prime minister of the difficulty of obtaining by friendly negotiation any concession sufficient to satisfy Italy.

Thus, while Macchio judged Salandra to be ambitious enough to go to war so as to save his government, Austrian public opinion was expressing itself in such a way as to discourage the remaining friends of the Triple Alliance in Italy from taking open responsibility.

The German government had no doubts. Bülow was told by Sonnino himself that Italian expectations had reached the point where, if Austria made no concessions, *c'est la guerre*. The Pope used the same words to the German Catholic deputy, Erzberger, who had come to Rome to give support to Bülow. Accordingly, in the Prussian council of ministers on 27 February, Bethmann Hollweg obtained a resolution to offer Austria–Hungary as compensation for the cession of the Trentino the Polish mining district of Sosnovice, and further, if she was still not satisfied, a rectification of the Prussian–Silesian frontier. But this never became necessary. On the day when the German Emperor approved the Chancellor's plan (6 March), the Austrian leaders themselves were on the point of deciding to cede the Trentino. On 3 March Burian noted in his diary: 'The Italian claim seems irrefutable today, because the military situation is bad'. On the same day Tisza told him that serious though the loss of the Trentino might be, he had decided to agree to it if it was the only way of preventing an Italo-Rumanian alliance. Tisza had previously blocked negotiations with Italy for fear of setting a precedent for Rumania, but he had now perceived that, on the contrary, it was Italian hostility that made the Rumanian attitude dangerous. And since for him the real enemy was Rumania, he began ardently recultivating Italian friendship, but without being able to pursue to the end the only road, however painful a one, which could lead to it.

A little later, Macchio's despatch of 5 March was received in Vienna, and, as with all diplomatic correspondence of any relevance, Tisza had a copy of it within a few hours. It described a conversation he had had with Facta, an influential deputy sent to him by Giolitti, who wished him to know that he had supported the Italian government in the negotiations with Vienna and that he advised the latter to 'make haste' to reach an agreement. Facta admitted that Italy did not want war, but she would find herself 'implacably constrained' to fight unless Austria–Hungary decided to offer the necessary compensation. This warning from the most faithful supporters of Italian neutrality was all the more serious for a reason which Macchio had already several times referred to: Giolitti's best means of bringing pressure upon Salandra and Sonnino was his power to force their resignation at any moment by a pronunciamento of his majority of followers among the deputies, and this method would become much more difficult to employ at the right moment because of the adjournment of parliament, some time before the end of March. There remained only two or three weeks of favourable conditions for the Austro-Hungarian government to reach an agreement. Sonnino himself was of this opinion, and on 10 March he instructed Avarna to propose that the negotiations should be concluded within two weeks.

At Vienna a decision was taken, but an inadequate one. On 8 March the cession of the Trentino was approved by the joint council of ministers. It was proposed by Burian, who reported that the Italian army expected to be ready for action by the middle of April, and that on 14 February the Italian government had, in accordance with article 7, vetoed any further Austro-Hungarian military action in the Balkans without previous agreement upon compensation for Italy. Once the German government had declared that, if Vienna would make the necessary concessions, it would obtain from Italy 'a free hand in the Balkans' for Austria-Hungary's projects there, Burian considered it was impossible to refuse to cede the Trentino. Tisza agreed, saying that the imminent fall to the Russians of the great fortress of Przemysl in Galicia, the Anglo-French landing in the Dardanelles, and the probability that Italy's intervention would be followed by Rumania's, had reconciled him to sacrifices which in January he had still rejected. He was now the more in favour of them because he was convinced that the maintenance of good relations with Italy 'will be of vital importance for us after the war also'. The Austrian ministers would not go so far as that; the sacrifices in question were to be made by Austria (while the Hungarians were losing nothing). Stürgkh agreed to the cession of the Trentino but not the line of the Isonzo, which it was now known that Italy was demanding as a minimum, and he added that it was only until the end of the war that he was prepared to make *bonne mine au mauvais jeu*; after that, he would see. Krobatin, the war minister, agreed, but with the reservation that he would like all those Italians, even if Austrian citizens, who had continued to be irredentists at Trieste or elsewhere, to be expelled and expropriated after the war. Burian observed that irredentism was being suppressed, but by less draconian methods, and that Italy too would have to make a concession: 'We have been informed by the Germans that Italy offers us a free hand in the Balkans', which might even imply Italy's renunciation of Albania. Conrad, resigned by now to losing the Trentino but prepared to fight 'to the death' to save the line of the Isonzo, was doubtful if Italy had ever offered Austria–Hungary *carte blanche* in Serbia: 'In his opinion, the first opportunity ought to be taken after the war to teach Italy a lesson'. Stürgkh, too, 'was of the opinion that the Serbian question would lead to war with Italy some day'. Tisza and Burian contested this thesis and reasserted the expediency of attempting to reach durable agreement with Italy. Their position was weakened, however, by the fact that, as Hungarians, they were opposed to any concessions to the Rumanians in Transylvania and had made it clear as early as 14 July that they were opposed to the annexation of Serbia or Montenegro because they were against any increase of the Slav population of the Dual Monarchy; whereas the generals and the Austrian ministers were in favour of annexing them, although well aware that it would be very difficult for Italy to consent to this. In the end, Burian was content with being authorized to offer the Trentino alone.

The same day he noted in his diary: 'The Trentino, but with a good strategic frontier. Isonzo out of the question. Transfer only after the war.' And yet he had been warned by Avarna on 22 February: *L'accord préalable doit être non seulement initié, mais terminé*. If Sonnino could have seen the minutes of the council meeting, he would have found his insistence upon the immediate transfer of the ceded territory completely justified. Vienna's decision to postpone the execution of the agreement until after the war implied in fact that it would then be for Germany to persuade Italy (or compel her, which would certainly be possible if the Central Powers won the war) to let Austria–Hungary take whatever she liked in the Balkans. Tisza was aware that Hungary and Italy had the same interest (though for different reasons) in preventing the annexation by Austria–Hungary of a large part of Serbia, but he failed to see that he ought to support the immediate transfer to Italy of the Trentino, both for this reason and also because it was the only way of concluding an effective agreement with Rome.

Admittedly, Sonnino was disloyal in deciding on 3 March, while Austria–Hungary was still Italy's ally in the Triple Alliance, to present to London his conditions for Italy's entry into the war on the side of the Entente. (These conditions included the, ethnically at any rate invalid, claim to districts like the South Tyrol and Dalmatia which were almost entirely inhabited by German–Austrians and South-Slavs respectively.) His haste was due to the recent Anglo-French landing at the Dardanelles, which brought the war into the Mediterranean. Had he waited a month he would have seen that nothing was happening there which need oblige him to treat, as he did at Salandra's insistence, simultaneously with both belligerents. Italy could first have denounced the Triple Alliance and then treated with the Entente. It is probable in that case that the Entente would not have allowed her claim to Dalmatia, which was also claimed by Serbia; but this would merely have spared Italy the disappointments of the Peace Conference. However, Sonnino need only have waited until 27 March, when Burian informed Avarna of what was expected from Italy in exchange for the Trentino – not only 'benevolent neutrality in political, military, and economic matters', but also 'full and entire liberty of action in the Balkans' for Austria–Hungary, except in regard to Albania – to reach the conclusion that the Trentino was not worth so much. The Austrian refusal of its immediate transfer, even though mitigated by Burian's offer of a German guarantee of transfer after the war, put too great an onus upon Italy; it would oblige her, simply in order to obtain one province, to remain neutral throughout a European conflict which might end in such a way that a victorious Habsburg monarchy would be in a position to complicate the execution of the agreement with clauses unacceptable to the Italians, or else, if Austria was totally defeated, might take away her freedom to dispose of her own territory.

Sonnino did indeed call Macchio's attention to the fact that, whereas the Italian parliament was expected to ratify the agreement immediately, the Austrian parliament had not assembled since the beginning of the war and would clearly not be called upon to ratify it before the end of hostilities in Europe. What would happen if the *Reichsrat* then refused to ratify the agreement? The only agreement that could make sense for Italy was one that would come into effect immediately. On 14 March the Italian ambassador had explained even more clearly to the German secretary of state for foreign affairs, who repeated it immediately to the Austro-Hungarian ambassador, that the negotiations must be concluded within a fortnight and by an agreement to come into effect immediately; otherwise the Italian government would consider them to have failed. But Burian, encouraged in his disastrous refusal by his own ambassador in Berlin, who was even more intransigent than he, stuck firmly to his position – up to the end of April according to Avarna's despatches – that the immediate transfer of the Trentino 'could not be discussed'. On 16 April Sonnino received Vienna's reply to his final, precise statement of Italy's demands (which comprised, in addition to the Trentino with Bolzano included, Gradisca, Gorizia, the establishment of Trieste as an autonomous Free State, the Curzolari islands, and Valona). The reply was that, apart from the Trentino, Austria–Hungary would leave Valona in Italian possession and would agree, according to what Burian told Avarna, to a rectification of the Isonzo frontier at the end of the war.

Sonnino could deduce from this that further negotiation with Vienna was useless; he quickly did so, and negotiated the London Pact instead. His conclusion is justified by another document which we have found in the Vienna archives. The head of the Austrian foreign ministry's cypher office felt obliged, after the revolution of 1918, to warn Otto Bauer, the new foreign secretary of state of the Austrian Republic, who was planning the union of Austria with Germany, that he had learnt by experience that the Entente had broken the German diplomatic codes. He was certain that in April 1915, the French had deciphered and communicated to Tittoni, the Italian ambassador, a German telegram from Berlin to its ambassadors in Rome and Vienna, in which the hope was expressed 'that Austria would make the desired concessions to Italy, which could easily be withdrawn after victory had been achieved'.[1]

We have not succeeded in tracing this telegram. We have, however, discovered, again in the Haus-, Hof-, und Staatsarchiv, another one which tends to confirm the statement of the Austrian cypher chief. On 9 May 1915, the Austro-Hungarian ambassador to the Vatican, Prince Schönburg, who was working with Benedict XV's approval to make acceptable to the Italian government the

---

[1] Haus- Hof- und Staatsarchiv, Wien. *Nachlass Otto Bauer*. K. 262 – X. *Varia*. Friedrich Probst, head of the cypher office to O. Bauer, on 7 April 1919.

latest concessions offered by Bülow and Macchio, telegraphed to Vienna suggesting that the Pope should be asked to guarantee the fulfilment, after the war, of the obligations assumed by Austria–Hungary towards Italy. The Austro-Hungarian ambassador in Berlin, Prince Hohenlohe, to whom his colleague's proposal was transmitted, telegraphed to Vienna on 11 May: 'If we are going to make a mental reservation about certain concessions we have offered, even to the extent of taking back, when we get the chance, what has been extorted – something which Prince Schönburg evidently does not know – it is quite unthinkable that we should invite the Pope himself to guarantee the concessions we have made'.[2]

Obviously, therefore, the Austro-Hungarian foreign minister did have a 'mental reservation' about adhering to the offers he made to Italy; and the ambassador in Berlin, who evidently would have to explain this in due course to the German government, at whose insistence Vienna had been induced to make the offers, was aware of this reservation. One may suppose that for Burian the 'mental reservation' did not apply to the Trentino but only to the additions (the Isonzo frontier, the autonomy of Trieste, and so on) which Bülow had extorted *in extremis* from Austria–Hungary. But in any case, even allowing for this, the Austrian 'mental reservation' justified the Italian government's insistence upon the immediate execution of the agreement.

The Austro-Hungarian documents also contain further information on how the Central Powers decided during the first days of May (when it was already too late, though Burian could not know this) to present to Italy, and to communicate to Giolitti before Sonnino saw them, those final offers which, if they had been made two months earlier, might have changed the whole course of events. The first to become aware of the inadequacy of the policy adopted on 8 March was Tisza, who was undoubtedly more gifted with political instinct than any of his colleagues. On 28 March he wrote to Burian that it was desirable to represent to Italy that if she would renew her friendship with Austria–Hungary, in exchange for the cession of the Trentino, then Austria–Hungary in turn would offer

2 Haus- Hof- und Staatsarchiv. *Politisches Archiv*. Rot 507. Liasse XLVII 5a. *Italien*. Prinz Schönburg, ambassador to the Vatican, to the Austro-Hungarian Foreign Minister, on 9 May 1915. Prinz Hohenlohe, ambassador in Berlin, on 11 May 1915.

friendship and also an immediate German guarantee of the loyal execution after the war of the agreed cessions of territory. If, after this, Sonnino still remained firm in demanding the immediate transfer of territory, Tisza suggested contacting Salandra, Giolitti, and the King of Italy.

By this time it was perhaps a little too late to change the course of events. The Italian chamber had been adjourned until May and the government, having made clear to Vienna that it found the Austro-Hungarian offers inadequate, felt that it enjoyed complete freedom of action. But Burian proceeded to lose more precious time. Receiving on 16 April his reply – which was not positive – to Sonnino's demands, Avarna confessed to Burian that Italy, to his extreme regret, would decide to go to war.

The next day Forgach wrote to Macchio that Burian's attitude had unexpectedly changed: he was tense, anxious, in favour of appealing for peace, and said that he had spoken about it to Conrad and the Germans. On that same 17 April Tisza, to whom Burian had expressed these views, wrote to him that the delaying tactic had clearly irritated Italy; it was now necessary to let her know that Austria–Hungary might be prepared to cede almost everything that Sonnino demanded, except Trieste. Meanwhile, the German government was impressing emphatically upon the Austro-Hungarian ambassador in Berlin the urgency of making the concessions.

On 4 May, the day on which Italy denounced the Triple Alliance, the German ambassador in Vienna formally requested Burian to authorize Bülow to offer the Trentino, the Isonzo line, autonomy for Trieste, and Albania. Burian replied that he had already authorized Macchio to discuss these concessions with the Italians, in company with Bülow. On 9 May Bülow persuaded Macchio to draw up a list of concessions, signed by the representatives of the two Central Powers, which were considerably more ample than any formulated hitherto, and to present it, in a quite irregular way, first to Giolitti, who had returned to Rome that day, then to Sonnino and Salandra. This list included the cession of the Trentino and of the right bank of the Isonzo wherever inhabited by Italians; the establishment of Trieste as a free city, with an autonomous Italian municipal council and university and a free port, though remaining a part of Austria–Hungary; Valona; the renunciation by Austria–Hungary of her interest in the rest of

Albania; friendly examination of Italian claims to Gorizia and the Curzolari islands; and a German guarantee of the loyal execution of this agreement.

To his government (all of whom, including Tisza, considered that too much had been promised, especially as regards Gorizia and the Curzolari islands), Macchio explained as follows his reasons for accepting Bülow's text: 'The arrival of Signor Giolitti in Rome, and the intense activity of the Holy Father, who has exposed himself in the interest of peace to the point of entering into relations with Giolitti, made it necessary to take some resolute decision immediately'. The list 'was sent to His Holiness, and forwarded by him to Giolitti', who showed it to the King. The Pope then told the Austro-Hungarian ambassador to the Vatican that on the strength of the new concessions he had already persuaded the minister of education, Grippo, to resign in order to bring about a governmental crisis and the return of Giolitti to power. But Giolitti, although he told the King, and others as well, that the latest Austro-Hungarian offers made it absurd for Italy to enter the war against her former allies, was unwilling to take up the reins of government again. Macchio believed in Giolitti's reluctance, 'because he will not yet consider it opportune to appear as a pro-Austrian prime minister'. He thought Giolitti simply proposed to get rid of Sonnino and arrange for Salandra to accept the Central Powers' proposals.

By refusing to take power, Giolitti left the way open for Salandra's reappointment; he undoubtedly had it in mind, however, that Austria–Hungary had not yet agreed to the immediate transfer of the territory she was ceding but only to the immediate exemption from military service of the inhabitants of territory to be ceded after the war – so that Italy (even if she had not been already bound by the London Pact, of which, as it now appears certain, Giolitti was still ignorant), would have had to face new and difficult negotiations before being able to sign the agreement. For example, if the offers made by Bülow and himself were accepted, Macchio proposed to submit to the Italian government an additional text, to be published immediately after signature, which, while reconfirming the concessions already listed (except that it postponed for later discussion the question of Gorizia and the islands) required Italy not only to pay an indemnity for the ceded territory but to forgo any further appeals to article 7 of the treaty of the Triple Alliance (necessarily renewed) in respect of *avantages territoriaux ou autres qui résulteraient pour l'Autriche–Hongrie du traité de paix terminant cette guerre*. Although this text prescribed *parfaite neutralité* for Italy (Sonnino had already explained on 31 March that the Italian government could not promise 'benevolent' neutrality, or at least not publicly, for fear of incurring economic reprisals from England), Macchio maintained in an explanatory memorandum when he returned to Vienna that, in fact, what was expected in return for the Austro-Hungarian concessions was 'benevolent neutrality throughout the war . . . and a completely free hand in the Balkans for us'.

There is no doubt that the Entente, who were evidently suspicious, would have interpreted an agreement between Italy and the Central Powers (even if Italy had not already committed herself in the opposite sense by the London Pact) precisely as a tacit Italian promise of aid to the Entente's enemies, which was in fact what the Austro-Hungarian ambassador thought the Italians ought to give in return for the agreed concessions. Even without the London Pact, therefore, the least that Italy could have expected from the Entente would have been hostile diplomatic relations and open support for those political forces in Italy which were opposed to the Triple Alliance. After the signing of the Pact the Entente could obviously bring formidable pressure to bear by threatening to make it public, so as to provoke an interventionist revolution in Italy with French republican support. But from Austria–Hungary herself, if Italy had promised her an effective benevolence throughout the war, she would hardly have received the same in return after the war if Austria–Hungary emerged from it victorious and therefore greatly strengthened (and all the stronger thanks to the agreement required from Italy, in advance, to allow Vienna a free hand in the Balkans). Again, on 15 May, the Austro-Hungarian foreign minister – who, as a Magyar, was much less Italophobe than his Austrian colleagues – telegraphed to his ambassador in Rome that he intended to carry into effect 'without any second thoughts, the cessions we have agreed to', in other words, those he had approved before Bülow drew up his list on 9 May, but that as regards the additional items (and here Burian mentioned Gorizia, the islands, the autonomy of Trieste, and the rights of Italian citizens of Austria–Hungary), 'these hasty additions oblige us, for the safeguarding of our vital interests, to think sooner or later of some restrictions'.

It may be, as Giolitti said, that if Italy had resumed or continued the negotiations, Austria–Hungary would have ended by giving her the necessary guarantees in order to keep her neutral. Macchio himself telegraphed to Vienna on 16 May to suggest the immediate transfer to Italy of the city of Trento. And, according to Forgach, Tisza was now 'completely convinced that war with Italy must be avoided à tout prix; and Conrad, too, has several times expressed the same opinion'.

But, even apart from the fact that Bülow heard once more from Berlin on 18 May that the government in Vienna was opposed to the immediate transfer of territory, which the Pope favoured, it was now too late for negotiations. And yet, except for the question of whether the transfer should take place immediately or after the war, the latest Austro-Hungarian offers did broadly meet Italy's earlier demands; if these offers had been made before the London Pact was concluded, there would have been the possibility, which Giolitti desired, of negotiations which might keep Italy out of the war. But once again Austria had arrived an hour too late.

(*This article is based both on the documents already published, and on original research in the still unpublished documents, for 1914–15, of the Italian and the Austro-Hungarian Foreign Offices, and also on other unpublished sources, as for example the diary of Burian, the Austro-Hungarian Minister for Foreign Affairs in 1915–16, and the private letters of Sonnino, the Italian Minister for Foreign Affairs, to Senator Bergamini, the editor of the daily* Giornale d'Italia, *which was Sonnino's mouthpiece.*)

German World Policy and the Reshaping of the Dual Alliance

Christopher Andrew

The Dual Alliance between France and Russia, as it existed at the outbreak of war in 1914, dated from 1899. In August of that year the terms of both the original political entente of 1891 and the military convention of 1893–94 were altered in an exchange of letters drafted by the French foreign minister, Delcassé. The duration of the Dual Alliance in its new form was no longer limited to the life of the rival Triple Alliance of Germany, Italy, and Austria–Hungary; and its object, formerly the maintenance of peace, now also included the preservation of the European balance of power. If the reasons for, and the significance of, these changes have never been adequately explained, it is perhaps principally because they have been interpreted within too narrow a context. The reshaping of the Dual Alliance was essentially a product of the diplomacy of imperialism: the first response of an emergent French imperialism, with its dream of a Greater France built round the shores of the Mediterranean, to the new challenge of German world policy.

In the last decade of the nineteenth century French imperialism ceased at last to be the preoccupation of a few enthusiasts, and acquired popular, if not mass, support. Comparing the French public's newly-discovered interest in its empire-builders with its apathy in the 1880s, the leading colonialist journal declared in 1899; 'At that time the return of a Brazza concerned only an interested minority; today the return of a Galliéni or a Marchand excites the crowd.'[1] This growth of imperial feeling coincided with the arrival at the French foreign office of Théophile Delcassé. Delcassé had been a founder member of the parliamentary *groupe colonial* and had for many years been closely identified with colonialist

---

1 *Bulletin du Comité de l'Afrique Française* (hereafter *BCAF*), July 1899.

policies. As minister of colonies in 1894 he had received a presentation from the *parti colonial* 'as a tribute to the services rendered by him to the cause of our colonial expansion since the start of his political career',[2] and he became foreign minister in June 1898 partly as a result of colonialist support. Delcassé remained at the Quai d'Orsay for seven years, a term of office since surpassed only once. For most of these seven years, the pre-occupation of successive French cabinets with the Dreyfus affair and with the bitter conflict between Church and State allowed him a greater freedom to shape French foreign policy than was granted to any of his successors.

As under-secretary and minister of colonies in the years 1893–95, Delcassé had seemed as concerned to promote French expansion in the Far East as in Africa. During the Siamese crisis in 1893 the rest of the French cabinet had been nervous of English reaction; Delcassé had called himself 'the man who stands up to John Bull', and hoped to bring Siam under a French protectorate.[3] By the close of the nineteenth century, however, Delcassé was identified with the small but growing body of colonialist opinion which believed that France's imperial effort should be concentrated in, and limited to, Africa: an attitude which came to be crudely expressed in the phrase '*lâchons l'Asie, prenons l'Afrique*'. As foreign minister he regarded Indo-China and Madagascar as no more than an unnecessary burden on French resources. He saw France, above all, as a Mediterranean power with an African empire stretching from Algeria and Tunisia in the north to the French Congo in the south, and he believed it vital to secure that empire by bringing Morocco under French rule.[4]

Almost at the same time as Delcassé's arrival at the Quai d'Orsay the sudden emergence of a German world policy, marked by the seizure of the Chinese port of Kiao-Chow in 1897 and the passing of the German Navy Law a year later, threatened to cause a major upset in the European balance of power. 'The German

[2] *BCAF*, December 1894.

[3] Delcassé to his wife, 24 and 27 July 1893, Delcassé Mss. I owe a great debt of gratitude to the late Mme la Générale Noguès for allowing me to use her father's papers and for much help and encouragement.

[4] M. Paléologue, *Un grand tournant de la politique mondiale 1904–6* (Paris, 1934), p. 202. Cte de Chambrun, *Traditions et souvenirs* (Paris, 1952), p. 72. O. Homberg, *Les coulisses de l'histoire* (Paris, 1938), p. 28. Mme la Générale Noguès, *Memoir on Delcassé* (Paris, unpublished), pp. 8, 14.

empire', the Kaiser declared, 'has become a world empire'. The ambitions of this new world empire seemed so vaguely defined that each of the powers of the future Triple Entente could feel its own vital interests threatened. The effect of the German challenge to British naval supremacy and to Russian influence in the Near East has been widely discussed. By contrast, the fact that German world policy had an equally important influence on French policy has been curiously ignored. Increasing French suspicion of Germany during Delcassé's seven years of office, in so far as it has been interpreted at all, has often been traced to his alleged Germanophobia. When Delcassé came to power in 1898, however, his attitude towards Germany was more moderate than that of most French politicians. In 1887 he had told his German friend, Louis Nordheim, that his newspaper articles showed 'how dispassionately I discuss German affairs'.[5] When the Kaiser came to the throne in 1888, he had a reputation as an apprentice warlord which understandably inspired most Frenchmen with apprehension and hostility, both of which were strengthened by his message to the army on his accession. Delcassé, however, refused to believe that William was 'the hothead painted by his friends', and wrote to Nordheim three years later: 'Your Emperor is no commonplace figure; he is a remarkable man. What direction will he take? I shall not venture to risk an opinion, but he fills me with a very lively curiosity.'[6] The origins of the increasing Franco-German antagonism in the early twentieth century lie not in Delcassé's alleged Germanophobia, but in the French fear of a new rival in the Mediterranean.

The single-mindedness with which Delcassé and many of his collaborators pursued their vision of France's destiny as a Mediterranean empire made them acutely, sometimes pathologically, suspicious of the Mediterranean ambitions of other powers. Even the United States of America did not escape suspicion. Almost Delcassé's first act as foreign minister was to mediate in the Spanish–American War. Although he was very conscious of the prestige a successful mediation would bring, his main motive was the fear, shared by many French colonialists, that America planned, if the war continued, to land in Morocco and to establish herself

---

[5] Delcassé to Nordheim, 28 January 1887, Nordheim Mss. I am very grateful to M. Rupert Nordheim for permission to use his grandfather's papers.
[6] Delcassé to Nordheim, 12 May 1891, Nordheim Mss.

as a Mediterranean power. The French ambassador in Washington later wrote to Delcassé; 'For both you and me, the whole purpose of our policy at the end of the war was to prevent the Americans from approaching Europe and entering the Mediterranean.'[7] French suspicion of English policy in Morocco ran deeper still. Paul Révoil, appointed French minister in Morocco in 1900, declared that England would stop at nothing to establish her influence at the Sultan's court; he believed that when persuasion, intimidation, and bribery failed, the wives of English diplomats would surrender their honour in the national interest.[8]

But the power whose Mediterranean ambitions were of most concern to Delcassé was Germany, who in the closing years of the nineteenth century had begun to establish herself at the eastern end of the Mediterranean as the dominant influence in the Turkish Empire. Delcassé viewed with particular anxiety the claims made by the Pan-German League, the most vociferous champion of the cause of German world empire. There was good reason to believe that a close connection existed between the aims of the League and the policy of the German government. The first acts of the new world policy, the seizure of Kiao-Chow and the passing of the Navy Law, both corresponded to declared Pan-German aims, and there was considerable co-operation between the League and the Navy Office in propaganda for the new navy.[9] Delcassé no doubt compared the role of the Pan-German League in Germany with that of the *parti colonial* in France. During his seven years as foreign minister, the *parti colonial* had a profound influence on the course of French foreign policy; it was the first group to support the idea of an Anglo-French barter of Egypt and Morocco, and it did much to bring about the *Entente Cordiale*.[10] Delcassé thus viewed with considerable concern the open designs of the Pan-German League on the Habsburg Empire, which at the close of the nineteenth century was widely believed to have begun the process of disintegration. His fears were summarized in a memorandum by the French military attaché in St Petersburg:

7 Jules Cambon to Delcassé, 17 March 1899, Delcassé Mss; cf. Jules Cambon to Delcassé, 8 July 1898, and *BCAF*, August 1898.

8 A. Combarieu, *Sept ans à l'Elysée* (Paris, 1932), p. 182.

9 J. Steinberg, *Yesterday's Deterrent* (London, 1965), pp. 143, 156.

10 This subject is discussed in detail in the author's unpublished Ph.D. dissertation, *The Foreign Policy of Théophile Delcassé to 1905* (Cambridge, 1965).

In view of the great age of the Emperor Francis Joseph and the absence of a direct heir at his death, there is a very real danger that the moment at which German ambitions and aspirations [in the Habsburg Empire] will seek realization may be relatively near, if not imminent.

If Germany is allowed, in one form or another, to bring about this annexation, she will constitute a massive state in the centre of Europe with a population of more than sixty million inhabitants, stretching from the North Sea and the Baltic to the Alps and the Adriatic, and as a result possessing an outlet on the Mediterranean for which she is already preparing, under the pretence of other preoccupations, a powerful fleet.[11]

Delcassé feared that Germany was waiting for the disintegration of Austria–Hungary to establish herself as a Mediterranean power. He believed that the new German fleet was secretly intended for the Mediterranean, and that the Mediterranean rather than the North Sea was the logical base for Germany's new policy of world empire. Charles Benoist, Professor of History at the *École des Sciences Politiques*, wrote in 1899:

Germany already has an outlet to the sea in the north, and she now wants an outlet to the south – for the principal reason that the North Sea leads nowhere, whereas the Mediterranean leads everywhere, being at the centre of the commercial world. Through this outlet to the south, Germany would become a *central* and *universal* power.[12]

The outlet on the Mediterranean for which the Pan-Germans were hoping and for which Delcassé, like Benoist, believed that the German fleet was being secretly prepared, was Trieste, the main port of the Habsburg Empire.

Delcassé's principal aim in 1899 in seeking to modify the Dual Alliance was his concern for the consequences of the possible disintegration of the Habsburg Empire. His purpose in redefining the aim of the alliance as the maintenance of the European balance of power was to prevent the irruption of Germany into the Mediterranean; the fact that the duration of the Dual Alliance was no

---

[11] *Documents Diplomatiques Français 1871–1914* (hereafter *DDF*), first series, vol. 16, appendix, pp. 590–1. Moulin, the author of this memorandum, had been instructed by Delcassé to make a special study of the likely consequences of the collapse of Austria–Hungary (*DDF*, first series, vol. 15, no. 115). This memorandum, prepared for the meeting of the French and Russian Chiefs of Staff in 1900, repeated the conclusions of an earlier memorandum submitted to the minister of war in the spring of 1899 and completely approved by him (*DDF*, first series, vol. 16, appendix, p. 593).

[12] C. Benoist, 'L'Europe sans Autriche', in *Revue des Deux Mondes*, 15 November 1899.

longer limited to the life of the Triple Alliance made sure that it would still be in force at the collapse of Austria–Hungary. Delcassé never believed that it would be possible to prevent Germany's absorption of at least most of the German-speaking parts of the Habsburg Empire if that Empire ceased to exist. He felt confident, however, after the reshaping of the Dual Alliance, that it would be possible to prevent Germany from acquiring any part of the Adriatic coast-line of Austria–Hungary, where Germans were a small minority, and hence from reaching the Mediterranean. Early in 1901, whilst briefing the new *généralissime désigné*, General Brugère, on the provisions of the Dual Alliance, Delcassé told him: 'We are fully prepared for the events which will follow the death of Francis Joseph. Germany wishes to take Trieste and she will have against her almost the whole of Europe.'[13] Nonetheless Delcassé continued to be concerned by Pan-German designs on Austria–Hungary. Early in 1902 Brugère found him 'still preoccupied by what will ensue at the death of the Emperor of Austria' and anxious that the French army should be ready for this eventuality.[14] The end of the Habsburg Empire was also discussed by the French and Russian chiefs of staff during their meetings in 1900 and 1901.

There now remains a problem of timing: the difficulty of reconciling the concern for the future of Austria–Hungary which, said Delcassé, 'had not ceased to preoccupy me since my arrival at the Quai d'Orsay',[15] with the hastily-arranged visit to St Petersburg in August 1899 during which he proposed the modification of the Dual Alliance. In 1878 Albert Sorel had predicted that the Eastern Question would be followed by an Austrian Question. By the end of the century the increasing unrest and rivalries of Austria–Hungary's eleven national groups had convinced many European statesmen that the Empire would not survive the death of its Emperor. Even Charles Benoist, who believed that if Austria did not exist it would be Europe's duty to invent her, wrote in 1899; 'Why hide the fact? From this moment the question of "the future of Austria–Hungary" confronts every cabinet in Europe'.[16] If the Empire did fall, Benoist feared it might be divided between

---

13 Diary entry by Brugère, 18 February 1901; cf. entry for 2 May 1901. I am very grateful to His Excellency, M. Raymond Brugère, for allowing me to use his father's unpublished diary.

14 Diary entry by Brugère, 25 January 1902.

15 *DDF*, first series, vol. 15, no. 255.

16 Benoist, *loc. cit.*

Germany and Russia with scant respect for French interests. Such a solution had already been suggested early in 1899 by the *Alldeutsche Blätter*, the organ of the Pan-German League.[17]

It was fear of a Russo-German division of Austria–Hungary, a fear brought to a head by the news that the Kaiser was seeking a meeting with the Tsar, which led to Delcassé's sudden journey to St Petersburg in August 1899. In Russia it was believed that the Kaiser's motive in seeking such a meeting was to propose a prospective partition of the Habsburg Empire.[18] This belief was probably passed on to Delcassé either by the Russian ambassador or by one of the Russian agents with whom he was in regular contact, although it is hardly likely that he needed any prompting to draw similar conclusions from the news of the Kaiser's overtures. French statesmen realized that the Tsar found it hard to say no, and were always profoundly distrustful of his meetings with the Kaiser.[19] Their suspicion was amply justified in 1905 when in a meeting at Bjorkoe the Kaiser cajoled the Tsar into signing an agreement which, had it not been later repudiated, would have meant the virtual destruction of the Dual Alliance. If in 1899 Delcassé's fears of a Russo-German understanding on the future of Austria–Hungary were groundless, it was because he anticipated, rather than misinterpreted, the direction of German foreign policy. Although at the close of the nineteenth century the German government's first reaction to the possible collapse of the Habsburg Empire was one of alarm at the loss of an ally, within a few years it had come to share Pan-German views on the desirability of an understanding with Russia. Early in 1905 the German Chancellor, Bülow, wrote to his ambassador in Russia, suggesting an approach to the Russians to determine a division of interests in Austria–Hungary, in the event of that Empire's disintegration.[20]

[17] *Alldeutsche Blätter*, 1899, p. 14 (cited by A. Chéradame, *L'Europe et la question d'Autriche*, Paris, 1901, p. 102); cf. *DDF*, first series, vol. 16, appendix, p. 591.

[18] *DDF*, first series, vol. 15, no. 258.

[19] President Faure wrote in 1896: 'The only cause for concern, in my opinion, is that the young Tsar, who is very gentle, appears easy to convince and makes commitments without perhaps sufficient thought' (Faure Mss. XIV). I am very grateful to M. François Berge for allowing me to use his grandfather's *notes personnelles*. On French reaction to the Tsar's meeting with the Kaiser in 1901 see *DDF*, second series, vol. 1, no. 281.

[20] *Die Grosse Politik der Europäischen Kabinette 1871–1914* (hereafter cited as *GP*), vol. xxii, ii, no. 7349.

First news of the Kaiser's attempt to arrange a meeting with the Tsar for the autumn of 1899 reached Delcassé in a despatch from Noailles, the French ambassador in Berlin, early in June. By late July, following press reports on the likelihood of such a meeting, Noailles reported it as probable that the two Emperors would meet. This last report was headed 'urgent – discuss with me together with the previous reports' by Delcassé's *directeur politique*.[21] No doubt the 'previous reports' also included information from a number of confidential French and Russian sources with whom Delcassé was in regular contact. The only sure way to prevent a Russo-German agreement on the future of Austria–Hungary was to forestall it, and with this object in mind Delcassé decided to arrange an immediate journey to St Petersburg. The first that Montebello, French ambassador to Russia, heard of Delcassé's plan was when Muraviev, the Russian foreign minister, told him on 26 July:

You are acquainted with M. Ratchkowsky, our agent in Paris. We have the fullest confidence in him, and he appears to have gained that of the French government. He has, in addition, known M. Delcassé personally for a long time and frequently has occasion to see him. In a conversation with him a few days ago on the general situation, on relations between France and Russia, and on the apparent German overtures to you, he gained the impression that M. Delcassé might have the idea, on a pretext which would be easy to discover, to spend several days in St Petersburg. He telegraphed the minister of the interior who passed his message to me. I do not think M. Delcassé announced any definite intention, but his idea is excellent.[22]

There is little doubt that on this, as on other occasions, Montebello was not told the full story. Montebello was only one of several elderly aristocratic ambassadors whom Delcassé preferred to by-pass in the conduct of confidential negotiations. In arranging his own visit to St Petersburg in 1899, as in arranging the Tsar's state visit to France in 1901 and President Loubet's return visit to Russia a year later, Delcassé preferred to indulge his penchant for secret diplomacy by working through the Russian agent, Ratchkowsky.[23]

21 Noailles to Delcassé, 3 June and 25 July 1899, Quai d'Orsay archives, *Allemagne NS 61*. The French ambassador in Russia reported on 28 July 1899: 'the Tsar's plans are still a complete mystery' (Delcassé Mss.). The Tsar eventually met the Kaiser at Potsdam in early November 1899.
22 Montebello to Delcassé, 28 July 1899, Delcassé Mss.
23 In St Petersburg Ratchkowsky was in touch with one of Montebello's

'*Le terrible Ratchkowsky*', as one French diplomat called him, was one of the most sinister figures in the underworld of European diplomacy during the generation before the Great War. He was officially stationed in Paris as head of the Russian secret police in Europe, but for many years also played an important part in Franco-Russian diplomacy. On his arrival in Paris in 1887, the veteran French agent, Jules Hansen, had found him 'a supporter of an alliance between France and Russia and ready to help towards this end', and he had been regularly used as an intermediary in confidential negotiations with the Russian Government.[24] Delcassé had known Ratchkowsky for several years before he became foreign minister and continued to have regular meetings with him until Ratchkowsky's recall in 1902. Ratchkowsky was described by the secretary-general of the Elysée as 'more anti-German than ourselves', and was therefore probably as apprehensive as Delcassé at the likelihood of a meeting between the Tsar and the Kaiser in the autumn of 1899. When in late July 1899 Delcassé decided that it was imperative to forestall such a meeting, it was through Ratchkowsky that he made urgent arrangements for a visit of his own to St Petersburg. The story that Delcassé had casually mentioned a visit as only a vague possibility in the course of a general conversation with Ratchkowsky, was no more than an attempt by Muraviev to conceal from Montebello the fact that on this, as on other occasions, Delcassé had preferred to conduct important business through other channels. Delcassé himself gave the lie to this story by arriving in St Petersburg only a week after Montebello had been told that his visit was not even definitely decided.

When the terms of the Dual Alliance, as it was modified in 1899, became known after the Great War, Delcassé was widely accused of having given French support to Russian designs in the Balkans. In fact almost the reverse is true. In 1899 it was not Russia who was seeking to involve France in the Balkans, but Delcassé who was trying to involve Russia by seeking her support against Germany's supposed ambitions on the coast of the Adriatic. By so doing Delcassé believed he had succeeded, where previous French statesmen had failed, in making the Dual Alliance serve the interests

deputies, Greigueuil, who corresponded secretly with Delcassé; see Greigueuil to Delcassé, 14 August 1901 and 8 January 1902, Delcassé Mss.

[24] J. Hansen, *Ambassade à Paris du Baron de Morenheim* (Paris, 1906), p. 129.

of France. Since the beginning of his political career he had been a partisan of a Franco-Russian alliance. When the Dual Alliance did come about, however, he was sickened by the attitude of those of his countrymen who looked on alliance with Russia simply as a refuge from the diplomatic isolation in which France had languished for twenty years. He spoke in a letter to his wife of 'what you have heard me say many times, that it was not solely for the satisfaction of Russia that we made the Dual Alliance, and that we should make use of her to serve our interests just as she uses us with so much success for her own'.[25]

After his exchange of letters with Muraviev in August 1899, Delcassé hoped that, so far from being a major threat to French security, the collapse of the Habsburg Empire could now be turned to France's advantage by giving her an opportunity to recover the provinces of Alsace-Lorraine lost to Germany by the Treaty of Frankfurt in 1871. From the start of the Dual Alliance France had made very clear to her ally the importance she attached to the return of the lost provinces. Although the terms of the military convention of 1893–94 appeared to commit France to general mobilization even in the event of Austria's involvement in a Balkan war which did not directly threaten Russia, President Faure warned the Russian Government in 1895 that France would support Russia in a Balkan war only if such a war offered her the opportunity to recover Alsace-Lorraine: '*ce jour-là tout est possible*'. Faure repeated this warning during the visits to France by the Tsar in 1896 and by Muraviev a year later.[26] Delcassé, however, hoped that France might win back the lost provinces without a war. He told the Russian ambassador soon after he became foreign minister in 1898 that France would never endanger the peace of Europe to recover Alsace-Lorraine – 'but may not circumstances come about which will spontaneously make a just solution possible?'[27] The 'circumstances' he had in mind were the boundary changes which would follow the collapse of the Habsburg Empire. He later expressed his belief that in the European crisis which he expected to follow the death of Francis Joseph, Germany would need the consent of France to her share of the Austrian inheritance.

25 Delcassé to his wife, 6 November 1895, Delcassé Mss; cf. letters to his wife of 3 November 1890, 20 October 1891, 14 September 1893, 7 October 1896.
26 Faure Mss. XVI, XII.
27 Note by Delcassé, 31 August 1898, Delcassé Mss.

'Is it unreasonable to think that in such circumstances Germany . . . would not consider the revision of the Treaty of Frankfurt too high a price to pay? History has seen stranger things.'[28] In the summer of 1899, however, Delcassé had feared to lose far more from the disintegration of Austria–Hungary than he could hope to gain. Hope of the recovery of Alsacc-Lorraine was overshadowed by a threat to the whole future of France as a Mediterranean power, and it was this latter consideration which was uppermost in Delcassé's mind when he set out for St Petersburg.

On his arrival there Delcassé found Muraviev sceptical of his fears of Germany's ambitions as a Mediterranean power. Muraviev later commented on these fears in a despatch which, said one Russian diplomat, 'destroyed with one stroke of the pen the web of imaginary suspicion directed by M. Delcassé against the Berlin cabinet's alleged designs on the possession of Trieste or another point on the Adriatic'.[29] Nonetheless, Muraviev agreed on the need to preserve the balance of power in the event of the collapse of the Austrian Empire and to extend the duration of the Dual Alliance to cover this eventuality.[30] His main reason, however, for wishing to strengthen the alliance, was general rather than specific. In the summer of 1899 the Russian government was showing a concern for the strength of the Dual Alliance which contrasted with its apparent apathy during the previous few years. Russia was alarmed by the effect on the alliance of the dissensions in France caused by the Dreyfus affair and of the new tendency of a considerable section of the French press to favour a rapprochement with Germany. Muraviev told Montebello that 'France's true friends were very concerned by these developments', and expressed the hope that a visit by Delcassé 'would give the impression that our relations are as close and as cordial as ever, and that we are more than ever in agreement'.[31]

Russia's desire for a strong Dual Alliance stemmed, as did Delcassé's, from fear of the ambitions of German world policy: but while France was principally concerned by the threat of a new

[28] Paléologue, *op. cit.*, p. 196; cf. Combarieu, *op. cit.*, p. 283.

[29] A.-F. Meyendorff, *Correspondance diplomatique du Baron de Staal 1894–1900* (Paris, 1929), vol. 2, p. 455. There was, however, some sympathy in the Russian army for Delcassé's fears.

[30] Montebello to Delcassé, 28 July 1899, Delcassé Mss; *DDF*, first series, vol. 15, no. 255.

[31] Montebello to Delcassé, 28 July 1899, Delcassé Mss.

rival in the Mediterranean, Russia was preoccupied by Germany's emergence at the end of the nineteenth century as the dominant influence in the Turkish Empire. The Russian government was particularly alarmed by the German plan for a Baghdad railway which would link the Sea of Marmora to the Persian Gulf, and from April to June 1899 unsuccessfully sought compensation from Germany in the form of her consent to Russian control of the Straits. Russian suspicion of the ambitions of German foreign policy was strengthened by the brashness with which it was sometimes conducted. The tsar was especially irritated by Germany's behaviour at the disarmament conference summoned on his initiative at The Hague from May to July 1899. By responding wholeheartedly to the Kaiser's command to bring 'healthy realism to bear on the mass of Russian hypocrisy, twaddle, and lies', the German delegation to the conference had succeeded in appearing largely responsible for the failure to discuss the disarmament proposal and for making recourse to the new arbitration tribunal voluntary and not compulsory. The Tsar was further annoyed to learn from Queen Victoria that 'William takes every opportunity of impressing upon [the English ambassador] that Russia is doing all in her power to work against us'.

Russia's acceptance of the modification to the Dual Alliance proposed by Delcassé, though due mainly to suspicion of Germany, also reflected her confidence in Delcassé and the fundamental improvement in Franco-Russian relations which had followed his arrival at the Quai d'Orsay. Delcassé's predecessor, Gabriel Hanotaux (perhaps the most overrated of all the Third Republic's foreign ministers), had displayed an increasing lack of enthusiasm for the alliance and had completely alienated Muraviev, whom he variously described at cabinet meetings as 'cheat' and 'traitor'.[32] The relationship between Delcassé and Muraviev was quite different; Muraviev visited Paris soon after Delcassé took office and quickly established close relations with him. A year later Delcassé told his wife; 'Personally we are increasingly in sympathy, and this personal friendship complements our political relationship'.[33] Many European statesmen combined a considerable contempt for French politicians in general with a considerable respect

[32] Faure Mss. XXIII, XXV. The Faure papers suggest that Hanotaux had a talent for making enemies.
[33] Delcassé to his wife, October 1899, Delcassé Mss.

for Delcassé in particular; Edward VII, for example, came to feel 'absolute confidence' in Delcassé, whilst being 'by no means favourably impressed' by the rest of the French government.[34] This dichotomy of attitude was even more marked among Russian statesmen. During Delcassé's seven years of office the Dreyfus affair and the bitter conflict between French Church and State transformed Russia's traditional distrust of France's republican government into thinly disguised disgust. But while Russian diplomats the world over treated their French colleagues with disdain,[35] Russian confidence in Delcassé himself increased steadily. The extent of this confidence was shown by Russia's secret and formal request in March 1905 for his good offices to end the Russo-Japanese War.[36] Lamsdorff, Muraviev's successor at the Russian foreign office, looked on Delcassé's fall from power three months later as little short of a disaster: 'I cannot adequately express my sorrow at the loss of Delcassé, an unfailing friend of Russia for so many years. May he return to power soon and take into his safe hands the great task of peace-making'.[37] Not merely the reshaping but the very survival of the Dual Alliance during the early years of the twentieth century depended on Delcassé. Nelidov, the Russian ambassador in Paris, told him in April 1905; 'I have the inner conviction that with your departure the whole alliance would perish'.[38] When the Tsar and the Kaiser met at Bjorkoe a month after Delcassé's fall from power, Nelidov's prophecy came close to fulfilment.

The motive which had led Delcassé to seek a modification of the Dual Alliance continued to shape French policy towards Germany in the years up to the Great War. Throughout his term of office he was constantly preoccupied by fear of Germany's ambitions in the Mediterranean, although the area where he most feared a German intrusion changed. Before 1903 German policy towards Morocco had been of only minor concern to Delcassé and to his friends in the *parti colonial*. In January 1903, however, a Moroccan Company

---

[34] Monson to Lansdowne, 15 May 1903, Lansdowne Mss; *DDF*, second series, vol. 5, no. 449.

[35] *British Documents on the Origins of the War 1898–1914*, vol. 1, no. 184; *DDF*, second series, vol. 1, no. 62.

[36] Note by Delcassé, 22 March 1905, Delcassé Mss.

[37] Manuscript letter from Lamsdorff to Nelidov, 8 June 1905 (new style). See C. Andrew, *op. cit.*, chapter 10.

[38] Nelidov to Delcassé, 22 April 1905, Delcassé Mss.

was founded in Germany with Pan-German and colonialist support. From the first it demanded that the German government seize a foothold in Morocco, and by the beginning of 1904 Morocco had become the chief preoccupation of the Pan-German League.[39] Once again Delcassé believed that Pan-German demands reflected, or at least anticipated, the official policy of the German government. And just as fear of German ambition in the Adriatic had led him to strengthen the Dual Alliance, so fear of German ambitions in Morocco did much to persuade him to seek an entente with England. In February 1903 Delcassé at last adopted the policy of Anglo-French exchange of interests in Egypt and Morocco which the *parti colonial* had been urging on him for almost five years. A few months later he told one of the original advocates of this policy:

The Moroccan question must be solved within three years, and given the way in which the Germans are talking and putting forward (through the Moroccan Company) the idea of a German seizure of Morocco, we must not allow them three years. In three years it would be too late; the German race, with its tendency to expand and overrun, would have given itself a historic and nationalist justification for what is still only the momentary demand of a minority.[40]

Delcassé believed that the later German challenge to French policy in Morocco which led in 1905 to the first of the pre-war Franco-German crises was an attempt to achieve at the western end of the Mediterranean the foothold she had so far failed to secure in the Adriatic. Delcassé's first *directeur politique* wrote to him on the eve of the first Moroccan crisis, resuming the evidence of the growth of German influence at the eastern end of the Mediterranean and of a fleet which he believed was secretly intended for the Mediterranean; he concluded: 'William II . . . considers that Germany is virtually, here and now, a Mediterranean power — whilst waiting for the opportunity to establish herself, by a lease or monopoly, either on the Muslim coast of the Mediterranean or at its gates, at, for example, an Atlantic port in Morocco.'[41]

The diplomacy of imperialism was very often based on suspicion and on myth created by suspicion. Governments were apt to attri-

[39] *BCAF*, February 1903, M.S. Wertheimer, *The Pan-German League 1890–1914* (New York, 1924), p. 169.
[40] Delcassé's words were recalled in a letter to him from Joseph Chailley-Bert written early in July 1903 (Delcassé Mss.).
[41] Nisard to Delcassé, 1 May 1905, Delcassé Mss.

bute to others their own imperial ambitions. The two great suspicions which shaped French foreign policy at the beginning of the present century – fear of Germany as a Mediterranean power, fear of British designs on Morocco – though grounded on some evidence, were principally a reflection of France's own dreams of empire. The imperial mission generated an imperial mythology, and it was the mythology rather than the mission that inspired early twentieth-century diplomacy. France's motive in modifying as in making the Dual Alliance was suspicion of Germany; but by 1899 her resentment at the past had been overshadowed by fear for her imperial future.

Hungary and the Crisis of July 1914

Norman Stone

Albert Sorel described the Austrian Empire as having not a government but a diplomatic service that also administered. The Habsburg dynasty traditionally conducted business with an eye turned towards Europe; and in Austria–Hungary foreign policy had a relevance to internal problems that was more immediate than in any other European state. In the years before 1914 men loyal to the Monarchy came increasingly to feel that their political debility could be cured only through foreign policy. No-one had much faith in the prospects for purely internal reform: the nationality problem was too complex to be solved merely through an emperor's longevity. Real patriots hoped that some great stroke of foreign policy would re-awaken the loyalty of the Habsburg peoples and the respect of the Monarchy's neighbours; and thus, while European statesmen believed that a civil war in Austria–Hungary would produce general conflict, official circles in Austria–Hungary calculated that general conflict in Europe was their only alternative to civil war. The mood of governing ministers in Vienna was a desperate one – 'better a terrible end than an endless terror', the phrase ran – and their quarrel with Serbia was endowed with a bitterness and irrationality that made compromise impossible. In itself, squalid bickering with Balkan states was an unworthy occupation for men who sat at Metternich's desk; but Serbia, with her challenge to Habsburg rule in Bosnia–Herzegovina, seemed to question the Monarchy's existence as a great power as well as aggravating the South Slav problem. The Monarchy's very existence depended, it was thought, on its European position; and a small Balkan state thus became an object on which the Habsburg dynasty could demonstrate its continuing vigour.

However, even the 'daring stroke' of July 1914 showed how far the Monarchy had declined. The strains that eventually broke the settlement of 1919–20 were already present under a dynastic carapace in 1914: in matters of moment, the peoples of Central Europe thought of Germany and Russia, not of the Monarchy. It was symptomatic of this development that the Hungarian Prime Minister, Count Stephen Tisza, agreed to go to war with Serbia only at the prompting of the German ambassador, Tschirschky, who made it clear that Germany would take her patronage elsewhere if Austria–Hungary did not take action. Tisza's first loyalties went to Hungary, and not to the Monarchy. He accepted the Monarchy's interests only in so far as they coincided with those of Hungary; describing the idea of war with Serbia as a 'fateful error', he refused to sanction it until German pressure made it necessary for him to do so. By 1914 Germany had acquired a decisive arbitrage in the Monarchy's affairs, and the grandly-trumpeted ultimatum to Belgrade had first to be haggled over in Budapest and finally brought about by Berlin. The role of Vienna was at times an ignobly passive one: as Seton-Watson said during the war, 'In August 1914 two currents met, the one from Berlin, the other from Budapest, over the prostrate body of Vienna; and it may safely be maintained that without Budapest the necessary circuit could not have been established'.[1] This was an exaggeration of Hungary's power; she had to choose between Russia and Germany, and she would prefer to obey Berlin. In July 1914 Berlin forced the moment of choice.

The humiliating triviality of Austro-Hungarian foreign policy had much to do with the power exercised by Budapest. Vienna thought of cutting a figure in Europe, while Budapest was quite content to see the Monarchy restrict its activities to the Balkans; as a result, the Monarchy had the capacities of a large power and the preoccupations of a small one. Hungarian influence on foreign policy had been guaranteed by article eight of the Compromise – Law XII of 1867, which laid down the Hungarian Prime Minister's right to be informed about and to shape decisions of foreign policy.[2] As long as Hungarian governments were dominated by politicians who had learnt caution and restraint in the 1850s and 1860s, the emperor's servants could conduct foreign policy almost

[1] R.W. Seton-Watson, *German, Slav, and Magyar* (London, 1916), p. 11.

[2] L. Bernatzik, *Die oesterreichischen Verfassungsgesetze*, 2nd ed. (Vienna, 1911), p. 324. A similar provision did not, apparently, exist for the Austrian Prime Minister. (The non-Hungarian lands of the Habsburg Monarchy are referred to here as 'Austria', a convenient though strictly illegitimate abbreviation.)

without reference to the Magyars; but in 1900 a new generation of politicians appeared in Hungary, prepared to argue seriously about foreign policy. Until 1913, Hungarian governments were relatively unstable, their chiefs mainly concerned with domestic affairs; but when Count Tisza became Prime Minister in June 1913, with his confidant Burian as Hungarian representative in Vienna, Magyar influence on the conduct of foreign affairs became significant as never before. Tisza was the greatest Magyar statesman in the age of Dualism, and in his understanding of the larger issues involved in Central European politics he was equalled only by Count Michael Karolyi, who saw them from an anti-dynastic point of view. Unlike most of his political contemporaries, Tisza had before 1914 a good sense of the implicit, and he recognized the power that Hungary might have under Dualism if she set about acquiring it with the necessary vigour.

The war of 1914 blew away much of the fog in which Central European politics were conducted. Domination by Germany of the Monarchy's military and foreign affairs was matched by a domination of her internal affairs by Hungarian interests. This now became more obvious than ever previously; under Tisza's direction the Magyars came to exercise a power they had not known since the middle ages. Hungarian landowners became of greater account than the Austrian population: Tisza refused to allow customs duty on food to be lowered so that the army authorities could buy cheap foreign wheat; he also prevented the municipality of Vienna from importing cheap meat from the Argentine, in competition with Hungarian meat, 'until conditions in the meat-markets here make this import convenient to us', meaning that the Viennese were to eat expensive food for the benefit of Magyar land-owners. In December 1915 the Austrian Prime Minister was reduced, in a letter to his Hungarian colleague, to the ridiculous assertion, 'I can only set up once more the incontrovertible axiom that you can certainly slaughter swine in Hungary, but not people in Austria'.[3] In foreign policy Hungary took the same preponderant role: Tisza negotiated on almost equal terms with the German General Staff, and on one occasion accepted an invitation to go to Berlin for this

---

[3] v. *Grof Tisza Istvan osszes munkai*, 6 vols. (Budapest, 1923–7), vol. 2, nos 129, 586. The text of Stürgkh's letter is to be found in the protocol of a ministerial conference of 17 December 1915, in the *Haus-Hof- und Staats-Archiv*, Vienna.

purpose without asking Francis Joseph's permission; early in 1915 Count Berchtold was casually dismissed from the foreign ministry over lunch with Tisza and the German ambassador: he went, wrote Tisza, 'in his usual way, like a good child'.[4] The events of the war years amply bore out the comment of Louis Eisenmann that

To make secure the existence, independence, and sovereignty of the Hungarian state by providing it with a permanent alliance, and, by virtue of this alliance, to give Hungary the strength of a great state to sustain the great role she can no longer play on her own: such is the chief political idea behind the Compromise.[5]

In July 1914 the power of Hungary, though less evident than it later became, was sufficient to block the suggestion of provoking war with Serbia; and it was a measure of the Monarchy's decline that Germany had to intercede before Tisza would give way.

One of the reasons for the weakness of the Dualist settlement was that conservatives in the two parts of the Monarchy were working towards different ends. Austrian conservatives wished to save the Monarchy, while Magyar conservatives wished to save Greater Hungary, with its archaic social structure and its ten million non-Magyars. Some Hungarian politicians of the opposition thought that Hungary should become an 'Eastern Switzerland', and hoped to co-operate with the Balkan peoples, on lines developed in exile by Louis Kossuth. Had the Magyars followed such lines, the South Slav problem as it existed in 1914 would have disappeared. But Hungary was dominated by its large gentry-class, which had all the pretensions and none of the tolerance of a great aristocracy; there was in fact no chance of reconciliation between the Magyars and their neighbours so long as this class was predominant in Hungary. Tisza, like the Austrian conservatives, was well aware of the fragility of the Dualist structure; but where the Austrians wished to strengthen the Monarchy, Tisza merely sought to avoid putting the system to a test. He knew that politics in Hungary were conducted in the shadow of a volcano. Parliament notoriously represented only six per cent of the Hungarian population, the 'political nation' with whom Francis Joseph had struck the bargain of 1867,

[4] v. *Graf Stefan Tisza: Weltkriegsbriefe 1914–18*, 2 vols. (Berlin, 1928), I, pp. 250, 150–3. These volumes contain the most important letters, some already in German, others in translation from the Magyar. Where there are alternatives, I cite the German rather than the Magyar version.

[5] L. Eisenmann, *Le Compromis austro-hongrois de 1867* (Paris, 1905), p. 640.

and social questions were reflected only at long remove in politics. The quarrels that rocked the Dualist system concerned matters of somewhat limited interest to the majority of the population – the language of command in the army, the statute of the Austro-Hungarian Bank, the nomenclature employed in common agreements, the existence of conjunctions in imperial titles. Some members of the opposition, radical nationalists for the most part, went beyond these ponderous frivolities and demanded control of foreign policy. In 1912 Tisza, as Speaker, expelled them by force from the Chamber, and thereby achieved an almost complete control of politics. With a large and stable majority he believed he could reassert the basic principles of Dualism, and since he was convinced of the historic mission of the Magyar gentry, he worked against democratic reform or national reconciliation. Buttressed by 'the national cause' – in a generous interpretation of the phrase – Tisza's party made its principal appeal to Magyar demagogues: universal suffrage, which would have destroyed the social structure and given political expression to the subordinate nationalities, was resolutely opposed. Tisza himself once said that it would be tantamount to 'castrating the nation'. Patriotism therefore required non-propertied Magyars to accept political repression.[6]

It was above all the nationality question that preoccupied the gentry-politicians. They believed that the ten million non-Magyars – Slovaks, Germans, Rumanians, Ruthenes, and Serbo-Croats – should be turned into Magyars as rapidly as possible. Every public institution in Hungary was used to this effect; and even Tisza, who was an enthusiastic supporter of the Monarchy, would not consider its interests if they clashed with Hungary's. The Austro-Hungarian army was commanded in German, but in its regiments the language of the soldiers was used for all other purposes, such as drill and instruction. Magyar patriots saw in this an assertion of that *Gesamtmonarchie* which had been ostensibly forgotten in 1867 when Hungary was given autonomy, for the army seemed to combine the dynasty's centralizing ambitions with favour towards the lesser peoples condemned by Budapest. Tisza maintained 'that no foreign national spirit should remain in the army, and furthermore that the common army in this land should be a

---

6 Literally, 'cut off the nation's life-force'. The speech is quoted in the four-volume collection of his parliamentary speeches published in Budapest, 1933–7, under the title *Grof Tisza Istvan Kepviselohazi beszedei*, iii, p. 765.

propagator and handmaiden of the Magyar national idea and spirit',[7] meaning that Slovaks would in future have to stammer at their officers in Magyar to serve the Magyar national cause. The Magyar propertied class approached the whole issue of nationalism with a violence and intolerance from which even the Bohemian Germans could have learnt much; and though Tisza dissociated himself from the ranting arrogance of many of his contemporaries, he held true to the course of magyarization. His attitude was in itself a sufficient illustration of the term 'master-nation': writing to Count Czernin, Austro-Hungarian minister in Bucharest, he condemned a German proposal that the Rumanian inhabitants of Hungary should be appeased by concessions. The Germans had suggested that Tisza appoint a Rumanian *Landsmannminister*, which Tisza dismissed as 'a fatuous idea'; the Germans had also urged Tisza to create a Rumanian university, which he rejected as 'a cultural absurdity that would prejudice the academic education and practical interests of Rumanian youth'.[8] In 1912 Tisza's party (nominally headed by Laszlo Lukacs) introduced in response to foreign pressure a bill to extend the suffrage. The extension promised – and not carried out – was in itself a gingerly approach to democratic ideals; it was to be supplemented in effect by bribery and intimidation of candidates and voters, and possessed the perhaps inevitable qualification that 'whoever attacks the national character of the Hungarian state loses ten years voting rights on the first offence and loses them permanently on the second' – a provision that automatically outlawed all nationality representatives. Not unnaturally, the various leaders of the nationalities objected to the bill, protesting to Archduke Franz Ferdinand that 'the dynasty is once more allowing itself to be trapped by the Magyar oligarchy'; the Archduke himself objected in a letter to his uncle that the bill would merely strengthen 'that urban semi-intelligentsia which has always been a preserve of Magyar chauvinism'.[9] A state organized on these lines was a fragile enough affair, and foreign complications would not help it towards stability. In 1914 Tisza was aware that the survival of Dualism depended upon several conditions –

---

[7] Ibid., vol. 4, p. 219 (April 1910).

[8] *Weltkriegsbriefe* I, pp. 254–7.

[9] *Pester Lloyd*, 31 August 1912; *Kriegsarchiv*, Vienna, *Akten der Militärkanzlei des Thronfolgers*, 1912 – PU.19: letters from Vajda-Voevod to Francis Ferdinand, 24 December 1912, and Francis Ferdinand to his uncle, 28 December 1912.

the Magyar propertied class must be united and determined to maintain its power; the Magyars themselves must accept social repression and political silence in the name of patriotic endeavour; the Habsburg dynasty must refrain from dreams of restoring the *Gesamtmonarchie* by intriguing with the national minorities in Hungary; the minorities must be kept in place and magyarized. Above all, there must be no European complications to upset the balance that had been achieved.

Austrian conservatives vaguely calculated that war would solve their nationality problems: once the Serbs had been crushed, the Czechs would no longer insist on having schools in non-Czech areas. Tisza on the other hand knew that war with Serbia would complicate the workings of Dualism in Hungary to an intolerable extent. Whatever its outcome, war would lead to a fatal disruption of the Compromise settlement. If Russia won, then Great Hungary would cease to exist, being partitioned among Slav and Latin states; while if the Central Powers won, the prestige of the Monarchy would be enhanced, and the destruction of Serbia might prove, as many members of the dynasty hoped, to be a prelude to the reduction of Hungary to the status of an Austrian province. Perhaps, too, if the war provoked all the trends implicit in Central Europe, Hungary might have to cope with a great extension of German power. At all events, Hungary might be ground between *Mitteleuropa* and *Gross-Oesterreich*. Tisza had recognized as early as 1889 that war would not be 'child's play for the Monarchy or the Hungarian nation', that 'it could easily become a life-and-death struggle for Hungary'[10]: and in July 1914 he clearly knew that Hungary had much to lose from a war that might destroy the existing balance of power, both in Europe and in Austria–Hungary.

Consequently, on hearing of the assassination in Sarajevo, Tisza's first reaction was to counsel caution. He was not much perturbed at the assassination of the Archduke, who had a reputation of being hostile to the Magyars: if anything, the assassination came as a relief to him. In Vienna, however, a mood of desperation seized the governing circles: as Josef Redlich recorded in his diary on 28 June, 'It should now be clear to everyone that peaceful coexistence (*friedliche Koexistenz*) is impossible to achieve between

---

[10] *Kepviselohazi beszedei*, i, p. 8.

this half-German Monarchy with its sister-relationship to Germany, and Balkan nationalism with its fanatical bloodthirstiness'.[11] The press in Vienna indulged itself at length in vituperation against the Serbs; various officials of the foreign ministry suggested that Serbia should be severely punished; and Conrad von Hötzendorf, Chief of the General Staff, manipulated his statistics to show that his army was ready for war as assiduously as he had manipulated them in a reverse direction when trying to extract money from the politicians. The foreign minister had however to take some stock of the realities, and although himself convinced that war was the only possible answer to the Serbian question, he did not know whether Germany would cover the Monarchy against Russia, or whether Italy and Rumania would approve. Berchtold's reaction was to delay diplomatic measures until the investigation in Sarajevo had provided some form of evidence against Serbia; when it did, 'a clear programme of action as regards Serbia should be drawn up'.[12] The idea of war was unquestionably in Berchtold's mind, and when Tisza heard on 30 June that it was being considered, he at once wrote in protest to Francis Joseph. In a memorandum of 1 July, he denounced Berchtold's 'intention of using the revolting murder in Sarajevo as an occasion for settling accounts with Serbia'; he had made no secret when talking to Berchtold of his conviction that this would be a 'fateful error for which I can in no event be responsible'. If war broke out, it would be 'a large-scale war under the most unfavourable conditions', for Russia would intervene, Rumania would not come to the Monarchy's aid, and Bulgaria, 'the only state on which we can rely', was for the moment 'exhausted'. Tisza urged a peaceful solution on the Emperor; war could be provoked at a later date, if really required. Meanwhile Rumania should be forced back to her allegiance in the Triple Alliance, and to provide the right threat to Rumania, the Monarchy should begin negotiations with Bulgaria.[13] This memorandum, together with the German ambassador's initial discouragement of the hotheads, threw the foreign ministry into confusion: on 2 July Redlich recorded, 'as usual they are beset by

[11] *Schicksalsjahre Oesterreichs: Das politische Tagebuch Josef Redlichs*, 2 vols. (Graz, 1953), I, p. 235.

[12] Quoted from Berchtold manuscripts in H. Hantsch, *Leopold Graf Berchtold*, 2 vols. (Vienna, 1963), II, pp. 558–9.

[13] *Oesterreich-Ungarns Aussenpolitik* (henceforth OeUAP), vol. VIII, no. 9978.

their beloved vacillation . . . they do not wish to hear a word about serious measures against Serbia'.[14]

It became clear that indecision in Vienna could be cured in Berlin alone, and the Austro-Hungarian foreign ministry accordingly sought advice there. A long memorandum on Balkan affairs had been prepared for Germany's benefit before the assassination of the Archduke: it contained a plea that Germany should reconsider her relations with Rumania, and should to this end make an approach to Bulgaria in the hope that the Rumanians would then run back to the Central Powers. This document was slightly refurbished to meet the situation created by the Sarajevo assassination; and although war was at no point directly mentioned, the Austro-Hungarian authorities were clearly flirting with it. Berchtold urged that Germany and Austria–Hungary should 'at this stage work forcefully and at the right moment against the developments being systematically planned and encouraged by Russia, which we will perhaps at a later date be unable to reverse'; and he also stressed to the Germans the 'necessity of resolutely tearing apart the cords which her [Austria–Hungary's] enemies are seeking to build into a net above her head'. This memorandum, taken to Berlin on 4 July by Count Hoyos, one of Berchtold's closest collaborators, was accompanied by a letter from Francis Joseph to the German Emperor, the tone of which was similarly bellicose without at any stage directly mentioning war.[15] In reality Austria–Hungary could on her own go no further than futile cavilling against Balkan states: everything depended upon the decision taken in Berlin. Hoyos, Forgach, and the other foreign ministry officials could preach war, but since Tisza opposed it and the German attitude was not clear, Austria–Hungary could scarcely go forward on her own.

During the Balkan Wars of 1912 and 1913 the German attitude had been one of restraint. Austria–Hungary had seen the danger of Serb nationalism for some time, and could easily have been pushed into war with Serbia had the Germans indicated their support. The real departure of July 1914 was that the Germans began to accept the Austrian thesis that the position of the Central Powers could be defended only by aggression. On previous occasions, the Germans had been more economical in their use of Pomeranian

[14] *Redlich*, I, p. 236.
[15] OeUAP, VIII, no. 9984 and *Beilage*. Tisza tried, too late, to tone down parts of the letter.

155

grenadiers, and in consequence the Austro-Serb conflict during the Balkan Wars had been reduced to dreary diplomatic haggling. In February 1913 the German Chief of Staff, Moltke, not usually an advocate of peace, wrote to Conrad that public opinion in Germany would not sympathize with Austria–Hungary 'if she were to provoke a war at this moment'.[16] At the same time, Bethmann Hollweg had warned Berchtold that 'to bring about a solution by force – even if many interests of the Monarchy recommend it – would be to my mind a mistake of inconceivable magnitude at a moment when prospects, however distant, exist of settling the conflict in conditions much more favourable to us'.[17] There was in effect no more to be said: without full German support even Conrad became cautious, while both Tisza and Archduke Franz Ferdinand declared their opposition to war. It was significant of the German government's usual attitude to Balkan affairs that Tschirschky, the ambassador, at first counselled caution after the murder of Franz Ferdinand: he reported on 30 June that he was engaged in warning Vienna 'gently but earnestly and with great emphasis against taking precipitate steps',[18] an attitude that was to earn him a reprimand from Berlin. The real significance of the early days of the July 1914 crisis was that Germany had changed her position and was determined to push the Habsburg Monarchy into action. The crisis showed also that the Monarchy could no longer act resolutely on its own: even when they had given Austria–Hungary their blank cheque, the Germans had to guide the hand of Austria as it traced out the figure and indeed the date.

For reasons of her own, Germany was now willing to attempt to reverse by force, and with full consciousness of the possible consequences, the developments that had led to Russia's domination, through her protégés, of the Balkan peninsula. The language used in Berlin was henceforth quite unambiguous. Count Hoyos and the Austro-Hungarian ambassador in Berlin, Count Szogyeny, were left in no doubt as to the German attitude. On 5 July Szogyeny had lunch with the Kaiser, showed him the documents prepared in Vienna, and reported the Kaiser as saying, 'if we [i.e. Austria-Hungary] are convinced of the need for military action against

---

[16] F. Conrad von Hötzendorf, *Aus meiner Dienstzeit 1906–18*, 5 vols. (Vienna, 1921–5), III, pp. 144–6.

[17] *Die Grosse Politik der europäischen Kabinette 1871–1914*, XXXIV, i, no. 12818.

[18] *Die deutschen Dokumente zum Kriegsausbruch* (henceforth D.D.), no. 7.

Serbia, then he would regret our not exploiting the present moment, which is so favourable to us'; earlier, the Kaiser had said 'should it come to war between Austria–Hungary and Russia, we can be absolutely certain that Germany will stand at our side with her accustomed loyalty'. On 6 July Szogyeny reported a similar conversation with Bethmann Hollweg:

> With regard to our relations with Serbia, the German government takes the view that we should determine how to proceed in order to clear up these relations; in this respect we can rely with certainty – whatever our decision – on Germany's support, as a friend and ally of the Monarchy. In the further course of this conversation I became convinced that the imperial chancellor, like his sovereign, regards immediate drastic measures on our part against Serbia as the most radical and best solution of our difficulties in the Balkans. From the international point of view he believes that the present moment is more favourable than a later one.

Tschirschky in Vienna was to be secretly informed of these remarks. Tisza was immediately informed, apparently by Hoyos, that 'In Kaiser Wilhelm's opinion we should not hesitate any longer with our measures against Serbia'.[19]

However, even with these unmistakably enthusiastic assurances of support from Berlin, Tisza was not convinced that war should follow. Judging affairs from the standpoint of his *politique de longue vue*, he knew that war on a European scale could easily be a disaster for Dualist Hungary; there were, besides, many immediate considerations arguing against war. Again, it was a measure of the contradictions in Austria–Hungary that Tisza and Berchtold's group reacted differently to the same facts: Tisza wished to avoid war with Rumania, which might explode the nationality problem in Hungary, and believed that Rumania would not remain neutral if the Monarchy were attacked by Russia. Berchtold on the other hand reacted to the Rumanian question with more arguments for war; and his *Aktion* against Serbia was as much designed to impress Rumania as to intimidate Serbia. Czernin had reported from Bucharest in March 1914 that the alliance with Rumania was 'a worthless scrap of paper'; and in the memorandum sent on 4 July to Berlin, Berchtold wrote: 'It must not be forgotten that Rumania is now bound by ties of friendship and community of interests to Serbia, the Monarchy's bitterest enemy in the Balkans'. In the

19 OeUAP,I, VII nos. 10058, 10076, 10091. Hantsch, II, 571–2.

Balkan Wars Rumania and Serbia had, jointly and under Russian patronage, acquired Bulgarian territory; both had thus a stake in the maintenance of the status quo in the Balkans, and both also stood to gain much from victory against Austria–Hungary. Conrad was aware of the disastrous effect that Rumanian adherence to Russia would have in time of war, and he warned Berchtold that it would unquestionably produce a situation 'where the Monarchy would be deprived of all chance of success in a conflict'.[20] Talk of this kind merely made Berchtold more anxious for a radical solution; but Tisza, with three million Rumanians to intimidate, was necessarily more circumspect about provoking a war with Rumania.

At a ministerial conference on 7 July[21] he made his objections plain, although he admitted a need for some kind of action against Serbia. The other ministers, elderly bureaucrats with little imagination, believed that war would clear the air and would not last long, and that Germany was invincible; they saw no sense in gratuitously throwing away an offer to profit at Germany's chariot-wheels. Berchtold said that a purely diplomatic victory over Serbia would be meaningless, and although there was a great danger that Russia would intervene, he was sure that in any case Russia would sooner or later pass to the offensive against the Monarchy. The Austrian Prime Minister, Stürgkh, thought that the situation was moving towards military conflict with the Serbians, and remarked that 'it should exert a great influence on our decisions if, on the part of those we regard as the most loyal supporters of our policy, we are promised absolute adherence to the alliance and, on top of this, as we have heard, recommended to take immediate measures'. At a later date the Germans might not offer such firm guarantees; therefore the Monarchy should go to war now. For the sake of appearances, there might be diplomatic preliminaries, but 'this should happen with a firm intention of concluding the whole affair with war'. The ministers present, with the exception of Tisza, agreed that 'far-reaching demands should be made to Serbia, acceptance of which must be regarded as out of the question, so that a radical solution by means of military interven-

[20] OeUAP, VIII, no. 9984, cf. no. 9995, and Conrad, III, pp. 417–19.
[21] OeUAP, VIII, no. 10118; Berchtold's report, no. 10116. J. Galantai, 'Tisza es a vilaghaboru', in: *Szazadok*, 98. evf. 4 szam (1964), makes many useful points, though excessively concerned with capitalism.

tion can be set in motion'. This was the position of Austria and, with increasing clarity, of Germany also. Tisza refused to recognize it as valid. He knew that Russia would intervene in a war between Serbia and the Monarchy; he thought that the entire Balkan peninsula with the exception of Bulgaria would be hostile to the Monarchy, and said, 'it is none of Germany's business to decide whether we should attack Serbia or not'. Germany's undertaking to negotiate with Bulgaria offered an opportunity to force Rumania back to her initial orientation; therefore it should not be necessary to go to war with Serbia, the more so as no Serbian territory could be annexed by the Monarchy. He was prepared to compromise to some extent, and thought that Serbia should be asked for assurances of future good conduct in a form that was 'stiff, but not unacceptable'. If Serbia refused to carry out the requested measures, then an ultimatum should be sent by the Monarchy, and war declared. If this programme and his own point of view were not respected, 'he would be obliged, for himself, to draw the consequences': and Tisza's resignation would have thrown the entire Hungarian political machine out of gear. When the conference broke up, having been unable to agree on war, Berchtold wrote to Francis Joseph reporting that Tisza would favour war 'only if we fail beforehand to humiliate Serbia by means of diplomacy'; Berchtold alleged that Tisza's attitude was dictated by his fear of Rumania.

On his return to Budapest, on 8 July, Tisza sent a further memorandum to Francis Joseph, explaining his position. Noting that all his colleagues wanted an armed conflict, he said that war with Serbia would 'in all conscience provoke Russian intervention and thus world war' (*nach aller menschlichen Voraussicht die Intervention Russlands und somit den Weltkrieg heraufbeschwören*), with Rumania on Russia's side. The possibilities for diplomatic activity were better, since Germany had agreed to work on Bulgaria; and by this means Rumania would return to the Central Powers. Tisza repeated that he would resign if Serbia were not given a chance to escape war by accepting diplomatic humiliation. He would ask the opinion of the Hungarian government,[22] but 'for the moment I can only make the declaration in my own name that,

[22] No record survives of his having done so *in extenso*. At a government meeting of 9 July, the cabinet merely re-affirmed article eight of Law XII (1867), the legal basis of Tisza's interventions. *V. Magyar minisztertanacsi jegyzokonyvek az elso vilaghaboru korabol 1914–18* (Budapest, 1960), p. 59.

despite my devotion to Your Majesty's service, or rather because of that devotion, I could not carry any of the responsibility for an exclusively and aggressively military solution'.

Shortly after sending his memorandum, Tisza received a letter from Berchtold, dated 8 July, in which Berchtold recounted a conversation with Tschirschky. Berlin had apparently told Tschirschky 'to declare with all possible emphasis that in Berlin they expect the Monarchy to proceed against Serbia, and that it would not be understood in Germany if we should let the present opportunity pass without showing fight'. Germany had given a positive guarantee that Rumania would not attack; and Berchtold said that from Tschirschky's attitude it was clear that 'in Berlin they would construe any attempt on our part to compromise with Serbia as a sign of weakness, which could not be without effect on our position in the Triple Alliance and on Germany's future policy'.[23] Under such pressure, Berchtold discussed with the German ambassador on 10 July what form the demands on Serbia should take 'to make acceptance quite impossible for Serbia' and provide an excuse for mobilization by Austria–Hungary; Berchtold even suggested various demands in this sense – among others the request for admission of Austro-Hungarian officials to superintend Serbian inquiries, which was the very point that Serbia refused to accept on 25 July. On 11 July Berchtold was able to inform Tschirschky that Tisza had become much more ready to consider his (Berchtold's) point of view, and by 14 July it had become clear that Tisza had entirely abandoned his objections to the plan.[24]

Tisza's change of front thus occurred between 9 and 14 July. It happened, evidently, because German pressure had become so strong; Berchtold merely transmitted the pressure to Tisza. It is quite possible that he changed his mind on 9 July, on receipt of Berchtold's letter, which clearly threatened German disapproval. No doubt also the arguments of Baron Burian, his closest political collaborator, who was in Budapest at the time, were important in determining Tisza's attitude.[25] At all events Tisza came to Vienna on 14 July and Berchtold was able to report to Francis Joseph that he had dropped all the objections which he had raised against 'an

[23] OeUAP, VIII, no. 10145.

[24] DD, nos. 29, 34a.

[25] *Weltkriegsbriefe* I, pp. 5–35; in his introduction, Wertheimer states his belief that Tisza was brought round by Burian. Forgach told Berchtold after the war that this was so (Hantsch, II, 586).

ultimatum with a short time-limit', having been convinced by Berchtold of the grave military disadvantages they implied.[26] Berchtold also reported that he had assured Count Tisza that war was highly probable, but might be avoided. It is curious that he should have talked in terms of probability: war was in fact certain, as Tisza knew. Presumably, in talking of war as 'probable', Berchtold was using euphemisms for the Emperor's benefit. Tisza at any rate had no illusions: he told Tschirschky on the same day that 'It was with difficulty that I decided to advise war, but I am now convinced of its necessity'; and the note to Serbia would be drawn up in terms that made acceptance a virtual impossibility. He ended the conversation with a hearty, 'Now let us look calmly and straight into the future'.[27]

No-one was under any illusion that Russia would stand aside. Krobatin, war minister in 1914, said without contradiction at a ministerial conference two years later, in the presence of most of his colleagues responsible for the decisions of July 1914, that 'in fact, in preparing our measures against Serbia, all competent authorities had counted upon the inevitability of Russian intervention'.[28] These considerations were vital for Tisza; his much dramatized fear of Rumania was in reality a reflection of his fear of a European war. Great Hungary, cushioned by Austria, could balance between Germany and Russia; but, if Germany or Russia emerged triumphant, Hungary would be the satellite of one or the victim of the other. None the less, Tisza had in the end no choice but to bow before German demands for his assent. He was conscious of a 'special relationship' between Berlin and Budapest, and in the last resort he had to respect exhortations from Tschirschky. Ever since 1867, Hungary had worked in favour of Prussia; the Compromise, intended to free Francis Joseph's hands for further action in Germany, in fact terminated that action. The catalyst became a preservative: in 1870 Andrassy prevented Beust from going to war to

26 It may perhaps be assumed from this report that up till the 14th Tisza – having accepted on the 9th or 10th at least some measure of 'forceful action' – had hoped that the time-limit of the note to Serbia would be longer than forty-eight hours. This would presumably have given Russia and Serbia a chance to avoid war through negotiations, as Tisza had hoped all along.

27 DD, no. 49. The Kaiser commented, 'na doch mal ein Mann'. Later (DD, no. 50) Tschirschky reported that Tisza had 'sogar in manche Punkte (of the note) eine Verschärfung hineingebracht'.

28 *Haus-Hof- und Staats-Archiv*, Vienna. Record of a conference, 7 January 1916.

save France from Prussia. The Magyars worked to maintain Prussian supremacy, since this entailed their own survival as a great state; and in 1914 Tisza similarly recognized the enduring value of a connection with Germany for the interests of Great Hungary. In this sense, it was not the alliance itself which caused the outbreak of war in 1914, but fear of losing the alliance: Germany was free to choose between Hungary and Rumania, whereas Hungary had no choice but to side with Germany. The alliance between Dualist Hungary and Germany was the diplomatic super-structure of an edifice shaped by Sadowa and Sedan: for the Germans it guaranteed that the Habsburg Monarchy would not return to the policies of Metternich and Schwarzenberg; for the Magyars, it meant that 1849 would not recur, since the German army would uphold Hungary against Russia. This political outlook, expressed in terms of solidarity against the Slavs, linked Budapest with Berlin from the humiliation of Olmütz to the second world war; and it was with full consciousness of this that Tisza gave way to German pressure in 1914. He had written in 1912:

It is the Hungarian nation that supports our intimate alliance with the German Empire, more directly perhaps than even the Austrian Germans. This is the cornerstone of our entire policy; we remain true to and proclaim the enduring principle, which is above day-to-day events, that the Hungarian nation must carry out its historic mission shoulder to shoulder with the great German nation in true political solidarity.[29]

Towards the end of the war, in October 1918, Tisza wrote to the Emperor Charles that he would have advanced still more convincing arguments against war had he not had to take 'higher points of view' into account.[30] No Magyar considered Vienna as having a 'higher point of view' than Hungary; if Tisza agreed to go to war with Serbia, it was exclusively due to the 'higher point of view' adopted in Berlin.

There was after 14 July little question that war with Serbia would be avoided, even if Russia intervened. Redlich was told by

[29] *Tisza osszes munkai*, I, p. 660. At a ministerial conference in October 1915 (*Haus-Hof- und Staats-Archiv*: record of a conference of 16 October 1915), Tisza remarked that the Germans would not wish to see Poland included in the Monarchy on an equal footing with Hungary, 'for the present direction of our foreign policy would no longer be guaranteed by the equality of Hungarian with other interests in the Monarchy'.

[30] Quoted in G. Gratz, *A dualizmus kora 1867–1918*, 2 vols. (Budapest, 1938), II, p. 296.

Hoyos on the 15th, 'in the greatest confidence, that war has been as good as decided upon . . . Berchtold has the agreement of Tisza, Stürgkh, and Burian . . . Hoyos said, "If the world war breaks out, it needn't matter to us" . . . Germany is in full agreement with us'; and on 23 July, once the note had been sent, Redlich was told that it was such 'as to make acceptance quite impossible for Serbia'.[31]

Tisza had tried to stop the *Aktion* against Serbia. It remained for him only to make it meaningless in practical terms. He was concerned that the Monarchy should not annex any part of Serbia, for he knew that the resultant difficulties would be grave: solution of the South Slav problem was in reality not compatible with the maintenance of Dualism. On 19 July, at a ministerial conference, he demanded from the conference a unanimous declaration that 'in the procedure against Serbia no plans for conquest by the Monarchy are involved and that the Monarchy does not wish to annex any part of Serbia except as regards frontier-rectifications required by military considerations'.[32] This declaration was made, and throughout the war respected – at Tisza's insistence. In January 1916, when Serbia had finally been conquered, he insisted on upholding the original declaration: with three million ungovernable Serbs already, annexation of Serbia and inclusion of a further two million Serbs would 'make the situation so difficult that the Hungarian government would take no responsibility for it'; and a year later, with Russia almost out of the war and the Rumanians in inglorious flight, Tisza again refused to entertain the idea of expansion in the Balkans: annexation of Serbia, he declared, 'would be not only for Hungary but for the whole Monarchy the greatest misfortune and would present us with the most catastrophic results'.[33]

It was a singular comment on Berchtold's Balkan policy that its chief practical result would have been at most a minor territorial rearrangement in favour of Bulgaria and Albania. As far as Austria–Hungary was concerned, the first world war began with an enterprise that had in advance been deprived of its tangible

[31] *Redlich*, I, pp. 237–7.
[32] OeUAP. VIII, no. 10393.
[33] *Haus-Hof- und Staats-Archiv:* records of conferences of 7 January 1916 and 12 January 1917. On the text of the former, where Conrad was reported in a discourse on *weitgehende Annexionen serbischen Gebietes*, Tisza added in his own hand, *welche die Situation sowohl in Kroatien wie in Bosznien (sic) unhaltbar machen und schwere innere Krisen für die Monarchie bedeuten würden.*

163

profits: in the most favourable case, the Austro-Hungarian army would march into Serbia; it would extract promises of good behaviour from the Serbians; and then it would go away. In July 1914 Austria–Hungary had in effect no policy, and she had to be supplied with one by Germany; and Germany's unambiguous promptings towards war cannot be explained away in terms of Tschirschky's unauthorized bellicosity or Szogyeny's senile inaccuracy. Without Tisza's support, the Vienna ministers could have done nothing; and if Tisza in the end sanctioned the war with Serbia, it was due above all to pressure from Germany that he did so. Austria–Hungary was required to transmit to the Balkans a policy inspired by Berlin; and in the war that followed, the Habsburg Monarchy, with no real interests, none the less incurred total losses.

Rumania and the Belligerents 1914-1916

Glenn E. Torrey

As the intention of Austria–Hungary to utilize the assassination of Archduke Franz Ferdinand for a reckoning with Serbia became increasingly evident during July 1914, the Rumanian government manifested corresponding concern. It was widely believed in Bucarest, and not without reason, that an Austro-Serbian conflict would lead to the aggrandizement of Bulgaria, thereby threatening Rumania's aspirations in the Balkans and her security as well. Even more disquieting was the possibility that the Austrian action would touch off a general European war in which Rumania might become merely a battleground for the great powers. But for King Carol I, a prince of the South German branch of the Hohenzollern family, an Austro-Russian conflict was especially unwelcome. His personal inclinations and a secret alliance of more than thirty years standing linked him to the Central Powers. Until recent years at least, Rumania's isolation and traditional Russophobia gave reasonable justification to Carol's association with the Triple Alliance. But in the decade before 1914 the memory of Russia's past iniquities and even the indignation over the treatment accorded the Rumanian minority in Bessarabia had been eclipsed in Bucarest by resentment over Austria's support of Bulgaria during the Balkan Wars, and especially by anger over the plight of the larger Rumanian minority 'languishing under the Magyar yoke' in Transylvania. The latter, together with the Austrian province of Bukovina, now became the prime object of Rumanian irredentism. The role of Vienna in championing Bulgaria's cause at the Peace of Bucarest (1913) unleashed an outburst of Austrophobia which was still re-echoing in the Rumanian press the following summer and which prompted the first steps towards a rapprochement with Russia.

Carol became acutely conscious of this contradiction between his personal inclinations and the interests of his adopted land when he realized, even before the delivery of the Austrian ultimatum, that Russia would probably intervene. His first response, completely justified by the circumstances, was to resist the application of the *casus foederis* in his alliance with Austria. Yet as the war became a reality, repeated appeals from his fellow monarchs in Vienna and Berlin persuaded him to advocate a declaration of war on Russia at the famous Rumanian crown council convened in his summer palace at Sinaia on the afternoon of 3 August. With only one exception, this assemblage of cabinet ministers, elder statesmen, parliamentary officers, and party leaders spoke out for neutrality, arguing that the aggressive and unilateral nature of Austria's action relieved Rumania of any obligation. Carol accepted this consensus with surprisingly little resistance.

One cannot avoid the conclusion that Carol welcomed this opportunity to shift the responsibility for Rumanian policy to other shoulders. In explaining his action to the German and Austrian ministers, he insisted that he was 'true to the alliance through and through', but that it was impossible for him to 'draw the sword' against the will of his people. Prime Minister Ion Bratianu, fearing censure and possible retaliation, likewise stressed his loyalty to the Central Powers and implied the intention to bring Rumania into the war as soon as public opinion and military preparations permitted. He sought to sweeten the bitterness in Berlin and Vienna over the decision of the crown council by renouncing any intention of impeding a Bulgarian attack on Serbia. In conversation with the Russian Minister S. A. Poklevsky, however, Bratianu spoke in a different strain. Although he declined the Minister's offer of Transylvania as an inducement for an immediate attack on Austria–Hungary, he said that Rumania's eventual co-operation with the Entente was not excluded and asked that the proposition be kept open. Thus, from the very beginning, Bratianu began to practise the diplomatic dissimulation for which he became justly famous. His duplicity should not be exaggerated, however. The German and Austrian diplomatic correspondence reveals that as a rule it was the Central Powers who were victims of his deception. His negotiations with the Entente, though cautious and guided exclusively by Rumanian interests, were relatively straightforward.

While Bratianu was quick to see the opportunity as well as the danger for Rumania in the Austro-Russian conflict, he avoided committing himself during the first month of the war, awaiting the outcome of the great battles then under way on both the eastern and western fronts.

By early September the initial results were in. In the east, the Russian army had smashed a precipitate Austrian offensive and was in the process of overrunning Galicia and Bukovina. Simultaneously in the west the myth of German invincibility was being demolished at the Marne. The victories of Hindenburg in East Prussia went hardly noticed.

The military success of the Entente, especially the Russian invasion of Austria–Hungary, had an electrifying effect on Rumanian irredentism. Whereas a month earlier a Rumanian attack on Austria–Hungary seemed remote, if not unthinkable, the Russian capture of the Galician capital of Lemberg on 3 September marked the emergence of a strong interventionist movement. A number of former Russophobes, including Constantin Mille, editor of the important Bucarest daily, *Adevarul,* now joined in the increasingly loud and insistent call to action. Mille, who only a few days previously had declared 'Not with Russia! Not with Austria!', utilized the 'moment of Lemberg' to demand an attack on Austria–Hungary, 'Now . . . Now . . .!' These sentiments were echoed in the other major Bucarest daily, *Universul,* and in a host of less important newspapers. Virtually drowned out by the clamour of the warmongers were the voices advocating neutrality. Professor Nicolae Iorga's *Neamul Romanesc,* the socialist *Lupta,* the government press, and those few newspapers oriented towards the Central Powers.

The universities, the popular cafés, and especially the streets provided settings for other manifestations of Rumanian chauvinism. More than forty professors at Bucarest university, sharing the opinion of the historian A.D. Xenopol that 'Rumania has had no greater enemy in one thousand years than Hungary', sent a manifesto to the king demanding the immediate invasion of Transylvania. Self-appointed experts, mostly reserve officers, held forth in prominent meeting places, explaining with maps and charts the daily progress of the French and Russian armies. Street demonstrations, many of them organized by professional agitators, were the order of the day. Not a few ended with a march on the German and Austrian legations, where windows were broken and the occupants insulted. The government was obliged to provide these buildings with continuous protection, giving them the appearance of besieged fortresses; the Austrian minister even felt constrained to distribute revolvers among his staff. The activity of a number of emigrés from 'across the mountains', among them the talented poet and future Iron Guardist, Octavian Goga, lent authenticity to the irredentist cause.

The interventionist current flowed across party lines, opening a schism in the ranks of the Conservatives and disturbing the unity of Bratianu's ruling Liberal Party. Nicolae Filipescu, a leading Conservative and former war minister, embraced interventionism with a fervour which can only be described as fanatical, and sought to persuade his party to utilize this issue to overturn Bratianu. Party chief Alexandru Marghiloman succeeded in keeping the Conservatives committed to neutrality, although Filipescu kept the party in an uproar by continuing to advocate an attack on Austria–Hungary. Together with Take Ionescu, the head of the splinter group of Conservative Democrats, he assumed the titular leadership of the warmongers. The Liberal Party, on the other hand, experienced less serious internal tension. Finance Minister Emil Costinescu, whose partisan use of official powers quickly earned him the title of 'Minister for the Entente', maintained close contact with Filipescu and Ionescu. On the other extreme of the Liberal spectrum stood the party theoretician and highly respected rector of the university at Iasi, Constantin Stere, an implacable Russophobe. (A Bessarabian, he had suffered deportation to Siberia before emigrating to Rumania.)

The extent to which the Rumanian people as a whole sympathized with the interventionist movement is impossible to determine. At least eighty per cent of them were illiterate, unfranchised peasants preoccupied with a bitter struggle for existence. No assessment of their feelings can be found in Rumanian newspapers, which were almost without exception either personal and party organs or irresponsible scandal sheets, all notoriously susceptible to bribery. Like so much in Rumanian public life, they were controlled by a relatively small number of intellectuals, large landowners, business leaders, and professional politicians. The leaders of the irredentist movement formed only a minority of this elite, albeit an extremely vocal one. But because they represented honest Rumanian nationalism (as well as sordid personal opportunism) their potential strength exceeded their formal support; but they would have needed the co-operation of the police and the army to enable them to force their will upon the government. Despite the fears of many, including the king, conclusive evidence of serious disloyalty in either arm of the security forces is lacking.

The role King Carol was forced to play in the interventionist crisis was a tragic one. Fatally ill, under continuous pressure from his family and peers in Germany to join them in the war against Russia, he was thrown into panic by the increasingly articulate demand to sanction war against the Central Powers. Early in September he let Berlin know indirectly that the hostile attitude of his people might be reversed if Austria–Hungary would offer a 'boundary rectification' in Bukovina and internal reforms in Transylvania. Later in the month, as the agitation reached its peak, he conceived of a foreign threat as a means of dampening the spirit of the warmongers and asked Berlin to 'stir up' Bulgaria. Deeply pessimistic, he confided to the German minister that he might be forced to countenance a 'preventive occupation' of Transylvania. Finally, he prepared an abdication manifesto to be used as his ultimate weapon against the interventionists or, if that proved ineffective, as an escape from his dilemma. While there is evidence that rumours of the king's intention to leave the country, possibly with the crown prince as well, sobered some of the moderate Austrophobes, his threat had little effect on the radicals. They took heart from a report that Crown Princess Marie had vowed to remain and carry on the fight should Carol depart, even if her husband went with him.

Carol's suggestion that Austro-Hungarian concessions might reverse the unfavourable trend in Bucarest, though totally divorced from reality, found a sympathetic reception in Berlin, and the German government sent a sharply-worded request to Austria–Hungary to make the requisite sacrifices. Initially the Habsburg leaders flatly refused 'to enter into Rumania's blackmail', pointing out quite correctly that appeasement would simply exacerbate Rumanian chauvinism. But after extremely heavy pressure from their German allies and a plea from the hard-pressed Austrian military, the Habsburg government agreed to make an offer if Rumania agreed in return to 'march against Russia with all its power'. Bratianu received the offer cordially but insisted that it would be insufficient to reverse the trend of public opinion. However, he held out the prospect of co-operation later and snggested that the same concessions be offered for neutrality alone.

The German leaders, depressed by their reverse at the Marne, now demanded in no uncertain terms that Austria–Hungary placate Rumania, at whatever cost was necessary, arguing that an attack from the latter would mean the 'end of both imperial monarchies'. Furthermore, the Germans advised their ally, in the event of an attempted invasion of Transylvania, to 'be satisfied with a protest and let Rumania enter without opposition'. The Austro-Hungarian leaders, possessing a superior insight into the situation in Bucharest, refused to accede to the German demands. Count Stephen Tisza, the Hungarian premier, did agree to introduce minor reforms relative to the status of the Transylvanian Rumanians, but these were not announced publicly at that time because, as the Austrian minister in Bucharest, Count Ottokar Czernin, aptly commented, they would sound like a 'bad joke' and would be as ineffectual as attempting 'to extinguish a burning house with a garden sprinkler'. The Austro-Hungarian government instead stiffened its attitude toward Bucharest. Bratianu and Carol were reminded that any attempt to enter Transylvania would mean war. Czernin visited Filipescu, Ionescu, and Princess Marie, threatening the complete destruction and partition of Rumania if it attacked the Dual Monarchy, and was supported by the German minister, Baron Hilmar von dem Bussche. Bulgaria and Turkey both assumed menacing attitudes. Rumours that German troops were already being sent to aid Austria were allowed to circulate because, as Czernin remarked, 'if General Hindenburg were only suspected [of being] in Transylvania with one company, no Rumanian would step over the boundary'.

Bratianu, too, was embarrassed by the interventionists and took energetic steps to keep them from getting out of hand. On 25 August he ordered his cabinet to see that anti-Austrian demonstrations were 'dispersed with all strictness', and through the Liberal Party press he issued warnings against intemperate action. His neutralism was not motivated by Germanophile sentiments or indecision. On the contrary, the available evidence indicates that after the battle of the Marne, if not before, he came to the conclusion that the Entente would ultimately be victorious. Determined to use their victory for the completion of Rumanian national unity, he did not waver from this purpose even at times when the war favoured the Central Powers. He showed no interest in their repeated offers of Bessarabia and at no time did he enter into serious negotiations to share in their possible victory. Bratianu's diplomacy becomes comprehensible only when understood, not as an attempt to play off the belligerents until the course of military operations indicated on which side Rumania should range herself, but as a cautious, steady preparation for joining in the partition of Austria–Hungary. The premier's aims, therefore, were identical with those of Filipescu and Ionescu, except that he realized, as they did not, the necessity of careful military and diplomatic preparation. Rumania was certainly in no condition for war. The army, as its French adviser found even two years later, was 'admirably disorganized'; ammunition was in short supply and the country produced none of its own; the only war plan possessed by the general staff, drawn up in accordance with the commitment to the Triple Alliance, called for an attack on Russia. Bratianu also realized that it would be equally foolish to enter into action without proper diplomatic preparation. Like most Rumanians he was haunted by the memory of Russia's treatment of Rumania in 1877–78 (when his father had been premier) and he was determined not to commit Rumania to action again without far-reaching guarantees.

While avoiding military action in the fall of 1914, Bratianu did not hesitate to press ahead with the diplomatic groundwork for such action, whenever it might come. His first step was to give formal shape to Rumania's community of interest with Italy. Mutual reluctance to take the initiative had prevented a written accord during the first month of the war, but in mid-September Rome responded favourably to Bratianu's suggestion that 'it would be best for Italy and Rumania to proceed in agreement to the liquidation of Austria–Hungary in their favour (if liquidation there must be)'. An agreement providing for consultation and, if necessary, joint action was signed in Bucarest on 23 September. Bratianu hoped to make close co-operation with Italy an integral feature of his foreign policy, thereby enhancing Rumania's bargaining power with the Entente and obtaining assistance in resisting Russian influence in the Balkans after the war.

Simultaneously, Bratianu dropped his reserve in negotiations with Russia. He refused to be seduced into the war by an invitation from the Foreign Minister, Sazonov, on 16 September to act jointly with the Russian army and 'occupy without delay the Southern Bukovina and Transylvania'. Instead he demanded the same compensation in return for a Rumanian promise of continued neutrality. What advantage there would be to Russia from such an agreement is difficult to discover. Rumania's attitude would be determined exclusively by self-interest and this dictated the destruction of Austria–Hungary. If the tide of war turned irrevocably against Russia, a written promise to remain neutral would no more determine Rumania's policy than the alliance with Austria did now, in the moment of Russia's victory. Nevertheless, Poklevsky, who seems to have overestimated the strength of the Germanophile element in Rumania, succeeded in persuading Sazonov to accede to Bratianu's wish. In an agreement signed in St Petersburg on 2 October, Rumania pledged herself to remain neutral towards Russia until the end of the war and received in return a guarantee of territorial integrity, the recognition of her right to annex those provinces of Austria–Hungary inhabited by a Rumanian majority, and the right to choose the moment to occupy these areas.

This was a major triumph for Bratianu. Active intervention later was of course still necessary; no one believed that the Entente would actually reward Rumania without a substantial military effort on her part. But the agreement did mark an important step towards recognition of Rumania's claims. It outlined a minimal price for Rumanian intervention, one at which Russia would be forced to begin the bidding at a later date. Furthermore, the agreement of 2 October, like the Italo-Rumanian accord, took some of the urgency out of Rumania's decision and gave her time to prepare. Bratianu did not hesitate to use this argument with the warmongers, and to good effect. On the other hand, it would be going too far to argue, as has been done, that if Sazonov had stood firm in his demand for active intervention and publicized the offer of 16 September, he might have 'stampeded Rumania into war'. As a matter of fact, the Russian offer was widely rumoured in the Rumanian press and known in detail by those few Rumanians who wielded political influence. Bratianu, the king, the vast majority of Liberals, and a good many Conservatives were opposed to immediate intervention. It is more than questionable that their resistance could have been overcome by a Russian attempt to 'make diplomacy in the streets'. Furthermore, the Austro-Hungarian army, assisted by German reinforcements, began to stabilize the Galician front before the end of September. Even Filipescu and Ionescu soon agreed that neutrality was now necessary.

The approach of winter meant that Rumania would remain quiet for several months. All observers in Bucarest agreed, however, that after this time of preparation she intended to enter into action in the spring, almost certainly in association with Italy. This view was correct. In October, Bratianu dispatched an ordnance officer to western Europe to purchase munitions; in January, he ordered the Rumanian general staff to prepare 'an offensive against Austria–Hungary in Transylvania . . .'; in February, he took the initiative in negotiating a more comprehensive agreement with Italy. All the while, in his contacts with the Central Powers, Bratianu assumed the role of loyal ally, impeded only by public opinion from placing Rumania alongside the Central Powers. While Czernin was not taken in, Bussche continued to insist that the premier's 'heart is on our side'.

Bratianu's position was eased by the death on 10 October of King Carol, who had acquiesced in the neutrality agreement with Russia but would hardly have been a party to a declaration of war on the Central Powers. His nephew and successor Ferdinand promised at his accession to be 'a good Rumanian', and, as he told a Russian diplomat, he intended to disregard his German background and act 'exclusively according to his duty and the interest of Rumania'. Lacking experience and indecisive by nature, Ferdinand appears to have welcomed the opportunity to turn over the direction of foreign affairs to Bratianu, whose policy had an influential advocate at court in the person of Queen Marie. Popular, spirited, clever – everything her husband was not – Marie emerged during the dark days of 1916–18 as the heart and soul of the regime. While her contribution to the determination of Rumanian policy during the period of neutrality is more difficult to document, it can hardly have been inconsiderable. The daughter of the Duke of Edinburgh, Marie was unwaveringly dedicated to the Entente cause, and urged her views on her husband and her lover, Prince Barbu Stirbey (Bratianu's brother-in-law and a close adviser to Ferdinand). Stirbey was used by the German legation as its secret liaison with the King. More than anything else it was his deliberately misleading reports which gave Bussche and, in turn, Berlin, such an inaccurate view of Ferdinand's intentions.

Convinced that 'if Italy remains neutral Rumania is hardly to be feared', the Central Powers concentrated their diplomatic efforts in Rome during the winter and spring of 1915. In Bucarest they concentrated upon propaganda and bribery, attempting to create an atmosphere favourable to a change in Rumanian policy. The Balkan tradition of bribery, one of the most unfortunate legacies of Turkish rule, encouraged them to think that anything could be accomplished with money. An official though incomplete audit made late in the war reveals that in the years 1914–16 the Wilhelmstrasse spent over 40 million marks in Rumania. This was more than the amount utilized to foment revolution in Russia and dwarfed the allocations for all other countries. The chief recipients of this largesse were newspapers and political figures, although at the time it seemed as if almost every important public figure, and many unimportant ones, were profiting in one way or another.

Ludwig Roselius, a Bremen importer and reputed inventor of caffeine-free coffee, who had extensive business experience in the Balkans, was sent to Bucarest at the beginning of the war to take charge of the German operation. He had virtually unlimited funds at his disposal and quickly built up an extensive organization with the aid of the directors and staff of large German corporations such as the Disconto-Gesellschaft and Deutsche Bank, men with years of business experience in Bucarest and well-versed in the art of dispensing *baksheesh*.

Attempts to bribe Filipescu, Costinescu, and Ionescu directly proved unsuccessful. The first two were millionaires and beyond reach. Ionescu, on the other hand, had a tarnished reputation and was more approachable. Early in 1915 he negotiated with the Austrian legation through a middleman for a bribe of 30 million but backed out before the deal was consummated. A more successful practice was to offer subsidies for political purposes, thus lessening the stigma of personal corruption. According to German sources, Bratianu accepted a gift 'for the next election'; Marghiloman received money for political and propaganda activity; Carp was given money to found a newspaper to campaign for a war against Russia. Newspapers founded or purchased with Austro-German money included *Ziua*, *Moldova*, *Minerva*, *Seara*. However, public knowledge of the source of their support made these newspapers the target of popular scorn and even physical violence; their value to the Central Powers appears to have been questionable. A more successful approach was to subsidize individual journalists and editors to publish stories favourable to the Central Powers, or simply to headline Austro-German victories in larger type. Even *Adevarul*, the mouthpiece of the interventionist movement, was influenced in this manner occasionally. At the same time Roselius and his organization worked to impede the publication of pro-Entente newspapers by cutting off supplies of newsprint, ink, and even by smashing press equipment. In general, however, Rumanian publishing establishments profited immensely. One Bucarest firm printed both the irredentist scandal sheet *Epoca*, and *Ziua*, the organ of the German and Austrian legations. A wide variety of other outlets for Austro-German propaganda activity were found. A well-organized team regularly staged anti-Russian street demonstrations. Not infrequently they came to blows with counter-demonstrations run by partisans of the Entente. The formation of a special wire service, the publication of a popular Sunday 'illustrated', the purchase of movie houses and the distribution of propaganda films, are but a few of the other methods by which Berlin and Vienna attempted to mould opinion in Bucarest.

But this indiscriminate use of money in fact damaged the already tarnished image of the Central Powers. The pro-Entente press took delight in exposing scandals involving Austro-German agents. In one *cause célèbre* late in 1915, one Rumanian and two Hungarians recruited by German military intelligence to destroy bridges in Russia, decided to use a portion of their explosives to blow up the homes of Filipescu and Ionescu. One of their number, quite possibly recruited by the Entente as a double agent, made a detailed confession to the police which created a major diplomatic incident. Roselius himself became so notorious that he was forced to return to Germany. Despite some accomplishments, his organization served rather as a happy hunting grounds for criminals, swindlers, and opportunists of all varieties. The Wilhelmstrasse was besieged by cranks like the one who argued that Rumania could be won for the Central Powers by sending 200 German *Koketten* to Bucarest. The authorities in Berlin commissioned too many of these adventurers, and Bussche warned his Berlin superiors against them. When their visits continued to proliferate despite his warnings, he threatened to resign.

It is not possible to document the propaganda activity of the Entente in such detail. Nevertheless, scattered evidence indicates that it was extensive though not, of course, on such a grand scale as that of the Central Powers. But in the final analysis one cannot avoid the conclusion that, despite the expenditure of enormous sums, neither side appears to have exercised a decisive influence on Rumanian policy.

Another attempt to influence policy by bribery concerned the Rumanian refusal to permit the transit of munitions intended for Turkey. The closure of this vital rail route between Berlin and Constantinople followed the Russo-Rumanian agreement of 2 October 1914, and indeed seems to have been the major benefit accruing to the Entente from this accord. The Russians applied continual pressure on Bucarest to keep it closed and Finance Minister Costinescu served as their watchdog. Bratianu answered every Austro-German démarche on the subject with the argument that acquiescence in the transit of munitions would provoke a Russian declaration of war. While this was an overstatement, abrogation of the transit ban would certainly have seriously estranged the Entente.

The Germans were able initially to smuggle through a small quantity of munitions after a liberal distribution of *baksheesh* among Rumanian railroad and customs officials. For each freight car successfully passed, the Germans paid 10,000 lei, but only 170 if the shipment was betrayed. This ceased when the Entente ministers assigned special agents to check all trains and Costinescu gave plenipotentiary power to an agent of the French legation for the specific purpose of monitoring the conduct of customs officials. After the struggle at Gallipoli began and the Turkish need for munitions became critical, German ingenuity increased. Munitions were encased in asphalt and concrete or buried in shipments of lime. False bottoms were installed in freight cars and munitions hidden in the lower compartments. All these methods failed, as did a novel attempt to ship explosives in beer kegs. Not infrequently the captured arms were put on exhibition, much to the embarrassment of the Austrian and German legations. No substantial amount of war material passed through Rumania until the defeat of Serbia opened an alternative route and reduced the transit issue to unimportance.

The Treaty of London (26 April) like the 'moment of Lemberg' some months previously, was widely interpreted in Bucarest as ushering in a new and decisive stage in the war. *Adevarul*, taking note of Italy's obvious intention to intervene, proclaimed on 28 April that the 'twelfth hour' for Rumanian action had come. A familiar pattern of agitation appeared: mass meetings, street demonstrations, and hysterical journalism. Filipescu and his followers made their long-expected break with the Germanophile wing of the Conservative Party and, if we can believe newspaper reports, the schism was accompanied by fisticuffs and revolver shots. Troops and police once again went into action to disperse unruly demonstrators, and the cartoonists pictured Bratianu as receiving his orders at the German legation.

Bratianu was, of course, not indifferent to Italy's example, having done everything to co-ordinate his policy with Rome. But despite two written agreements, the Italian leaders had never really taken the Rumanian government into their confidence. They proceeded to work out their own deal with the Entente without consulting Bucarest. Ignored by Rome, Bratianu pressed ahead on his own and on 3 May presented Rumania's demands in St Petersburg. The price he demanded for an attack on Austria–Hungary was high: Transylvania, Bukovina to the Prut, the entire Banat, and parts of Hungarian counties along the river Tisza. The Russians were angered at the extravagance of these claims, regarded as irreconcilable with their own interests in Bukovina and those of Serbia in the Banat. This resistance was short-lived. On the same day as Bratianu's démarche, an Austro-German offensive in Galicia pierced the Russian lines at Gorlice, throwing the Tsar's armies into a catastrophic retreat. As they continued to give ground, Sazonov's resistance to Rumania's claims gradually diminished. Finally, in late July, he agreed to accept them in full, provided Rumania agreed to enter the war within five weeks.

Despite the Russian retreat, Bratianu had been determined to intervene in mid-June. On the 19th he ordered his chief of staff, General Iliescu, to prepare mobilization plans in anticipation of Russia's acceptance of his demands. But a month later, with virtually all of Galicia and Poland in the hands of the Central Powers, the premier began to have second thoughts. On 23 July he reaffirmed his willingness to sign a political agreement but now pleaded that he could set no date for actual intervention. The continued deterioration of the Russian position, highlighted by the fall of Warsaw on 4 August, soon made Bratianu unwilling to sign even the political accord. However, he promised to consider the unsigned agreement as being in effect and reaffirmed his determination to prevent the transit of munitions for Turkey.

Although the negotiations of 1915 produced no written document, they mark what was perhaps the most crucial stage in Rumania's rapprochement with the Entente. St Petersburg's willingness to concede Bratianu's full territorial demands meant that any reasonable improvement in the Russian military position would make Rumanian intervention virtually inevitable.

The Central Powers also tried to draw Bratianu into an agreement in the summer of 1915. The German government, preoccupied with the threat posed by Italy's entry into the war and the munitions shortage at Gallipoli, thought it imperative to placate Rumania with Austro-Hungarian concessions. The Habsburg leaders considered appeasement dangerous as well as useless. The Foreign Minister, Count Burian, insisted that in view of the Gorlice breakthrough 'the jackal in them' would soon cause the Rumanian leaders to embrace the Central Powers. If not, he boasted to a German visitor, he planned to 'grab Rumania by the throat'. Bratianu was well aware of the danger in estranging Germany and Austria–Hungary at a moment when the Entente was impotent to aid him, and attempted to breathe new life into his well-worn role as a loyal partisan of the Central Powers. With complete composure he admitted his negotiations with Russia, but explained that the whole affair was a ruse to satisfy the 'war party'. The Austro-Hungarian leaders were not inclined to negotiate further with Bratianu, but the German government, bombarded with frantic pleas from Constantinople for the opening of a supply route, insisted that its ally seek to purchase Bratianu's acquiescence in the transit of munitions. Lobbyists were sent to Vienna and Budapest to mobilize support for an offer of concessions to Rumania. Chancellor Bethmann Hollweg invited Tisza to Berlin and gained his backing for a boundary cession in Bukovina and additional reforms in Transylvania. Burian, however, remained adamant and rejected the concessions approved by Tisza. Upon learning of this, Bethmann Hollweg decided to visit Vienna immediately. During three days of conferences, he exerted every form of pressure at his command to force concessions on Burian, but without success. The latter argued that a territorial cession was too high a price to pay for a promise of benevolent neutrality and pointed out, quite correctly, that Bratianu was unlikely to permit transit in any case, a view confirmed by Bratianu's continuing evasion of all attempts to draw him into negotiations. Finally, in response to a direct request that he name his price for transit, the Rumanian premier replied on 26 June that he saw 'no chance for an agreement now'. This episode marks the last attempt made by the Central Powers to deal with Bratianu on the basis of appeasement. Military developments soon permitted them to use a more peremptory tone.

The second half of 1915 saw the military initiative in Eastern Europe pass to Germany and Austria–Hungary. Their armies were deep in Russia and still advancing; the Entente admitted failure at Gallipoli and withdrew; Bulgaria joined the Central Powers in crushing Serbia. In these circumstances Bratianu wisely remained quiet. The Bulgarian mobilization, of course, touched off a demand by Filipescu and Ionescu that Rumania take counter-action, but the premier refused to heed their plea. It would be better, he told a few close advisers on 23 September, to delay action until the Entente was in a position to take up a general offensive, probably in the spring. Bratianu's inactivity earned him the censure of the interventionists, but they were still unable to mount a serious challenge to his direction of Rumanian policy. In response to repeated interpellations by Ionescu during the December session of parliament, the premier accepted full responsibility for his action but refused to discuss it, pleading *raison d'état*. With his party holding 80 per cent of the seats in the Chamber and 70 per cent in the Senate, Bratianu could afford to ignore his critics. On the other hand he was obviously worried lest the Central Powers, their triumph over Serbia nearly completed, now turn their armies against Rumania. This anxiety was heightened by the fact that the Bulgars made no secret of their desire to march into Dobrudja to settle old accounts, and by a chance remark of the Kaiser during an inspection tour of prostrate Serbia early in January, that 'Ruschuck is only sixty kilometers from Bucarest'. The words stirred a small panic in the Rumanian capital. Bratianu had no intention of submitting to intimidation but, on the other hand, he did everything possible to avoid provoking the Central Powers. When Octavian Goga and Father Vasile Lucaciu, like the former a Transylvanian emigré, stood as candidates for the Chamber of Deputies, he felt their election would be an incitement to Austria–Hungary and forced their withdrawal. But undoubtedly his most significant act of accommodation towards the Central Powers was to lift restrictions on the export of grain and oil.

From the fall of 1914 to the beginning of 1916 Rumania exported only negligible quantities of grain. Initially, restrictions had been imposed to insure domestic supplies, but they had been extended and tightened under Russian pressure and the influence of Costinescu. In August and September 1914, before the intentions of the Rumanian government were fully known, a German grain importer working with German diplomatic officials succeeded in buying up 750,000 tons of cereals. Only a small amount reached Germany before the imposition of restrictions; the remainder went into storage. This purchase temporarily eliminated an important means of applying economic pressure on Rumania and was generally viewed in Berlin as a colossal blunder. But the approach of the 1915 harvest restored this economic weapon to the Central Powers' arsenal. The Rumanian landowners, eager to profit from inflated wartime prices and lacking adequate storage facilities, demanded that the government permit free export, whereupon the Central Powers commissioned a special agent to harness this discontent for their own purposes, hoping that it might lead to the overthrow of the Bratianu government. During the summer and fall of 1915, Bussche and Czernin utilized this opening to promote the formation of a coalition government under the Conservative elder statesman Titu Maiorescu, which would initiate a policy of benevolent neutrality, permitting the transit of munitions, as a prelude to a declaration of war on Russia. The hope was a vain one; the Conservatives were discredited and the king gave full support to Bratianu and his policy of alignment with the Entente.

However, the agitation of the agriculturists and the military success of the Central Powers convinced the Bratianu government that it was expedient to sell grain. On 6 June Costinescu expressed willingness to do business and on 1 August the ban was lifted. But a high duty payable in gold was imposed on grain exports, which both moderated the effect of foreign sales on the domestic market and at the same time boosted Rumania's gold reserves. The Central Powers were far from happy about the higher prices and the outflow of gold, but their need for food made Rumanian imports imperative. On 27 December a contract for 500,000 tons of cereals was signed in Bucharest. The same agreement guaranteed export for the German-owned cereals stored since 1914. News of the Austro-German purchase touched off an attempt by the British government to forestall additional sales by pre-empting the entire remaining supply. Bratianu appears to have believed that it would be dangerous to provoke the Central Powers by agreeing to this, but he did allow the sale of 820,000 tons to reassure the Entente of his continued loyalty.

The German government was not mollified; the English sale was 'an unfriendly act from which Germany will draw the consequences'. Bussche, then on leave in Berlin, was sent back immediately with instructions to press for the dismissal of Bratianu. Despite an ominous warning that the prime minister's policy had brought Rumania's relations with the Central Powers 'near the breaking point', Ferdinand refused to sacrifice Bratianu. He had neither the desire nor the power to repudiate him. Although no ultimatum as such was actually delivered, the German démarche was interpreted in many quarters as a threat of war and Bratianu was worried enough to query St Petersburg about possible assistance. The German 'threat' was nothing more than a bluff. General Falkenhayn was firmly committed to the attack at Verdun and this meant that German troops would no longer be available for action against Rumania. German economic officials likewise opposed a hard line in Bucarest, insisting that early Rumanian grain imports were absolutely imperative for the army as well as the populace. A promise by Ferdinand that his government would end all 'chicanery' in meeting this demand for grain helped to melt German anger.

Thereafter, Rumanian trade with the Central Powers expanded rapidly. On 16 March, arrangements were completed for the purchase of an additional 1,400,000 tons of grain, and on 1 April a general trade agreement was signed for the exchange of goods other than war materials. Now it was Russia's turn to fulminate. Bratianu's reply to St Petersburg stressed the danger to his regime from agricultural discontent and insisted, less plausibly, that the grain sales would deceive the Central Powers about his true intentions.

To move the Austro-German purchases, totalling more than two and a half million tons, to the beleaguered populations of Central Europe was a colossal task, but it was accomplished in the few months of peace that remained, primarily via the Danube, but also on the famous 'cereal trains' organized by the German military railroad genius, Colonel Groener. The arrival of Rumanian grain gave a powerful lift to the hunger-conscious Central Powers. The production and export of Rumanian petroleum followed approximately the same pattern as for grain, although a shortage of railroad tank cars severely restricted its shipment to Germany and Austria–Hungary. Only 15 per cent of Rumania's oil production was exported in 1915–16, as compared to 65 per cent in 1913–14.

Bratianu had decided upon intervention, in principle, in 1914; he gained acceptance of his political demands in 1915; military arrangements, therefore, were all that remained in 1916. In regard to these, the allied attack at the Somme and the spectacular Russian offensive under General Brusilov went a long way towards fulfilling his basic precondition, a general offensive on all fronts. But he still refused to set a date for Rumania's intervention until two additional points were settled: an adequate supply of munitions and 'unconditional security' against Bulgarian attack. It was around these two issues that the final negotiations revolved. The Allies found it relatively easy to satisfy Bratianu on the first. Previously purchased munitions already en route were to be expedited through Russia, and in addition the Entente promised to supply 300 tons of war material per day to the end of the war. This promise was given and accepted without any real understanding of the difficulties involved in its fulfilment, as Rumania was soon to learn.

To immobilize Bulgaria, Bratianu and his military advisers had previously insisted on the assistance of a Russian force of 200,000 in the Dobrudja, supported by an Allied force of 500,000 taking the offensive from Salonika. When told in 1916 that the requirements of the Brusilov offensive would cut Russia's contribution to 50,000, Bratianu shifted his search for security to Salonika. The resolution of this issue, which lay at the heart of the negotiations over a military convention, delayed Rumania's entry into the war by several weeks. Meanwhile, the Brusilov offensive sputtered and stalled, so that when Rumania finally did intervene she contributed little to the Russian effort and suffered a military disaster herself. The Central Powers, who had intercepted a large number of Italian diplomatic radiograms concerning the Russo-Rumanian negotiations, made good use of this additional time for defensive preparations. The blame for this unfortunate delay has usually been placed at Bratianu's doorstep. True, he negotiated stubbornly and raised new demands at the last minute. But, as a recent Soviet study based on unpublished material demonstrates, the Allies were also responsible for the failure to reach early agreement. Unprepared themselves at Salonika, the British and French insisted that Rumania support their attack on Bulgaria with an offensive south from Dobrudja. This clashed with the Russo-Rumanian plan to remain on the defensive there while concentrating Rumania's power against Transylvania. The Allies eventually dropped their demand but irrecoverable time had been lost. As it turned out, their effort at Salonika was far from what Rumania expected.

The military convention and the political agreement were finally signed on 17 August 1916 in Bucarest. The most important terms of the first have been mentioned. Of prime importance in the second was article 4, which outlined Rumania's territorial gains, now slightly enlarged since the 1915 negotiations: Transylvania, Bukovina to the Prut, the entire Banat, and additional Hungarian counties bounded on two sides by the Tisza River and on the third by a line running just to the east of Szeged and Debreczen. Only one additional point merits attention. Article 6 incorporated Bratianu's insistence that Rumania be granted equal rights with the great powers in all peace negotiations. The emphasis which Bratianu placed upon this demand mystifies many commentators but seems entirely understandable when it is remembered that Rumania was excluded from the Congress of Berlin. The premier felt that a full voice at the peace conference was essential for the coming struggle to convert the treaty's promises into reality. Bratianu waited until 26 August, one day before the stipulated date for declaring war, before presenting the treaty to a crown council. And then it was to announce a *fait accompli*, not to seek approval. On 27 August, as scheduled, the Rumanian minister in Vienna visited the Ballplatz with a declaration of war.

Rumanian intervention was the logical and, by August 1916, inevitable climax of a policy Bratianu had pursued with great constancy since the autumn of 1914. He did not overvalue the Brusilov offensive and blunder into war, as has been often claimed. In fact, the immediate military situation seems to have played a secondary role in his decision. What seems to have been the case is that Bratianu became convinced that the last hour for intervention had arrived. To delay any longer would jeopardize the achievement of Rumania's war aims. He knew full well that he had exhausted the patience of the Entente with his repeated postponements and uncompromising insistence upon Rumania's full territorial claims. He believed that he had gone beyond the point of no return. There was no Russian ultimatum, as some believe, but Bratianu did recognize that Marshal Joffre's earlier warning of 'now or never' accurately represented the temper of the Entente.

Perhaps equally important in underlining the urgency of intervention was the widespread talk of peace. War weariness and the prospect of a third winter of conflict, had greatly increased the desire in all countries to end the bloodshed. The Austro-Hungarian empire was torn by internal dissensions, aggravated by defeat, hunger, and minority discontent. The government in Vienna was known to be dispirited and Hungarian negotiations for a separate peace were widely rumoured. German peace-feelers proliferated in 1916. Bratianu was certainly aware of the growing eagerness among the Central Powers for a negotiated settlement; there is some evidence that Czernin's secret memorandum of mid-July, conceding that the war was lost and calling for peace, even a costly peace, may have fallen into Rumanian hands. Disquieting signs were also emanating from France and especially from Russia, where Sazonov's replacement in July by Stürmer was widely interpreted as an indication that peace could thus be more easily achieved. Bratianu had good reason to wonder how long an Austro-Russian accord, which would be fatal to Rumania's aspirations, might be delayed. As he explained to his son a week before the crown council: 'The moment before us is decisive. If peace is concluded without us, we will be crushed between a great Hungary and a great Bulgaria. The world must be forced to see what we want. . . .'

This last phrase suggests that Bratianu conceived of Rumania's intervention, in part at least, as a way of dramatizing her demands. With a premonition of what lay ahead, he argued in the crown council that even a military reversal would advance this aim. As in the case of Italy at Novara, he pointed out, there are defeats which are steps to victory. 'The majority of Europe sanctions our historic claims . . . whatever the outcome of the war, the claims established will remain.' It was indeed through defeat, not victory, that Rumania authenticated her national claims.

Rumania's intervention, so decisive for her own national destiny, also had an important bearing on the fate of the Central Powers. The fact that it committed the Entente irrevocably to the partition of Austria–Hungary, thereby sealing the doom of the Dual Monarchy, is widely recognized. Not sufficiently appreciated, however, is the influence the Rumanian action exercised upon Germany's destiny. As Professor Ritter has recently pointed out so clearly, Rumania's declaration of war was the catalyst in a decision which proved momentous for German history. Bratianu's long record of indecision had led the German high command, especially General Falkenhayn, to believe, in spite of the revelations contained in the Italian radiograms, that Rumania's intervention would come somewhat later. Consequently, when the Austrians forwarded the news it fell like a bomb at German supreme headquarters. The Kaiser, who had just rejected a bid by Hindenburg and Ludendorff to unseat the Chief of Staff, was completely unnerved and now surrendered to the demand from Falkenhayn's critics that the war effort be turned over to the heroes from the east. The consequences of this event need no elaboration. Rumania's belligerency also seems to have deprived Bethmann Hollweg of a powerful argument against unrestricted submarine warfare and thus, it would appear, contributed indirectly to his capitulation on this issue. A full consideration of the influence of Rumania's intervention, and of her quick defeat, upon the peace negotiations of 1916–17, lies beyond the scope of this study but should prove equally interesting.

(*This article represents some tentative results of a longer study of Rumanian diplomacy 1914–18, which is being supported in part by grants from the American Council of Learned Societies and the American Philosophical Society. Detailed reference to the extensive archival material upon which it is based has not been attempted.*)

Gerhard Ritter and the First World War

Klaus Epstein

This is the third volume of the monumental work produced by
Gerhard Ritter on the problem of militarism in modern German
history.[1] The first volume, covering the years from the accession
of Frederick the Great to the dismissal of Bismarck (1740–1890),
won much praise for the breadth of its scope and for Ritter's clear-
cut stand in favour of the primacy of *Staatskunst* over *Kriegshandwerk*. (It was, however, in the opinion of this reviewer, far too
favourable to Bismarck, a point which will be developed later in this
essay.) The second volume, covering the Wilhelmian period (1890–
1914), was generally hailed for its forthright condemnation of the
anachronistic constitutional structure of the German Empire, the
excessive prestige enjoyed by the military among the leading strata
of Germany society, the irrational folly of the Tirpitz naval programme, and the disastrous results wrought by the Schlieffen Plan.
The third volume is far more monographic in character and
encyclopedic in source foundation than its two predecessors:
although it deals only with the three years from the outbreak of the
first world war (August 1914) to the fall of Chancellor Bethmann
Hollweg (July 1917), it is longer than the combined volumes I and
II dealing with the 175 years from 1740 to 1914.

Ritter's decision to provide a very full narrative is due partly to
the crowding of important and controversial events into the war-
time period; partly to the vast mass of primary materials available
for these years; and partly to Ritter's polemical purpose of de-
molishing what he considers to be the false conceptions of the
'Fritz Fischer school'. The topics covered by Ritter in separate
chapters – each almost monographic in character – are the follow-

[1] Gerhard Ritter, *Staatskunst und Kriegshandwerk. Das Problem des Militarismus in Deutschland*, vol. iii. *Die Tragödie der Staatskunst. Bethmann Hollweg als
Kriegskanzler* (1914–17). Munich, Oldenbourg Verlag, 1964, 707 pp.

186

ing: German war aims, official and unofficial, in 1914; the relation-ship between Chancellor Bethmann and Chief of Staff Falkenhayn 1914–15; Balkan policy in the autumn of 1915; plans for *Mittel-europa* and for solving the Polish question 1915–16; America and the first two submarine crises 1915–16; the failure of the Verdun offensive and the fall of Falkenhayn; the Polish Manifesto of 5 November 1916; the peace move of the Central Powers, the launching of the submarine war, and the break with America December 1916–April 1917; the militarization of the German economy, with special reference to the Auxiliary Service Law and the Belgian deportations in the winter of 1916–17; Austria's moves towards a separate peace in the spring of 1917; the Russian March Revolution and the programme of a 'peace without annexations and indemnities'; and, finally, the fall of Bethmann Hollweg in July 1917, which meant the complete triumph of German militarism.

It will be seen from this summary survey of the book's contents that Ritter's work comes close to being a general history of Ger-many during the three years 1914–17; it falls short of this only because his preoccupation with the relationship between Bethmann and the generals (inevitably) leads to the comparative neglect of other important topics, though it is in fact remarkable how much Ritter has to say about problems not directly connected with the relationship between *Staatskunst* and *Kriegshandwerk*. The book is comparatively weak on all aspects of domestic and socio-economic history: it has little to say on party politics and the work of the Reichstag; the part played by economic pressure groups in the shaping of war aims; the management of Germany's war-time economy; and the development of public opinion. The bulk of the work – the definitive analysis of civilian-military relationships apart – is devoted to a conventional diplomatic history in the some-what old-fashioned manner of 'what one diplomat (or statesman) wrote to another'; it should be stressed, however, that it is con-ventional history written in a magisterial style by a historian who combines critical attention to detail with luminous generalization and who is deeply concerned with history as a form of art to be appreciated by any interested reader.

Unlike his rival Fritz Fischer, Ritter was unable to go personally to East Zone archives, though his pupil Zmarzlik examined some materials for him there. He has, however, explored many archival collections available in West Germany (Bonn, Koblenz, Munich, Stuttgart, and Karlsruhe) and in Austria. (The Austrian chapters of the book, while not always germane to the main subject matter and hence an obstacle to its readability, contain much valuable new information from previously unexplored primary sources. They suffer, however, from too much contempt for the Austrians and an extreme hostility towards General Conrad.) The elaborate footnote apparatus – unhappily placed at the end of the volume, pp. 589–688 – provides a careful documentation in primary sources and gives evidence of the thorough assimilation of secondary sources.

In his footnotes Ritter subjects Fischer's *Griff nach der Weltmacht* to a merciless cross-examination and is successful in demonstrating that Fischer is often deplorably careless in detail and sometimes guilty of *a priori* prejudice in the interpretation of sources. Nothing in Ritter's treatment, however, refutes the *major* aim of Fischer's pioneering work: to show that Germany (or at least nearly all influential people in Germany) succumbed during the first world war to a collective megalomania which expressed itself in utterly unrealistic war aims and a grotesque inability to see the world as it actually was; but Ritter does succeed in the *lesser* task of showing – as have a distinguished group of Fischer critics which includes men of viewpoints as diverse as Dietrich Mende, K.D. Erdmann, Erwin Hölzle, Hans Herzfeld, and Egmont Zechlin – that Fischer tends to exaggerate the purposiveness, continuity, and consistency of 'Germany's drive for world power', and that he misunderstands the complex figure of Chancellor Bethmann Hollweg.

What of Gerhard Ritter's own point of view? It is very difficult to characterize it in any single phrase, because he is – in this respect avoiding Fischer's penchant for massive generalization – profoundly impressed by the multi-dimensional complexity of the problems presented by the war and the men (especially Bethmann) who dealt with them. Caution is the keynote of much – not all! – of Ritter's work, a caution which results from a scholarly ethos which has compelled him, in the course of a long life, to re-examine continuously the controversial problems of a period he personally experienced as a young man. He appears torn at times between the National Liberal outlook of his early manhood – with its instinctively apologetic attitude towards criticism directed against

Germany's conduct – and a distinctly post-1945 critical attitude towards Wilhelmian Germany which yields nothing to Fischer in the trenchancy of its accusations. The earlier outlook appears in an occasional relapse into outmoded nationalist views; an undue stress upon the defensive character of German intentions and aims; an obvious desire to relativize whatever was outrageous in German annexationist programmes by pointing to similar Allied programmes; and the attempt to build up Bethmann Hollweg as a 'tragic hero' who was generally moderate in his views despite occasional aberrations. The later outlook appears in his recognition of the problematical character of *all* German annexationism; his criticism directed against the anachronistic character of the entire 'power structure' of Wilhelmian society; his extraordinarily – for a German historian – sympathetic and fair-minded attitude towards Woodrow Wilson and America's policy in the submarine question; and his contemptuous characterization of Ludendorff and the 'militarist forces' which he represented. Ritter is sometimes inconsistent in his judgments because he is so obviously torn between the rival poles of old sentiment – expressed in delightful occasional autobiographical reminiscences (pp. 85, 118, 225) – and new insight promoted by his contemplation of the tragic course of Germany's post-1917 history and by an admirable receptivity to the fresh outlook of young historians born after the events described. His assimilation of books written by non-German experts on the first world war – for example, Arthur Link, Ernest May, Arno Mayer, and Karl Birnbaum – is a landmark in the deprovincialization of German academic history. In the last years before his retirement in 1955 Ritter himself trained an unusually able group of German specialists on the war of 1914–18 – for example, Wolfgang Steglich, Karl Heinz Jannsen, and Klaus Schwabe – whose researches have influenced his own work. It is regrettable, however, that he has not taken adequate cognizance of the writings of young historians trained by Fritz Fischer; for example, Imanuel Geiss' valuable monograph on *Der polnische Grenzstreifen 1914–18* (1960).[2]

2 In his two chapters dealing with Poland Ritter has remarkably little to say about the atrocious plans, discovered by Geiss, to expel hundreds of thousands of Poles from a frontier area to be annexed by Germany. Admittedly these plans never became official policy, but they are nonetheless highly indicative of the narrow chauvinist mentality conspicuous among prominent German civilians and soldiers alike.

A few examples may serve to demonstrate the fact that Ritter has 'two souls within his breast'. His residual sympathy with an old-fashioned nationalist outlook appears most clearly in his first chapter surveying 'The Chancellor and the Dreams of Power (*Machtträume*) of German Patriots'. To be sure, he condemns the notorious shift in German public opinion, following the early military victories, from a purely defensive outlook to one bent upon conquest (34); he also recognizes the military futility of frontier changes in an age of tanks and airplanes, and their immorality in an age of mass nationalism (35). He insists, however, that broad allowances must be made for a nation which sincerely believed itself to be the innocent victim of foreign encirclement (what provincialism!) and wanted to escape once and for all from a situation where it was continuously threatened by powerful neighbours (as if a country located in Central Europe could *ever* escape permanently from anything!). Ritter is unduly sympathetic to the numerous German professors who concocted elaborate theories on the political, historical, and even metaphysical significance of Germany's war effort, comparing these 'attempts at spiritual self-defence and self-justification' with the Allied 'crusade for democracy and freedom against tyranny' (39). He forgets the world of difference which existed between the parochial-nationalist ideals of German professors and the universalist democratic ideals of the Allied Powers (the fact that the latter may occasionally have been rationalizations for purely nationalist ends is irrelevant in this context). Ritter also betrays some residual Wilhelmian reflexes in his remarkably narrow view of what constitutes a German 'patriot'. He describes with approval the comparatively moderate early war aims of Loebell (Prussian Minister of the Interior) and Solf (Colonial Secretary), both of whom stressed the impossibility (not to say undesirability) of annexations in Europe while desiring the enlargement of Germany's overseas empire. Ritter comments that the demands of the two ministers are especially interesting because 'they state pretty precisely the minimum of what a patriotic German politician hoped, at the beginning of the war, to achieve from a future peace' (41). The implied corollary to Ritter's statement appears to be that anti-annexationists, i.e. the entire Socialist Party, were *not* patriots.

Ritter goes to considerable pains to stress the defensive character of Germany's war effort and war aims. This constitutes, no doubt, a valuable antidote to Fischer's theme of a Germany rationally and deliberately bent upon realizing the offensive goal of the position of a 'world power'; but both historians tend to forget – for opposite reasons – that in the German war-aims movement offensive and defensive elements were inextricably intertwined in the minds of most actors. The term 'offensive' covers motives like greed and the will to power; the term 'defensive', fear and concern about one's ability to cope with future contingencies. Those who insisted upon securing permanent domination of Belgium usually wanted control of Belgian industries (an offensive aim) *and* a better strategic position in the next war (a defensive aim); those who wanted to establish *Mitteleuropa* wanted to dominate a satellite empire (offensive) and secure protection against anticipated Allied economic discrimination in the post-war era (defensive); those who wanted vast Eastern annexations – however cloaked under the slogan of 'national autonomy' – wanted markets (offensive) but were also concerned about the often cited 'Russian-Asiatic-Mongolian danger' (defensive). What was true of specific war aims was also true of the general tenor of Germany's diplomatic and military policy, beginning with her conduct during the July 1914 crisis. Ritter – again in sharp and explicit opposition to Fischer – insists that Bethmann's policy was essentially defensive and pacific at that time (15–20); but he admits that the Chancellor's conduct was influenced by the fatalistic conviction that a showdown with Russia was inevitable sooner or later. Was it defensive or offensive to force such a showdown in 1914 in the belief that Russia might now – but no longer in 1917 – climb down peacefully and be sufficiently humiliated so that it could not hope to make new trouble in the foreseeable future? Are genuine 'preventive wars' – and the German decision to support Austria to the hilt contained some of the ingredients of a preventive war – offensive or defensive? They generally look very offensive, but their ultimate motivation may very well be defensive in the sense of springing from a feeling of insecurity. The question is certainly interesting when it comes to the evaluation of the subjective motives of statesmen, but it has little objective importance; it has been raised here only to point out the illegitimacy of Ritter's exclusive stress upon the defensive motives of Germany and the obvious apologetic purpose which this serves.

Ritter is much concerned – in sharp contrast to Fischer – to relativize the enormity of German annexationist plans by pointing to the similarly annexationist aims of Germany's enemies (see Section II of Ch. VIII: 'The Problem of Peace and the Allied Governments'). This survey is curiously unbalanced in devoting half a page to Russia, five pages to France, and fourteen to England – the length of each discussion stands in inverse proportion to the extent of the annexationist aims championed by the three countries; this appears to be a rare case in which Ritter's treatment was evidently governed by the available secondary literature. He has no difficulty in establishing the fact that Allied statesmen (and the public opinion behind them) were incorrigible annexationists and that they were even less willing than Bethmann to contemplate a 'peace of reconciliation' on the basis of the *status quo ante*. He is on questionable ground, however, in his major contention that there was no qualitative distinction between Allied and German annexationism. Ritter ignores two key facts of the 1914–18 situation: that German annexationism and *only* German annexationism threatened the complete overthrow of the European balance of power; and that *all* German annexationist plans were certain to violate the now fashionable principle of nationality.

Wilhelmian Germany – because of its size, population, geographical location, economic dynamism, cocky militarism, and autocracy under a neurotic Emperor – was feared by all other powers as a threat to the European equilibrium; this was an objective fact which Germans should have recognized, irrespective of whether Germany in fact did or did not have intentionally aggressive designs (as affirmed by Fischer and denied by Ritter). Allied annexationist ambitions were, of course, also in many cases morally outrageous, besides being undesirable because they precluded (equally with German annexationism) any negotiated peace; but their realization did *not* threaten the European equilibrium with the intolerable hegemony of a single Power, whereas the expansion of an already too powerful Germany did. The principle of nationality – increasingly accepted by 'enlightened' public opinion as the most satisfactory basis for international frontiers – was an additional barrier to *any* German expansion. The immediate Allied war aims (for example, France's desire for Alsace-Lorraine, Italy's for Trieste, and Serbia's for Bosnia) were substantially in accordance with the wishes of the populations affected, whereas *all* German territorial objectives were a violation of the right of self-determination. This is but to say that the bloated

German frontiers of 1914 already included a large number of un-assimilable and misgoverned Poles, Alsatians, and Danes.

Bethmann Hollweg is the tragic hero of Ritter's book – a man of high intelligence and basic moderation who failed because of a combination of objective circumstances and personal flaws. Ritter's portrait of Bethmann is by all odds the best that we possess – it is certainly truer to life than Fischer's picture of an unbending and inflexible annexationist who consistently adhered to the extreme war-aims programme he had drawn up on 9 September 1914, before he understood the significance of the Marne debacle. (Fischer, who scored a trump by discovering this sur-prising programme in the archives, exaggerates its importance by claiming that Bethmann at heart never deviated from it.) Although Ritter is generally sympathetic to Bethmann he nonetheless criti-cizes him on several scores: his extreme annexationism in 1914, his participation in the intrigue which replaced the sober Falkenhayn by the rabid Ludendorff in 1916, his failure to protest against the Belgian deportations of 1916, and his weakness in the crucial de-bate on submarine warfare. Bethmann's war aims in 1914 were not only fantastic in their ambitiousness but crazy in detail. To give only one example: he wanted to impose a treaty upon England de-priving her of the right to levy protective tariffs in the future – a provision which would not only benefit German exporters but so cripple England's finances as to make her incapable of introducing universal military service after the war (thereby perpetuating Germany's military superiority) (44). Ritter says in extenuation of this and other unrealistic plans that they were supported by an overwhelming public opinion – if true, a complete confirmation of Fischer's main theme; that they were subsequently modified or abandoned by Bethmann – a useful corrective of Fischer's views; and that even the great Bismarck made an annexationist mistake in the case of Alsace-Lorraine in 1871. This last consideration – which could be paraphrased in the question 'how can you expect Bethmann to be better than Bismarck?' – is surely irrelevant, and the implication that statesmen cannot learn from their pre-decessors' mistakes is not necessarily true and far from flattering to Bethmann.

We leave it to the reader to follow Ritter in his major pre-occupation of discovering the 'true historical Bethmann'. A concluding observation should, however, be made on this topic. It appears, at least to this reviewer, more important to consider what Bethmann was and what his position permitted him to be, than what he actually did. There is general agreement (or will soon be again, once the revisionist position of Fischer has been revised in turn) that, compared with Germany's other leaders, Bethmann was a man of high intelligence and basic moderation whose views were, to the misfortune of Germany, overridden by Ludendorff in 1916–1917. Why were his views overridden so easily by so incompetent and irresponsible a militarist – a man without the slightest qualification to rule Germany in her moment of extreme crisis? Partly because of the institutional weakness of the Chancellor's office under the Bismarckian constitution, under which the incumbent was nothing but an Imperial bureaucrat dependent – unless a national hero like Bismarck – upon Imperial favour; it was considered quite improper for a Chancellor to base his position upon an appeal to public opinion or upon a majority in the Reichstag. That position was bound to be weak in war because the principle of civilian supremacy over the military was completely contrary to German traditions. In Bethmann's case the weaknesses of the office were compounded by the weaknesses of the man. Bethmann lacked charisma and political finesse; he often radiated a contagious pessimism intolerable in a war leader; he became unsure of himself when confronted by the expertise of generals and admirals in the submarine question; and he lacked Lloyd George's megalomaniac – but invaluable – belief that he, and he alone, could extricate his country from its unparalleled difficulties. Bethmann succeeded only rarely in imposing his views upon others, either by persuasion or intimidation; he shrank from conflicts with Ludendorff – for example, on the crucial question of war aims – which he knew he could not win and believed to be premature, thereby creating a pattern of acquiescent surrender; and he permitted his power to be progressively undermined long before he was finally dismissed at Ludendorff's behest.

Even a stronger Chancellor in a stronger office would have encountered formidable opposition if he had sought – as Bethmann did, haltingly and ineffectively – an early peace based, if necessary, upon the renunciation of annexations. Ritter spends a great deal of effort exploring the state of Bethmann's mind and soul – his precise intentions at various times, his reaction to real and hypothetical events, the specific circumstances explaining his annexationist aberrations, etc. This effort certainly yields new insights concerning Bethmann, but it appears comparatively unimportant for the understanding of Germany's war-time policy. Ritter admits – though unlike Fischer he does not stress – the fundamental fact that the ruling elite of Germany: the officer corps, landowners, industrialists, bureaucrats, professors, and clergymen, plus a majority of the Reichstag until 1917, ardently favoured an annexationist policy and was prepared to sweep away any Chancellor who favoured genuine moderation. It is unfortunate that he pays such disproportionate attention to Bethmann as an individual, to the comparative neglect of an analysis of the basic political, social, and economic forces whose constellation reduced any particular personality – even that of Chancellor Bethmann – to virtual historical insignificance.

Ritter deplores the extreme annexationist outlook of broad German strata and the fact that this outlook was sometimes shared, and never effectively opposed, by Bethmann. He insists, however, that German annexationism was not responsible for the needless prolongation of the war (as charged at the time by the Independent Socialists); one of the main themes of Ritter's book (188 ff) is that a negotiated peace was an objective impossibility in an age when mass passions had replaced the calm *Staatsräson* of happier periods of European history. He argues persuasively that the Allied Powers were at no time willing to settle for a negotiated peace based upon the *status quo ante* – and an undefeated Germany obviously could not accept terms less favourable than the *status quo ante*, especially as its armies stood almost everywhere on enemy soil and its ruling class suffered from a bad case of collective megalomania. The valid charge against German annexationism is not that it *prolonged* the war since it takes two to negotiate a reasonable peace – but rather that it handicapped Germany's war-time position by promoting pro-war solidarity in the Allied countries, preventing Allied-American controversies about war aims, and embittering substantial sections of the German people who believed (incorrectly, it appears) that Germany could have had peace if it had only renounced annexations. Ritter fully realizes (337) that a generous German peace offer – preferably one explicitly calling for a return to the *status quo ante* – would have caused tremendous embarrassment to the Allied governments and strengthened the waning loyalty of Germany's lower classes to the war effort. Why, then, did Bethmann Hollweg – assuming he was at heart as moderate as Ritter thinks – never seriously contemplate such an offer? More especially since its inevitable rejection by the Allies need not have precluded large annexations in the case of a subsequent German victory? The reasons appear to be: (1) the refusal of Germany's allies (especially Bulgaria) to agree to a *status quo ante* peace – hence any peace move must put strains upon the existing Quadruple Alliance; (2) the fear that the Allied will to fight until total victory would be strengthened by any German 'confession of weakness'; (3) the belief that annexations would be more difficult to justify, in case of the subsequent victory, once the goal of a non-annexationist peace had been proclaimed; and – most important of all – (4) the intransigent opposition of the Supreme Command to such a move. The Supreme Command, in this speaking for the most influential groups of German society, was bent upon annexations; it even justified these by such preposterous arguments as the necessity of annexationist goals to maintain the fighting morale of the army. Bethmann refused to make a major effort to override these considerations, partly because he was impressed by the force of the first three arguments; partly because he never ceased to hope that Germany might achieve some annexations; but mostly because he feared a showdown with the Supreme Command which he believed he could not win. He probably had the intention of seizing upon any concrete chance of a negotiated peace if and when such a chance should come up, and hoped that he could then prevail against the Supreme Command with the help of the Emperor; but such a chance never came, and meanwhile Germany muffed the great propaganda chance of successfully indicting the Allies for the crime of needlessly prolonging the war for purely annexationist ends. A different Chancellor, of greater personal force and greater personal prestige, might conceivably have been strong enough to insist upon a peace offer embarrassing to the Allies; but Germany's constitutional structure (under which soldiers were not subordinated to civilians), its political power structure (under which all key positions of German society were held by annexationists), and its mental condition (already described as collective megalomania), would have made difficult any peace move by even a Chancellor of Bismarckian capacity.

Ritter insists that Bethmann's Peace Note of 12 December 1916 was sincerely meant, and not just part of the preparation for launching unrestricted submarine warfare – an argument which rehabilitates Bethman's integrity at the expense of his intelligence, for the specific terms of the Note were couched in arrogant and defiant tones which facilitated rejection. Ritter's two long chapters (V, VIII) dealing with the submarine question are among the best in the book, and are pathbreaking – so far as the German reading public is concerned – in following Ernest May and Arthur Link in their penetrating understanding of Wilson's truly neutral attitude in his peace moves. Ritter's passionate interest in the question arises from his understanding that *it* (not economic factors or fears for the European balance of power) was primarily responsible for America's entry into the war; and that America's decision was responsible for the defeat of Germany, since the Allied Powers would have been incapable of defeating Germany – especially after the Russian Revolution – without America's active support. Apart from these broad perspectives of world history, the submarine controversy is central in the context of Ritter's theme of the triumph of militarism in Germany during the war. The decision for the submarine war marked the clear-cut victory of military over political considerations; it showed the fatal role played by public opinion in deciding – in a manner unprecedented in German history – a military-diplomatic question upon which the future of Germany depended; and it demonstrated how technical judgments (on, e.g., the number and effectiveness of available submarines) could be clouded by nationalist passions. It also reveals Bethmann's deplorable self-doubt in the face of arguments advanced by experts; he made his first error by not preventing the initial launching of submarine warfare on 1 February 1915, being impressed by the dishonest, bragging claims of the Admiralty; his victories over the Admiralty in both the 'Lusitania' and 'Sussex' crises never went beyond half-measures, since they never led to the explicit and unconditional renunciation of illegal practices of submarine warfare; he allowed himself to be persuaded that an intermediary policy between unrestricted submarine warfare and total abandonment was impracticable; and he finally acquiesced in the crucial decision for unrestricted warfare – refusing to resign – because he was half persuaded that the Navy might be right in its claim that England could be starved out despite America's anticipated entry into the war. Ritter is curiously sympathetic to Bethmann's refusal to oppose the submarine war *à outrance*. 'It is demanding a very un-usual (not to say super-human) degree of political instinct and strength of will to expect a man to rely exclusively upon his per-sonal insight (more accurately, his instinct) to take upon his shoulders the terrible responsibility [of vetoing the submarine war] against the advice of all leading soldiers and naval experts, against the will of his monarch, against the majority of the Reichstag, and against the greater part of politically active Germans (extending even into the ranks of the Social Democrats) who expressed them-selves on the question' (384–5). Perhaps so: but this fact throws a glaring light upon the state of German public opinion which con-firms the views of Fritz Fischer. It did not require much political instinct, only an elementary understanding of America's strength (as indicated, for example, by readily available statistics on produc-tion and financial resources) to convince any rational person that America's entry must be avoided *at all costs*. Germany's rulers, Bethmann included, were, however, too parochial to understand the real world of 1917. Germany's Chancellor – a man rightly praised for his comparatively sensible views – thought that America's entry into the war would mean nothing more than America's 'delivering food to England, providing some financial help, and sending some airplanes and a corps of volunteers' (384, 657 n. 48). A man so ignorant of the facts supporting his position was helpless when Ludendorff insisted that the launching of un-restricted submarine warfare was the only way in which the war could still be won.

Whereas Chancellor Bethmann is the tragic hero of Ritter's work, General Ludendorff is cast for the role of villain. It is a weakness of the book that there is no elaborate character portrait of this baneful man – but he emerges from the narrative as the very stereotype of a militarist in terms of his brutality, his lack of under-standing of political problems, and his insistence upon the para-mountcy of purely military considerations. This was true in his insistence upon submarine warfare, his insistence upon a Polish proclamation (5 November 1916) motivated by the vain desire to recruit Polish soldiers, and his insistence upon the barbarous deportations of Belgian labourers in the winter of 1916–17 (a policy unfortunately and unaccountably not opposed by Bethmann). As a foil, Ritter draws a favourable portrait of Ludendorff's predecessor

Falkenhayn (Ch. VI), who – though he also at times interfered improperly in political affairs – was a man of sober judgment whose view of the world was at least as realistic as Bethmann's, thus providing comparatively few opportunities for serious quarrels. Why, then, did Bethmann actively support Falkenhayn's replacement by the Hindenburg–Ludendorff combination in August 1916, a mistake fatal for the rational conduct of Germany's war effort and Bethmann's retention of the Chancellorship? The reason seems to be (248 f.) that Bethmann did not like Falkenhayn and did not fear Ludendorff; that he was impressed by the military criticism directed against Falkenhayn's Verdun offensive; that he was – as usual – not insensitive to the clamour of public opinion; and most of all, that he hoped to use the legendary prestige of Hindenburg in order to make a 'reasonable peace' palatable to rabid German public opinion if such a peace should become feasible. Never was there so complete a miscalculation. Hindenburg and Ludendorff became the most intransigent foes of a reasonable foreign and domestic policy looking towards a 'peace of understanding' and the conciliation of the German masses through political reforms. They were, in fact, soon to take the lead in securing Bethmann's dismissal from the Chancellorship the moment he proposed the democratic franchise for Prussia and showed his willingness to work with the anti-annexationist Reichstag majority which emerged during the July 1917 crisis.

Ritter's account of this crisis (Ch. XII) is one of the less satisfactory parts of the book. He bemoans the complete triumph of the Supreme Command, yet refuses to criticize Bethmann's failure to fight to retain his office. If there was an alternative to Ludendorff's dictatorship, it consisted of Bethmann's making a frank and firm alliance with the left-wing Reichstag majority formed under Erzberger's guidance at that time. It is true that Erzberger behaved in a thoroughly irresponsible manner in the latter phase of the crisis by co-operating with the Supreme Command in bringing down Bethmann before making sure that there would be a better replacement[3]; but this should not have deterred the Chancellor

---

[3] Ritter has a strong prejudice against Erzberger throughout his book – the latter's pushing, self-advertising, and indiscreet personality is obviously extremely distasteful to him. He has no appreciation for Erzberger's great achievement during the July crisis: winning a parliamentary majority (however impermanent) for the sensible policy of a 'peace of conciliation' (however vague) by the only appropriate method available to him – the use of exposure and shock

from seeking to retain his position. Could Ludendorff have insisted upon Bethmann's dismissal if the latter had mobilized the
Emperor and the Reichstag majority on his own behalf, and had not
hesitated to expose Ludendorff's primary responsibility for the
submarine fiasco? Ritter had an inkling of this when he criticizes
Bethmann for (erroneously) denying before the Reichstag that
there had been a conflict of opinion between himself and the
Supreme Command on the submarine question: 'he thereby
deprived himself in his relations with the deputies of a weapon
which he might possibly have used to save both himself and his
policy' (561). This sounds like an accusation of weakness directed
against Bethmann; yet Ritter rather inconsistently accuses another
historian of a 'strange misunderstanding of the general German
situation of 1917' for suggesting that Bethmann showed weakness
in not standing up against Ludendorff by mobilizing Reichstag
support (688, n. 65). The fact of the matter is that Bethmann –
being the weak and incompetent man that he was – never seriously
thought of fighting for his position and feared above all that
Ludendorff's dismissal – the alternative to his own – would lead to
a terrible public outcry. So it would have, but Ludendorff's complete triumph led to something worse – the disastrous mis-
management of German affairs by a narrow-minded militarist. If
Bethmann had been convinced of his own indispensability – as all
great statesmen must be – and had recognized the full measure of
Ludendorff's incompetence – for which overwhelming evidence
was already available in July 1917 – he would have fought for his
position and the fate of Germany might have turned out more
fortunate.

Ritter considers Ludendorff's dismissal of Bethmann the final
triumph of German militarism and as such the climax of the story
of the relationship between *Staatskunst* and *Kriegshandwerk* in
modern German history. He has, however, promised a fourth
volume which will deal in detail with the final seventeen months of
the first world war and in more summary fashion with the period
1918 to 1945. It appears that Ritter exaggerates the importance of

tactics. Ritter shows his hostility to Erzberger by the erroneous suggestion that
the latter's extremely annexationist memorandum of 2 September 1914 was
influenced by his being a member of the Thyssen *Aufsichtsrat*; in fact Erzberger
joined Thyssen only in May 1915.

the events of July 1917, for Bethmann had for all practical purposes been the prisoner of the Supreme Command long before his fall. It made little difference whether Bethmann did Ludendorff's bidding reluctantly or Bethmann's successor Michaelis did it eagerly – the ascendancy of Ludendorff had been established, once and for all, by his victory in the submarine question in January 1917.

The phenomenon of militarism has – in Ritter's view – three aspects which are usually related to one another: the inadequate institutional subordination of soldiers to civilians; the excessive prestige attached to soldiers, warfare, and military ways of thought; and – as a consequence of both – undue weight being given, in policy decisions, to technical military factors at the expense of general political considerations. It requires stressing that the first two factors were a distinctive characteristic of Imperial Germany well before 1914; hence there was exceptional danger of the third when the war broke out. The subordination of soldiers to civilians was completely contrary to Prussian traditions, although this became explicit (and important) only after the constitutionalization of Prussia in 1850, having been previously concealed by the fact that the monarch was both Head of State and Commander-in-Chief. Moreover, in no country of the world were 'militarist' attitudes and ways of thought more prevalent, among soldiers and civilians alike, than in Imperial Germany. The army enjoyed tremendous prestige; a reserve officer's patent was indispensable for success in many civilian occupations; history books stressed victorious battles even more than was the case in other countries; the anniversary of Sedan – the day of the military humiliation of a great neighbour – was Germany's national holiday; and in no nation of the world were politics and politicians so disparaged at the expense of warfare and officers. These aspects of Germany's institutions and national outlook all contributed to the inevitable total triumph of militarism during the first world war. Ritter, when he comes to explaining the victory of unbridled and suicidal militarism over statesmanship, talks altogether too much about fate, destiny, and other metaphysical categories, instead of assigning specific responsibility to specific forces and figures in German history. He is right, no doubt, in stressing the limited alternatives which confronted a man like Bethmann Hollweg in view of the institutionalized power of the German army and the attitude of influential German public opinion. It appears to this reviewer, however, that Ritter accepts the structure of Wilhelmian society too much as a 'given' and pays insufficient attention to 'how it got to be that way'. The villain of his volume is Ludendorff, but Ludendorff was more a symptom than a cause; the real villain remains not only unindicted, but is even one of the main heroes of Ritter's first volume: Otto Prince Bismarck.

Needless to say, Bismarck was not a militarist, least of all in Ritter's definition of the term; he always believed in, and was successful in maintaining, civilian – that is to say, his own – supremacy over the soldiers. He generally subordinated narrow military to broad political considerations, always excepting the unfortunate annexation of Alsace-Lorraine in 1871; and he was basically a man of moderation who never dreamt of European hegemony – much less world power – but wanted only the aggrandizement of Prussia (or a Prussianized Germany) within the framework of the European equilibrium. Yet despite these virtues he must be considered the foster-father of German militarism in both the institutional and psychological senses mentioned above. In the Prussian constitutional struggle of 1861–66 Bismarck was responsible for preserving the position of the army as *imperium in imperio*; but for his acceptance of the Prime Ministership at a time when the King was on the verge of abdication, it is probable that parliament – and a government dependent upon parliament in an English-style constitutional monarchy under the liberal Crown Prince – would have secured full control over the army and thereby established civilian supremacy. Bismarck was responsible for perpetuating the anachronistic notion that the comprehension of military affairs exceeded the capacity of mere deputies, and for continuing the institutional arrangements under which the General Staff and the Military Cabinet were not subordinated to the Minister of War because the latter, though in no sense legally responsible to parliament, might fall under parliamentary influence because he was compelled to defend the military budget in the Reichstag.

Worse still was the encouragement given by Bismarck to the militarist mentality. He usually appeared in uniform when he gave Reichstag speeches; he declared on occasion that the Prussian lieutenant was the pillar of the German state (*den preussischen Leutnant macht uns niemand nach*); he regretted nostalgically that he had served his King too much sitting behind his desk instead of standing up against enemy bullets; and he proclaimed that only 'blood and iron', not speeches and parliamentary majorities, could solve the great questions of the day. He was only too happy to bask in the glory of three successful wars, and he did nothing to teach his countrymen the simple fact that war had become – at least in the eyes of enlightened men – a deplorable anachronism, to be employed only as a last resort, as an exceptional medicine to cope with exceptional evils; and that the theoretical glorification of war, and the practice of sabre-rattling, now offended 'the decent opinion of mankind'. He did much too little to educate his countrymen in the requirements resulting from Germany's extremely precarious position in the centre of Europe, a situation which could be successfully mastered only through exceptional political maturity in the form of moderation in policy and sympathetic deference to the interests of the other powers. Instead Bismarck tolerated, and at times even cultivated, a mood of narrow chauvinism, blatant arrogance, and self-centred provincialism – all qualities that were to contribute to the triumph of the militarism which is the main theme of Ritter's volume. Militarism can be curbed – if at all – only by the strenuous efforts of a politically mature nation which is trained, through the experience of self-government, in the necessity of civilian supremacy over a potentially irresponsible group like the officer corps. Bismarck, by perpetuating the political nonage of the German people, by buttressing the sagging position of the militarist Junker class, and by emasculating Germany's parliament, bears a heavy responsibility for the forces which made militarism victorious. The major weakness of Ritter's volume is that he does not adequately trace the historical roots of militarism back into the over-lauded Bismarckian era, and that he does not stress sufficiently the social factors behind the triumph of militarism – factors which are much more important than the condition of Bethmann Hollweg's soul. If Ritter had been more conscious of Bismarck's contribution to the spirit of militarism in modern Germany, he would have gained a better perspective for evaluating the forces which struggled with each other during the crucial years 1914–17; and there would have been less use of categories like 'fate' and 'tragedy' to explain the well-nigh 'inevitable' ascendancy of Ludendorff.

The Dismissal of Admiral Jellicoe

S. W. Roskill

The best known account of the seismic disturbance which shook Whitehall in December 1917 when Sir Eric Geddes, First Lord of the Admiralty, abruptly dismissed Admiral Sir John Jellicoe, the First Sea Lord, is that given in Lloyd George's autobiography.[1] But that brilliant *pièce justificative* is so obviously one-sided that it cannot be accepted without reservations. To arrive at a fair historical conclusion other contemporary sources, and the opinions of those who were near to the seat of power at the time, must be investigated.

Jellicoe came to Whitehall from command of the Grand Fleet in succession to Admiral Sir Henry Jackson at the end of November 1916. There is no doubt that 27 months in the most important and responsible sea command in time of war had taken severe toll of his physical and mental stamina. His temperament was basically cautious; he worried a good deal – sometimes over trifles – and he was incapable of any real decentralization of responsibility.[2] As to his physical condition, while in command of the Grand Fleet he was constantly troubled with piles and also with pyorrhea; and the care which he took over his diet, together with his worrying temperament, suggests that a careful clinical examination would have produced a diagnosis of peptic ulcers.[3] Nor was he allowed any real period of rest and recuperation before he took over the

---

[1] D. Lloyd George, *War Memoirs* (London, 1924), vol. iii, pp. 1160–70.

[2] The most balanced account of Jellicoe's mental attitude is A.J. Marder's *From the Dreadnought to Scapa Flow*, vol. iii (London, 1961). See especially pp. 410–11. 'Without doubt his most serious weakness ... was his inability to delegate authority ... He looked after the petty details of administering a fleet or a shore appointment himself.'

[3] These conclusions on Jellicoe's physical condition are derived from his official and private correspondence in the first volume of *The Jellicoe Papers* (ed. A. Temple Patterson), to be published for the Navy Records Society later this year.

most responsible appointment his service had to offer, and at a period of crisis in the war.

His pessimistic outlook has been commented on by several close and astute observers, including Sir Maurice (later Lord) Hankey, Lord Beaverbrook, and Dr Thomas Jones of the Cabinet secretariat.[4] It was probably aggravated by the physical ailments already mentioned.

The most critical issue with which Jellicoe had to cope immediately he took office was the increasing successes achieved by the German submarines against Allied merchant shipping. The Admiralty tried every possible counter-measure – except the introduction of convoy, to which naval opinion remained totally opposed even after the Germans had adopted unrestricted submarine warfare on 1 February 1917. However, chiefly thanks to the work of a quite junior officer in the Admiralty, Commander R.G.H. (later Admiral Sir Reginald) Henderson, on 17 May, the Admiralty appointed the Atlantic Convoy Committee to report on the feasibility of convoy. That body worked quickly. It reported on 6 June and produced a comprehensive scheme for the introduction of convoy. Eight days later the report was approved by Jellicoe. Meanwhile, on 10 May, an experimental convoy had been brought safely home from Gibraltar.[5] But the long delay over the adoption of convoy had by that time caused Lloyd George to take drastic action. On 30 April, according to Beaverbrook, he 'descended upon the Admiralty, and seated himself in the First Lord's chair . . . Lloyd George had staged a deliberate encounter with the Naval High Command, and had emerged triumphant. But he had lost faith in Carson, Jellicoe, and even his Board of Admiralty'. Though Beaverbrook cannot be classed as an impartial observer of those events, and probably over-dramatized them, the broad facts are as stated by him.

Jellicoe's pessimism, however, remained unabated. On 20 June

4 See Lord Hankey, *The Supreme Command* (London, 1961), vol. ii, pp. 553–4 and 645–8: Dr Thomas Jones, *Lloyd George* (London, 1951), p. 118; and Lord Beaverbrook, *Men and Power* (London, 1956), pp. 155–6.

5 The best account of the institution of convoy is in the Ministry of Shipping's undated but post-war publication, *The System of Convoys for Merchant Shipping in 1917 and 1918*. I have found no copy of this document in the Admiralty records, but one exists in the papers of Sir Norman Leslie, who was liaison officer between the Ministry of Shipping and the Admiralty at the time and had a large hand in the preparation of that work. I am grateful to his daughter Miss Cecil Mary Leslie for finding it and lending it to me. See also Sir Norman Leslie's

he informed the Cabinet Committee set up to consider the forth-coming offensive in Flanders that unless the Belgian coast was cleared of the enemy and the U-boat bases at Ostend and Zee-brugge were captured, 'we could not go on with the war next year through lack of shipping'.[6] Later Jellicoe impressed the same view on Haig; and the Admiralty of his time must therefore bear a share of the responsibility for the disastrous prolongation of the third battle of Ypres into the autumn of 1917. This serious misjudg-ment, coming so soon after the convoy crisis, was not likely to restore the confidence of Lloyd George and Geddes in the First Sea Lord.

Sir Eric Geddes has been made the subject of one of the more pungent of Beaverbrook's potted biographies. 'Punctuality was his passion and routine his practice . . . His way of life conformed to the teaching of the Shorter Catechism. He was looked on as the strong silent man of real influence. In his home a telephone was on the pay-box system.' By way of contrast, A.J.P. Taylor has re-cently described him as 'Lloyd George's best find in the business world'.[7] He had made his name in the field of railway management, and proved a successful Director-General of Transportation, British Armies in France 1916–17, after which he was appointed Inspector-General of Transportation in all the war theatres. In May 1917 Lloyd George recalled him to London to take over as Controller of the Navy, then a civilian post, with special responsi-bility for coping with the Admiralty's side of the rising crisis in merchant shipping. About two months later, on 20 July, Lloyd George appointed him First Lord of the Admiralty in succession to Sir Edward Carson, with the assurance of his support for any changes he found it necessary to make in the higher posts in the department.[8]

Geddes's position in the Admiralty as a potential new broom

lecture, 'The Mercantile Marine in a Future War', published in the *Journal of the Royal United Services Institution*, August 1929.

6 Quoted J.A. Terraine, 'Passchendaele and Amiens', I. *R.U.S.I. Journal*, May 1959. See also S.W. Roskill, 'The U-boat Campaign of 1917 and Third Ypres', ibid., November 1959.

7 *Men and Power*, pp. xvi–xvii; *English History 1914–45* (London, 1965), p. 86.

8 There is no biography of Sir Eric Geddes. The best available substitute is Chapter XVI of Lord Geddes's *The Forging of a Family* (London, 1962); but as that work contains factual errors regarding the events of World War I it must be used with caution.

was not easy. He knew little about the navy, and he was handicapped by political inexperience. All the signs are that his confidence in Jellicoe quickly reached vanishing point; and the Admiral's own minutes and papers of the latter part of 1917 certainly show little vigour or imagination. Even his handwriting had deteriorated markedly. To give one example, at the time when the Smuts Committee of 1917 was considering the reorganization of the air services which resulted in the formation of the Royal Air Force, he produced an almost incoherent paper.[9] It is not surprising that Geddes's copy is endorsed 'Better not use this argument'. Both Geddes and the Deputy First Sea Lord, Admiral Sir Rosslyn Wemyss, were irritated by Jellicoe's refusal to delegate authority or to use the naval staff in the manner intended.[10] By the closing weeks of 1917 matters were plainly moving to a crisis, and the First Lord certainly had grounds for wanting to change his principal naval adviser. The reader may be left to judge for himself whether, taking all the relevant circumstances into account, Geddes's method of making the change was judicious, and whether he was justified in claiming the political support for his action which he did claim.[11]

On Christmas Eve 1917 (a Monday) Jellicoe found the following letter from Geddes on his desk at the Admiralty.[12] The timing had no doubt been carefully chosen, for Parliament had risen and there would be no newspapers for the next two days. Moreover Geddes had evidently already arranged that Admiral Wemyss should take Jellicoe's place.

---

[9] 'Remarks on a Scheme of an Imperial Air Policy', dated 14 August 1917. P.R.O. Adm. 116/1806.

[10] Lady Wester Wemyss, *The Life and Letters of Lord Wester Wemyss* (London, 1935), p. 364.

[11] It is only fair to record that, after Jellicoe had been granted the period of rest and recuperation which by 1917 he so plainly needed, he made a great success of his Empire Mission of 1919 and was later a much respected Governor General of New Zealand.

[12] Except when otherwise stated, all documents here printed are Crown Copyright and are reproduced by kind permission of the Controller, H.M. Stationery Office. The correspondence relating to Admiral Jellicoe's dismissal is in the Public Record Office, Adm. 116/1807 (Geddes Papers). The correspondence with King George V is in RA. Gv G. 1239 A, and is reproduced by gracious permission of Her Majesty the Queen.

My dear Sir John Jellicoe,

After very careful consideration I have come to the conclusion that a change is desirable in the post of First Sea Lord. I have not, I can assure you, arrived at this view hastily or without great personal regret and reluctance. I have consulted the Prime Minister and with his concurrence I am asking to see The King to make this recommendation to him.

The Prime Minister asks me to tell you that in recognition of your past very distinguished services he proposes to recommend to His Majesty that a peerage should be bestowed upon you. I have thought that you would prefer me to convey this decision to you in writing but, should you wish to see me, I shall of course be at your disposal at any time. My regret at having to convey this decision to you is the greater in view of the very cordial personal relations which have existed between us throughout.

Yrs Sincerely E.C. Geddes[13]

Jellicoe replied on the same day as follows:

Dear Sir Eric Geddes,

I have received your letter. You do not assign a reason for your action, but I assume that it is due to a want of confidence in me.

Under these conditions you will realise that it is difficult for me to continue my work, as action taken by me may commit my successor and may be contrary to your own views. I shall therefore be glad to be relieved as soon as possible, and if you prefer that Admiral Wemyss should take my place temporarily I am ready to go on leave to facilitate matters.

Yours sincerely
J.R. Jellicoe

I am of course ready to do what is best for the service without regard to any personal feelings. That I am sure you will understand.

Geddes answered, still on the same day, as follows:

Dear Sir John Jellicoe,

Thank you for your letter. I am obliged to you for your assurance that whatever is best for the Service is acceptable to you. You suggest going on leave and I think that will be quite satisfactory. I am asking Admiral Wemyss to arrange accordingly.

Yours sincerely
E.C. Geddes

---

[13] Copy in the hand of Mr G.A. Steele, private secretary to Sir Eric Geddes. Steele had previously been one of the Private Secretaries to Mr A.J. Balfour when he was First Lord.

On Christmas Day Geddes wrote again to Jellicoe:

Dear Sir John Jellicoe,

I saw The King today and he has approved the proposals as to which I wrote to you yesterday. The King wishes to bestow a Peerage upon you in recognition of your very distinguished services and I shall be glad if you can let me know, before Cabinet tomorrow morning, whether this will be acceptable to you. After notifying His Majesty of your answer I propose to make an announcement forthwith.

Yours sincerely

E.C. Geddes

Jellicoe replied on 26 December 'I shall feel it an honour to accept the mark of approval of my services'. On the same day Geddes wrote to Sir Oswyn Murray, the Secretary of the Admiralty, and to the civilian members of the Board (the Earl of Lytton, Mr E.G. Pretyman, Dr T.J. Macnamara, and Sir Alan Anderson) that he had 'thought it desirable, with the King's and Prime Minister's approval, to make a change of First Sea Lord'. Sir John Jellicoe had, he said 'relinquished the post and will be succeeded at once by Sir Rosslyn Wemyss'. Geddes ended by saying, 'I am confident I can count on your support that there shall be no dislocation of Admiralty business as the result of this and consequent changes'.

Geddes next sent the draft of the announcement in the press, which was to appear on Thursday, 27 December, to Jellicoe for his concurrence, and the Admiral proposed that the last two paragraphs, which paid tribute to his services to the country and held out the prospect of use being made of him 'later on in another important appointment', should be omitted. The final paragraph, he said, 'has the appearance of being intended to "make it easy for me". I think it is unnecessary'. But Geddes let the paragraphs in question stand, merely adding the words 'with distinction' to the reference to Jellicoe's thirteen months at the Admiralty.

Meanwhile, on Christmas day, Jellicoe had written privately to Admiral Beatty, the C-in-C of the Grand Fleet, about his dismissal.

Admiralty, 25th Dec. 1917.

My dear Beatty,

I don't want you to learn through the press that I am being dismissed from the post of 1st S.L. I received a letter last night from the 1st Lord notifying me of this and giving no reason.

I have recently had to take exception to his method of dealing with senior officers, yourself amongst them, and although I have no doubt the country will be told I was war weary, lacking in the offensive spirit etc., I incline to the opinion that the true reason is that I will not agree to the Navy being run by an autocrat like a Railway!!

The offensive portions of the telegram ordering the convoy enquiry were inserted by the 1st Lord without my knowledge.[14] I got hold of the original and showed it to him.

I should like you to know this. If you like I can send you a copy made by Share[15] showing what he inserted.

I am not sorry to be relieved ['lay down' deleted] from a thankless job, but I only hope that my successor will make a stand against similar action in future.

I do not know who succeeds me, but I have "gone on leave" at the wish of the 1st Lord. May 1918 bring you and the Grand Fleet a complete and glorious victory.

Yours ever
J.R. Jellicoe[16]

Also on Christmas day Jellicoe wrote to the King at York Cottage, Sandringham.

Your Majesty
   Sir
   The First Lord has informed me that he considers it desirable to make a change in the post of 1st Sea Lord, and that he is asking for an audience of your Majesty in order to make the recommendation.

He gives no reason for his desire, and all that I can do in the matter is to beg that Your Majesty will understand that my actions throughout have been guided solely by what I conceived to be for the good of the country and the Service to which I am so proud to belong.

I have lately unfortunately had differences of opinion with the First Lord in one or two matters, notably his treatment of distinguished officers serving afloat, including Sir David Beatty, but it is difficult to believe that such action on my part would have led to the action he is taking.

In matters of Naval Policy I have every reason for assuring Your

[14] This probably refers to the events following either the first or the second German attack on the Scandinavian convoys (17 October and 11–12 December 1917). See H. Newbolt, *Naval Operations*, vol. v (London, 1931), pp. 149–59 and 184–94.

[15] Fleet Paymaster H.H. Share, one of Jellicoe's secretaries in the Grand Fleet.

[16] Original in Jellicoe's hand in Beatty papers. Reproduced by kind permission of the Earl Jellicoe.

Majesty that my opinions are in agreement with those of the other Sea Lords. I therefore hope that Your Majesty will not feel that I have failed in my duty. If I am assured of this, I am indifferent to other matters.

With deepest respect
I have the honour to be
Your Majesty's most loyal and devoted subject
J.R. Jellicoe
Admiral

The King drafted the reply in his own hand. The file copy is undated, but it must have been written on 26 December, the day after Geddes had his audience.

My dear J. (*sic*)

I have just received your letter. The First Lord came to see me yesterday and informed me of the changes he proposed to make at the Admiralty to which I agreed with great regret. He spoke in the highest terms of the loyal manner in which you had always worked with him and that it was not on personal grounds that these changes were being made. Having known you for over 30 years you will understand how much I sympathise with you at the present moment.

I wish to assure you of my great appreciation of the splendid services which you have rendered to the Navy and the Empire, especially during this war, during which you have held the most responsible positions of C-in-C of the Grand Fleet and First Sea Lord and your services are equally appreciated by your Countrymen. I can certainly assure you that you have not failed in your duty, and I know that history will agree with me.

In recognition of your distinguished services I have much pleasure in conferring a Peerage upon you and I know that the announcement of this honour will be received with the utmost satisfaction throughout the Empire.

I hope to have the pleasure of seeing you soon when I come to London.

Meanwhile, also on Christmas Day, Wemyss wrote to the King that he had just seen Geddes, who had told him that 'His Majesty had agreed to his appointment as First Lord'. 'I am fully aware of my limitations', he continued, and he had left the First Lord 'in no doubt regarding them'. 'But', he added, 'I do think I have certain qualities which should be useful'. 'On personal grounds', he went on, 'I am more sorry than I can say about Jellicoe. He is a splendid fellow, and I am afraid will feel the wrench terribly, and I wish to heaven I could have been relieving him under more auspicious circumstances'.

The King replied from York Cottage on 26 December. The draft is in his own hand:

My dear Rosy,

I hasten to thank you for your letter just received. I of course was surprised when the 1st Ld told me yesterday of the changes he proposed to make at the Admiralty, although for some time I have heard rumours that he and Jellicoe didn't agree on all questions. I am of course sorry for J. who has certainly rendered splendid services to the Navy and Empire, and I fear will feel leaving the Admiralty very keenly.

My dear R. you are one of my oldest friends, having known you for over 40 years, during this war wherever you have served and whatever you had to do, you have done *right well*. You have many excellent qualities, but you are too modest to mention them, anyhow I consider that you have three which will enable you to fill the very important and responsible post of 1st Sea Ld. namely common sense, great tact and you are an absolute gentleman. For these reasons I at once gave my consent to your appointment. I feel sure you will have the support and confidence of the whole Service

If at any time I can be of any help to you I am always at your service.

Hoping to see you as soon as I return to London, probably next week.

Believe me

Yr. sincere friend

G.R.I.

On 2 January 1918 the naval members of the Board, with the exception of Admiral Wemyss, forwarded the following memorandum to Sir Eric Geddes. It was initialled by Admirals H.L. Heath, L. Halsey, H.H.D. Tothill, and Commodore G.M. Paine, the 2nd, 3rd, 4th and 5th Sea Lords, and by Admirals H.F Oliver and A.L. Duff, the Deputy and Assistant Chiefs of Naval Staff. The italicized passages are underlined with the red pencil generally used by Geddes.

First Lord

On the 25th. December 1917 we became aware that Sir John Jellicoe had been requested to vacate his post as First Sea Lord and had acquiesced.

We had full confidence in Sir John Jellicoe's ability and fitness to perform his responsible duties and were most gravely concerned and disturbed by this sudden removal of a most able and distinguished officer, we therefore decided to request you, if you saw fit, to inform us of the reasons which had caused this step to be taken.

We fully recognised that we had no constitutional right to question the removal or appointment of any member of the Board, but we thought you might be willing to afford your naval colleagues some information as to the causes which had led to Sir John Jellicoe's removal; we also recognised that as members of the Board of Admiralty we also had responsibilities to our Country and to the Navy.

On the morning of 26th. December the 2nd Sea Lord saw you and laid our request for some information before you and you consented to see us two at a time.

Shortly afterwards you saw the 3rd. and 4th Sea Lords the 2nd. Sea Lord being also present. You informed them that some two or three months ago you had a meeting, by arrangement, with Mr. Balfour and Sir Edward Carson in the presence of the Prime Minister, and that both Mr. Balfour and Sir Edward Carson had informed you that they did not consider Sir John Jellicoe *to be the best man for the position of First Sea Lord.*

Your statement was then communicated to the D.C.N.S. and A.C.N.S., and after some consultation we accepted with regret, the view that you had good and sufficient grounds for requesting Sir John Jellicoe to vacate his post. We were much impressed by the opinions of Mr. Balfour and Sir Edward Carson, who had held the position of First Lord, who knew Admiral Jellicoe intimately and who were, moreover, most experienced and eminent Ministers of the Crown.

Circumstances have since arisen which have cast some doubt on the statement that Sir Edward Carson had said that he did not consider Sir John Jellicoe to be the best man for the position of First Sea Lord. In order to set this doubt at rest the 3rd. Sea Lord called on Sir Edward Carson today (1st. January, 1918) on behalf of the remainder of us. Sir Edward Carson informed Admiral Halsey that he had never told you that Sir John Jellicoe was not the best man for the position of First Sea Lord and that he had always said that Sir John Jellicoe was the only man for First Sea Lord.

Sir Edward Carson also authorised Admiral Halsey to inform us that he definitely denied the statement you imputed to him.

We feel with deep regret that we cannot allow this misunderstanding to continue; it is imperative that it should be cleared up. It is due to you and to us that it should be fully explained and all *doubts be set at rest, and we feel that we cannot continue to serve as your colleagues unless this is done.*

We wish to add that we have no desire to hamper the public service by our action and that we will continue to carry out our duties loyally until we are replaced or until a satisfactory explanation is afforded.

Two days later Geddes replied to the Sea Lords' somewhat minatory memorandum as follows. The file copy is initialled by Geddes and endorsed by his secretary 'As sent by hand 3 p.m. 4th Jan. 1918'.

SECOND SEA LORD

I have received a memorandum dated 2.1.18 signed by yourself, Admiral Oliver, Admiral Duff, Commodore Paine, Admiral Tothill, and Admiral Halsey.

The reasons which made me decide to recommend the retirement of Admiral Sir John Jellicoe from the post of First Sea Lord are not a matter which I am prepared to discuss officially with his late colleagues on the Board. The personal and private talk which I had with you, Admiral Halsey, and Admiral Tothill, at your request, in which I explained that I had come to the decision regarding Admiral Jellicoe without haste, without any difference of opinion with him, or pressure from elsewhere, and after consultation with the Prime Minister and my two immediate predecessors in office, has been most unfortunately repeated in breach of confidence, and for that breach I have received an ample apology from, at any rate, one officer.

Your letter states officially that the signatories accepted the view that I had good and sufficient grounds for the action taken. I would remind you that it is not part of the duties of the Sea Lords to have any official opinion as to the appointment or removal of any of their number. The appointment and removal of the Sea Lords individually is entirely a matter for His Majesty and His Majesty's Government. It is my duty as First Lord to make such recommendations as appear suitable to me, and I shall at no time hesitate to do so.

As to the two concluding paragraphs of the letter, I confess I read these with amazement. They imply that you and your co-signatories propose to tender your resignations unless the First Lord affords an explanation which you consider satisfactory upon a private and personal conversation which he had with you and Admirals Halsey and Tothill upon a matter in no way coming within the scope of your duties.

I would remind you and your co-signatories concerned that at this time more than any other, it is the privilege of every citizen loyally and whole-heartedly to carry out the duties assigned to him.

On 4 January, the same day that the Sea Lords received Geddes's memorandum, they beat a hasty retreat. According to one of their number, Vice-Admiral H.F. Oliver, this was because Sir Edward Carson, Geddes's predecessor as First Lord, asked them to take no further action.[17] But as Admiral Oliver's account of these events was written long afterwards, and contains at least one definite inaccuracy, one may doubt whether it should be regarded as reliable evidence. The Sea Lords' retraction was as follows:

First Lord
In reference to our joint letter to you of 2nd January we understand that the interpretation has been put upon that letter that it was our purpose to suggest misrepresentation by you at the interview of 26th December with three of our colleagues of the extent to which Sir Edward Carson committed himself beforehand to Sir John Jellicoe's retirement.

That was not our intention. We regret that such an impression was created, and in order to make that quite clear we unreservedly withdraw our joint communication of 2nd January.

On 5 January Geddes replied to Admiral Heath, the Second Sea Lord, as follows:

Since I sent you my reply to your joint letter of 2nd January I have received the letter signed by your colleagues and yourself of January 4th.

I certainly felt that your joint communication of January 2nd was capable of the interpretation to which you now refer, and fully accept its withdrawal.

May I at the same time say that I recognise that there has been an entirely honest misunderstanding between us of the impression I intended to convey in my reference to the opinions of others when we met on December 26th?

I need not say that I feel sure that the incident being closed, we shall now devote all our energies to our work.

An interesting sidelight on the Sea Lords' retreat is an entry in Admiral Sir Herbert Richmond's diary for 15 April 1918. Richmond wrote: 'Saw ... Heath (2nd Sea Lord) who shouts and blusters, the hearty seaman all over – as dense as mud and obstinate as a mule, but I suspect easily frightened, for Geddes was able to put him in his kennel when he threatened to resign over Jellicoe's dismissal'.[18] Richmond was, however, notoriously censorious in his views on his colleagues.

[17] Unpublished autobiography by Admiral Sir Henry Oliver, now in H.M.S. *Dryad*, vol. ii p. 198. Reproduced by kind permission of the late Admiral of the fleet Sir Henry Oliver and Dame Beryl Oliver.
[18] Richmond Papers, National Maritime Museum. Reproduced by kind permission of the Trustees.

The account of the foregoing events as described by Admiral Oliver is reproduced below. Although he ante-dates Jellicoe's dismissal by 24 hours, it does show how the Sea Lords regarded the issue, and to a large extent it confirms Geddes's own letters and notes. However, no confirmation of the last two sentences has been found in any other source.

On the evening of 23rd Dec. 1917 [actually 24th Dec.] about 8 p.m. Jellicoe came into my room with a letter and asked me to promise not to tell anyone of its contents. I promised and read it. It was from Geddes, the 1st Lord, to the effect that Lloyd George and he were replacing him by Wemyss as 1st Sea Lord and asking for his resignation.

The moment for replacing Jellicoe was very carefully chosen to keep the Press quiet till after Christmas, and get the job done when Parliament was up and Ministers were away from London.

I was very unhappy, but could do nothing in view of my promise.

Next day or the day after Halsey the 3rd Sea Lord asked me if Jellicoe had shown me a letter . . . I told Halsey I had read the letter, he had also read it and promised as I had. We decided to scrap our promises and got busy, and got up a meeting of Sea Lords in my room . . . It was agreed to send a deputation of two to see Geddes. Geddes told them . . . that before replacing Jellicoe he had discussed it with Balfour and Carson, two former 1st Lords.

This seemed unlikely as Balfour had been away ill for some time . . ., Carson was in London and one of us [Halsey] went to ask him if it was true. Carson came to see us and said it was a lie and he was writing to Geddes to tell him so.

We then drew up a memorandum to Geddes saying that as he had made an untrue statement to our deputation we could not continue to be his colleagues on the Board, and we all signed it. Nothing happened for a day or two, and then Carson came from the War Cabinet and asked us to take no further action, as if we resigned there would be a political crisis and most likely the Government would fall . . . So in the public interest we took no further action.'[19]

Geddes's hope that the whole storm would subside after his acceptance of the Sea Lords' retraction was quickly proved optimistic. As Admiral Oliver recounted, they had sent one of their number, Admiral Halsey, to call on Sir Edward Carson on their behalf, to ascertain the correctness of the statement Geddes had made to them to the effect that he had consulted the two previous holders of his office before deciding to dismiss Jellicoe, and that

[19] Oliver Autobiography, vol. ii, p. 198.

they had supported his decision. The Admiral's visit produced the following letter from Carson to Geddes, dated 29 December

Private
Dear First Lord,

I have been informed that you have recently stated that at a conference held between The Prime Minister, myself Mr. Balfour and you I had agreed that it was time that Admiral Jellicoe left the Admiralty. I do not of course believe that you made such a statement but I think it right to bring it to your notice.

The only conversation I had with you as to Ad: Jellicoe was when I saw you at your request at the Admiralty with ref: to certain articles in 'The Daily Mail' – you then expressed certain grounds of dissatisfaction with Ad: Jellicoe. I stated that I knew of no one to replace him and that in my opinion Ad: Wemyss whom you mentioned was not at all to be compared with Ad: Jellicoe and did not possess the qualifications necessary for the office of 1st Sea Lord – an opinion which I still hold –

Yrs Sincerely
Edward Carson

The draft of Geddes's reply, amended in three places in his secretary's hand, is also dated 29 December.

Private
Dear Sir Edward Carson,

You say you have been told that I have said and that you and I had agreed "that it was time Jellicoe left the Admy".

I have not said so.

You say you have only once discussed the matter with me at my request in the Admy.

Unless my memory is completely in error you met me and the Prime Minister and Mr. Balfour at my request in the Cabinet room to discuss this matter and also subsequently at my request – alone.

What I have said and I have confirmed this to a very limited circle in strict confidence which has been violated ['and I know by whom', deleted] is that my opinion of Adml Jellicoe was not come to hastily and that I had some 2½ months ago *I thought* consulted my two immediate predecessors about it and that from the interviews I felt that my opinion of him was confirmed.

I have always most scrupulously added that the change and the question of successor was not a matter upon which my predecessors had agreed at all and ['that that was', deleted] being entirely my own responsibility.

I have always understood that you personally disapproved of my

217

choice of a successor and that you saw no one better than Adml Jellicoe to be 1st SL and I have never stated or implied anything to the contrary.

Yours sincerely

E.G.G.[20]

Also on 29 December Mr Steele sent Geddes an account of an interview he had sought with Carson, to whom he had delivered Geddes's letter reproduced above.

Dear First Lord,

I gave your letter to Sir Edward Carson and then had a talk with him. He has no objection at all to Mr. Balfour seeing copies of his letter to you and your reply – so that I have sent them to Mr. Balfour tonight at Whittinghame with a covering note. Sir Edward says he has no recollection of a meeting with yourself, the PM and Mr. Balfour in the Cabinet Room and, from his personal point of view, he would have preferred that he should not have been brought into the matter at all, tho' he now understands the extent to which you used his name and the reasons why you did so, that is to say, he now understands that you only used his expressed opinion of Jellicoe's abilities and qualities to confirm your own, and that you did not make use of his opinion as a reason for getting rid of Sir J. Jellicoe or for sharing the responsibility for that decision with anyone else.

Sir Edward has no intention of disclaiming that he had spoken quite frankly to you about Sir J.J.'s shortcomings, but he would have deprecated that frankness being interpreted as meaning that Sir J.J. ought to go as in his opinion he was irreplaceable. [Underlined in Geddes's red pencil]

I told Sir Edward that such an interpretation was quite contrary to facts and to your intention, and that the only context in which you had quoted his opinion of certain defects was to show that you had not formed a hasty judgement or without corroborating your opinion by the views of others also well qualified to judge.

Sir Edward was very friendly and I do not think he will try to aggravate the position.

Yours very sincerely

Gerald Steele

This letter is endorsed by Geddes. 'Thanks. Quite satisfactory. E.G.'

On the last day of the year Carson wrote to the Prime Minister from the offices of the War Cabinet, evidently still in some indignation.

[20] The amendments actually incorporated in this letter are not entirely clear.

218

Confidential.

My dear Prime Minister,

Can I have a private interview with you to-day if possible?

I am very much concerned about the dismissal of Sir John Jellicoe and even more so at the appointment of Admiral Wemyss as First Sea Lord, and I greatly resent the manner in which my name has been brought into the matter. I am sorry to trouble you but I cannot allow the matter to pass in silence.

Yours sincerely,
Edward Carson

The copy of the foregoing in the Geddes papers is endorsed in Geddes's hand, as follows:

Sir Edward Carson saw the P.M. that day 31/12/17 and was told what [the] P.M. repeated to me in his letter of 4th Jan. 1918 on file about the meeting taking place between P.M., A.J.B. [Balfour] Carson and myself – He told Carson he had approved the changes in detail and in consultation with B.L. [Bonar Law] authorised me to go ahead.

Nor was Carson prepared to allow sleeping dogs to lie in the matter of what he evidently regarded as a misrepresentation by Geddes. On 1 January he answered Geddes's letter of 29 December from the Offices of the War Cabinet.

Private

Dear First Lord

I have carefully considered your letter. I find it difficult to understand why my name was introduced into the matter of Ad: Jellicoe's dismissal. As there appears to have been a good deal of misunderstanding may I ask if you are prepared to inform the 'very limited circle' to whom my name was mentioned that I had expressed the opinion that I saw 'no one better than Admiral Jellicoe to be 1st Sea Lord'?

Yours sincerely
Edward Carson

Geddes answered on 4 January from the Admiralty.

Dear Sir Edward Carson,

I have your letter of the 1st January. *You do not refer to your denial that a meeting took place with the Prime Minister which I understand you still maintain.*

The Prime Minister tells me that he has confirmed my recollection of the fact of the meeting and of what passed. He tells me that he did so to you at your request, so if you are satisfied that the meeting took place, I shall be glad to hear.

I have confirmed the fact of the *meeting having* been held otherwise than by the Prime Minister's memory.

I am practically certain of the date on which it actually took place viz on 26th October.

You saw me at my office on the 27th at my invitation.

As regards the close of your letter I have never stated that in your opinion there was anyone better than Admiral Jellicoe for the post of First Sea Lord, but I have read that portion of your letter to those to whom I had mentioned the matter, as that seemed the best way of giving effect to your wish.[21]

Also on 4 January the Prime Minister replied to Geddes's request for confirmation of what he had told Carson.

10 Downing Street

My dear First Lord,

You have asked me whether I can recollect a meeting taking place in the Cabinet Room at 10, Downing Street, between myself, Mr. Balfour, Sir Edward Carson and yourself at your request, in order to discuss the late First Sea Lord Admiral Sir John Jellicoe.

I cannot charge my memory with the date of the meeting, but I am perfectly clear that such a meeting took place at which the four of us were present – perhaps about two months ago – and that it was arranged at your request. My Private Secretary is able to confirm my recollection.

Ever sincerely

D. Lloyd George

On 5 January Carson fired at Geddes what he evidently hoped would prove a Parthian shot.

Private

Dear Sir Eric Geddes,

I have nothing to add to my former letter as to meetings with you. [Sidelined in Geddes's hand 'He had it amply confirmed on the 31st'.] The matter is not material as it is admitted that on no occasion did I agree or suggest that Ad. Jellicoe shd leave the Admiralty. I very much resent that my name shd have been brought into an explanation of his dismissal to some of the Sea Lords and that they shd have been given the impression that I had expressed approval of his leaving office.

During the few months I was at the Admiralty I felt it my duty to resist efforts made by a section of the Press and others to make changes

[21] Copy in an unidentified hand (not Steele's). The italicized sentences appear in the copy.

which I considered were not in the interests of the Service or of the nation and indeed I attribute my departure from the office of 1st Lord to the fact that I declined to be influenced against my own judgement. It is therefore painful to me to have been in any way introduced into the matter as if I were a contributory party to action of which I entirely disapproved. However I hope this correspondence may now cease.

Your sincerely,
Edward Carson

Meanwhile, on 29 December, Steele had written to Mr Balfour, who was at his home at Whittinghame, as follows:

Private
Dear Mr. Balfour,

At the First Lord's request and with the concurrence of Sir Edward Carson, I enclose copies of two letters which have passed today between them on the subject of Sir John Jellicoe's recent departure from the Admy.

The information which has been conveyed to Sir Edward Carson is not in accordance with the facts as you will see from the First Lord's reply.

When talking to a very small circle of officers at the Admy in strict confidence the First Lord did not say anything which would justify the assumption that he was acting on the advice of others in changing the First Sea Lord, or that he was seeking to share with others the responsibility for the decision.

On the contrary the First Lord made it absolutely plain that, whilst he had had a frank personal discussion about Sir John Jellicoe with the Prime Minister and Sir Edward Carson, the decision to make a change and the choice of a successor were entirely his own.

The First Lord wishes you to be assured of this at once in case any such misinterpretation of what he said should be conveyed to you from some other source.

Yours very sincerely
Gerald A. Steele[22]

It appears that Mr Balfour was unwilling to become involved in the controversy, and was anxious to pour oil on the troubled waters. He did not reply to Steele's letter until 8 January, and obviously wished to be dissociated from the whole dispute that had arisen over Jellicoe's dismissal.

[22] The enclosures to this letter were Carson's letter to Geddes of 29 December and the latter's reply of the same date. See above.

221

Whittinghame,
Preston Kirk
Scotland

Private. Dictated.

My dear Steele,

I ought long ago to have acknowledged your letter and the accompanying enclosure from the First Lord, but during the earlier part of my brief holiday Mr. Short was not here, and I deferred writing until after his arrival.

The only thing that perturbs me about the whole matter is that, as I gather from a letter received two days ago from Carson, the Sea Lords are much upset by the impression – a false one as I understand it – which they had gathered from the First Lord, that I was a party to Admiral Jellicoe's dismissal. This, of course, as you know, is not the case. But it may be that some trace of the legend still lingers about the Admiralty walls; and, if so, I should be greatly obliged if you, or the First Lord, would finally exorcise its ghost.

Last week was lovely here, but, though the sun shines brightly, we are now in deep snow.

Yours sincerely
Arthur Balfour

Two days later Steele replied, as follows:

Dear Mr. Balfour,

Many thanks for your letter of the 8th January.

The incident of last week is now closed, and the Sea Lords and other Naval Members of the Board have recognised that there was a frank misunderstanding and that there was no intention on the part of the First Lord to seek to share the responsibility with any other person for the decision to make a change of First Sea Lord.

I hope your brief holiday has done you good but I am sorry to see that you had to end it up with a speech in Edinburgh.

Yours sincerely
Gerald A. Steele

But Steele's statement that the 'incident' was closed proved as premature as Geddes's earlier statement to the same effect made to the Sea Lords. In fact the rumbles continued for another two months. On 8 March Geddes wrote again to Balfour, who was by that time back in the Foreign Office. Evidently the First Lord was still very anxious to prove the correctness of his statement that he had consulted his two predecessors over the dismissal of Admiral Jellicoe, and that they had supported his decision. Furthermore, there had been some agitation in the press over the change at the

Admiralty, and Geddes was evidently aware that the matter might be raised in the House of Commons.

Dear Mr. Balfour,

I send you a copy of a letter which I am *proposing* to send to the Prime Minister. I have tried to restrict myself in writing, so far as you are concerned, to the exact statement of facts upon which there can be no controversy, and you will see that I have not made any mention in it of your opinion, nor do I think it necessary or desirable that any mention of your opinion should be made.

The decision come to was my decision, and all I wish to establish is that the matter was discussed and considered in October, and the decision in December about Lord Jellicoe was not hastily come to.

If you would very kindly look through the letter, and have your Private Secretary send a note of any modifications you would wish, I should be very much obliged, and will if necessary come over and see you.

Yours sincerely,
E. Geddes[23]

The Right Hon. A.J. Balfour, O.M. Ll.D., M.P.,
Foreign Office.

COPY

Enclosure to Sir Eric Geddes's letter of 8th March to Mr. Balfour

My dear Prime Minister,

After I left you last night I saw Mr. Balfour on the subject of our meeting with Sir Edward Carson in reference to Lord Jellicoe. Mr. Balfour recollects talking over the subject with yourself and myself at Downing Street, and he recollects the tenor of the conversation. He does not remember any definite meeting being called with Sir Edward Carson, but he admits that his memory is not of the best. He asked Sir Eric Drummond in my presence whether he remembered any such meeting, and immediately, without any hesitation, Sir Eric Drummond confirmed the fact that a meeting of what he called the three First Lords and the Prime Minister had taken place by special appointment some months ago. It was quite obvious that he knew that Mr. Balfour, Sir Edward Carson, and myself, as the present and two past First Lords, were to meet you at a special meeting.

Mr. Balfour also asked another Private Secretary, and his recollection was equally clear of this meeting of the three First Lords and the Prime

[23] The typed copy of this letter is endorsed by Steele 'See Mr Balfour's reply attached, after receipt of which 1st Lord sent off his letter to P.M. as drafted plus a copy of Mr. Balfour's reply. G.A.S. 9th March 1918'.

Minister, and he says he is as certain as he can be that Mr. Balfour attended.

We therefore have this confirmation of the meeting which you and I attended, and at which Balfour and Carson were both present.

I remember asking for the meeting and arranging it for the specific purpose, and I remember the exact circumstances for which I asked for the meeting. Davies[24] remembers calling it and remembers it being held. Mr. Balfour remembers discussing the matter with you and me at Downing Street, but does not recollect the actual formal meeting. Sir Eric Drummond and another of Mr. Balfour's personal staff recollect a meeting which left the significance on their minds of the three First Lords and the Prime Minister, and one of the two is practically certain that Mr. Balfour attended. My Private Secretary has a note in my diary that a special meeting was held at 11 o'clock on Friday 26th. October at Downing Street, and that is the date which I can locate by the sequence of events. My Private Secretary knows that I asked for the meeting, has the note that it was arranged for 11 o'clock upon the 26th. and that Sir Edward Carson came to see me the next day as a result of the meeting at my request, because I had not completely cleared up the points I had raised regarding the Press attacks. My Private Secretary also knows that I asked for the meeting for the specific purpose of discussing Sir John Jellicoe, and that it was held.

It is quite clear that unless the whole question dies down, which is unlikely, this aspect of it may be pressed. I feel that although Sir Edward Carson has thought well to disclose the line he himself would have taken on the matter, it would be a great mistake to bring Mr. Balfour's opinion into the controversy or the discussion at all, and I am merely writing this to enable you to make good the point – and I hope you will make it good out of justice to me – that in October I raised the whole question with you and my two colleagues best able to give an opinion, and in spite of Sir Edward Carson's lapse of memory – and I consider it nothing else – that consultation took place and is evidence of the care and deliberation with which I came to the decision which caused the recommendation I made to you on 24th December.

As you know from what passed at the time Lord Jellicoe left the Admiralty, my Naval colleagues were told by Sir Edward Carson that there was no truth in the statement which I had made – which was made privately but the privacy of which was violated – that I had taken counsel with my predecessors in Office on the subject of Sir John Jellicoe before taking the responsibility which was my own, of advising

[24] Presumably J.T. (later Sir John) Davies, Principal Private Secretary to Lloyd George as Prime Minister. But Geddes might have been referring to David Davies, M.P. (later Lord Davies of Llandinam), Lloyd George's Parliamentary Private Secretary.

you as to his removal, and the difficulty which Sir Edward Carson's action caused was not easily removed.

I hope very much that in any statement you make you will bear in mind that it is essential that my bona fides and veracity in this case should be established as far as they possibly can, and that you will do what you can to accomplish this. On the other hand, should you think it better, I am quite prepared to make a statement myself on the subject. You I know, realise that I am feeling my position personally infinitely more than probably would be the case had I gone through the hardening process of some years in Politics.

Yours sincerely,
E. Geddes.

The Right Hon. D. Lloyd George, M.P.,
10, Downing Street,
S.W.

I enclose a copy of a letter from Mr. Balfour to whom I submitted my draft of the above – it speaks for itself and must be read with the above.

E.G.

The foregoing letter was evidently sent to the Prime Minister on 8 March, together with a copy of Mr Balfour's reply, reproduced below, to Geddes's letter of the same date.

Foreign Office,
8th March, 1918.

PRIVATE

My dear First Lord,

So far as my not very useful memory serves me, the account contained in your letter to the Prime Minister on the subject of your consultation with Sir Edward Carson and myself does not err in matters of fact. Taken however, by itself, it would I think produce a very misleading effect upon persons not conversant with all that happened.

What you insist on in your letter is the fact that you consulted your predecessors in office on the subject of Sir John Jellicoe; and to this statement, as far as I am concerned, I raise no objection. But would not anybody reading your letter draw the conclusion that those whom you consulted in October *approved* the course which you actually took more than two months later ? Such an inference would of course be quite untrue. I was not able to think of any one more qualified, either by experience or capacity to fill the very difficult post of First Sea Lord in time of war. It would have been strange indeed had it been otherwise, for I was myself responsible for his appointment; and as I left the Admiralty almost immediately after he came, I had no opportunity of revising the judgement at which, after most careful consideration, I had deliberately arrived.

In the course of one of the conversations to which you refer in your letter, I remember your making some very unfavourable comments on the procedure of the First Sea Lord in connection with the attack on a convoy in the North Sea. But, beyond this single episode, I did not at the time appreciate the reasons which, in your opinion, imperatively demanded a change in your Staff, though I received the impression that you found Sir John not very easy to work with in the new organisation which you had introduced in the Admiralty.

In our conversation last night you particularised more fully; and I realised that in your deliberate judgement Sir John, with all his great ability and experience, (perhaps partly in consequence of them), found it difficult to carry decentralisation as far as in your opinion decentralisation was rendered necessary by modern conditions.

On such questions, it seems to me that only the Head of the Department can judge, and that his judgment must be final. The experience of his predecessors does not really touch the question at issue. I still think, and very likely you agree with me, that Sir John Jellicoe (as he then was) had a unique experience both of work in the Admiralty and of work in the organisation of a seagoing Fleet, and had shown himself a master in both spheres of activity. You will probably also agree that in these respects he has no rival among living sailors. But, while holding these views, I am for my part quite ready to accept the judgment at which you have deliberately, (and I know reluctantly) arrived, namely, that a change in the office of First Sea Lord was necessary if the machinery which you had endeavoured to adapt to modern requirements was to work smoothly and efficiently, as you had designed it.

I make not the smallest criticism on the course which, much against your personal inclinations, you have felt it your duty to pursue. But, from the nature of the case, neither I nor, as I think, anybody outside the Admiralty can be in the least qualified to offer an independent opinion upon it.

This is rather a long screed. I trouble you with it only in order to make it quite clear that merely to say that you consulted me (Carson I leave to speak for himself) is likely to be very misleading, *unless you add* that I offered no opinion upon the wisdom or unwisdom of keeping Sir John as First Sea Lord, and that I did not myself know of any sailor who could possibly be described as having better qualifications for the post.

Personally, I am sure it is in the public interest that the whole matter should be allowed to sleep. In any case, you might perhaps with advantage send on this letter to the Prime Minister as a sort of appendix to your own.

Yours v. sincerely,
Arthur James Balfour.

Finally, after several drafts had been prepared and amended or rejected, on 28 April Geddes sent Lloyd George the text of a statement he might wish to use if the dismissal of Jellicoe was raised in the House in the debate on changes in the Air Ministry consequent upon the resignation of Sir Hugh Trenchard, the Chief of the Air Staff, which was to take place next day. But in fact the need for the Prime Minister to use it never arose. Although Sir Edward Carson did bring in the question of Jellicoe's future employment, the events leading to his dismissal, and the controversy that followed Geddes's action, were never mentioned.[25]

In retrospect it seems plain that Geddes did indeed discuss Jellicoe's suitability as First Sea Lord with the Prime Minister and his own two predecessors. But he did not do so in a manner which justified the implication that Balfour and Carson had agreed with his views on the Admiral or had supported his action in dismissing him.

Jellicoe himself undoubtedly showed great restraint and dignity throughout what must have been a bitter experience. He accepted his fate without protest or complaint, and had no hand in the organization of the protest made on his behalf by the Sea Lords. On 24 January he wrote again to Beatty, who had evidently expressed the intention of seeking an interview with Geddes. But he never lifted a finger on his own behalf, or allowed any publicity to be given to the manner of his dismissal.

29 Sussex Square, Hyde Park W.

My dear Beatty,

I fear you may be wondering at my not replying to the letter you wrote me just after Xmas, but in it you said that you would write again as soon as you had seen Geddes. You did not do so, and I concluded that something had passed at your interview with Geddes which made you consider it better not to write again.

If that is so please do not trouble to reply to this. But I did not want you to think that I had purposely refrained from writing to thank you for your letter and so do so now.

I am still in the dark as to why I left the Admiralty, though I gather from what has been told me by Sir E. Carson and others that the change was due to Northcliffe's pressure on the Prime Minister passed on to Geddes.

The odd thing to me is that Geddes has made so many different statements on the subject to different people.

25 Hansard, Commons, Fifth Series, vol. 105. Col. 1341.

However the matter is ended now and I am enjoying freedom from a very thankless task, though I naturally feel disgusted at being idle at such a time. I don't see how I can be employed under present conditions and so must be content to be idle.

I am very sorry that the destroyer losses have been so heavy of late. That, combined with the terribly slow output will handicap all operations terribly. Our building programme is hopelessly behind promises and I am afraid that the reorganisation of the Controller's Department has been a failure.

Carson's resignation is a great loss. He was a very steadying influence in the Cabinet and was quite strong in his support of Haig and Robertson. I see the Press campaign against them is in full blast.

I hope all goes well with the Fleet and send every good wish for a successful year.

Ever yours
J.R. Jellicoe[26]

As an appendix to the foregoing account of the flurry produced by the dismissal of Jellicoe, a letter which King George V wrote to Admiral Beatty on 10 February 1918 probably came near to the heart of the matter. For the King always had a sensitive finger on the naval pulse. 'I agree with you', he wrote, 'that the way Jellicoe was removed from the Admiralty was unfortunate. The Prime Minister has had his knife into him for some time and wished for a change. I think Wemyss will do well and he has some first rate young brains to help him, he is full of sound common sense and does not go into details so much as Jellicoe did. I am sure now there will be much more sympathy between the Admiralty and the Grand Fleet than there was formerly.'[27]

[26] Original in Jellicoe's hand in Beatty papers.
[27] Original in Beatty papers.

Russia in 1914

Hans Rogger

To speak of Russia in 1914 means, inevitably, to think of it in the light of 1917. The magnitude of what happened in the later year – and even more of what was to follow – overshadows the events of the last six months of peace Russia was to know for a long time. Yet they were agitated months, and whatever inclination there may be for nostalgia to invest them with the bitter-sweet of lost hopes or the glamour of a happier age, there is remarkably wide agreement that Russia in 1914 was in the throes of an internal crisis which might assume revolutionary proportions. The recollections of survivors – in which most often the last few pre-war years merge to form one general impression – are borne out by contemporary evidence. Disagreement concerns rather the nature and the probable outcome of the crisis, and the potential of the war for making inevitable or avoiding, speeding up or retarding, the country's decline into political and social disintegration. In order to attempt some answer to these questions it may be useful to cut across the usual chronological boundaries in order to see what Russian society's response to the war can tell us of its likely reactions to the internal crisis which war, temporarily, reduced to secondary importance.[1]

The Russian crisis was three-fold: political, social, and spiritual (or cultural); its most visible part, as 1914 opened, was the political one. 'Long before the war', Fedor Stepun recalled, 'all politically conscious people lived as on a volcano', a sentiment which was in 1914 no longer confined to the liberal or radical opposition. 'We live on a volcano', wrote the arch-conservative and chauvinistic *Kievlianin* in April, noting 'sharp displeasure with the present

---

1 In this summary of Russia's pre-war crisis, I follow, in general outline, Professor Leopold Haimson's 'The Problem of Social Stability in Urban Russia, 1905–1917,' *Slavic Review*, December 1964 and March 1965. I hope that my somewhat different approach may contribute additional materials, questions and perspectives to the debate which Mr Haimson has initiated.

regime' even on the part of the absolutely loyal classes of society. This displeasure, although it stemmed from different sources, was noticeable also on the far right of the political spectrum, where there was fear that 1905 might be enacted all over again, and the opposition recover the unity it had then displayed and quickly lost.[2]

Crisis had, of course, been endemic in Russian political life for some time; in heightened form at least since the assassination of Stolypin in 1911. Its intensification in early 1914 was due to actual and feared changes in government policy and personnel, changes which seemed to make a purely political solution of the crisis ever more difficult. The most dramatic of these was the sudden dismissal, at the end of January, of the Chairman of the Council of Ministers, Kokovtsev, who, although his popularity in the country at large and among the opposition in particular, had hardly been great, appeared now to be the last defender of Stolypin's legacy: qualified cooperation with the legislature in the work of constructive reform. His leaving, and the manner of it ('He was let go like a domestic', one of the Grand Dukes observed),[3] was widely interpreted as a victory for the forces of reaction. These had gained influence at court, would now dominate the government and use their new-won power to destroy what was left of the Stolypin compromise, and assume towards the Duma, the non-Russian nationalities and the working-class movement harsh and irreconcilable policies. 'A fire is burning under a relatively calm surface,' reported an Austrian diplomat, 'an unskilled hand may fan the flames and start a conflagration if the nationalist hotheads, together with the extreme Right, bring about a union of the oppressed nationalities and the socialist proletariat.'[4]

There were several members of the government who qualified for a *testimonium paupertatis* as far as their political skills were concerned. Shcheglovitov, the Minister of Justice, who had let the

---

[2] Fedor Stepun, *Byvshee i nesbyvsheesia* (New York, 1956), I, p. 304; *Ezhegodnik gazety* 'Rech' na 1915, pp. 235–6; S. Elpatevskii, 'Zhizn idet', *Russkoe bogatstvo*, January 1914, p. 299; Aleksei Badayev, *The Bolsheviks in the Tsarist Duma* (New York, 1929), p. 153; Otto Hoetzsch, *Russland*, 2nd ed. (Berlin, 1917), p. 136.

[3] Count Otto Czernin to Count Leopold Berchtold, 13 February 1914 (Haus-, Hof- und Staatsarchiv, Wien, Politisches Archiv X, Russland, Karton 140 [hereafter 'HHStA']).

[4] Ibid.

Beilis ritual murder case come to trial, was constantly infringing the rights of the judiciary and the bar and had used his office to render interpretations of the law which disqualified 'undesirable' electors and candidates. L.A. Kasso, the Minister of Education, besides harassing students and professors, blocked expansions of educational opportunity proposed by the Duma. The new head of government, I.L. Goremykin, was a relic of former days, remembered mainly for his struggles with the first Duma in 1906; his appearance before the fourth led to lengthy disturbances in the house. Above all, there was N.A. Maklakov, the Minister of the Interior and imperial favourite, who had made no secret of his sympathies for the parties of the extreme Right and was believed to favour a revision of the Fundamental Laws (tantamount to a coup d'état) which would convert the legislative institutions granted in 1905 into purely consultative bodies.

No coup took place, but while the Duma sat in the spring of 1914, signs multiplied that the government was determined to whittle away its rights of interpellation, of legislative initiative, and even of immunity for statements made from the rostrum of the lower house. The 'constitutional opposition', consisting of about 100 Constitutional Democrats (Kadets) and Progressists, and the Left (24 'Labourites' and Social-Democrats) were joined in some of their protests by members who sat to their right – primarily, Octobrists and Centrists. In discussing appropriations for the Ministry of the Interior, this opposition succeeded for the first time in the history of the Duma in rejecting a specific portion of the government's budget for the purpose of political protest, while by a majority of 186 to 95, it criticized the Ministry for arbitrary restrictions on the activities of local government, for provoking dissatisfaction and disturbances among peaceful sections of the population (i.e., the subject nationalities), and for not carrying out what was called (presumably with tongue in cheek) the Emperor's desire for fruitful collaboration between the executive and the legislature. The Ministry's policies, it was said, threatened the tranquillity and the safety of the nation. Just before it rose in June, the Duma did, however, accept the government's military programme (earning the Tsar's praise for its patriotism), but it also voted an amendment to the state budget which forbade ministries from expending at their discretion unused sums assigned for specific purposes. The amendment was rejected by the Council of

State whose appointed members helped to make the upper chamber a graveyard for liberal hopes.[5]

Protest was not limited to those whose rights were most immediately threatened. Baron Rosen, a conservative diplomat in the Council of State; congresses of industrialists, businessmen, and agronomists; representatives of municipalities; one or another pro-government newspaper or even, on occasion, a provincial gentry assembly, voiced alarm, concern, or anger over what looked like a concerted drive against rights and institutions which the Tsar had granted and vowed to uphold. The conflict between government and the political opposition seemed by way of turning into a conflict between government and 'society' (i.e., *obshchestvo*, its articulate, privileged and critical sectors), from which the latter, building an ever broader base inside and outside the Duma, would emerge victorious. This would be a political revolution after the manner of 1905 – unless the government sought to save itself by a coup d'état. Few thought that there was another way out of the impasse. There was talk that many opposition deputies were considering resigning their mandates in despair and applying their energies to more rewarding work outside the Duma, while others thought it best to provoke the government into dissolution, in hopes of bringing the crisis to a head. They had not succeeded in doing so by the time the two chambers adjourned for the summer recess in early June.[6]

With the legislature adjourned and the confrontation between the government and the opposition once more postponed, attention shifted to the social crisis which the political one had partially reflected and partly obscured. This reached its height with the massive strikes and disorders which took place in the industrial quarters of St Petersburg during the visit of President Poincaré in early July, raged for more than a week, required the use of troops to keep them out of the centre of town, and revealed a degree of aggressive-

---

[5] *Ezhegodnik gazety* 'Rech' na 1915, pp. 236–7; P.N. Miliukov, *Vospominaniia* (New York, 1955), II, p. 167; S.S. Oldenburg, *Tsarstvovanie Imperatora Nikolaia II* (Munich, 1949), II, pp. 135–8.

[6] Oldenburg, *op. cit.*, II, pp. 108–9; A. Petrishchev, 'Khronika vnutrennei zhizni', *Russkoe bogatstvo*, February 1914, pp. 290–1, March 1914, pp. 331–2 and June 1914, pp. 279–80; *Novoe Vremia*, 17 and 18 April 1914; I.F. Gindin, 'Russkaia burzhuaziia v period kapitalizma . . .', *Istoriia SSSR*, no. 3, 1963, p. 57; Ivan Menitskii, *Revoliutsionnoe dvizhenie voennykh godov (1914–1917)* (Moscow, 1924), I, pp. 27–9.

ness and exasperation on the part of the workers for which even sympathetic observers were unprepared. There had already been so many strikes during the year, commented a writer for the Kadet newspaper *Rech*, and they were due to so many different causes, that there was at first no reason to attach any special importance to this one. But although the number of strikes and strikers in July was greater than for any previous month of 1914, their determination (or desperateness) was not altogether new.[7]

The British ambassador had reported in March that the temper of the 50,000 men who had downed tools in St Petersburg to protest against the persecution of the labour press 'was distinctly menacing, the demonstrators going so far as to assault and disarm the police – a step which marks a distinct advance in the daring of the Petersburg mob who have hitherto stood in wholesome awe of that force'. His Austrian colleague, commenting in April on the prevalence of political strikes, predicted that the revolutionaries would be able to organize the workers for still more serious action, long before the authorities would be able to deal with them. On 1 May, almost all work in the industrial enterprises of the capital had come to a halt. In view of the 'epidemic' nature of the strike movement throughout the first half of the year, in the capital as well as a half dozen other industrial towns – and the inability either of government repression or employers' lockouts to prevent new outbreaks – it is difficult to see how the Minister of Finance, the Grand Duke Nicholas, and the French Ambassador could regard the July outbreaks (begun as demonstrations of support for striking comrades in the Baku oil fields) as totally unexpected, without motive, and due to German machinations.[8]

The Austrian chargé d'affaires (Count Czernin) was more perceptive when he attributed the extent and violence of the July days to the treatment the workers had received at the hands of the police and predicted that such means could only postpone, not avert, the threat of an explosion. 'If one continues to cling to such a senseless

[7] Quotation from *Rech* in D.M. Odinetz and P.J. Novgorotsev, *Russian Schools and Universities in the World War* (New Haven, 1929), p. 152.

[8] Sir George Buchanan to Sir Edward Grey, 29 March 1914, PRO, FO 371, Piece No. 2092, document 14329; Count Friedrich Szapary to Berchtold, 24 April 1914, HHStA; P. Bark, 'Vospominaniia', *Vozrozhdenie* (Paris), March 1965, p. 87; Oldenburg, *op. cit.*, II, p. 140; Maurice Paléologue, *La Russie des Tsars pendant la Grande Guerre* (Paris, 1921/22), I, p. 11; P. Graevenitz, *From Autocracy to Bolshevism* (London, 1918), p. 37.

principle and keeps all safety-valves closed, it can happen that the revolutionary organization of Russia will be completed before her military one.' It is certain that German gold played no role in the summer of 1914. It is less certain to what extent the rebuilding of revolutionary organizations shattered in the years after 1906 was responsible for the intransigence of the workers. Badaev, a Bolshevik Duma deputy, believed that even if they had not been interrupted by the war, the July demonstrations might not have led to the decisive point of the revolutionary struggle, for lockouts, mass arrests, and deportations had diminished the economic strength and weakened the political organization of the working class, making necessary a respite for the regrouping of its forces. Indeed, the Petersburg party committee of the Bolsheviks realized before the workers did that their strike was bound to be defeated and called on them to return to work.[9]

As early as April the political commentator of *Russkoe Bogatstvo* had written in his monthly survey that, besides the conflict being played out between government and opposition in the Duma, the country at large was full of combustible material of a less controlled, less controllable, and more elemental nature. 'In particular, it seems that the activism of the working masses is beginning to outgrow the organizational capabilities and possibilities of the working-class intelligentsia.' He, too, compared the situation to the building up of pressures in a hermetically sealed boiler, pressures which had reached a degree of intensity sufficient to inspire the stokers (the authorities) with fear of the consequences of a further increase.[10]

Those of the stokers who showed an awareness of the seriousness of the social crisis did not ascribe it to the efforts either of German or even primarily of Russian instigators. In a remarkable memorandum which he submitted to the Tsar in February, P.N. Durnovo, a reactionary member of the Council of State and former Minister of the Interior, gave warning of the danger of social revolution in case of war. Although his prescience was due at least as much to fear as to insight, he saw clearly that the political and the social crisis were quite distinct and that the latter was the more threatening. A political revolution, lacking broad support, was impossible; a social revolution, in a country where the masses were

[9] Czernin to Berchtold, 17 July 1914, HHStA; Badeyev, *op. cit.*, pp. 177, 195.
[10] A. Petrishchev, 'Khronika vnutrennei zhizni', *Russkoe bogatstvo*, April 1914, p. 290.

234

unconsciously, almost instinctively, socialist, was not. 'The Russian masses, whether workmen or peasants, are not looking for political rights, which they neither want nor comprehend. The peasant dreams of obtaining a gratuitous share of somebody else's land; the workman, getting hold of the entire capital and profits of the manufacturer.'[11]

Durnovo's definition of socialism may have been faulty; his appraisal of the mass mood and of the relationship between the two crises was not. It was shared by the Minister of Agriculture, Krivoshein, who had the reputation of being a moderate, perhaps even a liberal. He did not deny, speaking in May, that radical propaganda played its part in agitating the masses, but viewed its authors as helpless to guide the revolution which would surely come if Russia went to war. It would be not so much a revolution as a *pogrom*, a senseless, pitiless, anarchic rising which would make victims even of those who had conjured it up.[12]

The cultural crisis is seen as stemming from similar perceptions on the part of thoughtful men who felt that there was an air of unreality, of impermanence, to all the busy building and planning – political and economic – in which their countrymen were engaged. They, too, feared that whatever gains had been made or were still possible could all too easily be swept away by the mighty floods of popular resentment that were barely restrained by the feeble dikes of civilization and a decaying state. The intelligentsia had to admit to themselves that in the higher culture which they were developing and which was giving Russia a standing in the world, the masses had no share, and that they would probably sweep it away if given a chance. The cultural elite felt keenly the lack of contact with a people roused to anger and violence. Alexander Blok's diaries are often cited to convey a sense of the 'deep uneasiness that was gnawing at the loftiest and more sensitive minds', an uneasiness which was taken to indicate a loss of faith in the efficacy and benefits of progress. Stepun derided the facile optimism of the enlightened, their belief in the possibility of controlling men and events, mocked their conceit that a happy resolution of Russia's

[11] Frank Golder, ed., *Documents of Russian History, 1914–1917* (New York, 1927), pp. 3–23.

[12] Princesses Paley, 'En Russie à la veille de la guerre', *La Revue de Paris*, no. 22, 1923, pp. 247–8.

crisis could be the work of a mere handful of politicians, a matter of reformed ministries and parliaments. In Andrei Bely's vision (*Petersburg*, 1913), the Russia of the father (imperial and bureaucratic) and the Russia of the son (revolutionary, intellectual, and visionary) are both doomed, as is the city in which their confused struggle is carried on.[13]

For others, like the Kadet jurist I.V. Gessen, the crisis expressed itself in a feeling of fatigue and exhaustion, with the old guard of the intelligentsia still carrying on its work of political and cultural enlightenment by mere reflex and the younger generation losing itself in aesthetic innovation or sexual pursuits. The right-wing publicist and repentant revolutionary Lev Tikhomirov, spoke on 1 January 1914 of a most alarming inertia as the characteristic contemporary mood. 'Perhaps we are living quietly. But this tranquillity is lifeless. Not only is there no striving for greatness or for ideals that could carry along the whole nation; belief itself in such an impulse has died out.' Even many of those who did not share the cultural despair or sense of moral dissolution seemed afflicted by a spiritual malaise that made them question the meaning of their political or educational activities in the face of constant and often petty irritations on the part of government.[14]

These irritations and annoyances were cumulatively disheartening and debilitating, but were they capable of becoming rallying cries for revolution in the face of apathy or indifference on the part of much of society, especially in the provinces, and, above all, in the face of the gulf of hostility, fear, or incomprehension which divided the political opposition of the educated from the anger of the urban masses and the sullen discontent of the peasantry? Russia, as Stolypin had once put it, was dissatisfied with herself, she was morbidly irritable, on edge, full of symptoms of a deep-rooted distemper, but was she ready to translate irritation, dissatisfaction, uneasiness, into a revolutionary onslaught on the tsarist regime? And would the country follow the political opposition of 'society' in such an onslaught?

There could be no certainty on that point, for Russians might well ask whether their crisis was one of growth or of decay. Which

13 Wladimir Weidlé, *Russia: Absent and Present* (New York, 1961), pp. 112–13; Stepun, *op. cit.*, I, pp. 306–7, 315–20.

14 I.V. Gessen, *V dvukh vekakh (Arkhiv russkoi revoliutsii,* vol. xxii, Berlin, 1937), pp. 316–18; Oldenburg, *op. cit.*, II, p. 110.

was the truer reflection of Russian reality? The political crisis, the prospect of another 1905 with the country united against the government? The social crisis, with the urban working class embittered alike by official persecution and what it felt to be unofficial indifference? Or was it the evidence of progress and improvement in the economy, in education, in the activity of local governments and agricultural cooperatives? Was there not reason to expect that political stagnation and social hostility would in time be overcome by the massive weight of the changes taking place in an expanding economy and society? Would not the political opposition, embracing ever more of the central portion of the political spectrum, carry the day over the government because it was supported by the general trend of the country's social and intellectual evolution? Might not the government retreat once more from an untenable position and yield to the moderate demands and aspirations of the vast majority of well-meaning, educated Russians, as Baron Rosen and others were urging it to do in order to forestall explosions from below?

There were those, then and later, who saw the possibility of such a development, of peaceful evolution or of a limited, primarily political, revolution that could be kept within bounds, yet serve to restore hope to the embittered masses as well as the pessimistic cultural elite. 'It seemed,' Alexander Kerensky wrote in 1934, 'as though the time was close at hand . . . when the reins of government would be transferred into the hands of the democracy which was now mature.' Kerensky's congenital optimism, his retrospective confidence that Russia's rapid economic advance had to lead to new political advances, and 'that the revolutionary process was bound to come to its logical conclusion,' was shared by a former Social-Democratic deputy of the second Duma, Grigori Aleksinsky. Aleksinsky, a defencist, wrote in November 1914 that the crisis through which Russia had been passing when war began had been difficult but salutary, giving promise of a favourable outcome: 'The political emancipation of the Russian people was not, in the words of one of our proverbs, "behind the mountains".'[15]

More recently, Professor Alexander Gerschenkron and the late Michael Karpovich expressed the view that a peaceful solution of Russia's many and difficult problems was by no means excluded,

[15] Alexander Kerensky, *The Crucifixion of Liberty* (New York, 1934), pp. 184–5; G. Alexinsky, Letter to *The Nation* (London), 14 November 1914.

that the political struggle for a general and equal franchise and a cabinet responsible to the Duma had not made the labour movement more revolutionary but had helped to move it in the direction of reformism, and that from the point of view of economic development, revolution was not a foregone conclusion. 'In this sense,' Mr Gerschenkron concludes, 'it seems plausible to say that Russia on the eve of the war was well on the way toward a Westernization or, perhaps more precisely, a Germanization of its industrial growth.' And in Professor Karpovich's opinion it was the war, not the pre-war crisis, that made revolution probable while human folly made it inevitable.[16]

It is the shock of war that is usually taken to have led not only to a temporary suspension of the crises which held Russia in their grip, but also to have created the opportunity – if only the government had seized it – of their permanent solution. The astonishing absence of vocal dissent or large-scale disturbance when war came, the outpouring of patriotism by most of the regime's critics, surprised even them, leading in some cases to a reappraisal of the pre-war situation. Thus, Kerensky came to believe that the 'enthusiasm of the masses for the war' was the direct consequence of the new forms of political and social life introduced in 1905 and that through them and through participation in the country's 'wholesome, healthy' economy, workers and peasants had at last been integrated into the national community.[17] What appeared to be a promise of harmony giving way to conflicts of class, nationalities, and parties, had consciously or unconsciously made these conflicts seem less severe and divisive than they had seemed before August 1914. The moving tableau of vast crowds kneeling before their Tsar in Palace Square, of genuine and spontaneous demonstrations of loyalty and patriotism in the cities, of an end to strikes, doubts, and disorders, is indispensable to any assumption of Russia's peaceful evolution or her avoidance of the cataclysm that tore her apart in 1917 and after. Yet there is need to re-examine Russian reactions to the war in order to see whether such assumptions are warranted

[16] Alexander Gerschenkron, 'Problems and Patterns of Russian Economic Development', in C.E. Black, ed., *The Transformation of Russian Society* (Cambridge, Mass., 1960); Michael Karpovich, *Imperial Russia, 1801–1917* (New York, 1932), pp. 93–4.

[17] Kerensky, *op. cit.*, pp. 192–6.

and also to find what light they may shed on the pre-war crises and their probable outcome.

The picture sketched above – to be found in the accounts of opponents as well as supporters of the war and the regime – contains false notes which would give rise to doubt even without conflicting testimony. Does it seem at all likely 'that the veriest peasant felt the peril of Russia and of his brother Slavs in Serbia'; that on 28 July, in St Petersburg, 'a dangerous strike ended as if by some spontaneous impulse, that the workers returned to the mills shouting "Long live Serbia"' or worked overtime without thought of extra compensation? Who indeed, to echo the wonder of Rodzianko, the Duma President, and others, were those people marching with songs and banners to the Serbian legation and the Winter Palace or cheering on the troops as they passed the factories? Were they really the very workmen who had been on the point of an armed rising a few days earlier and now told Rodzianko that it had all been part of a family quarrel, pressure upon the Duma to speed reforms? 'But now all Russia is involved. We have rallied to our Tsar as to our emblem, and we shall follow him for the sake of victory over the Germans.' Those who described the crowds as being seized by hysteria or emotional intoxication rather than a conscious patriotism, or spoke of the people's quiet, sober acceptance of war and suffering as inevitable, reflected the popular mood more accurately. Yet theirs was still an incomplete rendering of the state of feeling of the masses in town and country.[18]

'Even in the beginning,' wrote the Chairman of the Military Commission of the Duma, 'I did not think that a certain access of patriotism, which at the moment of the declaration of war developed among the people of the capital, was any measure of the actual attitude of the nation.' This was without doubt true of the villages, from which came few reports of rejoicing and where, at best, there was passive obedience. There was no major trouble in the countryside during the first months of war, although the chief of the General Staff's Mobilization Section spoke of 'significant disturbances' among tens of thousands of reservists in four pro-

[18] See, for example F.P. Chambers, *The War Behind the War, 1914–1918* (London, 1939), p. 5; S.I. Shidlovsky, *Vospominaniia* (Berlin, 1923), II, p. 14; M.W. Rodzjanko, *Erinnerungen* (Berlin, 1926), p. 97 ff.; A. Lobanov-Rostovsky, *The Grinding Mill* (New York, 1935), pp. 17, 20; Bertram Wolfe, 'War Comes to Russia', *Russian Review*, April 1963; N.N. Golovine, *The Russian Army in the World War* (New Haven, 1931), p. 201.

vinces, and Soviet historians report 80 outbreaks in 42 provinces during July. But the significance of such figures is as difficult to assess as the specific cause or object of the peasants' turbulence, particularly in the absence of precise statistics on its extent and duration, and without comparable data for the months and years before mobilization. It takes no special insight or knowledge, however, to realize that it was foolish or ignorant to speak of Russian peasants as inspired to take up arms by the conviction that Germany was the aggressor from whom the Russian soldier – 'holding himself to be the protector of oppressed Slavonic nations' – had to rescue his 'little brothers' and his own country. One must doubt whether 'the connection was one absolutely clear to the common sense of the Russian masses'.[19] Many contemporaries speak rather of profound bewilderment on the part of the peasants as to what the war was all about and what concern it was of theirs. They speak of sullen resignation or discontent, of the absence of an informed patriotism which was more than mechanical or passing and could embrace the state or conceive of a just war against other Christian nations, especially one so remote as Germany. They record grumblings of anger, mutterings against the 'masters', as if these were responsible for the war, and the drawing of a line between themselves and 'them'. 'To believe that the immense mass of the population of the Empire – let alone the peasantry which had to furnish the bulk of the reserve forces, mobilized and torn from their labours in the middle of the harvest season – would be to any appreciable extent affected by such warlike enthusiasm, could only betoken a profoundly erroneous interpretation of the real feelings of the people.'[20]

Would the situation be very different among the urban masses? There is no reason to question the fact of manifestations of Slavic

[19] Golovine, op. cit., pp. 122; 205; Sergei Dobrorolski, Die Mobilmachung der russischen Armee (Berlin, 1922), p. 32; Iu.N. Danilov, Rossiia v mirovoi voine (Berlin, 1924), II, p. 111; B.M. Kochakov, 'Sotsialny sostav tsarskoi armii v period imperializma', in Iz istorii imperializma v Rossii (Moscow–Leningrad, 1959), p. 358; A.M. Anfimov, ed., Krestianskoe dvizhenie v Rossii v gody pervoi mirovoi voiny (Moscow–Leningrad, 1965), pp. 5–151.

[20] Stepun, op. cit., I, pp. 347–9; Graevenitz, op. cit., p. 35; A.I. Denikin, Ocherki russkoi smuty (Paris, 1921), I, p. 19; W.S. Woytinski, Stormy Passage (New York, 1961), p. 223; Allan Monkhouse, Moscow, 1911–1933 (London, 1933), p. 50; V.I. Gurko, Features and Figures of the Past (Stanford, 1939), p. 538; Roman R. Rosen, Forty Years of Diplomacy (London, 1922), II, p. 174; V.V. Karrik, 'Voina i revoliutsiia', Golos minuvshego, April/June 1918, p. 6.

solidarity and Russian nationalism in the cities from the time of the Austrian ultimatum to Serbia. Yet frequent assertions as to their spontaneity, and even more of a universality of participation in them by all classes, are not convincing. 'No one can say that the people were driven to the Winter Palace, or that their demonstration was organized by the police. No, one felt that the whole population was becoming as one and in a general access of emotion wanted to throw itself upon the enemy.'[21] There were sceptics and opponents of the war who thought that the authorities had taken a hand in arranging some of these processions with their banners and icons. When President Poincaré passed through St Petersburg, almost a month after Sarajevo, his reception, the French ambassador noted in his diary, was enthusiastic. 'The police had seen to that. At each corner, a group of poor devils shout "hurrah" under the eyes of a policeman.' On 4 August, M. Paléologue had not yet abandoned his scepticism, although it was weakening. Workers, priests, peasants, students, domestics, shop clerks who passed before his embassy all day shouting 'Vive la France!' seemed sincere. But when a mob sacked and destroyed the German embassy unhindered, he asked himself what role the police had played in staging these parades which passed his windows in such numbers and at such regular intervals.[22]

The German ambassador noted that there was no sign of public agitation in the capital the day Austria presented her ultimatum to Serbia, nor during the next few days. 'Although 24 hours have passed since the order for general mobilization was published,' Count Pourtalès recorded in his diary, 'St Petersburg was still remarkably quiet on 1 August.' Such patriotic demonstrations as there were took place in evening and night-time hours and were, he was convinced, anything but spontaneous. One passer-by learned from a group of half-drunken patriots that their pay was three rubles per evening and that after having visited the Austrian embassy, they had orders to proceed to the Serbian and German ones. The Spanish ambassador saw neither fervour nor eagerness among the men who had been called to the colours, or among those who accompanied them as they were marched through the town, and his impression of silent despondency was shared by Pourtalès.

[21] A.S. Lukomsky, *Vospominaniia* (Berlin, 1922), I, p. 53.
[22] Paléologue, *op. cit.*, I, pp. 6, 51; V.M. Vonliarliarsky, *Moi Vospominaniia* (Berlin, 1939), p. 214.

'There was no ostentation and show about any of those departures, no flags or military bands, and very little cheering,' wrote Sir George Buchanan's daughter, who had no thought of questioning the justness of the war or Germany's responsibility for it. It was not prejudice alone that caused Pourtalès to contrast what he had seen in St Petersburg with the holiday mood of Berlin.[23]

It was, of course, possible to interpret the absence of noisy flag-waving as calm determination and quiet composure, to point to the nearly total cessation of strikes – in the capital there were only 10 of them, mostly economic, between 1 August and the end of the year, with 4159 participants – and to interpret the marching and singing that did take place as proof that 'the masses had been caught up by the enthusiasm and fevers of war as much as – nay, more unreservedly than the leaders'.[24] But if there was a widespread outburst of patriotic exaltation, it was neither deep nor lasting. The numbing shock of war's reality, an attitude of watchful waiting, fear of reprisals made even more severe by the state of war – these are enough to explain acquiescence and the end of open defiance by some, while others unquestionably welcomed temporarily the heady hysteria that broke the monotony and drabness, promising excitement, adventure and, at any rate, change. Such expectations were, however, more common among students and intellectuals, politicians and solid citizens, than among most workers and peasants who did not, in all likelihood, make any conscious decision for the defence of the fatherland or against it. With some modification, a conservative bureaucrat's summation of the case appears apt: 'Although the war excited neither patriotism nor indignation among the peasants and factory workers, it deeply stirred the patriotic sentiments of the educated classes.'[25]

[23] J.L.F.W. Pourtalès, *Am Scheidewege.* . . . (Charlottenburg, 1919), pp. 16, 26, 57, 80; Gustav von Lambsdorff, ed., *Die Militärbevollmächtigten Kaiser Wilhelms II am Zarenhofe, 1904–1914* (Berlin, 1937), p. 436; W.K. von Korostowetz, *Lenin im Hause der Väter* (Berlin, 1928), p. 146; V. Sukhomlinov, *Vospominaniia* (Berlin, 1924), p. 303; Anibal de Cartagena, *Erinnerungen an meine Botschafterzeit in Russland 1914* (Berlin, 1934), p. 112; Meriel Buchanan, *Petrograd* (London, 1918), p. 22; S.P. Melgunov, *Na putiakh k dvortsovomu perevorotu* (Paris, 1931), pp. 29–33.

[24] Bertram Wolfe, 'War Comes to Russia-in-Exile', *Russian Review*, October 1961, p. 308; I.I. Krylova, 'K voprosu o statistike stachek petrogradskikh rabochikh v gody pervoi mirovoi voiny', in *Iz istorii imperializma v Rossii*, p. 431.

[25] Gurko, *op. cit.*, p. 538.

One may question the sweeping nature of the generalization, but it does appear that 'society', including the parliamentary opposition, rallied, if not to the government, then to the defence of the fatherland; in the circumstances, the effect was much the same. It is this quite unexpected closing of ranks after the bitter political confrontation of the spring that created the impression of unity and patriotic affirmation extending throughout all sectors of the population, demonstrating how much even Russian observers took the statements of politicians and publicists to be representative of the nation. They had been so much preoccupied with the political contest that the sudden and dramatic reconciliation of the contestants must have appeared to them as an almost miraculous escape from a hopeless situation. During the first six months of 1914, commented a liberal review in January 1915, the oppositional tendencies and the discontent of society grew steadily; they stopped at once with the outbreak of war, 'which like a magic knife divided the two halves of the year ... bringing the nation to its senses. What had appeared unattainable in time of peace, was achieved'.[26]

If a concern with formal politics tends to lead to an overvaluation of its weight in the life of a community, how much more was this true in Russia, where politics was conducted on an extremely narrow base by a small number of people and excluded most of the lower classes from active participation. When the Minister of Foreign Affairs told the Emperor that 'unless he yielded to the popular demand and unsheathed the sword in Serbia's behalf, he would run the risk of a revolution and perhaps the loss of his throne',[27] he was not merely guilty of such overvaluation but of a constriction of perspective which let him see the danger of a political revolution by the vocal and politically active sectors of society as more serious than the danger of a revolution from the *narod*. His reactionary colleague at the Ministry of the Interior, not otherwise noted for his perspicacity, saw things more clearly. He warned the Council of Ministers of a repetition of the consequences that war with Japan had caused, and when he was brought the mobilization order for

26 Oldenburg, *op. cit.*, II, p. 160.
27 Rosen, *op. cit.*, II, p. 173; D.I. Abrikossow, *Revelations of a Russian Diplomat* (Seattle, 1964), p. 225.

his signature said: 'War cannot be popular among the broad masses of the people who are more receptive to ideas of revolution than of victory over Germany.'[28]

However their followers or presumed followers in town and country may have reacted, those of Russia's political and intellectual leaders who were not captives of the government or irreconcilable revolutionaries accepted war willingly and in some cases gladly. If there was constraint or reservation in their attitude, it did not appear in their speeches, their conduct, or their writings. There may have been calculation in this acceptance, a hope that in a hard war, and one moreover fought on the side of democratic allies, tsarism would have to make its peace with the political opposition and turn to it for help and support or, at the very least, reward it at the end of hostilities for its loyalty. Yet if the opposition held such expectations, it did little to make them known. It exacted neither concessions nor promises from a government or ruler who spoke of strengthening in this hour of trial 'the ties that unite Tsar and people' and of setting aside internal disputes, but could be trusted to do neither.

During 1914, the Duma met for only one sitting – on 8 August – and if the members believed that the brevity of the session was harmful and its harmony specious, they gave no public sign of it. The Minister of Finance, Bark, asserted that the government, for its part, was perfectly prepared during this period to keep the legislature in session and have it discuss and decide measures demanded by the war, as well as general policy, but that Rodzianko assured him of the majority's preference for only a brief meeting. In time of war the administration would be overburdened by weighty decisions and unable to conduct its business in a normal way. 'We shall only hinder you; it is better therefore to dismiss us altogether until the end of hostilities.' Miliukov, the leader of the constitutional opposition in the Duma, did not go quite so far, but in his speech of 8 August called on his party's friends and followers to put aside their quarrels with the government and to remember that their first duty was to preserve Russia one and indivisible and to defend her position in the first rank of the great powers. 'In this struggle we are all as one; we present no

---

[28] E.D. Chermensky, *Istoriia SSSR: period imperializma* (Moscow, 1959), p. 414.

conditions or demands; we simply throw upon the scales of battle our firm determination to overcome the aggressor.'[29]

Newspapers, journals, town councils, scholarly societies, poets, liberal and minority deputies, echoed Miliukov. When, before very long, it became clear that the regime had not been moved to change its ways by this show of support, disappointment and dismay set in. Among the Kadets, these led in September to secret discussions which weighed an address to the throne. It was to point out the unhappy mood of society, ask for an end to its further alienation by the government, demand an amnesty, a change of course vis à vis the subject nationalities, and the recall of the Duma. In the event, no address was agreed upon or submitted and the project was dropped. In the central committee of the party only Fedor Rodichev wondered whether unqualified support was wise and whether, in fact, it was possible to win the war with such a government. Even its enemies found it difficult to conceive the stupidity and incompetence of which it was still to show itself capable. Until this became evident – and as long as there were still victories and the defeats were not yet catastrophic – Russian 'society', for a wide variety of emotional, intellectual, and political reasons, was either defencist or actively pro-war. At least during 1914, this brought some bridging of the gulf between government and nation, for to defend the latter meant, nolens volens, an increase of support for the former.[30]

On the radical Left, the picture was more complex. There was no unconditional support for the war, and when the Duma voted on the war credits, Bolsheviks, Mensheviks, and the Labour group walked out. But such action, as statements made by Kerensky (for the *trudoviki*) and the Menshevik Khaustov (for all the Social-Democrats) demonstrated, did not necessarily mean defeatism. In very similar terms, the two socialists vowed that the Russian democracy and proletariat would defend the native land and culture

29 P. Bark, 'Vospominaniia', *Vozrozhdenie*, March 1965, p. 87; see also Rodzianko's testimony in *Padenie tsarskogo rezhima* (Moscow–Leningrad, 1927), VII, pp. 153, 157, and Sir Bernard Pares, *The Fall of the Russian Monarchy* (New York, 1961), p. 188. Conflicting evidence is to be found in Shidlovsky, *op. cit.*, II, p. 21, who states that the majority of the Duma were for continuing in session. The speeches of Miliukov, Kerensky, and others in Golder, *op. cit.*, pp. 33–6.
30 Paul Gronsky and Nicholas Astrov, *The War and the Russian Government* (New Haven, 1929), pp. 27, 166; Melgunov, *op. cit.*, p. 14 ff.; B.B. Grave, ed., *Burzhuaziia nakanune fevralskoi revoliutsii* (Moscow–Leningrad, 1927), pp. 2–3.

from any incursions, from wherever they might come, and having defended their country, would set it free. Some of the most famous figures of the Russian revolutionary movement – Vladimir Burtsev, Kropotkin, Plekhanov – called upon their comrades to put the national before the class struggle. There had been nothing like it at the time of the Japanese war, but with Germany the enemy, it was different. Lenin might fume in his Swiss exile, but even among his Bolsheviks, patriotism or defencism took their toll. The proletariat, recalled a Petrograd Bolshevik, was abandoned at the beginning of the war by all its intellectual leaders, while the party's Paris centre disintegrated, with some of its members enlisting in the French army. The story among the Social-Revolutionaries was much the same, with their centre at Paris suffering a similar fate to that of the Bolsheviks. Inside Russia, none of the party's organizations had declared for defence, but there were large-scale defections to the pro-war side on the part of the intelligentsia. Particularly in Petrograd, the Social-Revolutionary workingmen were abandoned by the majority of their educated comrades. What remained of uncompromising defeatism, pacifism, or internationalism was silent or barely managed to survive abroad.[31]

The attitude taken by most of the regime's vocal and prominent critics created the impression of national and class solidarity to be found in many accounts of Russia in the summer and autumn of 1914. It was reinforced by the cultural elite's affirmation of the war, a wave of momentary exaltation as powerful as the hysteria that swept lesser men into the streets or against German shops. There was a tone almost of relief in many of the essays and poems occasioned by the war, a welcoming of it for having freed Russia of narrowness and pettiness and for opening new perspectives on greatness. Some viewed war as a spiritual awakening, the end of a moral crisis which had long separated the intelligentsia from the people. Others saw in it a chance to preserve Russia from the spreading infection of bourgeois secularism and materialism.

[31] Wolfe, 'War Comes to Russia-in-Exile', *loc. cit.;* Olga Gankin and H.H. Fisher, eds., *The Bolsheviks and the World War* (Stanford, 1940), pp. 134–7, 267; S.I. Murashov, ed., *Partiia bolshevikov v gody pervoi mirovoi voiny* (Moscow, 1963), p. 23; M.T. Florinsky, *The End of the Russian Empire* (New York, 1961), pp. 160–2; O.H. Radkey, *The Agrarian Foes of Bolshevism* (New York, 1958), p. 67 ff.; Melgunov, *op. cit.*, pp. 18–20; P.N. Krestinsky, 'Porazhencheskaia kampaniia bolshevikov vo vremia voiny', *Byloe*, kn. 47 (no. II, new series, 1933).

Bulgakov, the Marxist turned Orthodox theologian, hoped that Russia's sickness of spirit, which stemmed from that infection, would be cured as its source too was purified in the fires of war. 'The war is destroying . . . the roofs of the cosy cottages in which mankind has housed itself, leaving it again under . . . the dome of Heaven. Europe is still spiritually alive, the bourgeois spirit has proved to be a disease which her vital organs have escaped. Such are the glad tidings brought by the war.' Russia would at last be able to recover her soul, her true Russian and Slavic identity, and turn her back on that empty, imitative Westernism that had once and for all died under the blows of the Teutonic fist.[32]

The intellectual historian Mikhail Gershenzon spoke of the collective will to victory as a means to submerge for a time the play of individual energies and strivings, while Peter Struve hoped that state and nation, Great Russia and Holy Russia, might at last become one. A whole pleiad of writers – Leonid Andreev, Gorodetsky, Remizov, Sologub, Balmont, Severianin, Gumilev, Kuprin, and others – felt in varying degrees the call of Slavdom, of battle, of Russia, of fusion with her simple peasant soldiers, and some of them answered that call by one or another kind of service.[33]

There were not many who stood aside in the first months of the war. Blok, who had foretold doom and destruction, was repelled and horrified when it became reality and would have no part of it. Love of country took with him the form of sadness for all its victims. The poet Maximilian Voloshin, sobered by the calamity of civilization, asked 'that I cease not to love my enemy nor start to hate my brother.' Zinaida Hippius tried in vain to convince the St Petersburg Religious-Philosophical Society that any war is a debasement of humanity, but in the debate that followed, members who urged its 'religious acceptance' prevailed. The Literary-Artistic Circle of Moscow expelled Germans even before the government ordered such action, and there were philosophers who proved that Kant and Krupp were one and the same thing. Russians recovered more quickly from this psychosis than Frenchmen

32 Novgorotsev, *op. cit.*, pp. 167–8.

33 D. Maslianenko, 'Russkie poety o sovremennoi voine', *Istoricheskii vestnik*, January 1915; Orest Tsekhnovitser, *Literatura i mirovaia voina, 1914–1918* (Moscow, 1938), passim.; S. Makovskiy, 'Nicolas Gumilev', *Cahiers du monde russe et soviétique*, no. 2, 1962, p. 206; Ilya Ehrenburg, *People and Life* (London, 1961), pp. 119, 124.

or Germans, but it was surprising nonetheless, not least to themselves.[34]

In the light of the immediate effect which the outbreak of war had on the Russian crisis, it may be useful to look again at its state in the first half of the year and to ask what its future might have been if the country had remained at peace. The question, to be sure, is an artificial one, for it is impossible to exclude from history what did indeed take place. But such an inquiry may help our understanding of the elements which made up the troubled state of Russia, and of their likely fate and conduct, in peace or war.

The political crisis, which loomed so large in the eyes of contemporaries, was probably most readily susceptible of settlement. The attitude taken after July by the liberal and moderate opposition to the government suggests that the gulf between them was perhaps not unbridgeable, that an accommodation with at least part of the opposition was possible, and that it might have been achieved by relatively minor concessions on the part of the administration. The positions of the contestants look less rigid than appeared to be the case before July, with neither side as determined or unified as talk of an impending clash would lead one to believe. The reactionaries in the cabinet and their adherents had no love for the Duma, and would gladly have done without it. Yet neither before nor during the war was there enough resolution or confidence among them to dismiss it or, for that matter, ideological commitment to such a course. Maklakov, believed most favourable to such action, had recoiled from it; nor was it impossible that he and other reactionary ministers might be sacrificed in case of need, as was to happen in 1915.[35]

The appointment of Goremykin, taken at the time to be symbolic of the government's hostility to representative institutions, was thought by many observers to be purely temporary. It was widely expected that the Minister of Agriculture, Krivoshein, would shortly replace him and that he would heed the Tsar's injunction (contained in a rescript to Goremykin) to unify the

---

[34] Oldenburg, op. cit., II, pp. 160-2; Donald Lowrie, Rebellious Prophet: A Life of Nicolai Berdyaev (New York, 1960), p. 141; Melgunov, op. cit., p. 13.

[35] V.P. Semennikov, Monarkhiia pered krusheniem (Moscow–Leningrad, 1927), pp. 89-91; S.P. Beletsky, 'Vospominaniia', Arkhiv russkoi revoliutsii, XII, p. 37; Bernard Pares to Grey, 13 January 1914 PRO, FO 371, Piece no. 2090, Document 3312.

cabinet and seek collaboration with the Duma. Krivoshein was said to be a liberal and popular in Duma circles, or a conservative who saw the need for cooperation with society. It is difficult to fix his political allegiances, or even to determine whether he had any, but his reputation and the fact that he was careful to maintain contact with the opposition created expectations that by July he would initiate a more liberal course and pacify the critics. One cannot, of course, be sure of this, and Krivoshein is reported by one source as opposing the continued sitting of the Duma after its one-day ceremonial meeting. But such uncertainty (which conflicting testimony raises also about other members of court and cabinet), only reinforces a suspicion that while Krivoshein may not have represented a clear alternative to reaction, reaction itself was not clear about its goals or single-minded in their pursuit.[36]

Lack of unity and of a unified political complexion in the government make it possible to envisage a change of course for the better. Lack of unity on the part of the opposition creates doubt that the only way out of the impasse between the state power and public opinion was either a revolution or a reactionary coup. The Tsar, while making no secret in private of his irritation with the parliamentary opposition, continued to declare in public his commitment to the reforms of 1905. This presented his political opponents with insuperable difficulties in achieving unity among themselves and their followers. A call for full adherence to the October Manifesto and the Fundamental Laws would not have been enough to assure joint action with the revolutionaries, while there was disagreement even among the Kadets as to how far or how hard one should push for such a goal. They were not prepared to cut all ties to the cabinet, as is shown by their participation in secret meetings on the defence budget from which the Left was excluded. And chances of converting the two anti-government votes of the spring into a more permanent opening to the Right were almost non-existent. The Duma's right wing (some 150 deputies) could be counted upon to be subservient to whatever ministry was in power; a portion of the Centre group and the Octobrists (perhaps 100 members in all) were satisfied with the status quo, while a

[36] Czernin to Berchtold, 17 January and 28 March 1914; Szapari to Berchtold, 22 February 1914, HHStA; Buchanan to Grey, 23 February, 9 March, 21 March, 1914, PRO, FO 371, Piece no. 2091, Documents 8009, 8012, 10329, 12988; Hoetzsch, *op. cit.*, pp. 136, 178; Michael von Taube, *Der grossen Katastrophe entgegen*, 2nd ed. (Leipzig, 1937), pp. 297–9; Gurko, *op. cit.*, p. 542.

third group, consisting of Octobrists, some Progressists, and right-wing Kadets, were ready to settle for the 'regime of the 3rd of June' (i.e. 1905 as amended and restricted by Stolypin) if only the government gave some sign of moderating its conduct. This left only the main body of the Kadets and Progressists in principled opposition. This was the 'responsible' opposition (as Miliukov called it), which was supposedly capable of trying conclusions with the government, of engaging it in a contest from which one or the other would have had to emerge the victor. Even with the support of the Left (28 deputies) this was not likely. The Duma opposition lacked unity and strength and if its growth in early 1914 foreshadowed the Progressive Bloc of 1915, the latter also showed by its moderation what the price of unity would be.[37]

As far as the wider opposition of society is concerned, it too looks less formidable from a post-July perspective, with as much political lethargy or indifference as there was of conscious disturbance or sympathy for the opposition parties. Miliukov himself, who had viewed the anti-government votes in the Duma as some kind of turning point, in September looked upon the war as a boon for having shaken the public out of its political apathy. The quick rally to the side of the regime in July 1914 by most of the educated public is no guarantee that the political crisis *would* have been settled; the further conduct of court and cabinet suggest rather the opposite. It does indicate, however, that it *could* have been settled with a little more intelligence and flexibility on the part of the administration. In that sense it *was* human folly that made revolution inevitable, not the clash of immovable forces and determined antagonists.

Taking reactions to the war as a starting point, one must conclude that the social crisis would have been vastly more difficult to compose than the political one. Even if they had been possessed of greater tact and skill, Russia's rulers would have found it difficult with the means at hand to remove the grievances of workers and peasants with speed, and without deepening the political crisis by infringing the economic interests of the privileged classes. There are numerous indications that the militancy of the urban working classes had outrun the organizational capabilities of the leftist leaders, and mass discontent was bound to increase with the bur-

[37] A. Petrishchev, 'Khronika vnutrennei zhizni', *Russkoe bogatstvo*, January 1914.

250

dens imposed by war. The splits which developed among socialist politicians over the issue of the war reflect their own uncertainty about the mood of the masses, with those remaining in Russia (and presumably possessed of a greater awareness of what that mood was) more opposed to the war than those abroad. The factory elections of September 1915, although later reversed, demonstrate how deepseated was worker distrust of authority and privilege.

Nor, as Mr Haimson has reminded us, is there a basis for confidence that a non-revolutionary trade-unionism could have directed the workers' resentment into safe reformist channels. While trade unions became legal in 1906, they continued to be harassed by the police, restricted to the purely local level, opposed by the majority of employers, numerically weak and incapable therefore of offering the best means for improving the workers' social and economic position. In spite of the improvement in money and real wages since 1909, industrial wages remained at a level that was barely adequate to meet the basic necessities of food, shelter, and clothing. Any continued improvement in the non-agricultural sector of the economy which would not have been matched by a very substantial improvement in wages would only have underscored for the workers their continued exclusion from the general prosperity. The war – with its food shortages, inflationary pressures, and high profits – did not create this sense of exclusion and bitterness; it deepened it as well as the feeling of alienation from 'society'.

There is perhaps less reason to view the passive or negative reactions of the peasantry to the war as a clue to their overall attitudes than is true of their brothers in the factories. The peasants had been before July neither so rebellious nor so victimized as these, and even with fewer grievances than they actually did have, would hardly have responded to war enthusiastically. Yet they too felt a sense of exclusion from and a hostility to 'society' which the war exacerbated and made more visible. It showed itself, for example, in the peasants' refusal, after February 1917, to elect members of the intelligentsia to canton and village committees, even those who had worked closely with them in the cooperatives and schools. Reliable information about peasant attitudes and conduct is scarce on the ground and often contradictory, ranging from statements about the increasing frequency of disturbances in the years 1910–14 to estimates of their marked decline during these same years. It does not seem likely, however, that the Stolypin reform could have furnished the answer to peasant unrest in a reasonable period of time.

A reform which may require 100 (Kutler) or even 40 to 45 years (Hoetzsch) for its work of pacification has doubtful title to that name, especially if its authors expect during its execution to be freed of the disturbances which it is designed to correct. A recent student of the agrarian reform has concluded that its operations were slowing down well before the war, that it dealt least effectively with those areas of the country where peasant distress was greatest, and that it was resisted by the majority of the rural population, sometimes with great bitterness. 'In sum, the policy of land settlement at no time looked like providing an effective solution for Russia's peasant problem. . . . It must, in the circumstances, appear more than doubtful whether the results achieved would have been significantly different if Stolypin's legislation had operated for twenty years instead of nine.' Or as the Social-Revolutionaries, in the person of Victor Chernov, realized – as long as the estates of the nobility were excluded from the reform, there would be trouble in the villages and the opportunity for making more.[38]

The response which Russia's cultural elite made to the war was another revelation of the chasm that divided it from the urban and rural masses. It tells us little, however, about the spiritual malaise which was supposedly but another dimension of Russia's political and social crisis. No artist or intellectual can be indifferent to the tremors by which his environment is shaken. He may, indeed, register them more sensitively than most of his contemporaries. But what he makes of his perceptions in his art or thought, and how immediate a reflection his work is of social or political reality, is another and most complicated matter. The hallmark of Russian culture in its Silver Age was precisely its rich diversity, and any attempt to classify it as either optimistic or pessimistic would do it violence. The facts of biography, of inner feelings, may well be as important here as those of history, of outer forces, and it is only the examination of their interplay in many individual instances that would justify an attempt at summary judgments. Even then, the evidence will not always be conclusive, as the case of Blok, for example, indicates. There are his diaries for the years 1911 to

[38] W.E. Mosse, 'Stolypin's Villages', *Slavonic and East European Review*, June 1965, pp. 273–4; Hoetzsch, *op. cit.*, p. 174; Radkey, *op. cit.*, p. 83.

1913; but there is also his confident poem 'The New America' (dated 12 December 1913) with its vision of Russia transformed. It is doubtful, moreover, that cultural despair (where it existed) was a specifically Russian rather than a general European phenomenon, for no country's 'high' culture was more finely attuned to universal currents and expressions than that of Russia. After all, even America, that model of robust hope, had its 'cataclysmic thinkers'.[39] This is not to argue that the study of thought and letters furnishes no clues to the temper of an epoch or people. But these must be used with care and avoid a too rigid synchronization of political, social, and cultural phenomena.

It is possible, therefore, to view the spiritual or cultural crisis (if there was one) in a larger, European context, and not as a necessary outgrowth of Russia's social and political difficulties. As for the latter, it appears that the political opposition of the classes lacked coherence, that it could not join forces with the disaffected masses, and that their mutual alienation robbed the classes of confidence while confirming the masses in their hostility to all of privileged society, including its liberal sector. Under such circumstances, there was little prospect of a common front against tsarism which could exact true political liberty and representative government. Nor, for its part, did reaction have enough strength or confidence to impose a solution. Regarding the social crisis, Mr Haimson may be right in saying that, even without war, the possibility existed of a radical overturn of the kind Russia was to experience in October 1917. But in order to judge of its probability, one would have to know the relative strength of the forces available and ready to make use of or to resist the social explosion which made October possible. In the course of such an inquiry, one might discover still other possible issues to the Russian crisis, issues which would have brought neither a major advance towards constitutional government nor the outburst of peasant and worker violence that 1917 was to witness.

[39] F.C. Jaher, *Doubters and Dissenters; Cataclysmic Thought in America, 1885–1918* (New York, 1964).

Russians in Germany: 1900–1914

Robert C. Williams

In the summer of 1914 Europeans went to war not only at the urging of those crowned rulers, diplomats, army officers and industrialists who had set the stage for the conflagration that followed, but also for their own causes. Even when public opinion did not decisively alter public policy, it helped to convince policy-makers that their decisions enjoyed popular support. Wide-spread Russophobia was an important element in German public opinion in the decade before the war. Germans went off to war in the East in 1914 with the feeling that they were at best defending Western civilization against Eastern barbarism and at least defending economic progress against political autocracy. Russia was a political anachronism staving off the forces of revolution; as such she symbolized a bastion of despotism for the German left (except for a brief moment in 1905), and the threat of revolutionary Slavic upheaval for the establishment. Even the German middle-class reading public, with its new editions of Dostoevsky, Turgenev, Gogol, and Tolstoi, saw in Russia a fantasy-world both exotic and dangerous.

One of the most important contributing factors to widespread fear of Russia in Germany after 1900 was the mass migration of disaffected political refugees from Russia into Germany. Since the second quarter of the eighteenth century Germany had exerted a powerful cultural attraction on Russian intellectuals. But increasingly after 1881 Germany became a centre of Russian exile political activity as well. The newer generation of Russians in Germany came for two main reasons: to obtain a professional education unobtainable in Russia, and to carry on political activity suspect at home. Highly critical of the regime from which they had fled, these emigrés quite naturally passed along their own interpretation of events in Russia to those in Germany who cared to listen. Equally important, the fact that a large percentage of the emigration was Jewish and that emigré political activity was largely left-wing or, at best, liberal, made the emigration itself a distasteful symbol of Russia in the German mind.

The two most important groups within the prewar emigration were in fact not Russians but Baltic Germans and Jews. Both had deep ties to Germany of culture, language, and family, and both were at the same time in sharp political opposition to the Russian government. This combination of an ability to assimilate with relative ease into German life and a critical attitude toward the Russian autocracy brought them into no small prominence in German life as interpreters of Russia for German policy-makers and public opinion and as intermediaries for other Russians less familiar with Germany. Moreover, each came to symbolize a hostile 'Russia' to different segments of German society: the 'Baltic barons' represented the Russian autocracy to the German left; the Jews Russian radicalism to the conservatives, the middle class, and many socialists. Thus each contributed to prewar Russophobia in Germany both as hostile critics of Russia and as undesirable examples of Russians.

Until the 1890s Russia was a country of immigration, not emigration. Since the sixteenth century Europeans had come to Russia as military advisers, merchants, tutors, doctors, bureaucrats, court painters and architects. Often they were Germans. From 1828 to 1915 some 1,459,000 Germans had settled in Russia, representing 35·1 per cent of Russia's total immigration during that period. But in the 1880s and 1890s the repressive policies of the Russian government managed not only to stem the flow of immigrants into Russia but to increase sharply emigration from Russia. From 1860 to 1889 2,147,000 foreigners settled in Russia while 1,129,000 Russian citizens left the country; from 1890 to 1915 the process was reversed – while some 1,786,000 persons came to live in Russia, emigration rose steadily so that 3,348,000 people left Russia in these years.[1] Most of the new emigrés, nearly half of them Jews, settled not in Western Europe but in the United States. In Germany too there was a marked rise in immigration from Russia after 1881. The German census figures recorded

---

[1] V.V. Obolenskii (Osinskii), *Mezhdunarodnye i mezhkontinentalnye migratsii v dovoennoi Rossii i SSSR* (Moscow, 1928), 108, 110.

15,097 Russians living in Germany in 1880, 46,971 for 1900, 106,639 for 1905; by 1910 there were 137,697 Russians living in Germany – over half the total number in Western Europe.[2]

Not only was there a major political emigration of Russians to Germany after 1900; traditional cultural ties were also being caught up in prewar politics. The old marital relations between Russian and German royalty had once been the foundation of a conservative and anti-Polish alliance. They survived the diplomatic revolution precipitated by the Franco-Russian alliance of the 1890s unimpaired, but after 1900 German politicians were tempted to turn these old ties to political use.

After Alexander II married Princess Marie of Hesse-Darmstadt, members of the Russian royal family had come to Germany on numerous occasions. Many Romanovs became seasonal or permanent emigrés from Russia by marriage, Germanized or Anglicized considerably in thought, manners, and dress. In the 1870s the common stamping grounds for Russian royal visitors to Germany were the Schloss Heiligenberg in Hesse-Darmstadt and the nearby royal summer palace of the Dukes of Hesse-Kassel. But when Alexander's daughter Marie married Alfred, Duke of Edinburgh, in 1873, and her daughter Viktoria Melita married Grand Duke Ernst August of Hesse-Darmstadt in 1894, the locus of visits was extended to include Coburg, Karlsruhe, and a villa at Tegernsee south of Munich. Here in the decades before 1914 gathered the great clan of inter-married Russian, German, and English royalty to exchange the latest family news, to arrange future marriages, to gossip, and to enjoy an atmosphere of quiet isolation and cosy *Gemütlichkeit*. When Nicholas II married Alix of Hesse-Darmstadt in 1894 he became an intimate member of this little world.

It was not surprising that many Russian members of the royal family felt quite at home in Germany, despite ominous political developments. Grand Duke Kirill Vladimirovich, pretender to the Russian throne in the 1920s and 1930s, was surrounded by German maids, tutors, and relatives as a young man, and recalled that his aunt, Grand Duchess Alix of Saxe-Altenburg, 'always spoke German to us.'[3] Kirill himself was forced because of his

---

[2] *Statistik des deutschen Reichs* (Berlin, 1915), vol. 240, p. 153.
[3] Grand Duke Cyril, *My Life in Russia's Service – Then and Now* (London, 1939), p. 17.

marriage to his divorced cousin Viktoria to spend the years from 1905 to 1910 in exile at Coburg, where he indulged his passion for hunting and motor-cars. The Leuchtenbergs, a lesser branch of the Romanov family, spent considerable time before the war at their ancestral castle of Seeon in Bavaria; Duke Georg of Leuchtenberg lived there from 1906 until 1914 convalescing from wounds received during the Russo-Japanese War, and became fast friends with Duke Leopold of Bavaria. For many of these royal exiles Russia remained a land about which they knew all too little. 'We were brought up in a Fool's Paradise', one of them later admitted, 'carefully guarded from reality', so that even on visits to Russia they felt 'on guard, a little hostile, or anyhow watchful, so that we could not blend entirely nor feel quite at home'.[4]

After 1900 the family relationship between Russian and German royalty had diminishing influence on diplomacy. Some Germans continued to look back to the good old days of close Russo-German relations on the basis of dynastic intermarriage. Even in 1906 the German ambassador in St Petersburg, von Schoen, felt that 'at that time there was still reason to consider the close friendship which had existed for the last century between the reigning houses the strongest bond between Germany and Russia, as in the past'.[5] But German policy toward Russia was hardly determined by such sentimental considerations. 'The Russians will need us', predicted Friedrich von Holstein, head of the Wilhelmstrasse's Political Section, in 1895, 'before we will need them.'[6]

Accordingly, in the years before 1914 the bonds between the courts of Berlin and St Petersburg became a weapon of German policy, not its determinant. German pressure was no longer exerted on the level of official diplomacy but through the institution of personal military attachés of both Emperors which dated from the early nineteenth century. Two of these men, Major General Lambsdorff and naval attaché Hintze, were attached to the court of St Petersburg where they probably had a greater influence

[4] G. Botkin, *The Woman Who Rose Again* (N.Y., 1937), p. 64; Grand Duke Alexander, *Once a Grand Duke* (N.Y., 1932), pp. 151-3; 'Leikhtenbergskii gertsogskii dom', *Entsiklopedicheskii slovar* (Brockhaus-Efron) (St Petersburg, 189-), XVIIA, 506-7; Queen Marie of Roumania, *The Story of My Life* (London, 1934), I, 205, 217.

[5] Freiherr von Schoen, *The Memoirs of an Ambassador* (London, 1922), p. 32.

[6] Holstein to Hugo von Radolin, Berlin, 2 July 1895; N. Rich, M.H. Fischer, eds., *The Holstein Papers*, III (Cambridge, 1961), p. 528.

than the German ambassador. The German attachés in St Petersburg and the Russian naval attaché in Berlin, Captain Pauli, were the personal emissaries between William II and Nicholas II and the bearers of that touching exchange of letters known as the 'Willy-Nicky correspondence'. Lambsdorff, who served in this capacity from 1904 to 1914, was declared by William to be 'responsible for reports only to me personally, and is forbidden once for all to report or communicate with anybody else, either General staff or Foreign Office, or Chancellor'.[7] Similarly, William preferred dealing with his cousin through a Russian military attaché rather than the stout, somewhat pompous but amiable Russian ambassador in Berlin from 1895 to 1912, Count Nikolai Dmitrevich Osten-Sacken.

At first Holstein was annoyed by a separate correspondence between rulers which might interfere with policy as he saw it. But by the late 1890s the composing of the Willy–Nicky letters was in the firm hands of the Wilhelmstrasse.[8] The birthday congratulations, court gossip, and Easter eggs exchanged by the Admiral of the Atlantic and the Admiral of the Pacific became a carefully organized part of German plans to involve Russia in Asia against England and Japan, leaving Germany with a free hand against France. 'By cultivating dynastic ties', recalled Schoen, 'we were still able to keep on good terms with Russia on the whole, so long as her immense strength sought and found a wide field for expansion in the Asiatic East.'[9]

But the political use of dynastic ties only revealed their steady erosion. William might ramble on in his letters about the Yellow Peril, the 'old tradition which always united our families for the benefit of our countries', 'our old friendly relations with Russia' and 'the maintenance of peace and of monarchical institutions'.[10] But in fact such an appeal to the memory of past ties no longer overrode the more pragmatic considerations of power politics, as indicated by the refusal of the astounded foreign offices in both Berlin and St Petersburg to endorse the treaty of Björko agreed

[7] William II to Nicholas II, Berlin, 6 June 1904; *Die Grosse Politik der Europäischen Kabinette 1871–1914* (Berlin, 1921–), XIX, 1, 182–4. See also G. Lambsdorff, *Die Militärbevollmächtigten Kaiser Wilhelms II. am Zarenhofe 1904–1914* (Berlin, 1937).

[8] F. Rosen, *Aus einem diplomatischen Wanderleben* (Berlin, 1931), II, p. 10; J. Haller, *Philip Eulenberg: The Kaiser's friend* (N.Y., 1930), I, p. 307.

[9] Schoen, *op. cit.*, p. 222.

[10] N.F. Grant, ed., *The Kaiser's Letters to the Tsar* (London, 1920), 28 March 1898, 8 January 1909.

between the two Emperors personally in 1905. But these ties did promote common action in the face of a threat recognized by both Russia and Germany. The two governments continued to find it profitable to maintain a close watch on the forces of revolution and Polish nationalism. To this end the Russian *Okhrana* agents and the police presidium in every German city worked hand in hand in the years before the war.

The type of Russian student attending German universities was also changing after 1900. Since the 1730s Russians had come to Germany to sit at the feet of the great German thinkers and had returned with feelings of ambivalence toward 'the West'. Germany was the land not only of Kant and Schiller, but also of beer and bourgeois uniformity. The traditional attraction of German thought continued to exist for upper-class Russians after 1900; Boris Pasternak, Fedor Stepun, Nikolai Berdiaev, and Boris Vysheslavtsev were among those drawn to the Marburg school of neo-Kantianism headed by Hermann Cohen and Friedrich Lange. But after 1900 they were not typical of Russian students in Germany. The cultured few were replaced by a wave of lower middle-class students, many of them Jewish, who came to the technical high schools as well as the universities to study not philosophy but medicine, chemistry, engineering, and law. The number of Russian students enrolled in German universities and high schools nearly tripled between 1900 and 1914. In the universities alone some five thousand Russians registered during the summer and winter semesters of 1912-13, primarily at Berlin (1174), Leipzig (758), Munich (552), Königsberg (435), Heidelberg (317), and Halle (283).[11] Russians made up more than half the number of foreign students at most universities and often a majority of them was Jewish.

Russian intellectuals, writers, and artists who did settle in Germany before 1914, however, found that a veritable cult of things Russian had developed among middle-class intellectuals in Germany which reversed the traditional one-way attraction. The appearance in translation of the classics of nineteenth-century Russian literature was one factor in this revived interest in Russia; another was the mood of despair among the younger generation in Germany which led to a great fascination with Russia and 'the

11 B. Brachmann, *Russische Sozialdemokraten in Berlin, 1895-1914* (Berlin, 1962), p. 196.

East' as a way out of the boredom and sameness of bourgeois European society. The West was organized, civilized, repressed, mechanized, dehumanized; the East was still untouched, primitive, unrepressed, natural, religious, and wise. Russia was a symbol of this way out to the East, and Dostoevsky was a symbol of Russia. In contrast to England, where he had the reputation of a somewhat morbid and unsavoury novelist, Dostoevsky was read in prewar Germany as a visionary prophet who portrayed an underground world beneath the facade of modern society which was somehow more real and which, it has been suggested, provided a vicarious experience of forbidden emotions for German middle-class readers.[12]

It is striking to note that German interest in Russia before the war was based upon little more than cursory reading of the works of Russian writers. Russia was largely an unknown quantity, a mysterious country peopled by characters from Gogol, Turgenev, Tolstoi, and Dostoevsky, both backward and dangerous, exotic and terrible, capable of either revivifying or destroying bourgeois Europe. Because of this lack of information about Russia, many Russians in Germany in these years found themselves pressed into service as interpreters of Russian life.

The best known of these was the writer and literary critic Dmitri Merezhkovsky, considered a 'European' in Moscow literary circles but by virtue of his translated commentaries on Russian literature widely read in Germany. He provided for the German reading public precisely the interpretative and authoritative simplifications about Russia which it craved. He wrote knowingly of an imminent 'third kingdom' that would mark the final phase of world history, a phase in which the Holy Ghost would appear and reconcile Father and Son, spirit and flesh, into some new and ultimate unity. Through Merezhkovsky and his interpretation of Dostoevsky the young Moeller van den Bruck derived all his knowledge about Russia and much of the framework of his later work, Das Dritte Reich.[13] Thomas Mann borrowed wholesale from him the characterization of Pushkin, Dostoevsky, and Tolstoi

---

[12] T. Kampmann, Dostojewski in Deutschland (Munster, 1931); L. Lowenthal 'The Reception of Dostoevski's Work in Germany: 1880–1920' in R.N. Wilson, ed., The Arts in Society (Englewood, N.J., 1964).

[13] F. Stern, The Politics of Cultural Despair (N.Y., 1965), p. 239, 380 n. 9; H. Schwierskott, Arthur Moeller van den Bruck und der revolutionäre Nationalismus in der Weimarer Republik (Göttingen, 1962), p. 17.

respectively as the 'Goethe', 'Dante', and 'Michelangelo' of the East, as well as his enthusiasm for that mysterious 'third kingdom' that would replace Western civilization.[14] It was while reading Merezhkovsky, recalled Stefan Zweig, that he first heard the news from Sarajevo in the summer of 1914.

The contribution of Russian intellectuals to German life after 1900 was in sharp contrast to their previous experience as humble students of German thought. The modish mysticism of Rudolf Steiner's 'anthroposophy' movement, a branch of English theosophy, had an enormous appeal for Andrei Bely and other Russians, but also was itself greatly influenced by those Russians who introduced into the movement the writings of the religious philosopher Vladimir Soloviev. The colony of Russian artists in Munich – Kandinsky, Iavlensky, Grabar, Kardovsky, Marianne Verefkin – came to Germany in the late 1890s to study European impressionism and stayed on to contribute Russian themes and their own talents to German expressionism and the postwar *Bauhaus* movement. In many more cases Russians came to Germany to learn and stayed to teach.

These two types of Russians who had traditionally come to Germany – royalty and intellectuals – continued to participate in German life in the years before the First World War. But they were no longer alone.

The politics of the new emigration to Germany were quite naturally politics of the left. Since the death of Alexander II in 1881 Russian political exiles had lived mainly in England and Switzerland. The first Marxist party in Russia, Plekhanov's 'Group for the Emancipation of Labour', had its headquarters in Geneva in these years. But in the late 1890s, as more and more Russians were forced into exile either for educational reasons or for participation in the strikes and student riots that marked the turn of the century in Russia, Germany became an important centre of emigré politics. Germany offered relative safety from Russian police agents familiar with Swiss haunts, printing facilities, a common border with Russia across which illegal literature could be smuggled, and separation from the 'elders' of the Russian revolutionary movement on which the younger activists looked with mixed awe and disdain.

[14] L. Venohr, *Thomas Manns Verhältnis zur russischen Literatur* (Meisenheim/Glan, 1959), p. 80.

From 1900 until 1905 Germany became a key centre of Russian socialist and liberal exiles, looking to the German socialist movement for support and to the Russian student emigration for membership.

For decades Russian socialists had admired German social-democracy as the largest and best organized European workers' movement. Since the 1880s Plekhanov and Akselrod had been personal friends of Kautsky and Bernstein, contributed articles on Russia to the socialist daily *Vorwärts* and Kautsky's journal *Die Neue Zeit*, and received assistance from the SPD in shipping Marxist literature from Geneva into Russia. But many Russians, particularly the younger generation, were increasingly suspicious of the growing trend toward reformism and trade unionism within the German labour movement. In Russia coexistence with the dominant political system for economic motives was unthinkable. In fact in Germany the 'orthodox' counter-attack against Bernstein's first critique of Marx which had appeared in *Die Neue Zeit* in January 1898, was led not by Kautsky but by three emigré Marxists from Tsarism: Plekhanov, Rosa Luxemburg and Alexander Helphand (Parvus).

In 1898, however, the tiny 'Union of Russian Social Democrats Abroad' in Berlin was highly sympathetic to Bernstein's ideas. Organized as a link between Plekhanov's circle in Geneva and Russian social-democrats in St Petersburg, the Union soon resented the domination of the 'elders' and came increasingly under the control of the new emigrés. Between 1898 and 1900 the four leaders of the Union – Wilhelm Bucholtz, S. N. Prokopovich, E.D. Kuskova, and Grishin (Kopelzon), the *Bund* representative abroad – succeeded in breaking away from Plekhanov and in turning the Union and its new journal, *Rabochee delo*, into an independent organization not unsympathetic to German reformism. In April 1900 Plekhanov's group in Geneva withdrew from the Union and decided to establish a new organ of Russian Marxism abroad.

In the spring of 1900 members of the Russian Social-Democratic Workers' Party (RSDRP) began to leave Russia for Germany for this purpose. Potresov arrived in March and Lenin followed four months later. In August they met with Plekhanov, Vera Zasulich, and Akselrod in Geneva to discuss plans for setting up the new journal, *Iskra*. The 'elders' favoured Switzerland as a location for *Iskra*, the 'youngsters' Germany. In the end Lenin and Potresov won out. In late August 1900 Lenin arrived in Nürnberg, where a German socialist, Adolf Braun, helped to arrange for the publication of *Iskra* at Leipzig through a Polish typographer, Joseph Blumenfeld. On 6 September Lenin arrived in Munich, where he was shortly joined by Potresov and Zasulich, and later, in March 1901, by Martov. Plekhanov remained in Geneva, Akselrod in Zürich. From the end of 1900 to the spring of 1902, then, Munich became the home of Lenin and Krupskaia, the centre of operations for *Iskra* and a new colony of Russians abroad.[15]

As an illegal journal *Iskra* was forced to keep one step ahead of the German and Russian police, who were aware of its existence from the start. After four issues had appeared in Leipzig it proved necessary to move printing operations to Munich, then to Stuttgart, and finally in April 1902 to London. In Stuttgart *Iskra* and its theoretical and legal companion *Zaria* were printed by the SPD publisher Dietz, who also printed the first edition of Lenin's *What is to be Done?* and helped the *Iskra* circle arrange the channels necessary for moving RSDRP literature into Russia. The Munich circle, which began to call itself the 'League of Russian Revolutionary Social-Democrats Abroad' in October 1901, worked with the 'Group for Assisting Russian Revolutionary Social-Democracy' in Berlin in this matter. RSDRP literature was brought into Berlin, stored in the basement of the *Vorwärts* building, and sent off to Russia via East Prussia, Upper Silesia, and Austrian Galicia in the metal waistcoats and false-bottom suitcases of sympathetic Sunday 'travellers'. Even after *Iskra* had moved out of Germany in 1902, its lines of communication were to remain important for the Bolsheviks down to 1914.[16]

Political infighting and splitting were characteristic of Russian political exiles before 1905, and the Bolshevik-Menshevik schism after 1903 was but one example of this. In Germany in these years the presence of Bernstein's supporters, Lenin's circle, the Mensheviks, Polish socialists, Bundists, and liberals, made it particularly

15 L. Stern, ed., *Die Auswirkungen der ersten russischen Revolution auf Deutschland von 1905–1907* (Berlin, 1956), II, xvii; X. Streb, *Lenin in Deutschland* (Berlin, 1957); F. Donath, *Lenin in Leipzig* (Berlin, 1958).

16 D. Geyer, *Lenin in der russischen Sozialdemokratie* (Köln, 1962), p. 206; B. Nikolaevskii, ed., *A.N. Potresov; posmertny sbornik proizvedenii* (Paris, 1937), pp. 40–3; *Pisma P.B. Akselroda i Iu. O. Martova* (Berlin, 1925), 21 n. 9, 60 n. 2; O. Piatnitsky, *Memoirs of a Bolshevik* (N.Y., 1933), pp. 51–75.

difficult for the SPD to decide which of these groups to support. Dietz helped Peter Struve publish the liberal journal *Osvobozhdenie* in Stuttgart from 1902 to 1904 at the same time as he was assisting Lenin and Plekhanov. Struve had Plekhanov's permission to edit a supplement to *Zaria* with Dietz, but his publication of an article by Witte, the Russian Finance Minister, quickly ended his relationship with exile Russian Marxists. Instead he formed his own liberal journal abroad with the help of the historian Paul Miliukov, the *zemstvo* leader Petrunkevich, and a number of Russians in Germany also uneasy about the direction in which Russian socialism was moving: Bernstein's admirers Prokopovich and Kuskova, the economist Tugan-Baranovsky, Kistiakovsky, a student of George Simmel at Heidelberg, and a young student of philosophy later associated with the *Vekhy* circle, S.L. Frank. The liberals never struck deep roots in Germany, however. Except for Simmel and Max Weber, the Russians had few personal contacts there and after 1905 returned to Russia to pursue careers in parliamentary politics that revealed a new middle-class nationalism hostile to Germany.[17]

Thus the Russian emigration to Germany after 1900 found fertile ground for political activity. But what struck most Germans about the emigration when it was 'discovered' during the stormy events of 1904–5 in Russia was not that it was simply in radical opposition to the Russian government. Rather they were impressed by the association between radicalism and the Jewish student emigration, and between Pan-German sentiment and the Baltic German emigration.

The last two decades of the nineteenth century were years of great hardship for Russian Jewry. The assassination of the Tsar in 1881 was followed by the first pogroms and by new restrictive legislation: with only a few exceptions, Jews were limited to the towns of the Pale of Settlement; by the July 1887 circular of the Ministry of Education Jews could not exceed 10 per cent of the student body at schools within the Pale, 5 per cent outside it, and only 3 per cent in Moscow and St Petersburg; no business could be conducted on Sundays or on Orthodox holidays; in 1891 20,000 Jews were expelled from Moscow. As a result hundreds of thousands of

[17] D. Shakhovskoi, 'Soiuz osvobozhdenie', *Zarnitsy; literaturno-politicheskii sbornik*, no. 2, part 2 (1909), pp. 82–171; D. Geyer, *op. cit.*, pp. 275–85.

Russian Jews, denied even those civil liberties available to other Russian citizens, began to leave Russia in the 1880s and 1890s for Europe, the United States, and Palestine. Many of those who stayed behind, as well as many who left Russia, moved easily into the ranks of the radical opposition movement.[18]

Germany was an important place of refuge for Russian Jews. In the 1880s there began a virtual stampede to German universities and technical high schools, where a curriculum of medicine, engineering, science, and law provided both career opportunities and the possibility of work in the public service. Driven out of Russia for political reasons, they found German culture familiar and accessible. 'They knew Germany', recalled Chaim Weizmann, 'they spoke German, and they were vastly impressed by German achievement, German discipline and German power.'[19] The majority settled in the cities of Prussia and Saxony where they found jobs as factory workers, artisans, and craftsmen. Jewish students also were most in evidence in these two provinces. They soon formed their own clubs, circles, and reading rooms, Zionist and socialist alike.

The number of Russian Jews in Germany after 1900 was often overestimated. The total from Russia, Poland, Galicia, the Bukovina, Hungary, and Rumania, the so-called *Ostjuden*, did increase from 41,000 in 1900 to over 70,000 by 1910, and those coming from the Russian Empire from 13,000 to 21,000 in the same period. But the number of Russian Jews actually decreased relative to the number of non-Jewish Russians in Germany during the same time span. Moreover, some 70,000 German Jews left their homeland between 1900 and 1910, balancing the influx of *Ostjuden*; by 1910 only 79,000 out of 615,000 Jews in Germany (13 per cent) were foreigners.[20] The claim by some Germans that a tide of Eastern Jews was sweeping into Germany before the war was considerably exaggerated.

What produced such exaggeration was the involvement of the Jewish student emigration in both German and Russian social-

18 L. Shapiro, 'The Role of the Jews in the Russian Revolutionary Movement', *Slavonic and East European Review*, December 1961; L. Deich, *Rol evreev v russkoi revoliutsionnom dvizhenii* (Berlin, 1923).

19 C. Weizmann, *Trial and Error* (Philadelphia, 1949), p. 165.

20 S. Adler-Rudel, *Ostjuden in Deutschland 1880–1940* (Tübingen, 1959), pp. 2, 18, 22, 29, 163.

democracy. Although nearly half the number of Russians studying at some German universities and high schools in these years were Jews, the total number of Jewish students from Russia who lived in Germany at any given time before 1914 was never much more than one thousand. Their ability to move easily into both SPD and RSDRP circles made them not only useful go-betweens for Russian and German socialists but gave them prominence in the German mind despite their relatively small number.

Wilhelm Adolfovich Bucholtz was probably the most important example of a Russian Jew involved in both socialist movements before the war. Rosa Luxemburg and Alexander Helphand were better known, but Bucholtz was a more significant link between the SPD and Russian emigré circles. It was not clear whether Bucholtz, born in 1867 in Orenburg of German parentage, was a 'Russian' or a 'German' Jew. Formally a Prussian citizen, Bucholtz was educated in Russian schools, and for his part in the Kazan student riots of 1887 was exiled to Samara, where he first met Lenin. In 1891 the Russian government extradited Bucholtz; he came to Berlin for the first time. When Lenin arrived there in the summer of 1895 he was surprised to find that Bucholtz was already a figure of some importance in German socialist circles, a correspondent for *Vorwärts* on Russian affairs, and a friend of Kautsky and Wilhelm Liebknecht. In 1900 he was important in the organization of *Iskra* and *Zaria* because of his connections with the SPD and his Prussian citizenship. In arranging with Dietz and the SPD for the printing of Russian literature and the subsidizing of the financially desperate RSDRP he could avoid the police surveillance which would have followed any Russian engaged in the same activity. After the 1903 split within the RSDRP Bucholtz remained an important liaison between the SPD and the Berlin Mensheviks, with whom he met from time to time and whose literature he helped to smuggle into Russia. After 1910 he joined with another emigré from Riga, Alexander Stein, in editing the Menshevik *Russische Bulletin,* a journal carrying news of the Russian labour movement to the Berlin colony and its German friends.

Helphand-Parvus was a more familiar figure in German socialist affairs before the war. An emigré from Odessa who came to Germany in 1891, he began his career as a radical critic of Bernstein in the 1890s and ended it as a chauvinist and war profiteer after

1914.[21] As a *Vorwärts* contributor in the 1890s, he was among the first to bring the existence of a labour movement in Russia to the attention of German socialists. In the pages of the two SPD dailies which he edited in Saxony before 1905, the *Leipziger Volkszeitung* and the *Sächsische Arbeiterzeitung* in Dresden, he and his two Polish exile friends, Rosa Luxemburg and Julian Marchlewski, provided a running commentary on events in Russia and a critique of reformist tendencies within the German labour movement. Bernstein's followers were not unaware of a certain 'eastern' element among his detractors, and after 1898 Parvus for a time found Russian exile circles more receptive to him than his former German friends. For Lenin and Krupskaia he was almost their only tie to the world beyond the Russian colony.[22] Parvus and his friend Dr Lehmann received all incoming mail for *Iskra*. It was in Parvus' Schwabing apartment that Lenin first met Rosa Luxemburg, that Trotsky stayed when in Munich, and that eight numbers of *Iskra* were printed on a hectograph machine borrowed from SPD friends in Berlin. Parvus and Marchlewski also ran a publishing house in Munich for a time, designed to make the works of Russian authors, among them Gorki, available to German readers. Like other Russian Jews in Germany, Parvus became an 'intermediary between two worlds', a man who could 'write for the Russian press on the German socialist movement and took pleasure in introducing the young generation of the Russian socialists to his German comrades'. Among his German socialist friends in Dresden Parvus was known as 'the Russian', whereas Krupskaia remembered him as an 'extreme left-winger ... interested in Russian affairs'. To some Parvus was a Russian, to others a German. The fact that he was not quite either enabled him to appear to be both.

Like the Russian Jews, the Baltic Germans who emigrated to Germany in the years before 1914 were politically disaffected because of persecution by the Russian government and capable of assimilation because of cultural and linguistic ties to Germany. But within the social fabric of the Russian Empire they were quite

21 Z.A.B. Zeman and W.B. Scharlau, *The Merchant of Revolution; the Life of Alexander Israel Helphand (Parvus) 1867-1924* (London, 1965); K. Haenisch, *Parvus* (Berlin, 1925); H. Schurer, 'Alexander Helphand-Parvus – Russian Revolutionary and German Patriot', *Russian Review*, 1959, 18; W. Scharlau, 'Parvus und Trotskij; 1904-1914' *Jahrbücher für Geschichte Osteuropas*, October 1962.
22 N. Krupskaia, *Memories of Lenin* (N.Y., 1930), I, p. 67.

distinct, a conservative landholding aristocracy in the northwest which proudly traced their ancestry to the Teutonic Knights and the Livonian Order, and their loyalty to the Russian crown to the early eighteenth century. Since Peter the Great they had been an important servitor class within the government. The list of Benckendorffs, Lievens, Korffs, Stackelbergs, Kleinmichels, and Lamsdorffs who had served the Russian Empire as civil servants, diplomats, army officers, and professors was a long one. Most remained loyal to the crown until 1917. But toward the end of the nineteenth century there were growing signs of discontent among the Baltic nobility, and some of the more discontented found their way to Germany.[23]

The Great Reforms of Alexander II, the Russification policies of Alexander III, and the beginnings of industrialization, all wrought great changes in the Baltic. A new Russian professional class of educated men and women reduced the dependence of the state on the services of the Baltic Germans. Russification hit not only the native Latvian and Estonian population of the region but the German upper class as well. Industrial change brought a restless non-German labour force into the towns and encouraged both nationalist and socialist sentiments among the local peasantry and intelligentsia. The Russian government not only did not support the Baltic Germans in coping with these changes, but exacerbated them by its policies. Baltic Germans had traditionally looked upon the Russia which they served with the mixed disdain and fascination characteristic of the colonial and paternalistic master. But after 1900, and particularly after the revolution of 1905, the mood among the German upper class in the Baltic provinces was one of 'better dead than Slav'.[24]

Baltic Germans had traditionally come to Germany for study or travel. Here they found that while they were considered 'Germans' in Russia, they passed for 'Russians' in Germany. Their familiarity with both cultures gave them peculiar expertise in Germany concerning Russia. By the 1880s their message was becoming more hostile than friendly. Victor Hehn, in his widely read

[23] On the Baltic Germans see especially H. Rothfels, 'The Baltic Provinces: Some Historic Aspects and Perspectives', *Journal of Central European Affairs*, July 1944; C. Lundin, 'The Road from Tsar to Kaiser: Changing Loyalties of the Baltic Germans, 1905–1914'. Ibid., October 1950.

[24] E. Stackelberg-Sutlem, *Ein Leben in baltischen Kampf* (Munich, 1927), p. 105.

De Moribus Ruthenorum: Zur Charakteristik der russischen Volkscele
(Stuttgart, 1892), portrayed Russia as an oriental despotism in
which the cleanliness, prosperity, and organization of the German
population in the Baltic and South Russia contrasted with the
surrounding dirty, unorganized, and repulsive Slavic natives.
Julius Eckardt, editor of the liberal *Die Grenzboten* and informant
on Russian affairs for the Foreign Office, pointed out the dangers
facing the Baltic Germans in Russia and warned of the perils of
'Pan-Slavism'. In Bismarck's Germany there was little interest in
Auslandsdeutschtum, but after 1900 Baltic Germans found increasing sympathy in Germany, and their role in German society became an impressive one, especially where Russia was concerned.
Both the Russian ambassador in Berlin, Osten-Sacken, and the
German military attaché in St Petersburg, were Balts. But there
were many others. Paul Rohrbach, the Imperial Commissar for
Settlement in German Southwest Africa, who urged German expansion in the Near East in his *Die Bagdadbahn* (1902), flavoured his
many articles in *Preussische Jahrbücher* and other journals with an
anti-Russian condiment. The theologian Adolf Harnack became the
confidant of William II on religious matters and an active supporter
of nationalist campaigns to help the Balts. The 'Russian expert' of
the German General Staff was Hugo von Freytag-Loringhoven,
later Chief of Staff. Among the active supporters of the Pan-
German League were Alfred Geiser, its business manager, and
Friedrich Lezius, a professor of theology. Balts in the academic
world included Reinhold Seeburg, another professor of theology
at the University of Berlin, Johannes Haller, who taught medieval
history at Marburg and Tübingen, and the cultural historian
George Dehio, also at Tübingen. After 1914 many of these men
became advisers to the German High Command in the East on the
administration of the occupied Baltic provinces. But even before
the war their influence on German policy and opinion concerning
Russia was such that the historian Friedrich Meinecke later uttered
a warning against ever again accepting 'Balto-centric' views of Russia
which considered her inferior and underestimated her 'vitality'.[25]

25 F. Epstein, 'Friedrich Meinecke in seinem Verhältnis zum Europäischen
Osten', *Jahrbuch für die Geschichte Mittel- und Ostdeutschlands* (Tübingen, 1954),
pp. 134-5; A. Zahn-Harnack, *Adolf von Harnack* (Berlin, 1936), 339-55, 383;
H.C. Meyer, *Mitteleuropa in German Thought and Action 1815-1945* (The
Hague, 1955), pp. 95-102; F. Fischer, *Griff nach der Weltmacht* (Düsseldorf,
1961), pp. 346-52.

The most influential Baltic German of the Russophobic variety in prewar Germany was Professor Theodor Schiemann. Schiemann was primarily a historian specializing in Russia, and his seminar on East Europe at the University of Berlin was the first of its kind in Germany. But in the 1890s he also interpreted Russian events for the conservative reading public through his weekly foreign affairs column in the *Kreuzzeitung*, and became an adviser on Russia to Holstein at the Wilhelmstrasse, and a member of the court camarilla of William II. His personal influence on William was considerable. During the 1914–18 war he saw many of his ideas become reality for a time: the restoration of German power in the Baltic provinces, the colonizing of Poland, Galicia, and the Ukraine with Germans, and the reduction of Russia to her pre-Petrine boundaries. The so-called 'Schiemann school' within the German General Staff and the Foreign Ministry became synonymous with German aggrandizement in the East; in 1917 it was probably Schiemann who persuaded William to annex formally Latvia and Estonia. Until his death in January 1921 Schiemann remained an outspoken proponent of a German policy and a Russian system of government which would guarantee the rights of the German upper classes in the Baltic, 'one of those Balts', as Chancellor Bülow put it, 'who see the world and every event from the narrow angle of local patriotism'.[26]

Schiemann's views on Russia and the Russians were not unlike those of his close friend Victor Hehn. These may be paraphrased as follows: The Russians, like the Slavs in general, were a primitive and backward people; nomadic, uneducated, uncivilized, barbaric, but also innately religious. Until Peter the Great Russia resembled an Oriental kingdom, but Peter and the procession of German rulers, bureaucrats, and colonists who succeeded him managed to introduce some order into the country. This 'westernization' of Russia, however, was a superficial process. It created only a *Scheinkultur*, a layer of European influence beneath which lay traditional weakness and disorder. In particular, Russian military power was vastly overrated in Europe. Since the Polish uprising of 1863 deep anti-Western and anti-German forces had been unleashed in Russia, and it was this threat rather than that of Russia's

[26] *The Memoirs of Prince Bülow* (Boston, 1931), II, p. 594; on Schiemann see K. Meyer, *Theodor Schiemann als politischer Publizist* (Frankfurt-am-Main, 1956).

armies which was most dangerous for Germany. The old order was being eroded in Russia under the fire of anti-state elements: writers, intellectuals, socialists, nihilists, Jews. The delicate balance between Tsar and Empire, Russians and non-Russians, was tipping toward disaster for the Baltic Germans. The only solution was the creation in Russia of a government of law (*Rechtstaat*) which could guarantee the rights of the cultured, German element in Russian society.[27]

Schiemann's hostility toward the Russian government and his underestimation of Russian military power were a welcome message for some German policy-makers. Most Balts of any prominence in Germany agreed with his views to some extent; those who did were more apt to achieve prominence than those who did not. But not all Balts shared his colonial mentality. For many it was Russia's very primitiveness that attracted them, her untouched vastness, her religiosity, her soul, all those elements, in short, which European civilization could neither understand nor overwhelm. But all too often cultural attraction was mixed with political hostility.

Those Balts who did feel a deep attraction toward Russia were no less successful in disseminating their views abroad before 1914, not among policy-makers but among European intellectuals. The remarkable friend of Nietzsche and Freud, Lou Andreas-Salome, introduced the poet Rainer Maria Rilke to the magic of Russia on two long trips taken in 1899 and 1900. With her help Rilke was able to see Russia for himself, to visit Tolstoi, to see the churches of Kiev and the peasants along the Volga and to immerse himself in the exotic, sacred, dark, and untouched land which seemed to recall his own childhood.[28] Moeller van den Bruck had been introduced to Merezhkovsky in Paris in 1902 by two Baltic German sisters, Lucie and Less Kaerrick. Lucie later became Moeller's second wife, while Less translated the famous Piper-Verlag edition of Dostoevsky's works. Rudolf Steiner also married a Balt, Marie Sivers, who introduced the writings of Vladimir Soloviev into

---

[27] For Schiemann's views on Russia see K. Meyer, *op. cit.*, 88–115, and the collection of his *Kreuzzeitung* articles entitled *Deutschland und die grosse Politik* (Berlin, 1910–12).

[28] 'Letters of Rainer Maria Rilke to Helene***', *Oxford Slavonic Papers*, 1960; I.S. Mackey, *Lou Salome; Inspiratrice et Interprète de Nietzsche, Rilke et Freud* (Paris, 1956).

Steiner's circle and later translated a number of his works into German.[29]

The best known of the Russophile Balts, although his popularity came in the wake of the war, was the philosopher and mystic Hermann Keyserling. After two years at the University of Dorpat, Keyserling came to Heidelberg in 1900 to study natural science. But like many of his generation he found that science raised more questions than it could answer. He turned to more philosophic writings then in vogue: Houston Stewart Chamberlain's *Foundations of the Nineteenth Century*, the works of the Austrian mystic Rudolf Kassner, the writings of Kant and Schopenhauer. From science he passed to mysticism. After a period of 'frenzied reading in the British Museum', Keyserling learned that the revolution of 1905 in Russia had destroyed his family estate at Rayküll. From 1906 to 1908 he lived in Berlin, claiming to have visions and studying yoga. In 1908 he returned to the Baltic again where he lived as a gentleman farmer for the next three years.

In 1911 Keyserling decided to escape the confines of Europe by taking a long trip to the Far East. Upon his return he produced an enormous travel diary (*Reisetagbuch*) which has been compared with Oswald Spengler's *Decline of the West* and which ran through seven German editions between 1918 and 1923. 'Europe has nothing more to give me', Keyserling announced in his book, in which he portrayed the 'partially developed peoples' of the world as superior to Europe precisely because of their lack of 'civilization'. 'Yes, Russia', he wrote, 'the Russia of the simple peasant, is today probably the only province of Christendom which is near to God.' He rhapsodized about the 'delicate soul of the Slav' and 'the Russian peasant, that primitive man, who seems absolutely incapable of any organization, in whom no form of objectivity, not even that of the concept of duty, meets with understanding, who obeys exclusively his uncontrolled subjectivity'. Russia, in short, was a part of the non-European world, a world superior to Europe because it had not yet been Europeanized.[30]

The careers of Schiemann and Keyserling reflected a certain polarity in the Baltic German mind between hostility and fascination

[29] H. Weisberger, *Aus dem Leben von Marie Steiner-von Sivers* (Dornach, 1956).

[30] H. Keyserling, *The Travel Diary of a Philosopher* (N.Y., 1925), I, p. 16, 227; II, pp. 70, 337.

toward Russia. Those most critical of Russia found it somewhat exotic, and those familiar with Russian culture harboured
fears of the forces of Russian political life. It was indicative of both
types of Baltic German now leaving Russia, and of the mood of
prewar Germany that Schiemann's colonial attitude found a
strong resonance and Keyserling's musings on the Russian soul
went largely unheard. Most Balts in Germany before 1914 would
have agreed with Schiemann's ominous warning in 1906 that
'Russia is a danger that will remain and with which future generations will have to deal, unless we release them from this danger'.[31]
In 1905 they spelled out this danger in Germany.

The Russian revolution of 1905 made most Germans aware for the
first time of the size and composition of the Russian emigration to
Germany. German attitudes toward the emigration, however,
were determined not only by its 'radical' nature and its association
with events inside Russia, but by considerations of foreign policy as
well.

   From the outbreak of the Russo-Japanese War early in 1904 until the Algeciras conference at the beginning of 1906, Germany
made a last attempt to revive Bismarck's policy of alignment with
Russia. Russian involvement in the Far East and the outbreak of
revolution in the winter of 1904-5 made it clear that Russia could
pose no serious threat to Germany in Europe in the event of war
there. How Germany should take advantage of this situation was
less clear. The danger was that the Anglo-French *entente* might be
broadened to include Russia, leading to the 'encirclement' of
Germany by hostile powers. Two lines of policy suggested themselves to German leaders: William II favoured the creation of a
'continental alliance' of France, Germany, and Russia directed
against England; Bülow and Holstein favoured a more aggressive
policy directed against France over the issue of rights in Morocco,
perhaps with the idea of provoking a 'preventive war' against
France in the absence of effective Russian support. Both policies
assumed that the Russian government was crumbling, an assumption that Russians in Germany were eager to promote.

   In the end both policies were pursued in haphazard fashion and
neither produced the desired results. By 1907 the encirclement of

[31] K. Meyer, *op. cit.*, p. 204.

273

Germany was complete. The Russo-German Treaty of Björko, signed on board the Kaiser's yacht in the summer of 1905, proved abortive. But important conclusions were drawn concerning Russia by German policy-makers in 1905. Both the Wilhelmstrasse and the General Staff assumed that Russia, in the wake of a Japanese victory and revolution at home, could not be considered a serious threat in a future war and that the bulk of the German army could be directed against France. After 1905 Germany feared not Russian power but Russian weakness, the danger that the flames of revolution might not only topple the government of Nicholas II but spread to Germany itself. Some Russians in Germany gave warning of this danger; others exemplified it.

Until 1905 the German government was more aware of the existence of Russians in Germany than was German public opinion. Since the 1880s suspicious Russians had been kept under surveillance and a treaty between Russia, Prussia, and Bavaria signed in 1885 provided for the extradition of 'undesirable aliens'. After 1900 the Okhrana agent in Germany, Harting, and the Berlin police president, Georg von Borries, kept a close watch on the growing number of emigré student clubs and socialist circles. But few Russians were extradited, since there were advantages for the Russian government in having its political opponents out of the country. 'We have to put up with an officially recognized colony of anarchists in Berlin for the sake of the Russians,' William complained in 1903, 'in order to lighten for the "Little Father's" police agents the task of watching them'; he whimsically suggested to Bülow a 'mass execution of these rascals'.[32] On occasion Russian or Polish students were arrested, as in December 1901 when a group of them had broken up a lecture by Schiemann at the University of Berlin because of its anti-Slav tone. But it was only in the winter of 1903-4, when more arrests occurred, that the issue of Russians in Germany became a matter of public concern.

'Is the Imperial Chancellor aware', SPD Reichstag delegate Auer asked Bülow in January 1904, 'that the Russian government maintains police agents on German territory to keep Russian and German citizens under surveillance?' Bülow admitted as much, but added that since 1900 there had been only three cases of extra-

---

[32] William to Bülow, 27 December 1903; *Letters of Prince Bülow* (London, 1930), p. 24.

dition of known 'anarchists' from Prussia to Russia.[33] Expulsion, not extradition, was the more common penalty. Between 1902 and 1909 only seven Russians were actually turned over to the Russian police, although many were expelled. Such was the case with fourteen 'undesirable aliens' in the spring of 1904, after Borries had arrested and interrogated over one hundred Russian students. Others were expelled that summer after the trial of nine German socialists in Königsberg revealed the extent of SPD cooperation in the smuggling of illegal Russian literature out of Germany. By the time news of the Russian revolution reached Berlin the question of Russian radicals was already a hotly debated issue.

On 23 January 1905 the first reports of Bloody Sunday and the outbreak of revolution in Russia reached Berlin. In the following months the SPD and the German labour unions responded to the fresh wind from the East that revitalized the forces of radicalism against those of reformism within the movement. Over 500,000 German workers were involved in work stoppages, strikes, and lockouts in 1905 – more than the total for the previous five years. For all of 1905 and into 1906 German socialists followed the news from Russia with great interest through a daily column in *Vorwärts*. The SPD collected some 350,000 Marks to aid Russian revolutionaries inside Russia and abroad.[34] The fact that the ideological justification of the new radicalism, Rosa Luxemburg's *Mass Strike, Party and Trade Unions*, had been written by an 'easterner' was not lost on German opinion. The very enthusiasm of German socialists for the Russian revolution and the discovery of Russian revolutionaries within the SPD heightened the fears of similar violence in Germany. None were more eager to promote this fear of revolution and to draw attention to its evil effects than the Baltic Germans.

At first the Balts found little support in Germany for their cause. In early 1904 the editors of the Pan-German League's journal, *Alldeutsche Blätter*, refused to believe warnings that the Baltic Germans were in any danger, but by the spring of 1905 conservative circles showed a growing awareness of their plight. When one writer argued that German culture was disappearing in the Baltic

---

[33] *Stenographische Berichte über die Verhandlungen des Reichstags*, 4 February 1904, 1363–1407. Hereafter *Verhandlungen*.

[34] C. Schorske, *German Social Democracy 1905–1917* (Cambridge, Mass., 1955), 31; L. Stern, *Auswirkungen*, II, lix.

and that the area was 'no province of Germanism', he was sharply attacked by Alfred Geiser. By the autumn of 1905 the League was busy raising funds to help the Baltic Germans recover their land and property and to emigrate to Germany if they so desired. Throughout 1905 Schiemann and other Balts pointed out the dangers which the Russian revolution held for their countrymen in an area of the world where, as Georg Cleinow, a St Petersburg German, put it, 'the more powerful West European culture has won out over the semi-Asiatic'.[35]

The winter of 1905–6 brought a wave of looting, murder, and general destruction in the Baltic provinces. Baltic Germans in Germany lost no time in lobbying to help their homeland in its hour of need. In December 1905 members of the Pan-German League travelled to various cities making speeches on behalf of the Balts. At the annual meeting of the League in Leipzig on 16–17 December a resolution demanded that the German government send ships to Riga, Reval, and Libau to protect Germans in those cities and to bring back to Germany those who wished to emigrate. The League also recommended that a note be sent to the Russian government asking that law and order be preserved in the region. Two weeks later a formal call for monetary donations to help the Balts went out.[36]

The Balts cultivated sympathies far beyond the confines of the League, primarily in conservative circles, in the press, and within the government establishment. Schiemann urged that Baltic German refugees in the eastern provinces be moved into Prussian Poland as a bulwark of Germanism. Hans Delbrück in the *Preussische Jahrbücher* wrote that the 'oldest and greatest colony of Germanism' was in danger of being overwhelmed by the forces of revolution. In the Reichstag the conservative deputy Libermann von Sonnenberg urged the government to help 'the most valuable element in the whole Russian Empire', Baltic Germans both in Russia and in Germany, and feared that a 'less desirable immigration from Russia' of Jews might be expected. In socialist circles, of course, the Balts were the undesirable elements in Russia. For August Bebel they were simply eastern Junkers, an oppressive

[35] *Die Grenzboten*, 1905, 3, 451; *Alldeutsche Blätter*, 23 January 1904, 11 March, 3, 17 June, 16, 30 September 1905.
[36] Ibid., 2, 9, 30 December 1905. Schiemann, Geiser, and Harnack were among the Balts most active in the League campaign.

landowning class in the Baltic which for centuries had kept the native Latvian population under its thumb.[37]

The Baltic Germans had some effect on German policy, as well as on public opinion. In late December 1905 German transport ships arrived in Riga to evacuate Balts who desired to come to Germany and the cruiser *Lübeck* and some torpedo boats were held at Memel in case of further violence in the provinces. There was no direct intervention, but there was strong support for the Balts not only in their homeland but in Germany. The Prussian *Staatsministerium* observed that the revolution had increased the number of Russian refugees coming to Germany and that most were either Jews or 'Russian citizens of German origin'. Bülow cared little about the Jews ('the revolution in Russia is their work') but encouraged the admission of Balts. Schiemann urged raising the fees at German universities and high schools to keep out the 'less gifted Slavic and Jewish students', admitting only Orthodox Russian and Baltic German students.[38]. He also used his friendship with William II to put pressure on the Russian government to protect the Balts. In a letter of 29 January 1906 to Nicholas, William wrote that Berlin was 'full of noble families who have fled from the Baltic provinces', people who 'find themselves in a particularly sorry state, for they have lost everything: their castles have been burned, their property destroyed and their forests plundered'.[39] In 1906 the German government could do little more to help the Balts. But an irredentist cause had been established which was to become an important justification for war in 1914. 'I will never consent to leave the Baltic provinces in the lurch,' William is said to have told Schiemann in July 1906; 'I shall go to their assistance, and they must be incorporated in the German Empire. I shall not raise a finger to do this as long as the present Russian government maintains itself, but I could never leave the Balts to their fate.'[40]

German attitudes toward Russian Jews in Germany during

---

[37] *Preussische Jahrbücher*, January 1906, pp. 172–8; *Deutsche Monatschrift für das gesamte Leben der Gegenwart*, January 1906, pp. 544–5; *Verhandlungen*, 12 December 1903, p. 12, 14 February 1906, pp. 1213, 1272, 1291.

[38] R. Wittram, *Drei Generationen: Deutschland-Livland-Russland, 1830–1914* (Göttingen, 1939), pp. 314–36; L. Stern, *Auswirkungen*, I, pp. 139, 152.

[39] W. Goetz, *Briefe Wilhelms II an den Zaren 1894–1914* (Berlin, 1920), p. 222.

[40] B. Bülow, *Memoirs*, II, p. 266.

1905–6 were quite different. William pointed out to Nicholas, as if he did not already know, that Jews like Trotsky, Parvus, and Luxemburg were the 'leaders of the revolt' in Russia. This was a strong impression in Germany too. Of the 360 Russian students at the University of Berlin in 1905, 261 were Jewish. Were not many of them being trained for revolution? Early in 1904 the Pan-German League had already suggested limiting the number of Jews entering Germany from Russia. 'Why doesn't Rosa Luxemburg go back to Russia?', wrote Friedrich Naumann in *Die Hilfe* in October 1905. Was this 'Jewish foreigner' not already a dominant influence within German social democracy?, echoed the *Konservative Korrespondenz*. For many Germans 'Russian', 'radical', and 'eastern Jew' became linked together after 1905 as a single type of undesirable.[41]

The fear of an influx of revolutionary Jewish students from the East never quite disappeared from the German mind after 1905. It did not become pathological until after the war, but until 1914 it remained a powerful part of general Russophobia. On 31 August 1906 Bülow wrote to William that the expulsion of all 'Russian immigrants, especially Jews', was desirable. The aim of Russian socialists, wrote the *Kreuzzeitung*, was nothing less than an 'organized Jewish proletariat' in Russia and Germany. 'The political police,' Sonnenberg said in the autumn of 1907, 'must pay close attention to the machinations of the Russian-Jewish students who study revolutionary propaganda at our universities and dynamite at our technical high schools, who set up seminars for the science of revolution and laboratories for dynamite bombs in our midst.' One Reichstag delegate even recommended 'blocking the border against any Russians who do not come here with evidence of certain positive attitudes toward us'. In the spring of 1908 the conservative deputy Lattmann still felt there was a 'rising danger of an immigration from the East' of Russian Jews. The terms 'Russian', 'Jew', 'revolutionary', 'easterner' became almost interchangeable for some. When SPD deputy Ledebour protested against the expulsion of a Russian Jew named Montag from Germany in the spring of 1911, his reference to him as a 'Russian' provoked only anti-semitic remarks on the right.

But after 1907 the issue of Russians in Germany never assumed

---

[41] Cf. L. Stern, ed., *Die russische Revolution von 1905–1907 im Spiegel der deutschen Presse* (Berlin, 1961).

the proportions it had reached during the revolutionary events of 1905. While the number of Russians in Germany increased until it reached a peak in 1912–1913, their political activity was less noticeable. There were two reasons for this. First, with the institution of the Duma and the legalization of political parties greater activity became possible within Russia itself. Many Russians had returned from exile at the beginning of the 1905 revolution and were able to remain. Second, the German police and Russian agents in Germany tightened their watch on all suspicious activity. In the spring of 1907 they raided a 'reading room' in the Berlin suburb of Charlottenburg, discovered stores of Bundist and Bolshevik literature, and expelled one student. Several months later Maxim Litvinov and two other Bolsheviks were expelled from Prussia for running an illegal printing press. In Dresden the police expelled five Russians from Saxony because they participated in the Reichstag election campaign for the SPD. In June 1909 twelve Russian socialists went on trial in Dresden and arrests followed in Mannheim, Darmstadt, Heidelberg, and Braunschweig.

Thus emigré political activity died down after 1907. From 1909 to 1912 the Bolshevik journal *Proletarii* was brought to Leipzig from Geneva and Paris, stored in the basement of the SPD daily *Leipziger Volkszeitung*, and sent to Russia. But the police were now well aware of such activities. It became more difficult for Jewish students to enter a German high school or university and easier for them to be expelled. By 1908 the number of Russian students at the University of Berlin had declined almost to its 1901 level of 250, a drop of 200 since the summer of 1906. In April 1911 the Bavarian government reduced the number of Russian students at the University of Munich from 393 to under 200.[42] The SPD also found it more and more difficult to assist the many factions of Russian socialists who refused to be united. Mensheviks, Bolsheviks, Social Revolutionaries, Bundists, Polish and Lithuanian socialists. By the summer of 1914 the Russian emigration to Germany appeared to be not so much a danger as a weapon in case of war.

In 1914 most Germans shared a common feeling of fear and antipathy toward the 'Russian danger'. Political Russophobia was an important factor in initial support of the war not only among conservatives, liberals, and centrists, but within the SPD as well.

42 B. Brachmann, *op. cit.*, pp. 102, 185.

Most Russian citizens left Germany that summer either for other places of exile or to return home, but some remained. A symbiotic relationship quickly developed between the emigration and the German government; each thought the other could help to hasten the fall of the Russian government. From the start the German war effort in the East was two-pronged: military operations were supplemented by a remarkable campaign to give support to any dissident political movement within the Russian Empire, national or socialist. At one time or another during the war the German government supported Ukrainian nationalists in Constantinople, Finnish emigrés in Stockholm, Prince Matchabelli's Georgian colony in Berlin, a 'Ruthenian national committee' in Lemberg, a 'Union for the Emancipation of the Ukraine' in Vienna and Berlin, a Zionist committee in Galicia, the Social Revolutionaries, and the Bolsheviks. In supporting these anti-Russian emigré circles, German officials quickly discovered the utility of the Baltic Germans and the Jews as intermediaries.

The Baltic Germans did not create German *Annexationspolitik* in the East in 1914, but none were more vociferous in approving it and in helping to carry it out. To convince an English journalist of the dangers of war between Germany and Russia in the spring of 1914, the Wilhelmstrasse only had to produce Schiemann in London's Carlton Hotel and to have him pound out warnings of the barbarian threat. The organization of the disparate non-Russian committees into a single group was put in the hands of two more Balts, von Uexküll and von der Ropp. Schiemann remained throughout the war a consistent and influential advocate of German expansion eastwards. Paul Rohrbach portrayed Russia as an orange whose non-Russian sectors should be carefully peeled away into that series of German-dominated *Randstaaten* from the Baltic to the Black Sea which had long captured the imagination of German policy-makers. The Baltic German professors, among them Harnack, Dehio, and Lezius, eagerly returned to their homeland as advisers and administrators when the German army occupied the area.

Russian Jews also assisted the German war effort in several instances. As a group they found life in Germany without German citizenship difficult during the war. Many were treated as enemy aliens, forced to report periodically to the local police, and subjected to abuse in pamphlets that portrayed Russia as a sea of

'Mongolized Slavs' and Jews which threatened a barbarian inunda-
tion of Germany.[43] But some were invaluable to the government,
particularly as contacts with the emigré committees. Parvus was
the major figure in the programme of supporting dissident political
movements in Russia. It was in his Constantinople apartment in
the summer of 1914 that the first contact was made with the
Ukrainian, Georgian, and Armenian separatists. And it was Parvus
who put the Germans in touch with Lenin and his circle in Switzerland and arranged for their transportation into Russia in the
spring of 1917.

Parvus was ideal for such work: a man who spoke both Russian
and German, who knew Russian revolutionaries personally, and
who was willing to work for a German victory in the East. Other
Jews were also useful. Paul Litvin, a businessman who came to
Germany in 1909 and founded a heating company, the 'Deutsche
Evaparator A.G.', conducted the secret peace negotiations with
Russian representatives in Stockholm in 1917 and a year later
helped to work out the terms of the supplementary treaties of
Brest-Litovsk in Berlin. Russian Jews, like the Baltic Germans,
also acted as advisers in the occupied areas of the Russian Empire.
In Poland, Belorussia, and the Ukraine, Oberost used them as
interpreters and local administrative assistants because their
Yiddish was understood by the majority of the population in these
areas, including the peasants.[44]

Thus the two groups within the Russian emigration most familiar
with Germany and hostile to the Russian government thought
German policy could be used to further their own ends: autonomy
and protection for the German population in the Baltic and the
collapse of the Russian autocracy. Both were of great help to the
Germans. Insofar as the German war effort and Lenin's arrival in
Petrograd set the stage for the October Revolution, both helped to
reap the whirlwind.

In 1914 Germany went to war against a Russia which it feared but
did not quite comprehend. The emigration was not the only factor

[43] For example, G. Fritz, *Die Ostjudenfrage; Zionismus und Grenzschluss*
(Munich, 1915).
[44] A Mendelssohn Bartholdy, *The War and German Society* (New Haven,
1937), p. 104; H. Gatzke, 'Zu den deutsch-russischen Beziehungen im Sommer
1918', *Vierteljahreshefte für Zeitgeschichte*, 1955, 3; 'Streseman und Litwin',
Ibid., 1957, 5.

in generating this fear. The old images of the Russian steamroller, of Cossack cavalry and peasant hordes riding out of the East, of a revolution which would unleash Polish discontent, still remained. But the Russian emigration made a major contribution to prewar Russophobia. Most Germans knew Russia largely from the pages of Russian literature. What Russians in Germany before the war said and what they did made a great impression. They not only filled in an information gap concerning Russia; they were themselves examples of 'Russians'.

But both the Russians and the 'Russias' which they portrayed were more diverse after 1900 than previously. Royalty still recalled the good old ties between Russia and Prussia, intellectuals the joys of German philosophy and the lure of the Russian soul. But for the new political emigration of socialists and non-Russians, the Russian government was a hostile and despotic force. The Baltic Germans and the Jews were culturally most suited to convey this attitude and for political reasons eager to do so. For German conservatives and the middle classes the Balts portrayed a Russia dangerous because it was weakened by revolution; for the German Left the Jews described a powerful and brutal autocracy. Each reflected broader sentiments of nationalist and socialist dissent; each was in part the object of criticism by the other, the Balts by the Jews because of their association with the Russian state, the Jews by the Balts because of their involvement in the revolutionary movement. Neither created anti-Russian sentiment in Germany; both reinforced it. The fascination of some German intellectuals for Russian culture notwithstanding, Germany went to war in 1914 in part to defend itself from dangers in the East.

Liman von Sanders and the German–Ottoman Alliance

Ulrich Trumpener

Shortly after the end of the 1914–18 war, General Otto Liman von Sanders,[1] whose dispatch to Constantinople in December 1913 at the head of a German military mission had provoked so much suspicion and resentment in Russia, revealed in his memoirs that during his five years service in the Ottoman empire he had had to cope with constant attempts to 'minimize the influence' of his mission, that both the Turks and various German government agencies had repeatedly ignored his advice and recommendations, and that on several occasions he had not even been consulted on major military questions.[2] Although the memoirs quickly became a standard source for historians of the Ottoman war effort, few writers outside Germany believed or paid much attention to his remarks about the limited influence he had possessed in Constantinople. Instead, many historians have continued to depict him as a key figure in the preparation, conclusion, and implementation of the German–Ottoman alliance of 1914 and/or as the *de facto* commander of the entire Ottoman army.

The opening of the German archives makes it possible to re-assess Liman's role. The purpose of this article is to review his activities during his first year as an Ottoman marshal and to clarify why his military and political influence in Constantinople was indeed as limited as he had asserted in his memoirs. When he and about forty other German officers took service in the Ottoman empire in the winter of 1913–14, they did so officially to advise and assist the Turks in the reorganization of their army.

[1] Just before his transfer to the Ottoman army, Liman was ennobled and added the name of his late wife (von Sanders) to his family name. He came on his father's side of a converted Jewish family, a rare case among Prussian generals. See Siegmund Kaznelson, ed., *Juden im deutschen Kulturbereich* (rev. ed., Berlin, 1959), p. 816.

[2] *Five Years in Turkey* (Annapolis, 1927), pp. vii, 8–10, 16–17, 20–7, 31–2, and *passim*. The original German edition of Liman's memoirs appeared in 1920.

Liman, for one, took that official purpose seriously. Indeed, having been explicitly told by the Kaiser that the military mission should stay out of politics, Liman concluded that his primary task was to reform the Ottoman army, not to serve as an agent for the German foreign office or German business interests. As a result, friction quickly developed between the official representative of the Reich in Constantinople, Ambassador Hans von Wangenheim, and his superiors in the Wilhelmstrasse on the one hand, and General Liman on the other. After initial skirmishes early in 1914 over questions of personnel policy, serious trouble between Wangenheim and the chief of the military mission erupted in May in connection with the unorthodox conduct of the mission's railroad expert, a certain Major Kübel.

Shortly after joining Liman's staff in the spring of 1914, Kübel had seen fit to launch a vitriolic attack on the German-controlled Anatolian and Bagdad Railway Companies for their alleged failure to provide the kind of services which the Ottoman armed forces needed and were, in his opinion, entitled to. The major's brusque demands for extensive technical improvements – which were likely to cost the Deutsche Bank and others in the railroad consortium up to 100,000,000 Marks – and, more particularly, his subsequent threat that he would arrange to have the lines placed under military management unless the companies became more cooperative – naturally provoked an uproar among the German concessionaires and at the Berlin foreign office. In response to Wangenheim's urgent request to get the major out of the Ottoman empire before he supplied the Porte with any more ammunition against the German companies, the Wilhelmstrasse presented the case to the Kaiser, but found to its dismay that Liman had meanwhile taken sides with Kübel. Despite a reminder from the Kaiser that the representation of Germany's political and economic interests was properly the concern of the ambassador, Liman reacted strongly to Wangenheim's 'interference' in the internal affairs of the military mission and announced that he would not set foot in the embassy until this issue had been settled. The general's boycott of his own country's embassy produced a great deal of diplomatic embarrassment for Wangenheim, and although – after weeks of procrastination – the Kaiser finally had Kübel recalled (thereby vindicating the ambassador's original judgment), the affair left a legacy of bitterness between Wangenheim and Liman which was never fully erased.[3] Parenthetically it should be added that Kübel's successor, a Lt. Col. Böttrich, proved to be equally unsympathetic towards the railroad concessionaires. Indeed, during the war years this German officer, as head of the Railroad Department at Ottoman GHQ, sided quite regularly with the Turks in their periodic disputes with the Deutsche Bank and the German directors-general of the line.

It has often been suggested that General Liman and the steadily expanding staff of his military mission played a crucial role in pulling the Ottoman empire into its war alliance with the Reich, and that this had been one of their assigned tasks all along, but the evidence hardly supports such conclusions. To begin with, it is clear that before the July crisis Germany's leaders were not even sure that an alliance with the Turks was desirable. As Carl Mühlmann has pointed out, Berlin was well aware of their weakness, military and economic, after the Balkan Wars; and as late as May 1914 the chief of the Prussian general staff, General Helmuth von Moltke, explicitly ruled out an alignment with the Turks 'in the foreseeable future'. Although during the following two months Liman's periodic reports to Berlin concerning the condition of the Ottoman armed forces became somewhat more positive than they had been previously, there is no evidence that Germany's military and political leaders abandoned their reserve. In fact, if they did have any thought of securing Ottoman military support in the weeks following the Sarajevo incident, they obviously did not inform Liman; for only a few days before Germany declared war on Russia, he and the other German officers in Ottoman service applied for their recall to the Reich.[4]

Although it cannot be determined how soon and how much Liman knew about Wangenheim's alliance negotiations with the Porte (which started in earnest on 28 July), it is clear that he

---

[3] For a detailed discussion of the Kübel affair and previous incidents involving the mission, see George W.F. Hallgarten, *Imperialismus vor 1914* (2 vols., rev. ed., Munich, 1963), II, 439–46, 561–74.

[4] Cf. Carl Mühlmann, *Deutschland und die Türkei 1913–1914* (Berlin, 1929), pp. 1–43; *Das deutsch-türkische Waffenbündnis im Weltkriege* (Leipzig, 1940), pp. 9–14; *Oberste Heeresleitung und Balkan im Weltkrieg 1914–1918* (Berlin, 1942), pp. 21–3, 32–4; F. Fischer, *Griff nach der Weltmacht* (Düsseldorf, 1961), pp. 133–4. Under Article II of Liman's original contract with the Porte, the German government was entitled to call him and the rest of the mission home if the Reich became involved in a European war.

personally was not involved in them until 1 August. On that day, the chief protagonist of the pro-alliance faction in the *Ittihad ve Terakki* (Union and Progress) regime, War Minister Enver Pasha, met Liman and Wangenheim at the German embassy to discuss the military implications of the proposed German–Ottoman pact. While the basic outline of the treaty had already been agreed on during the preceding three days, this conference of 1 August was crucial in terms of clarifying how exactly the Turks meant to contribute to Germany's impending war effort against Russia. Such a clarification had been expressly demanded by Chancellor Bethmann Hollweg the previous evening as a *conditio sine qua non* for the conclusion of the alliance – an indication that even at this juncture Germany's leaders were still harbouring doubts as to Turkish intentions and military capabilities.

The upshot of the conference was Enver's and Liman's assurance to Wangenheim that within about thirty days after the beginning of mobilization an army of 120,000 men could be assembled in Thrace for a joint Turco-Bulgarian advance against Russia, and that a second army, of 90,000 men, would probably be ready for the same purpose – or for a campaign against Greece - roughly one month thereafter. The three conference participants agreed, furthermore, that the Ottoman empire should assume a basically defensive posture on the Transcaucasian border with Russia, and that the flagship of Germany's Mediterranean Squadron, the modern battle cruiser *Goeben*, should immediately be brought to the Straits to strengthen Ottoman naval power in the Black Sea.[5]

It should be obvious, and it was certainly recognized by Wangenheim at the time, that the main features of this war plan were highly theoretical; there was as yet no assurance that the Bulgarians would wish to march with the Turks, nor was it at all clear whether the Bucharest government would permit either of them to cross Rumanian territory. Although aware of these obstacles, Wangenheim decided that Berlin's basic condition, namely Ottoman willingness to do something worthwhile against the Russians, had been met, and on the following day, 2 August, he formally signed the alliance treaty with the Porte.[6]

[5] *Akten des Auswärtigen Amtes 1867–1920, Politisches Archiv* (microfilm), hereafter cited as AA, file *Deutschland 128 Nr. 5 secr.*, Bd. 3, Wangenheim to Berlin foreign office (hereafter cited as FO), 2 August 1914, nos. 406, 407.

[6] See ibid., nos. 407, 408; *Verträge IE, Nr. 94*, same to same, 2 August 1914, no. 409. Mühlmann, *Deutschland und die Türkei*, p. 43, suggests that Wangen-

All the evidence points to the conclusion that the war plan of 1 August was an *ad hoc* arrangement and not the fruit of careful planning. Neither the correspondence between Liman and the Prussian general staff, nor that between Wangenheim and the Wilhelmstrasse, contains the slightest reference to any pre-arranged plan of action, and Liman specifically inquired on 2 August whether the dispositions he had made with Enver were agreeable to Moltke. As for Liman's own role in the projected Ottoman war effort against Russia, there was utter confusion on all sides. While, at Berlin's insistence, the alliance treaty contained a clause that the military mission would remain 'at the disposal of Turkey', and that the Porte, in turn, would grant the mission 'an effective influence on the general conduct of the army, in accordance with the understanding arrived at directly between ... the [Ottoman] Minister of War and ... the Chief of the Military Mission', Liman actually never received a clear-cut definition of the authority which this clause was supposed to confer upon him. As a result, he and Enver soon became embroiled in heated discussions concerning the status and functions of the military mission; a dispute which continued off and on throughout the war. In these altercations with Enver, Liman received virtually no support from the Kaiser or other German governmental figures; and Enver successfully maintained the position that he, and he alone, was in command of the Ottoman armed forces (of which he became 'vice-generalissimo' in October 1914).

Although the Porte's official declaration of neutrality in the rapidly spreading European war was justified by the country's military unpreparedness, the uncertain attitude of Bulgaria and Rumania, and a host of other problems, Liman and many of his German subordinates quickly became impatient with what they regarded as unwarranted procrastination on the part of the Turks. Liman's growing suspicion that none of the Ottoman leaders favoured intervention in the foreseeable future was, as we now know, largely justified (with Enver probably being the only exception),[7] but whereas Wangenheim reacted to this situation with

heim signed the treaty because of the encouraging reports about the Ottoman army which he had received from Liman on 27 July and perhaps even earlier, but it now seems clear that the ambassador did not make up his mind until after the meeting with Enver and Liman on 1 August.

[7] On the political situation in Constantinople after the outbreak of the European war see especially Yusuf Hikmet Bayur, *Turk inkilabi tarihi* (History

more or less polite admonitions to the Porte, Liman became daily more cantankerous. By the middle of August, word reached Wangenheim from several quarters that the impatient general had been talking of challenging both Enver and the navy minister, Djemal Pasha, to duels; and on 19 August the embassy received a dispatch for transmission to the Kaiser, in which Liman formally requested his own and his mission's recall. In justification of his unusual request, Liman pointed out that Enver's recent statements and military dispositions had confirmed his suspicion that the Turks would not intervene in the foreseeable future (certainly not until Russia had been 'decisively beaten' by the Central Powers); that the Ottoman army was bound to collapse for lack of money and food if it was kept much longer in a state of mobilization inside the Ottoman empire; and that the whole atmosphere in Constantinople made it well-nigh unbearable for German officers to continue their service there.[8]

Wangenheim was profoundly disturbed by the general's conduct and views, but couched his recommendations to Berlin in rather mild terms. He explained that Liman was obviously a victim of bad nerves and suggested that the mission chief might mend his ways if he received a friendly reminder from the Kaiser that his continued service in the Ottoman empire was both necessary and as meritorious as a combat assignment in the German army. Hardly had Wangenheim sent this message to the Wilhelmstrasse when Liman availed himself again of the embassy's telegraph to notify General von Lyncker, of the Kaiser's *Militärkabinett*, that Enver had meanwhile agreed to the withdrawal of 'myself and of one-third to one-half of the military mission'. This piece of news really exasperated Wangenheim. As he informed the Wilhelmstrasse in a follow-up dispatch, he had just received word from Enver that he regarded even a partial withdrawal of the mission as totally unacceptable, and that Liman's impatience and political obtuseness were 'simply incomprehensible'. Despite Liman's increasingly dangerous meddling in questions of high policy, Wan-

of the Turkish reform) (Istanbul & Ankara, 1940–), III:1, pp. 62–193. Cf. Ulrich Trumpener, 'Turkey's Entry into World War I: An Assessment of Responsibilities', *Journal of Modern History*, XXXIV (1962).

[8] See AA, *Türkei 139*, Bd. 33, Wangenheim to FO, 19 August 1914, no. 546; same to same (transmitting message from Liman to Wilhelm II), 19 August 1914, no. 547. Liman's statement in his memoirs, p. 23, that he sent his request for recall on 11 August appears to be an error.

genheim concluded, it was inadvisable for the Kaiser to be too blunt with the excitable mission chief; for an 'excessively sharp reprimand would cause him to lose his head completely'.[9]

Following Wangenheim's recommendation, the Kaiser sent a mild reply to Liman, exhorting him and the other members of the mission to carry on with their duties 'until I issue other orders', and assuring them that they were being given full credit for the difficult and frustrating job they were doing.[10] According to Liman's memoirs, there was 'much gloom' among the members of the mission when he informed them of the Kaiser's decision, but it would appear that at least some of them, particularly those working directly under Enver at Ottoman GHQ, were sufficiently aware of the obstacles still facing the Turks not to be too upset about the procrastinating policy of the Porte. They knew, among other things, that the mobilization and deployment of the Ottoman army was still far from complete, that the defences at the Straits were in woeful shape, and, most important, that the Turkish alliance talks with Bulgaria had all but bogged down.[11]

After lengthy negotiations by the Minister of the Interior, Talaat Bey, and the President of the Ottoman Chamber of Parliament, Halil Bey, with the Bulgarian government, a defensive pact between the two countries had been signed in Sofia on 19 August, but despite subsequent efforts by the Porte, as well as by Berlin and Vienna, to push the Bulgarians into an offensive alliance against Russia, this was all the Turks could get. Simultaneous attempts to secure a pledge of friendship or even of military collaboration from the Rumanian government proved similarly futile.[12] In view of this, Talaat and Halil suggested to Berlin and Vienna at the end of the month that it might be more profitable to aim for a Turco-Bulgarian pact against Greece and Serbia and to scrap the planned trans-Balkan offensive against the Russians. Berlin immediately notified the Porte that it did not like this alternative plan, especially its anti-Greek

9 AA, *Türkei 139*, Bd. 33, Wangenheim to FO, 20 August 1914, no. 555; same to same (transmitting message from Liman to Lyncker), 20 August 1914, no. 556.

10 See ibid. Bethmann Hollweg to FO, 20 August 1914, no. 17.

11 Cf. AA, *WK*, Bd. 27, Wangenheim to FO, 19 August 1914, no. 553; *Deutschland 128 Nr. 5 secr.*, Bd. 3, same to same, 22, 24, 26 August 1914, nos. 575, 595, 609.

12 Cf. Bayur, III: 1, pp. 99–133, and the copious correspondence on this subject in AA, *Deutschland 128 Nr. 8 secr.*, Bde. 1–2; and *Bulgarien Nr. 17*, Bd. 20.

orientation, but the Turks nevertheless sent a colonel to Sofia to discuss the project with the Bulgarian general staff.[13]

Both Moltke and his Austro-Hungarian counterpart, General Conrad von Hötzendorf, had made it abundantly clear since early August that they wished to get the promised Ottoman assistance at the earliest possible date, and their requests became more emphatic at the beginning of September. Faced with an increasingly critical situation on his own front in Galicia, Conrad sent an urgent call for action to Constantinople, asking especially for large-scale Ottoman landings on the Russian Black Sea coast at or near Odessa. The feasibility of such an amphibious operation had been studied at Ottoman GHQ for several weeks, but despite Liman's strong support of such a project nothing had yet been settled.

Liman had meanwhile accepted command of the newly-formed First Army, garrisoned in Thrace and in the Straits region, and though his headquarters continued to be in Constantinople, he could not participate in strategic planning at Ottoman GHQ as regularly as he might otherwise have been able to do. In any event, after the receipt of Conrad's call for help he was unable to persuade Enver or, for that matter, his German colleagues, that the Odessa operation was feasible and necessary. As Wangenheim explained to the Wilhelm-strasse on 6 September, Admiral Souchon and other German naval officers in Constantinople regarded the proposed operation as far too risky, and, even if successful, the presence of some Ottoman troops in the Odessa region would be of little help to the Austro-Hungarian armies in far-away Galicia, and the 'German agencies here' were, therefore, concentrating on preparations for 'action against Egypt'. What Wangenheim failed to mention was that Liman, for one, was adamantly opposed to this whole strategic concept and greatly annoyed by the way his advice was being ignored.[14]

Liman's frustration was further heightened on 5 September when he asked Wangenheim to show him the text of the German–Ottoman alliance treaty. As Liman explained, there were indications that the Turks were planning something against Greece, and

[13] AA, *Deutschland 128 Nr. 8 secr.*, Bd. 2, Waldthausen to FO, 30 August 1914, no. 211; Bethmann Hollweg to FO, 1 September 1914, no. 29; Michahelles to FO, 9 September 1914, no. 131; *WK*, Bd. 32, Zimmermann to Waldthausen, 31 August 1914, no. 249.

[14] Cf. AA, *WK*, Bd. 25, Wangenheim to FO, 18 August 1914, no. 530; *Deutschland 128 Nr. 5 secr.*, Bd. 4, same to same, 6 and 8 September 1914, nos. 725, 752; Liman, pp. 24–7.

he needed to know what the treaty said about such an eventuality. The ambassador replied that he could not show him the treaty as this would be contrary to international custom and the treaty's secrecy clause. Instead, he offered the perplexed general the assurance that the Turks had no obligation to move against Greece unless the latter came to the aid of Serbia or some other country at war with Germany (which was a highly arbitrary reading of the treaty), and let it go at that. It is not entirely clear whether Liman managed at a later date to familiarize himself with the treaty, but that at the beginning of the war he actually did not know the details of his own country's alliance treaty with the Turks can no longer be disputed.[15]

Despite the indifference or outright opposition to his advocacy of an amphibious assault on the Russian Black Sea coast, Liman refused to give up, and for a brief moment it looked as though he would prevail after all. As Wangenheim wired to Berlin on 13 September, the Odessa project was apparently gaining favour with Enver, although he himself had made it repeatedly clear that an advance against Egypt and other anti-British projects were far more important to Germany. To Wangenheim's satisfaction, his own view was promptly upheld by the Kaiser and his advisers. On 14 September they informed Liman that they did not approve of the Odessa project (because it was too risky) and regarded an expedition against Egypt as particularly important – the very project which he had consistently opposed.[16]

By the time this message arrived in Constantinople, Admiral Souchon had received permission from Enver to take the Ottoman fleet into the Black Sea for 'manoeuvres'. Judging from the available evidence, Enver had furthermore made it clear that he did not mind if these led to hostile encounters with Russian ships, but before the admiral could take advantage of this blank cheque, Enver's colleagues at the Porte turned against him and forced him to countermand his instructions. The collapse of the enterprise produced a series of heated arguments between Wangenheim, Souchon, and other Germans on the one hand, and the Grand Vizier and his associates on the other. After prolonged haggling, the Porte agreed on 21 September that henceforth it would not oppose strictly

15 Cf. AA, *Deutschland 128 Nr. 5 secr.*, Bd. 4, Wangenheim to FO, 6 September 1914, no. 726; Liman, p. 22.

16 AA, *Deutschland 128 Nr. 5 secr.*, Bd. 4, Wangenheim to FO, 13 September 1914, no. 795; Bethmann Hollweg to FO, 14 September 1914, no. 43; Liman, pp. 26–7.

peaceful training manoeuvres in the Black Sea on the part of the *Goeben* and *Breslau*, but this and certain other concessions apparently made little impression on Liman. Heedless of previous admonitions, he drafted and sent out a new request that he and his officers be allowed to return to Germany.[17]

Although it is unlikely that anyone in Germany thought seriously of approving the request, Wangenheim was asked for advice. The ambassador responded on 24 September with considerable candour, asserting among other things that the Turks were not really ready for war, and that therefore 'benevolent Turkish neutrality is presently far more valuable to us than a premature . . . declaration of war'. In the meantime, he continued, the military mission served a highly useful function in keeping the Turks in Germany's orbit, and Liman's renewed attempt to get himself and his officers out of the Ottoman empire was plain foolishness.[18]

While Wangenheim's remarks about the advantages of continued Ottoman neutrality occasioned considerable dismay in Germany – a special emissary, Richard von Kühlmann, was shortly thereafter sent to Constantinople to put some fire into the ambassador – his recommendation with regard to the mission was heeded. On 26 September Lyncker sent a curt notice to Liman that his request had been denied, that the Kaiser had given strict orders that he must subordinate his personal views to the officially authorized policy of the ambassador, and that he would do well to 'put up with your situation once and for all'.[19]

As he had done once before during the Kübel affair, Liman reacted to this endorsement of the ambassador's authority by severing relations with Wangenheim. Since his relations with Souchon and several other German dignitaries in Constantinople had become similarly strained, Liman spent the following five weeks in virtual isolation and devoted himself primarily to his duties as the commanding general of the First Army. According to the evidence we now have, he had no part in the German negotiations with

[17] See Trumpener, pp. 371–3; Bayur, III; I, pp. 84–93; Liman, p. 23; and *Oesterreichisches Staatsarchiv, Abt. Haus-, Hof- und Staatsarchiv*, Vienna, Austro-Hungarian Foreign Ministry files (hereafter cited as AHFM), *PA I Karton rot 941*, Pallavicini to Vienna foreign ministry, 15 and 18 September 1914, nos. 589, 605; same to Berchtold, 22 September 1914, no. 57/P.

[18] AA, *Deutschland 128 Nr. 5 secr.*, Bd. 4, Wangenheim to Jagow, 24 September 1914, no. 3.

[19] Cf. AA, *Türkei 139*, Bd. 33, Jagow to Zimmermann, 27 September 1914; Liman, p. 23.

Enver, Talaat, Djemal, and Halil during October, which led to their commitment – half-hearted in the case of Talaat and Halil – to bring the Ottoman empire into the war even if the majority of the cabinet persisted in their opposition to intervention. Liman's assertion after the war that the provocation of hostilities with Russia by Admiral Souchon's ships on 28–9 October came as a surprise to him is, therefore, entirely credible.

The opening of hostilities without the knowledge and consent of the Grand Vizier and a majority of the ministers naturally caused an uproar at the Porte and dangerous dissensions in the committee of the Ittihad ve Terakki Party. The situation was aggravated by a temporary split in the ranks of the very ministers and party officials who had been involved in, or known of, the preparation of the raid. Unlike Enver, who had been the central figure in the plot, Djemal, Talaat, and Halil were greatly annoyed that Souchon had carried the attack all the way to the Russian coast; they had expected the clash with the Russians to occur on the high sea, where Ottoman provocative intent would have been far less evident. However, after giving the Germans some very uneasy moments on 30 and 31 October, Enver's fellow-plotters in the cabinet and a majority of the Party's committee closed ranks behind him, and by 2 November Wangenheim received assurances from Halil that the supporters of intervention had prevailed, and that the Grand Vizier, for once, had meanwhile agreed to accept the *fait accompli*.[20]

We have very little information on what Liman was doing during the hectic days following Souchon's Black Sea raid. That he performed any valuable services for the Germans at this juncture – for instance, by rounding up support for Enver – appears highly unlikely; for on 31 October, at the height of the Ottoman cabinet crisis, Wangenheim thought it appropriate to apply for Liman's immediate transfer to another post. As the ambassador explained to Bethmann Hollweg, Ottoman participation in the war made it doubly important to have full cooperation and harmony among all German agencies in Constantinople, and this was out of the question if Liman remained in command of the military mission. Indeed, given his 'great nervousness' and persistent tendency to go

20 Cf. Trumpener, pp. 378–80; Bayur, III: 1, 238–59; AHFM, *PA I Karton rot 942*, Pallavicini to Berchtold, 29 October, 5 November 1914, nos. 63/P, 64/P; same to Vienna foreign ministry, 31 October, 1 November 1914, nos. 762, 766.

his own way, he was bound to cause trouble all round. An obvious successor, Wangenheim continued, was Field Marshal Colmar von der Goltz (who had worked for many years as a military adviser in the Ottoman empire), and even though Enver would deem it improper to get directly involved in a personnel issue like this, there were indications that he would just as soon have somebody else in charge of the military mission.[21]

Although the Kaiser and his advisers agreed to the proposed switch – and Goltz himself was more than willing to leave his thankless job as military governor of Belgium – the project quickly ran into a snag because of Enver's reluctance to lose Liman's talents as a field commander. There were other complications as well, and after weeks of correspondence on this delicate subject, the Kaiser decided to leave Liman in charge of the mission, but to send Goltz to Constantinople anyway, where the Porte had meanwhile offered to make him an adjutant-general in the Sultan's entourage.[22] Wangenheim was not at all happy with this arrangement; for though he could expect moral support from Goltz, the embassy would still have to contend with Liman – and he had meanwhile become more uncooperative than ever. As Wangenheim wired to Zimmermann on 25 November, the military mission chief was not only continuing his boycott of the embassy, but had also begun to pursue its entire staff with the 'most incredible acts of chicanery'. To heighten the ambassador's disappointment, an attempt by Enver to interest Liman in a new command position on the Transcaucasian front proved useless. As Liman explained to Lyncker on 27 November, no major operations were feasible in that theatre until after the winter season; there was no need to replace the present Turkish commander there; he himself had lots of work left in his present sphere of authority; and – most important – the idea of sending him out of Constantinople had obviously originated with Wangenheim, and he had no intention of playing into the ambassador's hands.[23]

[21] AA, *Türkei 139*, Bd. 33, Wangenheim to FO, 31 October 1914, no. 1178.

[22] Cf. ibid., Bethmann Hollweg to FO, 3 November 1914, no. 94; Wangenheim to FO, 5, 18, and 25 November 1914, nos. 1240, 1371, 1425; Zimmermann to Wangenheim, 22 November 1914, no. 1314; Stumm to FO, 28 November 1914, no. 414; Generalfeldmarschall Colmar Frhr. von der Goltz, *Denkwürdigkeiten* (Berlin, 1929), pp. 377–8.

[23] Cf. AA, *Türkei 139*, Bd. 33, Wangenheim to FO, 25 November 1914, no. 1425; same to Zimmermann, 25 November 1914, no. 1426; Liman to Lyncker, 27 November 1914.

Shortly after Liman had made it clear that he did not want the Transcaucasian command and that he considered the winter season unsuitable for any major operation on that front, Enver announced his determination to launch an offensive there anyway, and stated that he would now personally direct the attack. On 6 December, the vice-generalissimo set out for the remote Transcaucasian front – much to the dismay of Wangenheim. As he explained to Berlin, the prospect of having Enver absent from Constantinople for an indefinite period of time was 'extraordinarily regrettable', for Enver was after all a key member of the cabinet and, in addition, in charge of all Ottoman operations; but what really irked the ambassador was that in the meantime Liman would be given further opportunity to defy and harass him and his staff. If we are to believe Wangenheim's reports during the next four weeks that was, indeed, what happened. The military mission chief, he complained to Berlin on 16 December, was obviously gaining increased influence at Ottoman GHQ while Enver was gone, but while he kept the Austro-Hungarian embassy informed of what was being planned there, he continued to ignore the German military attaché and the rest of the German embassy staff. 'Under these circumstances,' the ambassador said, 'I can for the time being no longer accept responsibility for the proper consideration of our military-political wishes'; would the Kaiser order Liman to exchange places with Enver at the Transcaucasian front?[24]

To Wangenheim's chagrin, his superiors in Berlin initially refused to get involved and advised him instead to work out a *modus vivendi* with Liman. This, he wrote back on 30 December, was a useless piece of advice; for Liman was generally suspected by his own officers of being no longer in full possession of his mental faculties, and 'I have ... not yet acquired the qualifications of a mental specialist [*Irrenarzt*]'. His troubles with the military mission chief, Wangenheim emphasized, were not just a matter of personal friction, but pregnant with political repercussions. Thus it was of vital importance for the embassy to be kept *au courant* with the plans and projects of the Ottoman military, particularly as regards its domestic security programmes; for many Ottoman measures – against Greek espionage rings or those aimed at enemy aliens, for example – needed to be watched constantly lest they

24 Ibid. Wangenheim to FO, 6, 11, and 16 December 1914, nos. 1542, 1580, 1629.

cause political damage abroad. As long as Enver had been in charge, the embassy had usually been able to exert a moderating influence at Ottoman GHQ, but this was no longer possible, since Liman had meanwhile given strict orders that no information must be passed on to the embassy. Altogether, Wangenheim concluded, the situation was intolerable, and unless Goltz succeeded in correcting Liman's ways there was no telling what would happen.[25]

Fortunately for the ambassador, his superiors in Berlin and the Kaiser himself had meanwhile finally recognized that Liman's conduct was, indeed, dangerous, and sent him an appropriate reprimand. After prolonged negotiations via some of his subordinates the general consented in early January 1915 to resume personal contacts with the embassy. This truce was from the outset shaky, and Liman was soon to cause Wangenheim new problems by drifting into feuds with Bronsart, Goltz, and ultimately Enver himself.[26]

As the foregoing survey suggests, the German military mission played a rather limited role in the conclusion and implementation of the German–Ottoman alliance treaty of 1914, and its chief was by no means in control of the Ottoman army. It was in other ways that Liman and his officers rendered valuable service to Germany as well as Turkey in 1914. As instructors and staff officers they were in large measure responsible for the revitalization of the Ottoman army during the first half of 1914 and for the relative success of Ottoman mobilization at the beginning of the war. Moreover, once the Turks intervened, they provided experienced leadership for the conduct of many campaigns. Whether, in addition, the military mission had been intended to secure Germany's political and economic predominance in the Ottoman empire is debatable, but it is obvious that Liman was unaware of such a policy objective and, in any event, an unsuitable person to achieve it.

[25] Ibid., Jagow to Wangenheim 16 December 1914, no. 1545; Wangenheim to FO, 21 December 1914, no. 1683; ibid., Bd. 34, same to 'Dear Friend' (probably Zimmermann), 30 December 1914 (private letter); AHFM, *PA I Karton rot 942*, Hohenlohe to Vienna foreign ministry, 23 December 1914, no. 785. See also Feldmarschall Conrad, *Aus meiner Dienstzeit* (5 vols., Vienna, 1921–5), V, pp. 738–41, 840–1, 937.

[26] AA, *Türkei 139*, Bd. 34, Wangenheim to 'Dear Friend', 6 January 1915 (private letter); same to FO, 23 and 26 January, 25 February, 2 March 1915, nos. 200, 226, 459, 502, 509; *AHFM, PA XII Karton 209*, Pallavicini to Berchtold, 7 January 1915, no. 2D/P.

hARPER ⚜ ⲦORChBOOKS

HUMANITIES AND SOCIAL SCIENCES

American Studies: General

THOMAS C. COCHRAN: The Inner Revolution. *Essays on the Social Sciences in History* TB/1140

EDWARD S. CORWIN: American Constitutional History. *Essays edited by Alpheus T. Mason and Gerald Garvey* △ TB/1136

CARL N. DEGLER, Ed.: Pivotal Interpretations of American History TB/1240, TB/1241

A. HUNTER DUPREE: Science in the Federal Government: *A History of Policies and Activities to 1940* TB/573

A. S. EISENSTADT, Ed.: The Craft of American History: *Recent Essays in American Historical Writing* Vol. I TB/1255; Vol. II TB/1256

CHARLOTTE P. GILMAN: Women and Economics: *A Study of the Economic Relation between Men and Women as a Factor in Social Evolution.* ‡ *Ed. with an Introduction by Carl N. Degler* TB/3073

OSCAR HANDLIN, Ed.: This Was America: *As Recorded by European Travelers in the Eighteenth, Nineteenth and Twentieth Centuries. Illus.* TB/1119

MARCUS LEE HANSEN: The Atlantic Migration: 1607-1860. *Edited by Arthur M. Schlesinger* TB/1052

MARCUS LEE HANSEN: The Immigrant in American History. TB/1120

JOHN HIGHAM, Ed.: The Reconstruction of American History △ TB/1068

ROBERT H. JACKSON: The Supreme Court in the American System of Government TB/1106

JOHN F. KENNEDY: A Nation of Immigrants. △ *Illus.* TB/1118

LEONARD W. LEVY, Ed.: American Constitutional Law: *Historical Essays* TB/1285

RALPH BARTON PERRY: Puritanism and Democracy TB/1138

ARNOLD ROSE: The Negro in America TB/3048

MAURICE R. STEIN: The Eclipse of Community. *An Interpretation of American Studies* TB/1128

W. LLOYD WARNER and Associates: Democracy in Jonesville: *A Study in Quality and Inequality* ¶ TB/1129

W. LLOYD WARNER: Social Class in America: *The Evaluation of Status* TB/1013

American Studies: Colonial

BERNARD BAILYN, Ed.: Apologia of Robert Keayne: *Self-Portrait of a Puritan Merchant* TB/1201

BERNARD BAILYN: The New England Merchants in the Seventeenth Century TB/1149

JOSEPH CHARLES: The Origins of the American Party System TB/1049

LAWRENCE HENRY GIPSON: The Coming of the Revolution: 1763-1775. † *Illus.* TB/3007

LEONARD W. LEVY: Freedom of Speech and Press in Early American History: *Legacy of Suppression* TB/1109

PERRY MILLER: Errand Into the Wilderness TB/1139

PERRY MILLER & T. H. JOHNSON, Eds.: The Puritans: *A Sourcebook of Their Writings* Vol. I TB/1093; Vol. II TB/1094

EDMUND S. MORGAN, Ed.: The Diary of Michael Wigglesworth, 1653-1657: *The Conscience of a Puritan* TB/1228

EDMUND S. MORGAN: The Puritan Family: *Religion and Domestic Relations in Seventeenth-Century New England* TB/1227

RICHARD B. MORRIS: Government and Labor in Early America TB/1244

KENNETH B. MURDOCK: Literature and Theology in Colonial New England TB/99

WALLACE NOTESTEIN: The English People on the Eve of Colonization: 1603-1630. † *Illus.* TB/3006

LOUIS B. WRIGHT: The Cultural Life of the American Colonies: 1607-1763. † *Illus.* TB/3005

American Studies: From the Revolution to 1860

JOHN R. ALDEN: The American Revolution: 1775-1783. † *Illus.* TB/3011

MAX BELOFF, Ed.: The Debate on the American Revolution, 1761-1783: *A Sourcebook* △ TB/1225

RAY A. BILLINGTON: The Far Western Frontier: 1830-1860. † *Illus.* TB/3012

W. R. BROCK: An American Crisis: *Congress and Reconstruction, 1865-67* ○ △ TB/1283

EDMUND BURKE: On the American Revolution: *Selected Speeches and Letters.* ‡ *Edited by Elliott Robert Barkan* TB/3068

WHITNEY R. CROSS: The Burned-Over District: *The Social and Intellectual History of Enthusiastic Religion in Western New York, 1800 1850* △ TB/1242

GEORGE DANGERFIELD: The Awakening of American Nationalism: 1815-1828. † *Illus.* TB/3061

CLEMENT EATON: The Freedom-of-Thought Struggle in the Old South. *Revised and Enlarged. Illus.* TB/1150

CLEMENT EATON: The Growth of Southern Civilization: 1790-1860. † *Illus.* TB/3040

LOUIS FILLER: The Crusade Against Slavery: 1830-1860. † *Illus.* TB/3029

DIXON RYAN FOX: The Decline of Aristocracy in the Politics of New York: 1801-1840. ‡ *Edited by Robert V. Remini.* TB/3064

FELIX GILBERT: The Beginnings of American Foreign Policy: *To the Farewell Address* TB/1200

FRANCIS GRIERSON: The Valley of Shadows: *The Coming of the Civil War in Lincoln's Midwest: A Contemporary Account* TB/1246

---

† The New American Nation Series, edited by Henry Steele Commager and Richard B. Morris.

‡ American Persectives series, edited by Bernard Wishy and William E. Leuchtenburg.

* The Rise of Modern Europe series, edited by William L. Langer.

¶ Researches in the Social, Cultural, and Behavioral Sciences, edited by Benjamin Nelson.

§ The Library of Religion and Culture, edited by Benjamin Nelson.

Σ Harper Modern Science Series, edited by James R. Newman.

○ Not for sale in Canada.

△ Not for sale in the U. K.

FRANCIS J. GRUND: Aristocracy in America: *Social Class in the Formative Years of the New Nation*   TB/1001
ALEXANDER HAMILTON: The Reports of Alexander Hamilton. ‡ *Edited by Jacob E. Cooke*   TB/3060
THOMAS JEFFERSON: Notes on the State of Virginia. ‡ *Edited by Thomas P. Abernethy*   TB/3052
JAMES MADISON: The Forging of American Federalism: *Selected Writings of James Madison. Edited by Saul K. Padover*   TB/1226
BERNARD MAYO: Myths and Men: *Patrick Henry, George Washington, Thomas Jefferson*   TB/1108
JOHN C. MILLER: Alexander Hamilton and the Growth of the New Nation   TB/3057
RICHARD B. MORRIS, Ed.: The Era of the American Revolution   TB/1180
R. B. NYE: The Cultural Life of the New Nation: 1776-1801. † *Illus.*   TB/3026
FRANCIS S. PHILBRICK: The Rise of the West, 1754-1830. † *Illus.*   TB/3067
TIMOTHY L. SMITH: Revivalism and Social Reform: *American Protestantism on the Eve of the Civil War*   TB/1229
FRANK THISTLETHWAITE: America and the Atlantic Community: *Anglo-American Aspects, 1790-1850* TB/1107
ALBION W. TOURGÉE: A Fool's Errand. ‡ *Ed. by George Fredrickson*   TB/3074
A. F. TYLER: Freedom's Ferment: *Phases of American Social History from the Revolution to the Outbreak of the Civil War. 31 illus.*   TB/1074
GLYNDON G. VAN DEUSEN: The Jacksonian Era: 1828-1848. † *Illus.*   TB/3028
LOUIS B. WRIGHT: Culture on the Moving Frontier   TB/1053

American Studies: The Civil War to 1900

THOMAS C. COCHRAN & WILLIAM MILLER: The Age of Enterprise: *A Social History of Industrial America* TB/1054
W. A. DUNNING: Essays on the Civil War and Reconstruction. *Introduction by David Donald*   TB/1181
W. A. DUNNING: Reconstruction, Political and Economic: 1865-1877   TB/1073
HAROLD U. FAULKNER: Politics, Reform and Expansion: 1890-1900. † *Illus.*   TB/3020
HELEN HUNT JACKSON: A Century of Dishonor: *The Early Crusade for Indian Reform. ‡ Edited by Andrew F. Rolle*   TB/3063
ALBERT D. KIRWAN: Revolt of the Rednecks: *Mississippi Politics, 1876-1925*   TB/1199
ROBERT GREEN MC CLOSKEY: American Conservatism in the Age of Enterprise: 1865-1910   TB/1137
ARTHUR MANN: Yankee Reformers in the Urban Age: *Social Reform in Boston, 1880-1900*   TB/1247
WHITELAW REID: After the War: *A Tour of the Southern States, 1865-1866. ‡ Edited by C. Vann Woodward*   TB/3066
CHARLES H. SHINN: Mining Camps: *A Study in American Frontier Government. ‡ Edited by Rodman W. Paul*   TB/3062
VERNON LANE WHARTON: The Negro in Mississippi: 1865-1890   TB/1178

American Studies: 1900 to the Present

RAY STANNARD BAKER: Following the Color Line: *American Negro Citizenship in Progressive Era. ‡ Illus. Edited by Dewey W. Grantham, Jr.*   TB/3053
RANDOLPH S. BOURNE: War and the Intellectuals: *Collected Essays, 1915-1919. ‡ Edited by Carl Resek*   TB/3043
A. RUSSELL BUCHANAN: The United States and World War II. † *Illus.*   Vol. I TB/3044; Vol. II TB/3045
ABRAHAM CAHAN: The Rise of David Levinsky: *a documentary novel of social mobility in early twentieth century America. Intro. by John Higham*   TB/1028
THOMAS C. COCHRAN: The American Business System: *A Historical Perspective, 1900-1955*   TB/1080

FOSTER RHEA DULLES: America's Rise to World Power: 1898-1954. † *Illus.*   TB/3021
JOHN D. HICKS: Republican Ascendancy: 1921-1933. † *Illus.*   TB/3041
SIDNEY HOOK: Reason, Social Myths, and Democracy   TB/1237
ROBERT HUNTER: Poverty: *Social Conscience in the Progressive Era. ‡ Edited by Peter d'A. Jones*   TB/3065
WILLIAM L. LANGER & S. EVERETT GLEASON: The Challenge to Isolation: *The World Crisis of 1937-1940 and American Foreign Policy*
   Vol. I TB/3054; Vol. II TB/3055
WILLIAM E. LEUCHTENBURG: Franklin D. Roosevelt and the New Deal: 1932-1940. † *Illus.*   TB/3025
ARTHUR S. LINK: Woodrow Wilson and the Progressive Era: 1910-1917. † *Illus.*   TB/3023
GEORGE E. MOWRY: The Era of Theodore Roosevelt and the Birth of Modern America: 1900-1912. † *Illus.*   TB/3022
RUSSEL B. NYE: Midwestern Progressive Politics: *A Historical Study of Its Origins and Development, 1870-1958*   TB/1202
WILLIAM PRESTON, JR.: Aliens and Dissenters: *Federal Suppression of Radicals, 1903-1933*   TB/1287
WALTER RAUSCHENBUSCH: Christianity and the Social Crisis. ‡ *Edited by Robert D. Cross*   TB/3059
JACOB RIIS: The Making of an American. ‡ *Edited by Roy Lubove*   TB/3070
PHILIP SELZNICK: TVA and the Grass Roots: *A Study in the Sociology of Formal Organization*   TB/1230
IDA M. TARBELL: The History of the Standard Oil Company: *Briefer Version. ‡ Edited by David M. Chalmers*   TB/3071
GEORGE B. TINDALL, Ed.: A Populist Reader ‡   TB/3069
TWELVE SOUTHERNERS: I'll Take My Stand: *The South and the Agrarian Tradition. Intro. by Louis D. Rubin, Jr., Biographical Essays by Virginia Rock*   TB/1072
WALTER E. WEYL: The New Democracy: *An Essay on Certain Political Tendencies in the United States. ‡ Edited by Charles B. Forcey*   TB/3042

Anthropology

JACQUES BARZUN: Race: *A Study in Superstition. Revised Edition*   TB/1172
JOSEPH B. CASAGRANDE, Ed.: In the Company of Man: *Twenty Portraits of Anthropological Informants. Illus.*   TB/3047
W. E. LE GROS CLARK: The Antecedents of Man: *Intro. to Evolution of the Primates.* ○ △ *Illus.*   TB/559
CORA DU BOIS: The People of Alor. *New Preface by the author. Illus.*   Vol. I TB/1042; Vol. II TB/1043
RAYMOND FIRTH, Ed.: Man and Culture: *An Evaluation of the Work of Bronislaw Malinowski* ¶ ○ △ TB/1133
DAVID LANDY: Tropical Childhood: *Cultural Transmission and Learning in a Puerto Rican Village* ¶   TB/1235
L. S. B. LEAKEY: Adam's Ancestors: *The Evolution of Man and His Culture.* △ *Illus.*   TB/1019
ROBERT H. LOWIE: Primitive Society. *Introduction by Fred Eggan*   TB/1056
EDWARD BURNETT TYLOR: The Origins of Culture. *Part I of "Primitive Culture."* § *Intro. by Paul Radin*   TB/33
EDWARD BURNETT TYLOR: Religion in Primitive Culture. *Part II of "Primitive Culture."* § *Intro. by Paul Radin*   TB/34
W. LLOYD WARNER: A Black Civilization: *A Study of an Australian Tribe.* ¶ *Illus.*   TB/3056

Art and Art History

WALTER LOWRIE: Art in the Early Church. *Revised Edition. 452 illus.*   TB/124
EMILE MÂLE: The Gothic Image: *Religious Art in France of the Thirteenth Century.* § △ *190 illus.*   TB/44

3

w. o. HASSALL, Ed.: Medieval England: *As Viewed by Contemporaries* △   TB/1205

DENYS HAY: Europe: The Emergence of an Idea   TB/1275
DENYS HAY: The Medieval Centuries ° △   TB/1192
J. M. HUSSEY: The Byzantine World △   TB/1057
ROBERT LATOUCHE: The Birth of Western Economy: *Economic Aspects of the Dark Ages.* ° △ *Intro. by Philip Grierson*   TB/1290
FERDINAND LOT: The End of the Ancient World and the Beginnings of the Middle Ages. *Introduction by Glanville Downey*   TB/1044
G. MOLLAT: The Popes at Avignon: 1305-1378 △   TB/308
CHARLES PETIT-DUTAILLIS: The Feudal Monarchy in France and England: *From the Tenth to the Thirteenth Century* ° △   TB/1165
HENRI PIRENNE: Early Democracies in the Low Countries: *Urban Society and Political Conflict in the Middle Ages and the Renaissance. Introduction by John H. Mundy*   TB/1110
STEVEN RUNCIMAN: A History of the Crusades. △
Volume I: *The First Crusade and the Foundation of the Kingdom of Jerusalem. Illus.*   TB/1143
Volume II: *The Kingdom of Jerusalem and the Frankish East, 1100-1187. Illus.*   TB/1243
FERDINAND SCHEVILL: Siena: *The History of a Medieval Commune. Intro. by William M. Bowsky*   TB/1164
SULPICIUS SEVERUS et al.: The Western Fathers: *Being the Lives of Martin of Tours, Ambrose, Augustine of Hippo, Honoratus of Arles and Germanus of Auxerre.* △ *Edited and trans. by F. O. Hoare*   TB/309
HENRY OSBORN TAYLOR: The Classical Heritage of the Middle Ages. *Foreword and Biblio. by Kenneth M. Setton*   TB/1117
F. VAN DER MEER: Augustine The Bishop: *Church and Society at the Dawn of the Middle Ages* △   TB/304
J. M. WALLACE-HADRILL: The Barbarian West: *The Early Middle Ages, A.D. 400-1000* △   TB/1061

History: Renaissance & Reformation

JACOB BURCKHARDT: The Civilization of the Renaissance in Italy. △ *Intro. by Benjamin Nelson & Charles Trinkaus. Illus.*   Vol. I TB/40; Vol. II TB/41
JOHN CALVIN & JACOPO SADOLETO: A Reformation Debate. *Edited by John C. Olin*   TB/1239
ERNST CASSIRER: The Individual and the Cosmos in Renaissance Philosophy. △ *Translated with an Introduction by Mario Domandi*   TB/1097
FEDERICO CHABOD: Machiavelli and the Renaissance △   TB/1193
EDWARD P. CHEYNEY: The Dawn of a New Era, 1250-1453. * *Illus.*   TB/3002
G. CONSTANT: The Reformation in England: *The English Schism, Henry VIII, 1509-1547* △   TB/314
R. TREVOR DAVIES: The Golden Century of Spain, 1501-1621 ° △   TB/1194
G. R. ELTON: Reformation Europe, 1517-1559 ° △   TB/1270
DESIDERIUS ERASMUS: Christian Humanism and the Reformation: *Selected Writings. Edited and translated by John C. Olin*   TB/1166
WALLACE K. FERGUSON et al.: Facets of the Renaissance   TB/1098
WALLACE K. FERGUSON et al.: The Renaissance: *Six Essays. Illus.*   TB/1084
JOHN NEVILLE FIGGIS: The Divine Right of Kings. *Introduction by G. R. Elton*   TB/1191
JOHN NEVILLE FIGGIS: Political Thought from Gerson to Grotius: 1414-1625: *Seven Studies. Introduction by Garrett Mattingly*   TB/1032
MYRON P. GILMORE: The World of Humanism, 1453-1517. * *Illus.*   TB/3003
FRANCESCO GUICCIARDINI: Maxims and Reflections of a Renaissance Statesman (Ricordi). *Trans. by Mario Domandi. Intro. by Nicolai Rubinstein*   TB/1160
J. H. HEXTER: More's Utopia: *The Biography of an Idea. New Epilogue by the Author*   TB/1195

HAJO HOLBORN: Ulrich von Hutten and the German Reformation   TB/1238
JOHAN HUIZINGA: Erasmus and the Age of Reformation. △ *Illus.*   TB/19
JOEL HURSTFIELD, Ed.: The Reformation Crisis △   TB/1267
ULRICH VON HUTTEN et al.: On the Eve of the Reformation: *"Letters of Obscure Men." Introduction by Hajo Holborn*   TB/1124
PAUL O. KRISTELLER: Renaissance Thought: *The Classic, Scholastic, and Humanist Strains*   TB/1048
PAUL O. KRISTELLER: Renaissance Thought II: *Papers on Humanism and the Arts*   TB/1163
NICCOLÒ MACHIAVELLI: History of Florence and of the Affairs of Italy: *from the earliest times to the death of Lorenzo the Magnificent. Introduction by Felix Gilbert* △   TB/1027
ALFRED VON MARTIN: Sociology of the Renaissance. *Introduction by Wallace K. Ferguson*   TB/1099
GARRETT MATTINGLY et al.: Renaissance Profiles. △ *Edited by J. H. Plumb*   TB/1162
MILLARD MEISS: Painting in Florence and Siena after the Black Death: *The Arts, Religion and Society in the Mid-Fourteenth Century.* △ *169 illus.*   TB/1148
J. E. NEALE: The Age of Catherine de Medici ° △   TB/1085
ERWIN PANOFSKY: Studies in Iconology: *Humanistic Themes in the Art of the Renaissance.* △ *180 illustrations*   TB/1077
J. H. PARRY: The Establishment of the European Hegemony: 1415-1715: *Trade and Exploration in the Age of the Renaissance* △   TB/1045
J. H. PLUMB: The Italian Renaissance: *A Concise Survey of Its History and Culture* △   TB/1161
A. F. POLLARD: Henry VIII. ° △ *Introduction by A. G. Dickens*   TB/1249
A. F. POLLARD: Wolsey. ° △ *Introduction by A. G. Dickens*   TB/1248
CECIL ROTH: The Jews in the Renaissance. *Illus.*   TB/834
A. L. ROWSE: The Expansion of Elizabethan England. ° △ *Illus.*   TB/1220
GORDON RUPP: Luther's Progress to the Diet of Worms ° △   TB/120
FERDINAND SCHEVILL: The Medici. *Illus.*   TB/1010
FERDINAND SCHEVILL: Medieval and Renaissance Florence. *Illus.*   Volume I: *Medieval Florence* TB/1090
Volume II: *The Coming of Humanism and the Age of the Medici*   TB/1091
G. M. TREVELYAN: England in the Age of Wycliffe, 1368-1520 ° △   TB/1112
VESPASIANO: Renaissance Princes, Popes, and Prelates: *The Vespasiano Memoirs: Lives of Illustrious Men of the XVth Century. Intro. by Myron P. Gilmore*   TB/1111

History: Modern European

FREDERICK B. ARTZ: Reaction and Revolution, 1815-1832. * *Illus.*   TB/3034
MAX BELOFF: The Age of Absolutism, 1660-1815 △   TB/1062
ROBERT C. BINKLEY: Realism and Nationalism, 1852-1871. * *Illus.*   TB/3038
ASA BRIGGS: The Making of Modern England, 1784-1867: *The Age of Improvement* ° △   TB/1203
CRANE BRINTON: A Decade of Revolution, 1789-1799. * *Illus.*   TB/3018
D. W. BROGAN: The Development of Modern France. ° △
Volume I: *From the Fall of the Empire to the Dreyfus Affair*   TB/1184
Volume II: *The Shadow of War, World War I, Between the Two Wars. New Introduction by the Author*   TB/1185
J. BRONOWSKI & BRUCE MAZLISH: The Western Intellectual Tradition: *From Leonardo to Hegel* △   TB/3001
GEOFFREY BRUUN: Europe and the French Imperium, 1799-1814. * *Illus.*   TB/3033
ALAN BULLOCK: Hitler, A Study in Tyranny. ° △ *Illus.*   TB/1123

4

E. H. CARR: German-Soviet Relations Between the Two World Wars, 1919-1939   TB/1278

E. H. CARR: International Relations Between the Two World Wars, 1919-1939 ° △   TB/1279

E. H. CARR: The Twenty Years' Crisis, 1919-1939: An Introduction to the Study of International Relations ° △   TB/1122

GORDON A. CRAIG: From Bismarck to Adenauer: Aspects of German Statecraft. Revised Edition   TB/1171

WALTER L. DORN: Competition for Empire, 1740-1763. * Illus.   TB/3032

FRANKLIN L. FORD: Robe and Sword: The Regrouping of the French Aristocracy after Louis XIV   TB/1217

CARL J. FRIEDRICH: The Age of the Baroque, 1610-1660. * Illus.   TB/3004

RENÉ FUELOEP-MILLER: The Mind and Face of Bolshevism: An Examination of Cultural Life in Soviet Russia. New Epilogue by the Author   TB/1188

M. DOROTHY GEORGE: London Life in the Eighteenth Century △   TB/1182

LEO GERSHOY: From Despotism to Revolution, 1763-1789. * Illus.   TB/3017

C. C. GILLISPIE: Genesis and Geology: The Decades before Darwin §   TB/51

ALBERT GOODWIN: The French Revolution △   TB/1064

ALBERT GUÉRARD: France in the Classical Age: The Life and Death of an Ideal △   TB/1183

CARLTON J. H. HAYES: A Generation of Materialism, 1871-1900. * Illus.   TB/3039

J. H. HEXTER: Reappraisals in History: New Views on History and Society in Early Modern Europe △   TB/1100

STANLEY HOFFMANN et al.: In Search of France: The Economy, Society and Political System in the Twentieth Century   TB/1219

A. R. HUMPHREYS: The Augustan World: Society, Thought, & Letters in 18th Century England ° △   TB/1105

DAN N. JACOBS, Ed.: The New Communist Manifesto and Related Documents. Third edition, revised   TB/1078

HANS KOHN: The Mind of Germany: The Education of a Nation △   TB/1204

HANS KOHN, Ed.: The Mind of Modern Russia: Historical and Political Thought of Russia's Great Age   TB/1065

WALTER LAQUEUR & GEORGE L. MOSSE, Eds.: International Fascism, 1920-1945. ° △ Volume I of Journal of Contemporary History   TB/1276

WALTER LAQUEUR & GEORGE L. MOSSE, Eds.: The Left-Wing Intelligentsia between the Two World Wars. ° △ Volume II of Journal of Contemporary History   TB/1286

FRANK E. MANUEL: The Prophets of Paris: Turgot, Condorcet, Saint-Simon, Fourier, and Comte   TB/1218

KINGSLEY MARTIN: French Liberal Thought in the Eighteenth Century: A Study of Political Ideas from Bayle to Condorcet   TB/1114

L. B. NAMIER: Facing East: Essays on Germany, the Balkans, and Russia in the 20th Century △   TB/1280

L. B. NAMIER: Personalities and Powers: Selected Essays ^   TB/1186

L. B. NAMIER: Vanished Supremacies: Essays on European History, 1812-1918 °   TB/1088

JOHN U. NEF: Western Civilization Since the Renaissance: Peace, War, Industry, and the Arts   TB/1113

FRANZ NEUMANN: Behemoth: The Structure and Practice of National Socialism, 1933-1944   TB/1289

FREDERICK L. NUSSBAUM: The Triumph of Science and Reason, 1660-1685. * Illus.   TB/3009

DAVID OGG: Europe of the Ancien Régime, 1715-1783 ° △   TB/1271

JOHN PLAMENATZ: German Marxism and Russian Communism. ° △ New Preface by the Author   TB/1189

RAYMOND W. POSTGATE, Ed.: Revolution from 1789 to 1906: Selected Documents   TB/1063

PENFIELD ROBERTS: The Quest for Security, 1715-1740. * Illus.   TB/3016

PRISCILLA ROBERTSON: Revolutions of 1848: A Social History   TB/1025

GEORGE RUDÉ: Revolutionary Europe, 1783-1815 ° △   TB/1272

LOUIS, DUC DE SAINT-SIMON: Versailles, The Court, and Louis XIV. ° △ Introductory Note by Peter Gay   TB/1250

ALBERT SOREL: Europe Under the Old Regime. Translated by Francis H. Herrick   TB/1121

N. N. SUKHANOV: The Russian Revolution, 1917: Eyewitness Account. △ Edited by Joel Carmichael   Vol. I TB/1066;   Vol. II TB/1067

A. J. P. TAYLOR: From Napoleon to Lenin: Historical Essays ° △   TB/1268

A. J. P. TAYLOR: The Habsburg Monarchy, 1809-1918: A History of the Austrian Empire and Austria-Hungary ° △   TB/1187

G. M. TREVELYAN: British History in the Nineteenth Century and After: 1782-1919. ° △ Second Edition TB/1251

H. R. TREVOR-ROPER: Historical Essays ° △   TB/1269

ELIZABETH WISKEMANN: Europe of the Dictators, 1919-1945 ° △   TB/1273

JOHN B. WOLF: The Emergence of the Great Powers, 1685-1715. * Illus.   TB/3010

JOHN B. WOLF: France: 1814-1919: The Rise of a Liberal-Democratic Society   TB/3019

Intellectual History & History of Ideas

HERSCHEL BAKER: The Image of Man: A Study of the Idea of Human Dignity in Classical Antiquity, the Middle Ages, and the Renaissance   TB/1047

R. R. BOLGAR: The Classical Heritage and Its Beneficiaries: From the Carolingian Age to the End of the Renaissance △   TB/1125

RANDOLPH S. BOURNE: War and the Intellectuals: Collected Essays, 1915-1919. △ ‡ Edited by Carl Resek   TB/3043

J. BRONOWSKI & BRUCE MAZLISH: The Western Intellectual Tradition: From Leonardo to Hegel △   TB/3001

ERNST CASSIRER: The Individual and the Cosmos in Renaissance Philosophy. △ Translated with an Introduction by Mario Domandi   TB/1097

NORMAN COHN: The Pursuit of the Millennium: Revolutionary Messianism in Medieval and Reformation Europe △   TB/1037

C. C. GILLISPIE: Genesis and Geology: The Decades before Darwin §   TB/51

G. RACHEL LEVY: Religious Conceptions of the Stone Age and Their Influence upon European Thought. △ Illus. Introduction by Henri Frankfort   TB/106

ARTHUR O. LOVEJOY: The Great Chain of Being: A Study of the History of an Idea   TB/1009

FRANK E. MANUEL: The Prophets of Paris: Turgot, Condorcet, Saint-Simon, Fourier, and Comte △   TB/1218

PERRY MILLER & T. H. JOHNSON, Editors: The Puritans: A Sourcebook of Their Writings   Vol. I TB/1093;   Vol. II TB/1094

MILTON C. NAHM: Genius and Creativity· An Essay in the History of Ideas   TB/1196

ROBERT PAYNE: Hubris: A Study of Pride. Foreword by Sir Herbert Read   TB/1031

RALPH BARTON PERRY: The Thought and Character of William James: Briefer Version   TB/1156

GEORG SIMMEL et al.: Essays on Sociology, Philosophy, and Aesthetics. ¶ Edited by Kurt H. Wolff   TB/1234

BRUNO SNELL: The Discovery of the Mind: The Greek Origins of European Thought △   TB/1018

PAGET TOYNBEE: Dante Alighieri: His Life and Works. Edited with Intro. by Charles S. Singleton △   TB/1206

ERNEST LEE TUVESON: Millennium and Utopia: A Study in the Background of the Idea of Progress. ¶ New Preface by the Author   TB/1134

PAUL VALÉRY: The Outlook for Intelligence △   TB/2016

9